Environmental Taxation and Green Fiscal Reform

CRITICAL ISSUES IN ENVIRONMENTAL TAXATION

Series Editors: Larry Kreiser, *Cleveland State University, USA*, Hope Ashiabor, *Macquarie University, Australia* and Janet E. Milne, *Vermont Law School, USA*

The *Critical Issues in Environmental Taxation* series provides insights and analysis on environmental taxation issues on an international basis and explores detailed theories for achieving environmental goals through fiscal policy. Each book in the series contains pioneering and thought-provoking contributions by the world's leading environmental tax scholars who respond to the diverse challenges posed by environmental sustainability.

Previous volumes in the series:
Original book published by CCH Incorporated
Volumes I–IV published by Richmond Law Publishers
Volumes V–VIII published by Oxford University Press

Titles in the series include:

Volume IX Environmental Taxation in China and Asia-Pacific
Achieving Environmental Sustainability through Fiscal Policy
Edited by Larry Kreiser, Julsuchada Sirisom, Hope Ashiabor and Janet E. Milne

Volume X Environmental Taxation and Climate Change
Achieving Sustainability through Fiscal Policy
Edited by Larry Kreiser, Julsuchada Sirisom, Hope Ashiabor and Janet E. Milne

Volume XI Carbon Pricing, Growth and the Environment
Edited by Larry Kreiser, Ana Yábar Sterling, Pedro Herrera, Janet E. Milne and Hope Ashiabor

Volume XII Green Taxation and Environmental Sustainability
Edited by Larry Kreiser, Ana Yábar Sterling, Pedro Herrera, Janet E. Milne and Hope Ashiabor

Volume XIII Market Based Instruments
National Experiences in Environmental Sustainability
Edited by Larry Kreiser, David Duff, Janet E. Milne and Hope Ashiabor

Volume XIV Environmental Taxation and Green Fiscal Reform
Theory and Impact
Edited by Larry Kreiser, Soocheol Lee, Kazuhiro Ueta, Janet E. Milne and Hope Ashiabor

Environmental Taxation and Green Fiscal Reform

Theory and Impact

Edited by

Larry Kreiser

Professor Emeritus of Accounting, Cleveland State University, USA

Soocheol Lee

Professor of Economics, Meijo University, Japan

Kazuhiro Ueta

Professor of Economics, Kyoto University, Japan

Janet E. Milne

Professor of Law, Vermont Law School, USA

Hope Ashiabor

Associate Professor of Law, Macquarie University, Australia

CRITICAL ISSUES IN ENVIRONMENTAL TAXATION
VOLUME XIV

Edward Elgar

Cheltenham, UK • Northampton, MA, USA

Published by
Edward Elgar Publishing Limited
The Lypiatts
15 Lansdown Road
Cheltenham
Glos GL50 2JA
UK

Edward Elgar Publishing, Inc.
William Pratt House
9 Dewey Court
Northampton
Massachusetts 01060
USA

A catalogue record for this book
is available from the British Library

Library of Congress Control Number: 2014938837

This book is available electronically in the ElgarOnline.com
Law Subject Collection, E-ISBN 978 1 78347 817 0

MIX
Paper from responsible sources
FSC® C013056

ISBN 978 1 78347 816 3

Typeset by Servis Filmsetting Ltd, Stockport, Cheshire
Printed and bound in Great Britain by T.J. International Ltd, Padstow

Contents

Figures

Tables

Editorial review board

The 19 chapters in this book have been brought to publication with the help of an editorial review board dedicated to peer review. The 12 members of the board are committed to the field of environmental taxation and are active participants in environmental taxation events around the world.

Contributors

Antón Antón, Álvaro, University Cardenal Herrera CEU, Spain

Brandimarte, Cristina, Italian National Institute of Statistics, Italy

Butcher, Bill, The University of New South Wales, Australia

Cottrell, Jacqueline, Green Budget Europe, Germany

He, Yanmin, Kyoto University, Japan

Joseph, Sally-Ann, The University of New South Wales, Australia

Kawakatsu, Takeshi, Kyoto Prefectural University, Japan

Kettner, Claudia, Austrian Institute of Economic Research (WIFO), Austria

Kitagawa, Susumu, University of Yamanashi, Japan

Kletzan-Slamanig, Daniela, Austrian Institute of Economic Research (WIFO), Austria

Köppl, Angela, Austrian Institute of Economic Research (WIFO), Austria

Lerch, Achim, Hessian University of Cooperative Education, Germany

Liu, Xianbing, Institute for Global Environmental Strategies (IGES), Japan

Milne, Janet E., Vermont Law School, USA

Moinuddin, Mustafa, Institute for Global Environmental Strategies (IGES), Japan

Pearce, Prafula, Curtin University, Australia

Pirlot, Alice, FNRS Research Fellow, Université Catholique de Louvain (UCL), Belgium

Rudolph, Sven, Kyoto University, Japan

Sasao, Toshiaki, Iwate University, Japan

Shah, Rajiv V., T.A. Pai Management Institute (TAPMI), Tata Institute of Social Sciences, India

Suk, Sunhee, Kyoto University, Japan

Tan, Seck L., National University of Singapore, Singapore

Thampapillai, Dodo J., National University of Singapore, Singapore

Villar Ezcurra, Marta, University San Pablo CEU, Spain

Weishaar, Stefan E., University of Groningen, The Netherlands

Yano, Takashi, Hiroshima Shudo University, Japan

Zhao, Yuhong, The Chinese University of Hong Kong, Hong Kong

Zhou, Xin, Institute for Global Environmental Strategies (IGES), Japan

Foreword

Environmental taxation (or environmental tax reform) includes not only the reform of carbon and energy taxes but also reform of taxation on environmental pollutants and resource use that is not related to energy. Along with environmental taxation, green fiscal reform is also important. Governments should provide companies with stronger incentives to pursue the innovation of low-carbon processes and low-carbon products while shifting the focus of government expenditures from subsidies for fossil energy and nuclear energy toward support for renewable energy and reducing spending on the highly politicized construction of large-scale dams, roads and other questionable energy projects.

Environmental taxation and green fiscal reform are challenges that are difficult to achieve based on a short-term perspective. Necessary first steps are to present to the public a long-term vision for greening fiscal measures in an understandable manner and to gain public support for environmental sustainability.

Governments can deal with industrial pollution, urban environmental issues, and other environmental problems with market based instruments such as taxes and fees. It is difficult to say, however, that companies and other economic entities are sufficiently motivated to act in a responsible way by the current level of taxes and fees. Also, revenues collected by environmental taxes and fees are often earmarked for other than environmental purposes.

Environmental sustainability requires strong conviction and leadership that cannot be swayed by short-term economics. Governments must persistently provide the public with appropriate education and accurate information on the limits of an economy dependent on fossil energy, on the need for internalizing environmental pollution by proper means and on the risks associated with the use of nuclear energy. Volume XIV of Critical Issues in Environmental Taxation expands the discussion of these topics and explores the various ranges of environmental and energy policy for an environmentally sustainable future.

Soocheol Lee
Professor of Economics, Meijo University, Japan

Preface

A noted author, Thomas Pynchon, once said 'If they can get you asking the wrong questions, they don't have to worry about the answers.' In this line, there are many confusing questions being asked today about environmental sustainability.

Some politicians say let market forces decide energy policy. Eliminate all renewable energy standards and energy efficiency mandates. Natural gas producers advertise that natural gas is the 'clean energy' choice despite the fact that natural gas is a fossil fuel which creates carbon pollution. Electric utilities are petitioning to eliminate energy efficiency mandates since these mandates are reducing the demand for electricity. Isn't that what these mandates are supposed to do? One airline says it flies on 'eco-friendly skies' even though airplanes cause considerable pollution. In the current situation, it is more important than ever to publish high quality research on environmental sustainability, which is the mission of Critical Issues in Environmental Taxation.

Volume XIV of Critical Issues in Environmental Taxation contains 19 chapters on environmental taxation issues and green fiscal reform. These chapters have been prepared by environmental experts from around the world. We hope you find these studies to be enlightening and worthy of serious consideration by policy makers thoughout the world.

Larry Kreiser, Lead Editor
Soocheol Lee, Co-Editor
Kazuhiro Ueta, Co-Editor
Janet E. Milne, Co-Editor
Hope Ashiabor, Co-Editor
September 2014

PART I

Theory

Section A

Exploring theoretical assumptions

1. Environmental taxes and fees: wrestling with theory

Janet E. Milne*

Since the publication of Pigou's *Economics of Welfare* almost one hundred years ago, policymakers, scholars and environmental advocates have explored using economic instruments to internalize environmental externalities, particularly since the 1960s. Yet Pigou's call for internalization set a high standard that may be difficult to meet in actual implementation. This chapter poses questions that probe the gap between the underlying economic theory of environmental taxes and their actual execution. In light of a possible gap, it offers a preliminary inquiry into whether governments should consider an enhanced role for environmental fees in the continued evolution of the theory of environmental economic instruments.

A complete analysis of environmental pricing instruments inevitably must draw upon multiple disciplines often beyond the reach of any one author, and it should consider the unique legal, environmental and political circumstances of each country, which are known best to those who work within each country. Hence, this chapter provides an analytical framework and identifies questions for research and debate. This inquiry into fees is not meant to suggest that fees should displace environmental taxes, but rather that an expanded concept of fees might offer an alternative.

1. IS THERE A NEED FOR NEW RATIONALES FOR ENVIRONMENTAL PRICING?

The threshold question is why one should consider an enhanced role for environmental fees when the academic literature over past decades has concentrated on environmental taxes as a key way to attach prices to negative environmental externalities.[1] The answer lies in the potential gap between the economic theory and actual execution of environmental taxes.

As is well known, the economic theory of environmental taxes originated with A.C. Pigou in 1920, when he proposed imposing 'extraordinary restraints' on the private sector's damaging acts to capture their external social costs (Pigou 1920, p. 149). His gloriously elegant economic theory that a tax can internalize the external costs of environmentally damaging activities, however, can encounter practical implementation problems, given the complexities of accurately calculating external costs (see, e.g., Preiss 2012; Fullerton, Leicester and Smith 2010, pp. 425–6), and the political challenges of enacting taxes that approach full internalization (OECD 2010, p. 96).

Recognizing the challenges of valuing externalities, Baumol and Oates in 1971 suggested a second-best approach that is also a very elegant economic theory (Baumol and Oates 1971). They proposed that environmental taxes should serve as regulatory substitutes. Under their approach, the tax rate would be set at a rate designed to achieve a specific emissions reduction goal (or standard). This standard-pricing approach took a step away from classic Pigouvian theory and it nourished the concepts of least-cost abatement and taxes as an alternative to regulation.[2]

The Swiss carbon tax presents an example of a standard-pricing approach. The government set a goal for the reduction of greenhouse gas emissions, imposed a carbon tax, and has increased the tax rate when reductions did not meet the target (Speck 2013, p. 174). The tax will rise to 60 Swiss francs (49 euros[3]) in 2014 (Office fédéral de l'environnement 2013), and the law sets a cap of 120 Swiss francs, so more increases are still possible (Speck 2013, p. 174). Nonetheless, in general practice it may sometimes be difficult to accurately calculate the standard-based tax rate and to shepherd a theoretically correct rate through the political process. In addition, environmental taxes may remain static even if they do not meet explicit or implicit performance requirements and hence stray from Baumol–Oates' theory.

If a gap occasionally, or often, exists between the theory of internalization or standard-pricing taxes and actual execution, the next question is whether the existence of a gap bears significant implications for environmental taxes as an environmental policy instrument. This author's assumption is that the gap warrants attention because the *raison d'être* of environmental taxes is that they operate as economic instruments and achieve their environmental purpose by implementing economic theory. Consequently, if implementation falls short of theory, it seems to follow that a significant question arises about whether their use is still warranted. However, the answer should not turn on this simple logic but rather on a more sophisticated analysis that draws on the expertise of different disciplines.

Environmental economists, who are the intellectual guardians of the economic theories behind environmental taxation, are best positioned to determine whether the gap between Pigouvian and Baumol–Oates' theories for environmental taxes and the actual translation into specific environmental tax instruments is troubling. They can determine how pervasive the gap is and whether *ex post* analyses can demonstrate that theoretically imperfect environmental taxes are nonetheless delivering significant levels of environmental protection.[4] Political economists in turn can evaluate whether a real or perceived gap between theory and execution impairs the ability to convince policymakers that environmental taxes are a legitimate instrument for advancing environmental protection. This chapter poses these questions, but does not attempt to answer them. In wrestling with theory, it sets a framework for further research.

If the gap between theory and execution is significant from the economic and political perspectives, the analytical focus then turns to possible alternative responses.

One response might be to argue that environmental taxes should not be held to a higher theoretical standard than other types of taxes and other environmental policy instruments. Compared to other taxes, environmental taxes are somewhat anomalous. Pigou's internalization and Baumol–Oates' standard-pricing approaches impose a burden of exactitude on the tax rate, whereas other taxes are more likely to be set according to government discretion. Economists and policymakers consider whether other taxes stimulate or impair the economy or equitably distribute the burden of taxation across income levels, but there is much more debate and less of a precise theoretical basis for the 'right' level of taxation. Although Pigou and Baumol–Oates' theoretical brilliance has boxed environmental taxation into a bit of a difficult corner not shared by other taxes, one could argue that some level of discretion should be afforded environmental taxes. Similarly, other environmental instruments often do not operate in a theoretically perfect manner. For example, within the sphere of environmental economic instruments, the European Trading Scheme for greenhouse gas emissions has illustrated the challenges of executing economic theory, yet policymakers have thus far remained committed to the scheme. The acceptance of flaws may be inevitable in the second- or third-best world, but it still begs the question, identified above, of whether the flaws excessively erode environmental taxes' *raison d'être*.

Another approach is to continue to document and publicize the positive environmental impacts of environmental taxes that are less than theoretically perfect in order to reduce the significance of the gap between theory and execution. In addition, continuing *ex post* research can highlight the ways in which the design and implementation of environmental taxes can be improved to reduce the gap in the future.

A complementary alternative might be to add another component to environmental pricing theory and rhetoric to supplement, but not replace, environmental tax theory. If it is difficult to achieve pure execution of theory, and if the gap between theory and execution is significant (both of which are threshold questions taken as assumptions for analytical purposes), should we further develop our theories to better suit the realities of the time and our experience to date? The remainder of this chapter explores the idea of expanding the use of environmental fees as a complement to environmental taxes in the environmental pricing toolbox.

2. 'ECO-FEES' AS AN ECONOMIC RATIONALE

Fees have been used in the environmental context for decades. However, they traditionally have taken the form of administrative charges that cover the cost of the governmental permitting or enforcement process and user charges, such as payments for municipal waste treatment (see, e.g., Määttä 2006, p. 17). The possibility explored in this chapter is whether one could view environmental fees more broadly as a charge for the use of the environment, rather than a charge for some specific, traditional government service. This chapter refers to this broader concept as 'eco-fees', although other terms, such as user fee, charge or levy could be used as well.[5]

2.1 The Distinction between Taxes and Fees

Exploring an eco-fee approach involves drawing a conceptual line between taxes and fees. Defining the line is particularly important because an eco-fee for the use of the environment would bring the environmental charge conceptually close to a tax that attempts to capture the cost of environmental externalities. Long-standing definitions of environmental taxes provide useful guidance.

When discussing environmental taxes, the Organisation for Economic Co-operation and Development (OECD) has defined taxes as 'any compulsory, unrequited payment to general government . . .. Taxes are unrequited in the sense that benefits provided by government to taxpayers are not normally in proportion to their payments.' (OECD 2001, p. 15.) Thus, a critical, traditional distinction between taxes and fees (or other charges) is that fees provide a benefit back to the payers. Although other features, such as whether the payment is compulsory and whether the payment is to 'general government', are also significant, the following analysis focuses on the benefit aspect. The issues, however, can be conceptually linked. For example, a payment dedicated to a particular purpose that relates to the payers' activities may be more likely to bear a linkage to a benefit to the payers.

Direct benefit to the payers is obvious with traditional environmental fees, where the payers receive in return a very identifiable, concrete service, whether it is the cost of processing a permit application or the cost of waste treatment. If, however, the government is charging for the use of the environment, as explored here, a fee approach requires finding that the use of the environment offers a benefit to the payers. This approach is conceptually different from taxes that try to execute Pigouvian theory and Baumol–Oates standard-pricing: those taxes rely primarily on the burden of the tax itself as the means to achieve the environmental goal. The theory and vocabulary of fees instead require supporting rationales that concentrate on the benefit to the payers. The distinction between taxes and fees is already murky (as also illustrated in discussion of legal distinctions below), but exploring this shadowy forest between taxes and fees can help determine whether there is a way to adjust the theoretical framework around environmental fiscal payments to include a broader fee concept.

2.2 Benefits That Might Justify an Eco-Fee

Under the 'benefit' (or 'requited') approach to fees, the economic rationale for fee-oriented environmental price signals needs to be framed in terms of a benefit to the payers. If a benefit is not present, then the payment is more likely to constitute a tax than a fee, leaving the proponent with the potential burden of justifying the validity of the environmental tax under the theories of Pigou or Baumol–Oates. Several possible alternatives are presented below to help explore the theoretical feasibility of this approach, and others might be possible as well.

2.2.1 Government as trustee of environmental resources

One possibility is to consider whether government can use its legal ownership stake in the environment to impose a fee.[6] If so, then conferring the right to use that interest could provide tangible benefit to the recipient of the right, who would pay an eco-fee.

In a number of countries, the government holds some environmental assets in a public trust for the benefit of the public. The government does not have unrestricted ownership of the asset, because it must manage the asset for the public, but at the same time the private sector is not necessarily unilaterally prevented from using it. The government as trustee is charged with the responsibility of managing the asset in a way that will protect the public interest (see generally Blumm and Guthrie 2012). For example, in the United States (US), some states hold navigable waters in public trust (see generally Frank 2012, pp. 671–3). This public trust can limit the private sector's direct use of water but also limit activities that will more indirectly affect water.[7]

Under the public trust approach, one might argue that the government could attach an eco-fee to the use of environmental resources that it holds as trustee for the public. The private payers would obtain the right to use that resource in return for the payment, a clear 'benefit' in fee terminology. The government could charge according to its perception of the value of the right to use the public asset or according to the cost of any mitigation measures the government feels it should undertake.[8]

A fundamental issue under this approach is how far into the environment government can extend the reach of its public trust. Some have argued that the public trust doctrine covers air and, therefore, serves as a basis for government's authority over and obligation to protect air quality, including the obligation to reduce greenhouse gas emissions (Wood 2012; McGinley 2013).[9] If so, governments holding the air in public trust[10] could use their authority as trustees to charge fees for greenhouse gas emissions that enter the atmosphere.[11]

This approach to showing a benefit under an eco-fee system would require significant legal research in each jurisdiction to determine whether government holds environmental resources in public trust and, if so, the scope of government's obligations as trustee.

2.2.2 Government as the licensor of limited-entry industries

Alternatively, government may control a field of limited entry where significant environmental assets are at stake. The government's strong regulatory interest – not a quasi-proprietary interest – can cause it to impose significant licensing procedures and substantive requirements. In this instance, it could use its regulatory authority to impose an eco-fee, giving the payer the benefit of the right of access to a limited field. For example, the nuclear power industry is highly regulated, given the importance of the public interest. Government could attach a one-time eco-fee or ongoing eco-fees to the right to enter the field, a clearly identifiable benefit.[12] Such a fee would go beyond the traditional administrative permitting fee and could reflect government's assessment of costs it may assume as a result of the activity, such as response measures in the event of an emergency.[13] The fee in essence would be a payment for the possibility that the licensed activity might use environmental resources.

2.2.3 Government as environmental regulator

A third opportunity to apply eco-fees could arise when government uses its traditional power to regulate day-to-day commerce in order to protect the environment, such as the regulation of pesticides or the regulation of greenhouse gas emissions.[14] If government were to attach eco-fees to polluting activities, one would need to identify benefits that justify the fees. Unlike Pigouvian or Baumol–Oates' taxes, the fees are not designed primarily to change the payers' behavior, although the price increase may also have that effect (Opschoor and Vos 1989, pp. 14–15). The rationale for the eco-fees must instead link to specific benefits to the payers. Benefits are clear in the case of traditional fees, such as user charges where the government has assumed the responsibility of managing wastewater treatment plants. The following lines of reasoning might justify the use of fees for less tangible benefits, such as a fee on a manufacturer of pesticides or gas-guzzling cars, but each still involves a payment for use of the environment.

One could argue that the manufacturer or some other entity has no inherent right to pollute[15] and, therefore, government is allowing the benefit of the use of the environment, which it might otherwise restrict.[16] The eco-fees offer the payers the opportunity to conduct an activity that might degrade the environment.[17]

Alternatively, one could argue that the government can impose eco-fees in return for its commitment to engage in related environmental mitigation or adaption measures, such as government investments in alternative vehicle technology research that could fairly directly benefit the manufacturers. In some cases, however, government might want to engage in broader mitigation efforts with less or no direct return for the payer, such as investments in public transit that would offset the increased emissions resulting from gas-guzzling vehicles. In that event, the right-to-pollute rationale would be more appropriate.

Finally, a very different approach would be to shift the focus from the benefit offered to the payers to the burden that the payers are putting on the environment. In this case, the regulated entities would pay fees that enable government to mitigate the damage caused by the regulated activities. For example, a fee on lead paint manufacturers imposed by the State of California was used in part to fund government programs that addressed the health risks of children exposed to lead paint. When deciding whether the payment was a tax or fee for California's constitutional purposes, the California Supreme Court found that the payment was a 'regulatory fee' that was imposed under the government's police power, not a tax.[18] The court did not require a showing of benefit to the payers but rather focused on the fact that the government was trying to regulate the burdens on society imposed by the industry and would use the revenue to address those burdens. This broadening of fees to include payments directly tied to burden, not benefit, would be a step away from the

OECD's tax/fee distinction, which focuses on benefit, and it would bring the fee concept considerably closer to the Pigouvian internalization or a Baumol–Oates' standard-pricing approach. However, it is one that might warrant exploration.

3. THE EFFECT OF THE BENEFIT RATIONALES ON THE DESIGN OF ECO-FEES

The benefit-related rationales for eco-fees carry implications for the design of eco-fees, in particular the level at which the fees are set and how the revenue is used. The following discussion explores some of the possibilities at a preliminary, conceptual level. However, it is subject to the important caveat that design choices may be heavily influenced by the law in any particular jurisdiction, which can introduce a series of nuances that lie beyond the scope of this chapter.

An eco-fee approach may give government more latitude to set the amount of the payment imposed on polluters than an environmental tax. While Pigouvian taxes theoretically should capture the value of externalities and Baumol–Oates' taxes should set the price that will achieve an environmental standard, an eco-fee would usually correlate with the value of the benefit provided. These correlations may allow government more discretion. At the same time, the rationales for eco-fees could allow for the imposition of higher payments than traditional environmental fees, giving policymakers the ability to send a stronger price signal.

Table 1.1 summarizes the approaches government might take to setting the rate. Note, however, that setting the level of the eco-fees may not be entirely standardless. For example, if a fee is based on the public trust doctrine, the government is acting in its fiduciary capacity and may want to ensure that it receives a fair public return for the private sector intrusion on the public goods.[19] Similarly, depending on the law of the particular jurisdiction, government may need to show under other rationales that the amount of the fee is somewhat proportional to the benefit (or burden under the last rationale).[20] Nevertheless, from a purely theoretical perspective, governments may have a greater degree of discretion in deciding the rate for an eco-fee than for a theoretically correct Pigouvian or standard-pricing tax.

The benefit rationales may also significantly influence the question of whether the revenue from eco-fees is earmarked for an environmental purpose. Under the public trust approach, the trustee may have an obligation to use the revenue to protect the public asset held in trust.[21] Under the licensing rationale, if the fees reflect government's assessment of the

Table 1.1 Summary of environmental tax and eco-fee design components

Theory	Triggering Event	Rate	Use of Revenue
Pigouvian tax (tax effects results; no private benefit required)	Environmentally damaging activity	External costs	Open-ended (Note: Pigou's writing could also be interpreted to suggest earmarking)
Baumol–Oates' tax (tax effects results; no private benefit required)	Environmentally damaging activity	Rate necessary to achieve standard	Open-ended
Public trust eco-fee (private benefit is access to public assets)	Intrusion into public asset	Governmentally determined value of public asset made available for private use	Possible fiduciary obligation to compensate public
Licensing eco-fee (private benefit is access to limited market)	Environmentally damaging activity	Cost government decides to impose to achieve desired level of funding for related environmental purposes	Monitoring, remediation, mitigation
Regulatory eco-fee (private benefit is right to pollute)	Environmentally damaging activity	Cost government deems appropriate	Open-ended – but perhaps stronger policy basis if dedicated to remediation
Regulatory eco-fee (private benefit is government mitigation program)	Environmentally damaging activity	Cost government decides to impose to achieve desired level of funding	Mitigation program

Note: The design components of fees may vary depending on a country's law.

environmental costs it may assume as a result of the activities, the revenues presumably should be earmarked. Under the right-to-pollute rationale, government might argue that its allowance of activities provides sufficient benefit, leaving it free to use the revenue as it wishes, but as a matter of policy, the fees may be more attractive if the revenue is dedicated to environmentally related programs. Finally, where the benefit takes the form of a governmental promise to engage in certain activities, earmarking is essential.

In sum, the eco-fee approach tends to suggest earmarking of the revenues (see Table 1.1). As the benefits to the private sector become more attenuated, earmarking can provide a more concrete benefit, particularly if government is also providing the private sector with some relief from costs it would otherwise have to assume. However, policymakers might have more freedom in how to use the revenue than with traditional environmental fees, such as fees for permit processing and waste management services.

4. IMPLICATIONS OF A BROADER APPROACH TO FEES

4.1 A Shift in Theoretical Focus

As discussed above, an eco-fee approach would relieve analysts and policymakers of the obligation to design environmental taxes that meet Pigouvian or standard-pricing standards. Eco-fees could instead provide a form of rough justice, based on various rationales for why government has a right to charge for the use of the environment, often in return for using the revenue to protect the environment. Yet at the same time, the eco-fee approach would allow analysts and policymakers to venture beyond the boundaries of traditional environmental fees. The shift in design focus also carries significant environmental implications. The actual environmental return would come largely from the use of the revenue, but as recognized above, any price signal may also affect behavior, therefore potentially allowing eco-fees to serve two environmental functions.

4.2 A Shift in Public Perception

If the gap between the theory and execution of Pigouvian and standard-pricing taxes undercuts the political viability of environmental taxes (a threshold question posed in section 1 above), the design freedom that could come with eco-fees might be politically useful – a question again for political economists. It would also be important to consider whether eco-fees' tendency to dedicate revenue to the related environmental problem is a politically positive or negative development. On the positive side, there is some evidence that using revenue from environmental fiscal instruments to address the environmental problem increases public support (Brett and Keen 2000, pp. 336–7; Kallbekken and Aasen 2010, p. 2184; Soares

2012, p. 110). On the other hand, such earmarking would shift the public discourse away from revenue-neutral environmental fiscal reform or the search for new revenue to reduce budget deficits during periods of fiscal austerity.

The choice of terminology may also affect the public debate about the enactment of measures and the measures' ultimate effectiveness. For example, given the current toxicity of the word 'tax' in some countries, the eco-fee option might be more palatable. From an effectiveness perspective, there is the question whether 'tax' or 'eco-fee' (or some comparable term) sends a stronger behavioral message. A tax may carry a sense of penalty, while an eco-fee could suggest either a moral obligation to pay for and protect the environment or a license to pollute. If fees are preferable, which specific term (fee, eco-fee, charge, payment, levy or something else) is most effective? Political and behavioral economists are in the best position to evaluate the merits of these implications.

4.3 Legal Implications of the Tax-Fee Distinction

Whether payment obligations are legally characterized as taxes or fees can have significant legal consequences. The legal line between taxes and fees is often shadowy and can vary from jurisdiction to jurisdiction. The following discussion draws on US law to illustrate how one country draws legal lines between taxes and fees and the resulting legal implications. Although the law to date has developed largely around traditional taxes and fees, the legal implications are important when considering an expanded concept of fees and highlight the need to research the law in any particular jurisdiction.

4.3.1 Federal legislative and administrative procedures

The legal distinction between taxes and fees plays a significant role in determining federal legislative procedures for enactment. Federal taxes are subject to a procedural requirement that does not apply to fees.

The US constitution provides that bills 'for raising Revenue' must originate in the House of Representatives (the 'origination clause').[22] The House is the chamber of Congress elected based on population and therefore brings tax issues closer to the people, unlike the Senate where representation is equally divided among the states (see generally Kysar 2014). Taking a functional approach in interpreting the origination clause, the US Supreme Court has often reiterated that 'revenue bills are those that levy taxes, in the strict sense of the word, and are not bills for other purposes which may incidentally create revenue'.[23]

The allocation of the revenue to a specific program has emerged as a key factor in determining that a measure is not 'for raising Revenue'. After stating that the origination clause applies to taxes 'in the strict sense', the Court in *United States v. Munoz-Flores* explained: 'The Court has interpreted this general rule to mean that a statute that creates a particular governmental program, as opposed to a statute that raises revenue to support Government generally, is not a "Bil[l] for raising Revenue" within the meaning of the Origination Clause.'[24] However, the dedication of the funds to a particular program may not be determinative. In 2013 a lower court decided that the regulatory purpose of a tax (in that case a federal tax on people who do not obtain health insurance) precluded the measure from being a tax for purposes of the origination clause even though the revenue was not dedicated to a specific program.[25]

The analysis above suggests that eco-fees designed to raise revenue for a dedicated purpose might likely be designated as fees for constitutional purposes, that the legislative choice of words (tax or fee) is not constitutionally determinative, and even that taxes with a regulatory intent, such as standard-pricing taxes, might nonetheless be fees in the eyes of the law if the regulatory purpose dominates.[26] Legal characterization as a fee would give legislators in the Senate the freedom to approve a measure prior to action by the House, thereby creating potentially significant political opportunities.

The tax/fee distinction is also relevant to other federal legislative and administrative procedures. Under federal congressional procedures, tax proposals are referred to the congressional tax-writing committees in each chamber, and environmental proposals are referred to the committees that have jurisdiction over environmental protection. Thus, the tax/fee distinction will determine which committee has jurisdiction to review a legislative measure (Milne 2008, pp. 143–4). A more expansive approach to fees could open up opportunities for action by committees with jurisdiction over environmental measures. Once a measure becomes law, the Internal Revenue Service ordinarily is responsible for administering tax provisions, whereas other agencies, such as the Environmental Protection Agency, have jurisdiction over environmental matters. Thus, more expansive use of environmental fees would put more revenue responsibility in the hands of environmental agencies. In addition, a law's designation of a specific agency as responsible for administering a payment scheme may influence whether it is legally characterized as a tax or a fee.[27]

4.3.2 State procedural limits on new taxes

The tax/fee distinction may also be legally relevant to state procedural requirements. For example, California's constitution requires that a two-thirds majority of both chambers of the legislature approve a 'tax',[28] unlike a fee which is only subject to approval by a simple majority. California's constitution explicitly excludes reasonable charges for benefits, government services and regulatory costs, as well as charges for the use or transfer of state property. Consequently, eco-fees that meet these criteria would avoid the supermajority requirement.[29]

4.3.3 States' power to impose costs

The federal government's constitutional power to regulate interstate commerce under the 'commerce clause'[30] means that states cannot adopt measures, including revenue-generating mechanisms, that interfere with interstate commerce. Constitutional law may look more favorably on state pricing instruments that have fee-like attributes.

Recent US Supreme Court cases have looked at various factors to determine whether a state tax violates the commerce clause, including whether the interstate company's payment was related to services that the state government provided for that company and therefore did not unduly interfere with interstate commerce.[31] This factor means that constitutionally justifiable state taxes on interstate commerce are likely to bear more of the characteristics of user fees, even when the instrument is clearly a tax.[32] In striking down annual flat taxes on interstate trucking, the Court found that the flat taxes 'do not even purport to approximate fairly the cost or value of the use of Pennsylvania's roads'.[33] However, earmarking the revenues may not be necessary.[34]

If states want to maximize their power over interstate commerce, the eco-fee approach (or a tax structured approach like an eco-fee) may be appealing, particularly if the revenue is earmarked for a related state expenditure. This approach, however, would still entail the potentially difficult question of how to define the cost fairly allocable to the payers and the range of purposes for which the government can use the revenue under commerce clause jurisprudence.

In sum, the law of any particular jurisdiction will significantly affect the extent to which a fiscal instrument will qualify as a fee rather than a tax and how far one can stretch the meaning of a fee. The tax/fee distinction in turn can affect legal procedures for enactment, design requirements and issues of the authority of different levels of government to impose fees.

5. A 'CARBON POLLUTION FEE' PROPOSAL

A bill introduced into the US Senate in 2013 provides a contemporaneous example of how the fee issue has entered the political landscape and the potential challenges of distinguishing between a tax and a fee. The Climate Protection Act of 2013[35] calls for a 'carbon pollution fee' that would impose a price on fossil fuels equal to US$ 20 per ton of carbon dioxide content and an equivalent fee on imported carbon pollution-intensive goods.[36] The fee operates much like a carbon tax, but it would be imposed through the Clean Air Act, not the Internal Revenue Code, and it would be administered by the Environmental Protection Agency, not the Internal Revenue Service. Revenue would be used for a variety of purposes, including a per-capita rebate to US citizens, deficit reduction, climate change adaptation, transition relief for energy-intensive industry and low-income individuals, and research.

The proposal illustrates some of the substantive complexities and procedural implications of the tax/fee distinction. Although the fee looks much like a carbon tax, one could argue that the fee is a payment for the use of the environment under one or more of the rationales described above. In addition, the placement of the fee within the environmental legal regime of the Clean Air Act gives it a strongly regulatory nature that might overshadow its revenue-raising features. However, some of the uses for the revenue lend a tax flavor to the extent that they fund rebates to US citizens, which could be akin to environmental tax reform, and deficit reduction – putting squarely on the table the question whether dedication of the revenue for a related purpose is legally essential to the definition of a fee. From a procedural perspective, the proposal has been referred to the Senate Committee of Environment and Public Works, implying a procedural judgment that the measure is a fee, not a tax. Perhaps not coincidental to the design of the measure, the bill's sponsor, Senator Bernie Sanders, is a member of the Committee and the bill's co-sponsor, Senator Barbara Boxer, is the Committee's chair.

Although Congress has not acted on this proposal, it shows how some policymakers have an interest in extending the use of environmental fees in ways that bring them much closer to traditional environmental taxes, and the potential political opportunities that fees might offer.

6. CONCLUSION

The discussion above started with the premise that environmental taxes may not always achieve the economic ideals of Pigou and Baumol and Oates. Having explored the possibility of expanding the concept and use of environmental fees, it is useful to return to the basic question. As we move forward, should we accept imperfect execution of environmental taxes and continue to present environmental taxes as a mechanism for imposing costs on polluters in a more generalized, less perfect sense – or should we shift on occasion to a fee approach that conveys the notion that government is giving a benefit for which polluters should pay? The theoretical roots of the tax approach leave it open to challenge, but the tax approach is now familiar. The fee approach can avoid the potentially abrasive 'tax' language, convey a sense of public command over natural resources, and imply a greater public commitment to setting aside funds to protect the environment.

This discussion highlights the need for answers to questions from different disciplines to help determine whether pursuing the concept of a broader definition and more expansive use of fees is warranted:

- For economists, given the difficulties of fully executing the Pigouvian and Baumol–Oates' theories, do we need to look for other theories of environmental pricing, or are Pigouvian and Baumol–Oates' approaches still defensible?
- For political and behavioral economists, are 'fees' more appealing and effective than 'taxes' and if so, what specific terms – eco-fees, eco-charges, environmental fees, or something else – are most effective with the general public and policymakers? Or do 'fees' legitimize pollution in a way that will inhibit change?
- For lawyers, to what extent does the law of different jurisdictions allow for a broader interpretation of fees, and are the procedural and substantive ramifications positive or negative?
- For those involved in public finance, would a trend toward more earmarking, which might come with fees, be a useful development or would it threaten the integrity of the budget-making process?
- For those concerned about environmental policy from any perspective, would a greater use of fees, with the earmarking that might go alongside, yield a better environmental result?

This chapter does not propose answers. It instead seeks to press for answers as we move into the next century of experiences with environmentally related market-based instruments and continue to wrestle with theory.

NOTES

* The author thanks Scott Sakowski, Zephyr Jost and Andrew Homan for their comments and research.

1. Literature and practice have also focused heavily in recent years on the use of tradable permits, market-based instruments that take a quantity-based approach. This chapter, however, considers only market-based instruments that take a price-based approach. For a discussion of the evolution of the theory of environmental taxes, see Milne and Andersen 2012.

2. According to one analyst, governments have tended to design environmental taxes based on pollution-reduction targets (Vollebergh 2012, p. 15).
3. Using September 2013 currency values.
4. One example of *ex post* analysis is the COMETR project's study of the effects of environmental tax reform in Europe (Andersen and Ekins 2009).
5. This analysis does not attempt to trace the usage of and basis for various terms (tax, fee, charge, levy) in different countries over recent decades, a topic left to continuing research.
6. This analysis does not address the situation where government holds outright ownership of an environmental asset that it can sell or lease. In that case, government's revenue takes the form of a sales price or lease payment, not a fee. For example, in the US, the State of Alaska leases access to oil reserves in Prudhoe Bay. Its constitution requires that 25% of the revenue be held in the Alaska Permanent Fund for the benefit of current and future generations in recognition of the long-term public interest at stake when a finite, public natural resource is consumed (Westin and Bach 2009, pp. 32–3).
7. *See Just v. Marinette County*, 201 N.W. 2d 761 (Wis. 1969); *see generally* Scanlan 2000, pp. 157–63.
8. If the government determines that value according to the harm of the activity to the public asset, the calculation would assume a Pigouvian internalization flavor. The underlying rationale, however, is quite different from a Pigouvian tax, because the payment as a matter of policy is designed as a right to use rather than as a price incentive unattached to legal rights to use.
9. A court in the US state of Texas found that the public trust doctrine covers all of the state's natural resources, not just water, relying on broad language in the Texas constitution. Letter from Judge Gisela D. Triana to Adam Abrams and Cynthia Woelker, dated July 9, 2012, *Angela Bonser-Lain, et al. v. Texas Commission on Environmental Quality*, Cause No. D-1-GN-11–002194 (201st Judicial District Court of Travis County, Texas). The US Alaskan Supreme Court heard arguments in October 2013 about whether the Alaska constitution requires the state to hold the atmosphere in public trust: *Kanuk v. State of Alaska, Department of Natural Resources*, Supreme Court Case No. S-14776.
10. Note that the public trust doctrine may apply differently at different levels of government. For example, in the US, the doctrine is primarily a matter of state law. *See PPL Montana, LLC v. Montana*, 132 S. Ct. 1215, 1234–5 (2012); Frank 2012, pp. 680–1. Recent litigation dismissed a claim asserting that the federal government has an obligation to reduce greenhouse gases under a federal public trust doctrine: *Alec L. v. Jackson*, 863 F. Supp.2d 11 (D.D.C. 2012). From an environmental perspective, a federal right would be preferable for a natural resource that crosses state boundaries, such as air.
11. This example raises interesting issues about which governments can assert quasi-legal interests in the atmosphere when the atmosphere (and its pollutants) functions on a trans-boundary basis. It also leads to questions about the rationales for a fee regime versus a cap-and-trade system. A public trust eco-fee theory posits that the government has a quasi-ownership interest in the atmosphere itself. A cap-and-trade system posits that the government can create quasi-property instruments (tradable allowance) that allow polluters to emit into the atmosphere. In the first instance, the government has the quasi-ownership interest, which it is 'selling'. In the second, the government creates a new form of quasi-property (the allowances) using its regulatory power and that property becomes the means to the end.
12. This rationale also links to the compulsory-versus-voluntary distinction between taxes and fees. When an actor voluntarily chooses to enter a line of business, the payment obligation seems more voluntary than compulsory and hence more like a fee.
13. If the fee represented merely payment for access to a limited market without linkage to governmental remediation obligations, government could be susceptible to the argument that it is using its permitting power to extort. The fee would have a stronger rationale if it were based on the public costs associated with the grant of permission, such as the environmental costs government might choose to assume.

14. The question of which governments have this power may vary from country to country. For example, under the US Constitution, states retain the residual 'police powers' to protect the common welfare. However, the federal government has the right to regulate interstate commerce. *See, e.g., National Federation of Independent Business v. Sebelius*, 132 S. Ct. 2566, 2577–80 (2012).
15. For examples of case law finding that the private sector has no inherent right to pollute, see *Mobil Oil Corp. v. Superior Court*, 59 Cal. App. 3d 293, 305 (1976); *Communities for a Better Environment v. South Coast Air Quality Management District*, 226 P.2d 985, 995 (Cal. 2010).
16. Alternatively, the benefit might be regulatory forbearance. If the government were to impose the fee in lieu of regulatory action, such as a direct regulation limiting the environmentally damaging activity, the benefit could take the form of that regulatory forbearance. This approach raises questions of the extent to which government would need to, and can, agree to limit its regulatory authority.
17. The US Supreme Court used a similar rationale when it evaluated public access exactions associated with the development of land. It reasoned that if government could have denied an application, it can (under certain circumstances) instead attach a mitigating condition to the grant of the application. See *Nollan v. California Coastal Commission*, 483 U.S. 825 (1987). A recent case explored the application of this concept to development impact fees: *Koontz v. St. Johns River Water Management District*, 133 S. Ct. 2586 (2013).
18. *Sinclair Paint Co. v. State Board of Equalization*, 937 P.2d 1350 (Cal. 1997) (deciding whether the fee was subject to California's constitutional supermajority requirement for taxes).
19. One could argue, however, that the government still has substantial latitude. The public doctrine in the US allows private sector interferences with assets held in trust to some extent, with courts playing the key role in defining what is a permissible intrusion (Scanlan 2000, pp. 163–5; Sax 1970, pp. 488–9). If government charges for an interference that it could have allowed without charge, it arguably may not have a fiduciary duty to determine the exact value of the private-sector benefit it is providing. However, one commentator has suggested that transfers of property held in public trust for less than fair market value might be an indicator of potential abuse that would warrant closer judicial scrutiny (Sax 1970, p. 562). Legal fiduciary obligations would depend on the law of each country.
20. For example, the California constitution explicitly imposes a reasonableness requirement (article XIII A, section 3).
21. Under traditional trust theory, trustees should hold any assets in trust for the beneficiaries. In the case of the public trust doctrine, the beneficiaries are the general public. If one defines the general public broadly, one could argue that government could have the freedom to use the fees for any public purpose, but the intuitively stronger argument would seem to be that the government, as trustee of specific environmental resources, should use the revenue for purposes related to those resources. The answer will depend on the legal requirements of any particular jurisdiction.
22. US Constitution, Article I, Section 7, clause 1. *See generally* Saturno 2011.
23. *United States v. Munoz-Flores*, 495 U.S. 385, 399 (1990) (quoting *Twin City Bank v. Nebeker*, 167 U.S. 196, 202 (1897), which in turn cited Justice Joseph Story, Commentaries on the Constitution of the United States, § 880). *See also United States v. Norton*, 91 U.S. 566, 569 (1876); *Millard v. Roberts*, 202 U.S. 429, 436 (1906).
24. *United States v. Munoz-Flores*, 495 U.S. 385, 399 (1990). For examples of taxes deemed not to be subject to the origination clause because they served a non-tax purpose, see *Twin City Bank v. Nebeker*, 167 U.S. 196, 203 (1897) (tax on banks to support currency system); *Millard v. Roberts*, 202 U.S. 429, 436 (1906) (a tax on property to pay for railroad construction projects); *Millard v. Roberts*, 202 U.S. 429, 436 (1906) (a monetary assessment for a violation of criminal law paid into a victims' fund). *See also* Kysar 2014 (dedication of revenue serves as judicial proxy for origination clause purposes).

25. *Sissel v. US Department of Health and Human Services*, Civil Action No. 10–1263 (BAH) (D.D.C. June 28, 2013), 2013 WL 3244826. The court found that Supreme Court precedent could be interpreted to mean that the use of the revenue was not dispositive.
26. Such regulatory fees would deviate from the OECD's definition of the tax/fee distinction cited above, because they would not require a benefit.
27. The US Supreme Court recently found that a 'penalty' for failure to purchase health insurance was legally a tax, in part because it was administered by the Internal Revenue Service. *National Federation of Independent Business v. Sebelius*, 132 S. Ct. 2566, 2596 (2012).
28. Cal. Constitution, article XIII A, section 3.
29. Prior to 2010, the supermajority applied to 'state taxes enacted for the purpose of increasing revenues'. That language generated litigation over the meaning of 'tax'. *See, e.g., Sinclair Paint Co. v. State Board of Equalization*, 937 P.2d 1350 (Cal. 1997) (regulatory fees on paint companies to protect children from lead paint not a 'tax' for constitutional purposes); Joint Ruling on Submitted Matters, *California Chamber of Commerce v. California Air Resources Board*, Case No. 34–2012–80001313 (Cal. Super. Ct.), consolidated with *Morning Star Packing Company v. California Air Resources Board*, Case No. 34–2013–80001464 (Cal. Super. Ct., November 12, 2013) (auctioned greenhouse gas allowances not a 'tax' for constitutional purposes) (appeal pending).
30. Article I, § 8.
31. *American Trucking Associations, Inc. v. Scheiner*, 483 U.S. 266, 277 (1987); *Complete Auto Transit, Inc. v. Brady*, 430 U.S. 274, 278 (1977).
32. In one case, the Court referred to the 'user-fee defense': *American Trucking Associations, Inc. v. Scheiner*, 483 U.S. 266, 289 (1987).
33. *Ibid.* at 290.
34. *Evansville-Vanderburgh Airport Authority District v. Delta Airlines, Inc.* 405 U.S. 707, 720 (1972). In that case, half the revenues from a US$ 1-per-passenger airport fee went to the state aeronautical fund and half to the airport's municipality or airport authority. For the half not dedicated to the fund, the Court only required that the payments not exceed the airport costs. *Ibid.*
35. S. 332, 113th Cong. (2013).
36. The fee would increase by 5.6% annually until the twelfth year.

REFERENCES

Andersen, M.S. and P. Ekins (eds) (2009), *Carbon Energy Taxation: Lessons from Europe*, Oxford, UK: Oxford University Press.

Baumol, W.J. and W.E. Oates (1971), 'The use of standards and prices for protection of the environment', *Swedish Journal of Economics*, 73 (1), 42–54.

Blumm, M.C. and R.D. Guthrie (2012), 'Internationalizing the public trust doctrine: natural law and constitutional and statutory approaches to fulfilling the Saxion vision', *UC Davis Law Review*, 45, 741–808.

Brett, C. and M. Keen (2000), 'Political uncertainty and the earmarking of environmental taxes', *Journal of Public Economics*, 75, 315–40.

Frank, R.M. (2012), 'The public trust doctrine: assessing its recent past & charting its future', *UC Davis Law Review*, 45, 665–91.

Fullerton, D., A. Leicester and S. Smith (2010), 'Environmental taxes', in J. Mirrlees, S. Adam, T. Besley, R. Blundell, S. Bond, R. Chote, M. Gammie, P. Johnson, G. Myles and J. Poterba (eds), *Dimensions of Tax Design: The Mirrlees Review*, pp. 423–518.

Kallbekken, S. and M. Aasen (2010), 'The demand for earmarking: results from a focus group study', *Ecological Economics*, 69, 2183–90.
Kysar, R.M. (2014), 'The "shell bill" game: avoidance and the origination clause', *Washington University Law Review*, 91, 659–720.
Määttä, K. (2006), *Environmental Taxes: An Introductory Analysis*, Cheltenham, UK and Northampton, MA: Edward Elgar.
McGinley, P.C. (2013), 'Climate change and the public trust doctrine', *Planning & Environmental Law*, 65(8), 7–11.
Milne, J.E. (2008), 'New instruments on old turf: the institutional challenges of environmental taxation', in N.J. Chalifour, J.E. Milne, H. Ashiabor, K. Deketelaere and L. Kreiser (eds), *Critical Issues in Environmental Taxation*, Vol. V, Oxford: Oxford University Press, pp. 139–69.
Milne, J.E. and M.S. Andersen (2012), 'Introduction to environmental taxation concepts and research', in J.E. Milne and M.S. Andersen (eds), *Handbook of Research on Environmental Taxation*, Cheltenham, UK and Northampton, MA: Edward Elgar, pp. 15–32.
OECD (2001), *Environmentally Related Taxes in OECD Countries*, Paris: OECD.
OECD (2010), *Taxation, Innovation and the Environment*, Paris: OECD.
Office fédéral de l'environnement (2013), 'Objectif de réduction 2012 non tenu: hausse de la taxe CO2 sur les combustibles dès 2014', available at http://www.bafu.admin.ch/dokumentation/medieninformation/00962/index.html?lang=fr&msg-id=49576, accessed March 31, 2014.
Opschoor, J.B. and H.B. Vos (1989), *Economic Instruments for Environmental Protection*, Paris: OECD.
Pigou, A.C. (1920), *The Economics of Welfare*, London: Macmillan.
Preiss, P. (2012), 'Externality research', in J.E. Milne and M.S. Andersen (eds), *Handbook of Research on Environmental Taxation*, Cheltenham, UK and Northampton, MA: Edward Elgar, pp. 139–57,
Sax, J.L. (1970), 'The public trust doctrine in natural resource law: effective judicial intervention', *Michigan Law Review*, 68, 471–566.
Saturno, J.V. (2011), *The Origination Clause of the US Constitution: Interpretation and Enforcement, CRS Report RL31399*, Washington, DC: Congressional Research Service.
Scanlan, M.K. (2000), 'The evolution of the public trust doctrine and the degradation of trust resources: courts, trustees and political power in Washington', *Ecology Law Quarterly*, 27, 135–213.
Soares, C. (2012), 'Earmarking revenues from environmentally related taxes', in J.E. Milne and M.S. Andersen, *Handbook of Research on Environmental Taxation*, Cheltenham, UK and Northampton, MA: Edward Elgar, pp. 201–1.
Speck, S. (2013), 'Carbon taxation: two decades of experience and future prospects', *Carbon Management*, 4 (2), 171–83.
Vollebergh, H. (2012), *Environmental Taxes and Green Growth: Exploring Possibilities Within Energy and Climate Policy*, The Hague: Netherlands Environmental Assessment Agency.
Weston, B.H. and T. Bach (2009), *Recalibrating the Law of Humans with the Law of Nature: Climate Change, Human Rights and Intergenerational Justice*, South Royalton, VT: Vermont Law School.
Wood, M.C. (2012), 'Atmospheric trust litigation across the world', in K. Coghill, C. Sampford and T. Smith (eds), *Fiduciary Duty and the Atmospheric Trust*, Farnham, UK: Ashgate, pp. 99–163.

2. Environmental taxation for a sustainable future: perspectives from environmental macroeconomics

Seck L. Tan and Dodo J. Thampapillai

1. INTRODUCTION

The aim of this chapter is to present a case for the generalized adoption of the environmental-macroeconomic model for policy analysis – specifically, in fiscal policy analysis. This argument is made comparing the outcomes of a standard macroeconomic model with those of an environmental-macroeconomic model. The hypothesis is that the beneficial effects of environmental taxes are understated in a standard macroeconomic model compared to the environmental-macroeconomic model. This is clearly illustrated in the environmental-macroeconomic model, which explicitly accounts for the depreciation of environmental capital. In this chapter, we consider the context where environmental taxes are used to finance an environmental capital investment, which would offset the depreciation of environmental capital. In this context, the overall macroeconomic gains that include the reduction in environmental capital depreciation would be captured in the environmental-macroeconomic model and not the standard macroeconomic model.

The chapter is structured as follows. The next section deals with the presentation of the standard macroeconomic and environmental-macroeconomic frameworks, and the basis for testing the hypothesis. In Section 3, these frameworks are applied and tested with reference to the Australian economy. For this test, we consider the time series data on macroeconomic aggregates spanning the period 1980 to 2011. We then use these aggregates to estimate trends of pertinent coefficients in our frameworks. Such trends enable the resolution and simulation of specific macroeconomic outcomes, namely income (Y) and inflation (p). Central to the test is the insertion of a hypothetical marginal tax for an environmental capital investment for an initial period. We nominate 2011 as this period and then track the possible outcomes that could emerge following the introduction of the tax and its return on the environment as an investment. For illustrative purposes, we suppose that the investment is reforestation, which, when established, would add to the environmental capital sink capacity to sequester greenhouse gas emissions.[1]

2. THE MACROECONOMIC FRAMEWORKS

Following Thampapillai and Sinden (2013) and Thampapillai (2012), both the standard and environmental-macroeconomic frameworks are exposited in terms of aggregate demand (AD), aggregate supply (AS) and factor utilization. The differentiating feature between the two frameworks is the presence of environmental capital (KN) and its depreciation in the environmental-macroeconomic framework. AS is differentiated into a short-run function (AS_{SR}) and a capacity function (AS_F). It is assumed that AS_{SR} is strictly Keynesian – that is, production of as much output as possible would be endeavoured at a given set of prices. The definition of AD rests on the Fisher–Money equation. A Cobb–Douglas function of constant returns to scale describes factor utilization involving manufactured capital (KM) and labour (L) in the standard framework and in addition KN in the environmental-macroeconomic framework.

The two sets of frameworks are defined below.

2.1 The Standard Framework

$$AS_{SR}\text{: } \{(\pi = \pi_t) \mid (Y \to \infty)\} \tag{1}$$

$$AS_F\text{: } \{(Y = Y_F) \mid (\pi \to \infty)\} \tag{2}$$

$$AD\text{: } \pi_t = \left[\frac{M_t V_t}{Y_t P_{t-1}}\right] \tag{3}$$

In (3), Y is determined by the components of aggregate expenditure as follows:

$$\text{GDP} = \Phi + \beta Y(1 - \tau) \tag{4}$$

In (4): Φ is a constant comprising of investment, government spending and net exports, whilst β, and t are respectively the marginal propensity to consume and the rate of taxation. Factor utilization is defined as:

$$\text{Y} = \alpha\, \text{KM}^{\Theta}\, \text{L}^{\lambda} \tag{5}$$

In (5), θ and λ represent respectively the shares of Y that accrue to KM and L. The assumption of constant returns to scale dictates that $(\theta + \lambda) = 1$. Given that the income statements in national accounts is bounded by the identity defining payments to KM – namely Operating Surplus (OS) and payments to L – namely Compensation of Employees (CE), the point-estimate values of θ and λ can be elicited respectively as: (OS/Y) and (CE/Y).

2.2 The Environmental-Macroeconomic Framework

The environmental-macroeconomic framework differs from the standard framework by the recognition of KN in the definition of factor utilization and that of gross domestic product (GDP). That is, expressions in (4) would be redefined as follows:

$$GDP = (1 - \eta)\ \{\Phi + \beta Y\ (1 - \tau)\} \qquad (6)$$

In (6), η is the share of expenditure in GDP that accounts for the depreciation of KN – namely D_{KN}. The definition of factor utilization now becomes:

$$Y = (1 - \eta)\ \alpha\ (KM + KN)^{\theta}\ L^{\lambda} \qquad (7)$$

Note that should $(KN \rightarrow 0)$, then $(D_{KN} \rightarrow 0)$ and hence $(h \rightarrow 0)$. In such a context (6) and (7) would revert to (4) and (5). The basis for the formulation in (7) is provided in Thampapillai (2012) and rests on the recognition of the principles of entropy and ecological resilience. In Thampapillai (2012) and Thampapillai and Sinden (2013), the distinction is drawn between the accumulation of KN and the utilization of KN. The quantum of KN referred to in (7) pertains to the utilization of KN.

As illustrated in Thampapillai and Sinden (2013), when point-estimate data is available for the components of (6) and (7) barring of course KN, it is possible to estimate the quantum of KN utilized as follows by dividing (5) by (7):

$$KN = \left[\left(\frac{1}{(1 - \eta)}\right)^{\frac{1}{\theta}} - 1\right] * KM \qquad (8)$$

Consider Figure 2.1, the environmental-macroeconomic framework, which includes the internalization of KN.

In the environmental-macroeconomic model, GDP is now revised as per (6) to account for the depreciation of KN. The constituents of income Y

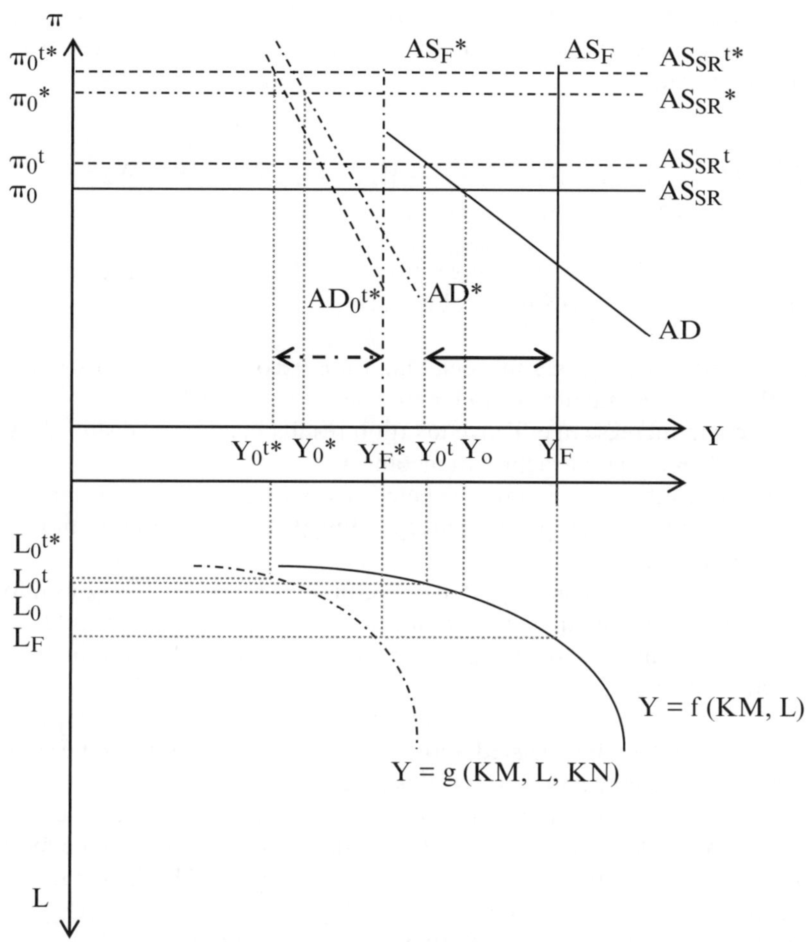

Figure 2.1 Environmental-macroeconomic framework

now include KM, L as well as KN (as a third factor in the factor utilization function). The resulting output gap is now represented by $(Y_F^* - Y_o^*)$ as opposed to $(Y_F - Y_o)$ in the standard macroeconomic model. The increase in inflation, π, would be $(\pi_o^{t*} - \pi_o^*)$ as opposed to $(\pi_o^t - \pi_o)$ in the standard macroeconomic model. An increase in effective taxation in this context will shift the AD^* curve leftwards to AD_o^{t*}. The increase in the level of unemployment would be $(L_o - L_o^{t*})$ as opposed to $(L_o - L_o^t)$ in the standard macroeconomic model.

It is apparent from Figure 2.1 that the changes in the level of Y, π and L will be different when the environmental-macroeconomic model is used as opposed to the standard macroeconomic model. In the section below we illustrate the application of the two frameworks with reference to Australian data.[2]

3. THE ILLUSTRATION – ENVIRONMENTAL TAXES

We envisage the following sequence of events/outcomes with reference to our illustration on environmental taxes.

1. The introduction of a marginal tax for environmental purposes raises the effective rate of taxation, and taxes (T) collected.
2. Such an increase in effective taxation results in a leftward shift of AD and thereby a contraction in income Y.
3. If the contraction is not remedied – for example, by returning the additional taxes as government spending (G) – then both inflation and unemployment would rise.
4. If the marginal taxes collected are returned soon enough, say, as reforestation, then apart from adding to the KN stock, there would be a reduction in D_{KN} following an appropriate lag time. We nominate this lag time as six years.[3]

The final point (point 4) listed above is not readily captured in the standard macroeconomic model as we illustrate below.

To begin with, we estimate the value of Australia's income Y in terms of both frameworks and illustrate that the standard macroeconomic model has overstated economic performance; see Figure 2.2. This is of course to be expected.

Second, we also employed (8) to estimate the quantum of KN that was utilized between 1980 and 2011. The utilization of KN is proxied to sink capacity as greenhouse gas emission. It was estimated based on the data obtained from World Development Indicators (World Bank 2013) for emission of carbon dioxide (CO_2), methane (CH_4), nitrous oxide (N_2O), and other greenhouse gases (which include hydrofluorocarbons (HFC), perfluorinated compounds (PFC), sulphur hexafluorinated compounds (PFC) and sulphur hexafluoride (SF_6)). All greenhouse gas emissions are expressed in tons of CO_2 equivalent and were costed at US$ 100/tonne – as per Stern (2007), Ackerman et al. (2009), Hope (2011), and Karstad (2012). The resulting value of the total cost of air pollution and abatement is regarded as the depreciation of environmental capital, D_{KN}.

The KN empirical test for Australia shows that KN utilization has been

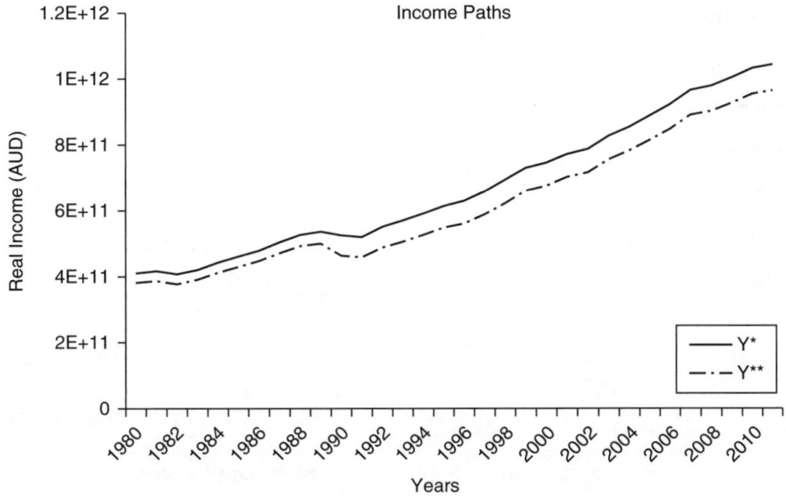

Figure 2.2 Comparison of the income paths of both frameworks

on the increase. In line with the increasing income functions in Figure 2.2, one can infer that utilization of the environment is necessary for the growth of an economy.

3.1 Simulations

We also simulated potential outcomes with reference to both models. For this purpose, we nominate 2011 as an initial year and use the pertinent coefficients of the two models to resolve for income Y and inflation p. These coefficients, together with the expectations concerning their changes until 2020 are presented in the Appendix as Tables 2A.1 and 2A.2. The tables also include the results of the analysis with reference to the outcome variables.

The expectations concerning the coefficients are gleaned from the time series data used in this study. The data reveals that the only coefficients likely to increase in the foreseeable future are F, KM and L_F. Because the others show modest to marginal changes, we have set them to be constant.

The key outcomes with reference to income Y and inflation π are illustrated in Figures 2.3 and 2.4.

3.2 Analysis

The analysis rests on the introduction of a marginal tax of 1 percent[4] in 2011. As can be seen in both model outcomes ($Y^*_{t2011} < Y^*_{2011}$) and

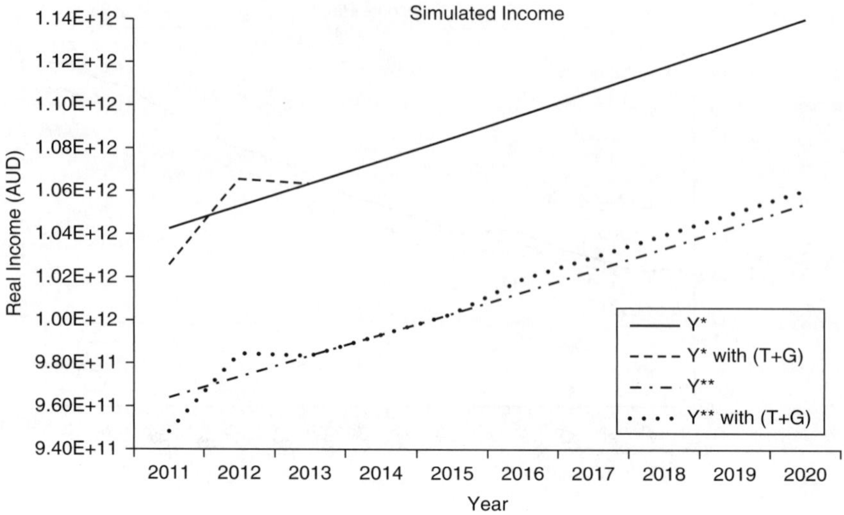

Figure 2.3 Simulated income comparisons (2011 – 2020)

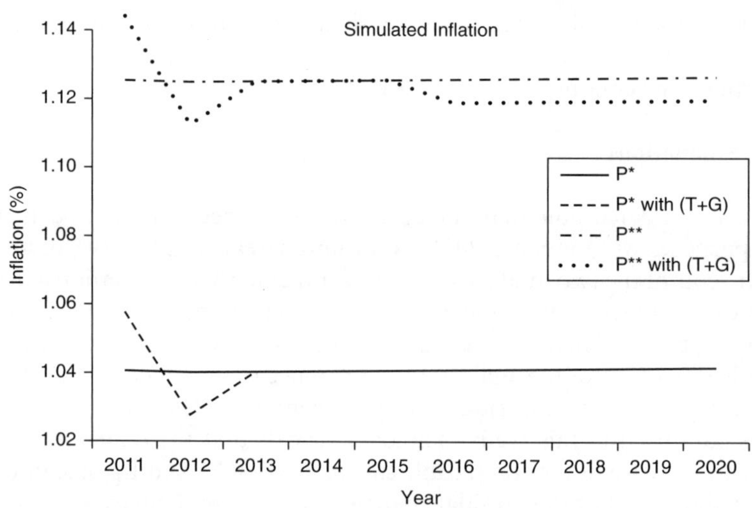

Figure 2.4 Simulated inflation paths (2011 – 2020)

($Y^{**}_{t2011} < Y^{**}_{2011}$). We then assume that 50 percent of the tax revenue collected in 2011 will be returned as an environmental capital investment in 2012. The spike in {Y^{*} with T+G} and {Y^{**} with T + G} for both models represents this return. As this investment is in forestry, we suppose that

Table 2.1 2011 snapshot of macroeconomic indicators

	Standard Macroeconomic Model	Environmental-Macroeconomic Model
Income	1.04E+12	9.64E+11
Inflation	1.04	1.13

Table 2.2 2011 snapshot of macroeconomic indicators with taxes re-invested

	Standard Macroeconomic Model	Environmental-Macroeconomic Model
Income	1.03E+12	9.48E+11
Inflation	1.06	1.14

the coefficient pertaining to D_{KN}, namely η would decrease by 3 percent after six years.

As can be observed, with the standard macroeconomic model, barring the changes in 2012 due to the return of a portion of tax revenue, the outcome variables $\{Y^*, [Y^* \text{ with } T + G]\}$ and $\{p, [p \text{ with } T + G]\}$ show no variation whatsoever. This is not the case with the results of the environmental-macroeconomic model. From both Tables 2A.1 and 2A.2 (Appendix) and Figures 2.3 and 2.4, it is clear that the enhanced sequestration capacity of KN can lead to clear benefits which are captured in the environmental-macroeconomic model. These benefits are increased income and stabilized inflation levels. The benefits are illustrated in Tables 2.1 and 2.2 – where snapshots for year 2011 of the two macroeconomic indicators in both the standard macroeconomic and environmental-macroeconomic model are presented.

3.3 Policy Implications

It is clear from Tables 2.1 and 2.2 that the two models displayed significantly different policy domains. In a report by United Nations (2013), tax revenues can be used to finance economic and social inclusion programs. The re-investment of taxes will work better in combination with well-defined regulatory measures and complementary measures designed to compensate the regressive effects of taxes (United Nations 2013). The revenue from taxes can cut budget deficits while meeting environmental objectives. Environmental taxes are defined as ‘green taxes’ by Hecht

(2005). 'Green taxes' can be recycled to allow other forms of taxes, for example, income tax, to be reduced towards a 'green income'. Collier (2010) advocates a carbon tax because it allows taxation on other economic activity to be reduced, and would be better than a heavily compromised emissions trading scheme (Garnaut 2008) where the issue of accumulated carbon in the environment is not addressed. However, the success of policy initiatives will be dependent on the type of macroeconomic frameworks used. The standard macroeconomic model does not capture the full benefits from environmental taxation. The effects of environmental taxation will only be captured in the environmental-macroeconomic model. Hence, the policy option of expanding environmental capacity and reducing environmental capital depreciation would be explicit in the environmental-macroeconomic model.[5]

4. CONCLUSION

Environmental taxation for a sustainable future requires policymakers to carry out fiscal reforms. Environmental fiscal reforms is a range of taxation and pricing measures which can raise fiscal revenues and increase efficiency while furthering environmental goals (OECD 2013). Fiscal consolidation and climate policy can reap sustained welfare gains for future generations (Rausch 2013). However, such reforms are often restricted by politics and institutions (Besley, Ilzetzki and Persson 2013) and such taxes need to be reinvested within the confines of fiscal balance (Thampapillai, Wu and Tan 2010).

In the case of Australia, such taxes can be reinvested into the sensitive ecosystem and agricultural technology to address food security challenges, and towards an effective transport infrastructure (Cadden 2013). It is obvious that there are multi-faceted considerations for each policy option. Tax revenues can be reinvested towards a portfolio of environmental assets or could simply be saved for wealth preservation. But, more importantly, the argument should lie in applying an environmental-macroeconomic framework which will address the macroeconomic objectives of income and inflation towards a sustainable future.

NOTES

1. The choice of reforestation as a proxy for KN is prompted primarily by the available data. However, the framework developed and tested is such that it can be extended to include other components of KN in the context of data availability.

2. Although our illustration pertains to Australia, the framework can easily be extended to industrial economies such as the European Union, Japan, and the United States. Perhaps the role of reforestation in sequestering pollution is higher with industrialized economies relative to less industrialized ones.
3. The nomination of six years follows earlier studies from Thampapillai, Thangavelu and Quah (2006).
4. The choice of 1 percent as the marginal rate of taxation was purely arbitrary and is displayed only for illustrative purposes. If this model is extended to include feedback loops that clearly define the effects of reforestation on the economy, then the determination of a desirable tax rate becomes feasible. Such feasibility would be guided by an iterative process.
5. The model developed and applied in this study is indeed a simple comparative-static one. There are several ways by which the model could be extended. These include dynamics of AD based on changes in population and, more importantly, attitudinal changes that recognize preferences towards environmental stewardship. Besides, such dynamics could also be extended to the analytics of factor utilization to capture changes inherent in KN.

REFERENCES

Ackerman, F., E.A. Stanton, S.J. DeCanio, E. Goodstein, R.B. Howarth, R.B. Norgaard, C.S. Norman, and K.A. Sheeran (2009), 'The Economics of 350: The Benefits and Costs of Climate Stabilization', *Economics for Equity and the Environment Network*, October 2009, p. 4.

Besley, T., E. Ilzetzki and T. Persson (2013), 'Weak States and Steady States: The Dynamics of Fiscal Capacity', *American Economic Journal: Macroeconomics*, 5(4), 205–35.

Cadden, J. (2013), 'RBA official calls for better transport', *The Australian*, November 26, 2013.

Collier, P. (2010), *The Plundered Planet*, Oxford, UK: Oxford University Press.

Garnaut, R. (2008), *The Garnaut Climate Change Review, 2008*, 'Final Report', September 2008, Cambridge, UK: Cambridge University Press.

Hecht, J. E. (2005), *National Environment Accounting – Bridging the Gap between Ecology and Economy*, Washington DC: Resources for the Future.

Hope, C.W. (2011), 'The Social Cost of CO_2 from the PAGE09 Model', Economics, Discussion Paper 2011–39, September 2011, available at http://www.economics-ejournal.org/economics/discussionpapers/2011-39.

Karstad, P.I. (2012), 'The Price on Carbon should Increase', Statoil Innovate Blog, April 24, 2012, available at http://innovateblog.statoil.com/2012/04/24/the-price-on-carbon-should-increase/.

Organisation for Economic Co-operation and Development (OECD) (2013), 'A Toolkit of Policy Options to Support Inclusive Green Growth', Submission to the G20 Development Working Group by the Asian Development Bank, the OECD, the United Nations and the World Bank.

Rausch, S. (2013), 'Fiscal Consolidation and Climate Policy: An Overlapping Generations Perspective', *Energy Economics*, doi: 10.1016/j.eneco.2013.09.009.

Stern, N. (2007), *The Economics of Climate Change: The Stern Review*, Cambridge, UK: Cambridge University Press.

Thampapillai, D.J. (2012), 'Macroeconomics versus Environmental-Macroeconomics', *The Australian Journal of Agricultural and Resource Economics*, Vol. 55, 1–16.

Thampapillai, D.J. and J. Sinden (2013), *Environmental Economics: Concepts, Methods and Policies*, Melbourne, Australia: Oxford University Press.
Thampapillai, D.J., S.M. Thangavelu and E. Quah (2006), 'The Value of Nature in Thailand', *International Journal of Environment Workplace and Employment*, Vol. 2, No. 4, 359–72, September 2006.
Thampapillai, D.J., X. Wu and S. Tan (2010), 'Fiscal Balance: Environmental Taxes and Investments', *Journal of Natural Resources Policy Research*, Vol. 2, No. 2, pp. 137–147, April 2010.
United Nations (2013), 'World Economic and Social Survey 2013 – Sustainable Development Challenges', Department of Economic and Social Affairs, United Nations Publication.
World Bank (2013), World Development Indicators, online edition, 2013, available at: http://databank.worldbank.org/data/views/variableSelection/selectvariables.aspx?source=world-development-indicators.

APPENDIX

Table 2A.1 Standard macroeconomic model

	2011	2012	2013	2014	2015	2016	2017	2018	2019	2020
Pt	1.28	1.3312	1.384448	1.439826	1.497419	1.557316	1.619608	1.684393	1.751768	1.821839
M1	2.63E+11	2.71E+11	2.79E+11	2.88E+11	2.96E+11	3.05E+11	3.14E+11	3.24E+11	3.33E+11	3.43E+11
V	5.07E+00	5.17E+00	5.28E+00	5.38E+00	5.49E+00	5.60E+00	5.71E+00	5.82E+00	5.94E+00	6.06E+00
Pt−1	1.23E+00	1.28E+00	1.33E+00	1.38E+00	1.44E+00	1.50E+00	1.56E+00	1.62E+00	1.68E+00	1.75E+00
Φ	4.22E+11	4.26E+11	4.31E+11	4.35E+11	4.39E+11	4.44E+11	4.48E+11	4.53E+11	4.57E+11	4.62E+11
β	6.65E−01	6.65E−01	6.65E−01	6.65E−01	6.65E−01	6.65E−01	6.65E−01	6.65E−01	6.65E−01	6.65E−01
τ	1.05E−01	1.05E−01	1.05E−01	1.05E−01	1.05E−01	1.05E−01	1.05E−01	1.05E−01	1.05E−01	1.05E−01
θ	4.69E−01	4.69E−01	4.69E−01	4.69E−01	4.69E−01	4.69E−01	4.69E−01	4.69E−01	4.69E−01	4.69E−01
λ	5.31E−01	5.31E−01	5.31E−01	5.31E−01	5.31E−01	5.31E−01	5.31E−01	5.31E−01	5.31E−01	5.31E−01
α	2.06E+02	2.06E+02	2.06E+02	2.06E+02	2.06E+02	2.06E+02	2.06E+02	2.06E+02	2.06E+02	2.06E+02
LF	1.21E+07	1.23E+07	1.26E+07	1.28E+07	1.31E+07	1.33E+07	1.36E+07	1.39E+07	1.41E+07	1.44E+07
Capital Stock (KM)	4.96E+12	5.01E+12	5.06E+12	5.11E+12	5.16E+12	5.21E+12	5.26E+12	5.32E+12	5.37E+12	5.42E+12
Y*	1.04E+12	1.05E+12	1.06E+12	1.07E+12	1.08E+12	1.10E+12	1.11E+12	1.12E+12	1.13E+12	1.14E+12
Y*t	1.03E+12									
Y* with (T+G)	1.03E+12	1.07E+12	1.06E+12	1.07E+12	1.08E+12	1.10E+12	1.11E+12	1.12E+12	1.13E+12	1.14E+12

Table 2A.1 (continued)

	2011	2012	2013	2014	2015	2016	2017	2018	2019	2020
YF	1.07E+12	1.09E+12	1.10E+12	1.12E+12	1.14E+12	1.16E+12	1.17E+12	1.19E+12	1.21E+12	1.23E+12
L	1.15E+07	1.16E+07	1.17E+07	1.18E+07	1.19E+07	1.20E+07	1.22E+07	1.23E+07	1.24E+07	1.25E+07
L with T+G	1.11E+07	1.18E+07	1.17E+07	1.18E+07	1.19E+07	1.20E+07	1.22E+07	1.23E+07	1.24E+07	1.25E+07
Π*	1.04E+00	1.04E+00	1.04E+00	1.04E+00	1.04E+00	1.04E+00	1.04E+00	1.04E+00	1.04E+00	1.04E+00
Π* with T+G	1.06E+00	1.03E+00	1.04E+00	1.04E+00	1.04E+00	1.04E+00	1.04E+00	1.04E+00	1.04E+00	1.04E+00
PF	1.01E+00	1.01E+00	1.00E+00	9.97E−01	9.92E−01	9.87E−01	9.82E−01	9.77E−01	9.72E−01	9.67E−01
LF−L	6.11E+05	7.38E+05	8.68E+05	1.00E+06	1.14E+06	1.28E+06	1.43E+06	1.58E+06	1.73E+06	1.89E+06
LF−L with T+G	9.57E+05	4.74E+05	8.68E+05	1.00E+06	1.14E+06	1.28E+06	1.43E+06	1.58E+06	1.73E+06	1.89E+06

Table 2A.2 Environmental macroeconomic model

	2011	2012	2013	2014	2015	2016	2017	2018	2019	2020
Pt	1.28	1.3312	1.384448	1.439826	1.497419	1.557316	1.619608	1.684393	1.751768	1.821839
M1	2.63E+11	2.71E+11	2.79E+11	2.88E+11	2.96E+11	3.05E+11	3.14E+11	3.24E+11	3.33E+11	3.43E+11
V	5.07E+00	5.17E+00	5.28E+00	5.38E+00	5.49E+00	5.60E+00	5.71E+00	5.82E+00	5.94E+00	6.06E+00
Pt−1	1.23E+00	1.28E+00	1.33E+00	1.38E+00	1.44E+00	1.50E+00	1.56E+00	1.62E+00	1.68E+00	1.75E+00
Φ	4.22E+11	4.26E+11	4.31E+11	4.35E+11	4.39E+11	4.44E+11	4.48E+11	4.53E+11	4.57E+11	4.62E+11
β	7.26E−01	7.26E−01	7.26E−01	7.26E−01	7.26E−01	7.26E−01	7.26E−01	7.26E−01	7.26E−01	7.26E−01
τ	1.13E−01	1.13E−01	1.13E−01	1.13E−01	1.13E−01	1.13E−01	1.13E−01	1.13E−01	1.13E−01	1.13E−01
η	7.53E−02	7.53E−02	7.53E−02	7.53E−02	7.53E−02	7.53E−02	7.53E−02	7.53E−02	7.53E−02	7.53E−02
η revised	7.53E−02	7.53E−02	7.53E−02	7.53E−02	7.53E−02	7.31E−02	7.31E−02	7.31E−02	7.31E−02	7.31E−02
θ	4.69E−01	4.69E−01	4.69E−01	4.69E−01	4.69E−01	4.69E−01	4.69E−01	4.69E−01	4.69E−01	4.69E−01
λ	5.31E−01	5.31E−01	5.31E−01	5.31E−01	5.31E−01	5.31E−01	5.31E−01	5.31E−01	5.31E−01	5.31E−01
α	2.06E+02	2.06E+02	2.06E+02	2.06E+02	2.06E+02	2.06E+02	2.06E+02	2.06E+02	2.06E+02	2.06E+02
LF	1.21E+07	1.23E+07	1.26E+07	1.28E+07	1.31E+07	1.33E+07	1.36E+07	1.39E+07	1.41E+07	1.44E+07
Capital Stock (KM)	4.96E+12	5.01E+12	5.06E+12	5.11E+12	5.16E+12	5.21E+12	5.26E+12	5.32E+12	5.37E+12	5.42E+12
KN Utilized	9.00E+11	9.09E+11	9.19E+11	9.28E+11	9.37E+11	9.46E+11	9.56E+11	9.65E+11	9.75E+11	9.85E+11
Y**	9.64E+11	9.74E+11	9.83E+11	9.93E+11	1.00E+12	1.01E+12	1.02E+12	1.03E+12	1.04E+12	1.05E+12
Y**t	9.48E+11									
Y** with (T+G)	9.48E+11	9.84E+11	9.83E+11	9.93E+11	1.00E+12	1.02E+12	1.03E+12	1.04E+12	1.05E+12	1.06E+12

Table 2A.2 (continued)

	2011	2012	2013	2014	2015	2016	2017	2018	2019	2020
YF	9.91E+11	1.01E+12	1.02E+12	1.04E+12	1.05E+12	1.07E+12	1.09E+12	1.10E+12	1.12E+12	1.14E+12
L (EM)	9.88E+06	9.98E+06	1.01E+07	1.02E+07	1.03E+07	1.04E+07	1.05E+07	1.06E+07	1.07E+07	1.08E+07
L with T+G (EM)	9.58E+06	1.02E+07	1.01E+07	1.02E+07	1.03E+07	1.05E+07	1.06E+07	1.07E+07	1.08E+07	1.09E+07
Π**	1.13E+00	1.12E+00	1.13E+00	1.13E+00	1.13E+00	1.13E+00	1.13E+00	1.13E+00	1.13E+00	1.13E+00
Π** with T+G	1.14E+00	1.11E+00	1.13E+00	1.13E+00	1.13E+00	1.12E+00	1.12E+00	1.12E+00	1.12E+00	1.12E+00
PF	1.09E+00	1.09E+00	1.08E+00	1.08E+00	1.07E+00	1.06E+00	1.06E+00	1.05E+00	1.05E+00	1.04E+00
LF−L	2.18E+06	2.33E+06	2.47E+06	2.62E+06	2.78E+06	2.93E+06	3.10E+06	3.26E+06	3.43E+06	3.61E+06
LF−L with T+G	2484036	2115079	2471490	2621713	2775947	2815435	2976779	3142400	3312394	3486860

3. The role of the precautionary principle in designing energy taxes in Australia

Prafula Pearce

1. INTRODUCTION: THE NEED FOR ENERGY TAXES

The precautionary principle as defined in Principle 15 of the 1992 Rio Declaration on Environment and Development states:

> In order to protect the environment, the precautionary approach shall be widely applied by States according to their capabilities. Where there are threats of serious or irreversible damage, lack of full scientific certainty shall not be used as a reason for postponing cost-effective measures to prevent environmental degradation.[1]

The precautionary principle has been widely used in international environmental law, but it has not been employed to judge political decisions for the conservation of oil. The call to conserve oil for future generations can be identified from the United Nations (UN) Brundtland Report, which states that the needs of the present must be met without compromising the ability of future generations to meet their own needs.[2] In designing and implementing oil policy in Australia, the precautionary principle dictates that measures to ensure sustainability should take the long term view and not be postponed on the grounds that scientific certainty has yet to be achieved. This chapter examines the sustainability of oil within the principles laid down by the global community through UN declarations and resolutions and how Australia has applied these principles. This chapter also demonstrates that the Australian government has a moral imperative and arguably also a legal obligation to adopt policies for the sustainability of oil, and that the precautionary principle can assist in designing energy taxes in Australia.

The author of this chapter, in an earlier book of this series proposed that the Australian government should take the lead and replace its transportation taxes with a luxury energy tax (LET).[3] The idea of using energy taxes to promote energy efficiency and consumption of more environmentally friendly products is now gaining momentum in Europe. The European Union proposes to revise the Energy Taxation Directive to allow its member states to make the best possible use of taxation and support sustainable growth.[4] The OECD 2013 Report on Taxing Energy Use has also now adopted the view that carefully designed energy taxes can assist in bringing about a change in behaviour and counteract the price elasticity of energy as a whole, which is relatively low in the short term.[5]

2. PRINCIPLES ENDORSED BY THE GLOBAL COMMUNITY

By participating in global discussions initiated by the UN, Australia has shown its intent and commitment to care for future generations of humanity, and that the sustainability of oil should form part of that commitment. Although the UN declarations and resolutions are non-binding instruments, they can become legally binding under customary law due to their wide acceptance.

Australia is a founding member of the UN and has consistently supported the UN's role in global sustainable development discussions since the 1970s. Australia participated in the 1972 UN Conference on Human Environment in Stockholm, which established a number of principles. Principle 5 stated that 'The non-renewable resources of the earth must be employed in such a way as to guard against the danger of their future exhaustion and to ensure that benefits from such employment are shared by all mankind'.[6] This chapter submits that Principle 5 should apply to the preservation of energy, in particular energy from oil.

From 1983 to 1987, the UN organized the World Commission on Environmental Development that produced the Brundtland Report. The key message from the Brundtland Report is sustainable development with an emphasis on the needs of the future generations. It states:

> We borrow environmental capital from future generations with no intention or prospect of repaying. They may damn us for our spendthrift ways, but they can never collect on our debt to them. We act as we do because we can get away with it: future generations do not vote; they have no political or financial power; they cannot challenge our decisions.[7]

The Brundtland Commission examined the dilemma of fossil fuels, in particular oil, and acknowledged forecasts that oil production will level off by the early decades of the twenty-first century, which is about now, and then gradually fall during a period of reduced supplies and higher prices.[8] The Brundtland Commission promoted energy efficiency and conservation measures so that waste of primary energy sources is minimized.[9] This applies to oil as it is a primary energy source for most countries.

The preservation of oil also falls within the discussion that occurred at the 1992 UN Conference on Environment and Development held in Rio de Janeiro, called the Earth Summit.[10] Twenty-seven principles were declared at the Rio conference, of which Principle 15 is the precautionary principle as defined above.

Further calls for sustainable development came from the resolutions adopted by the UN General Assembly declared at the 2000 Millennium Summit,[11] the 2002 World Summit[12] and also the 2012 Rio+20 Summit.[13]

The sustainability of oil should form part of caring for our environment and the needs of future generations. Unless people change their behaviour and governments bring about change through appropriate policies, there could be ramifications for survival and quality of life in the long run.

3. THE NEED TO INCLUDE OIL SUSTAINABILITY WITHIN THE GLOBAL COMMUNITY PRINCIPLES

The sustainability principle recommended by the Brundtland Commission focuses on intergeneration equity, requiring the present generation to ensure the wellbeing of future generations. The resource of conventional oil is finite and irreplaceable and therefore its current use should be examined to ensure that it is sustained for the wellbeing of future generations. The geological timing of some of the major oil reserves in the world and in Australia dates back to between 100 and 300 million years ago in the Palaeozoic and the Mesozoic eras and these reserves have been almost depleted in a matter of 100 to 150 years.[14] As discussed below, Australia has almost used up its known economic demonstrated oil reserves except for the balance ten years of supply, based on current demand.[15] Australia is now participating in using up the global oil reserves as it is heavily dependent on imports of both refined petroleum products and crude oil to meet its liquid fuel demand.[16] Many organizations have reported on the status of world oil reserves and although there are variances in their estimates of outstanding reserves, these variances would only give a few more decades of available oil for consumption. The Australian government in its 2010 Australian Energy Resource Assessment stated that, based on current production, the estimated world proven oil reserves are enough to last for around 42 years.[17] This confirms the predictions made by many international agencies that global oil production has already peaked. The Australian primary oil production peaked in 2000–2001.[18]

This timeframe indicates that all countries including Australia should be preserving conventional oil and using it sparingly. With a limited supply of conventional oil, the needs of future generations will have to be met through new discoveries of oil or unconventional oils that are more expensive to extract and with a much lower ratio of 'energy return on energy invested'. This leads to the next question of whether the sustainability of conventional oil falls within the precautionary principle, whereby policymakers should not postpone measures to prevent environmental degradation even though there is lack of full scientific certainty as to when the oil supplies will no longer be able to meet demand.

The precautionary principle is a well-known principle and has its origins in the German concept of '*Vorsorgeprinzip*', which literally means the 'foresight principle'.[19] The principle has been widely applied in many different forms and incorporated in multilateral agreements, international laws, domestic laws and policies.[20] The area where the precautionary principle has been most commonly applied is environmental and public health, for example climate change, biodiversity, endangered species, fisheries management, wildlife, trade, food safety, pollution control, chemical regulation and exposure to toxins,[21] but it has not been applied to oil conservation.

The precautionary principle focuses on uncertainty and irreversibility and the threat of serious or irreversible damage. The uncertainty concerning conventional oil is the timeframe when the global oil production has peaked and the oil supply crunch is likely to occur, although it is reasonably certain that conventional oil is finite and the oil supply will not last forever.

Besides transportation, we are dependent on oil to produce many products and without oil some of these products will be hard to replace. More importantly, a dwindling oil supply will affect our food supply and our ability to feed a global population of almost 7 billion people and increasing,[22] and, of this, 95 per cent of the increase will occur in developing countries.[23] The Australian population is expected to increase from 21.6 million in 2008 to 28.5 million by 2030.[24]

The precautionary principle calls for an understanding of the value of oil as a finite resource in order to eliminate its wastage. In addition to providing humanity with the cheapest source of energy in its history, oil has also enabled us to produce tens of thousands of products that it was not otherwise possible to bring into existence before the discovery of fossil fuels. Thus precautionary policies should be adopted to at least prevent the wastage of oil where its use can be curtailed, for example, in driving large and powerful motor vehicles and sports utility vehicles (SUVs) for personal transportation. The precautionary principle should trigger international treaties or agreements within the global community for the reduction of oil use, similar to international agreements and treaties for the prevention of pollution and climate change.[25]

If policymakers are aware of the fact that conventional oil supplies are dwindling, then they should be duty-bound to set policies to curtail oil consumption, reduce wastage and preserve it for future generations. There is a call to take sustainable development out of the environment box into fields of energy.[26] It is submitted that oil, being a non-renewable energy resource, should take priority, as the loss of oil could have a drastic impact on life. The extent to which Australia has adopted the sustainability and precautionary principles for the conservation of oil is explored in the next section.

4. AUSTRALIA'S NATIONAL STRATEGY FOR SUSTAINABLE DEVELOPMENT AND THE CONSERVATION OF OIL

Australia does not have an oil conservation policy despite the fact that the Australian government is aware that Australia has less than ten years of economic demonstrated oil reserves[27] and that it is heavily dependent on imports of both refined petroleum products and crude oil to meet its liquid fuel demands.[28] The Australian Energy Resource Assessment provides some startling facts about the status of Australia's oil position: that Australia has about 0.3 per cent of world oil reserves; that Australia's oil consumption is projected to increase over the next two decades; that Australia's crude oil production is projected to continue to decline; that, in the absence of major new discoveries and the development of alternatives, Australia's net imports on liquid fuels are projected to increase; and that to date around 80 per cent of the crude oil reserves in Australia have already been depleted.[29] The oil consumption in Australia is forecast to increase from 2359PJ in 2012–2013 to 2888PJ in 2034–2035 (a 22 per cent increase) and 3391PJ in 2049–2050 (a 44 per cent increase).[30] Oil remains the major energy source of consumption as demonstrated in Figure 3.1.

Since Australia relies heavily on imported oil, it can become vulnerable if the oil supplies are disrupted due to circumstances beyond the government's control. Australia's oil vulnerability can be gleaned from a recent National Roads and Motorists' Association (NRMA)-commissioned report[31] released on 28 February 2013, which states that Australia has sufficient fuel for about three weeks (23 days) at its disposal and if the

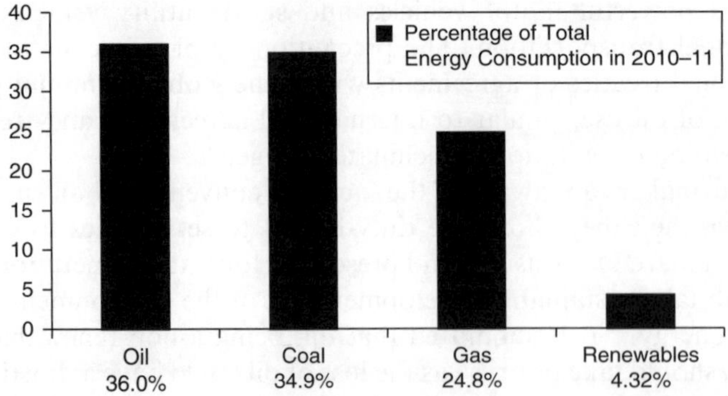

Source: Australian Government Department of Resources, Energy and Tourism (2013), Energy in Australia 2013, ABARE, Canberra, p. 4.

Figure 3.1 Energy consumption in Australia (2010–2011)

liquid fuel supply were to be disrupted, the road transport network would be crippled within weeks. The report further states that without adequate transport, shops will run out of chilled, frozen and dry food within seven to nine days, chemists will run out of medicine within a week, hospitals within three days, and fuel supplies for motorists will be exhausted in three days.[32]

This raises the question as to whether there is an obligation on the part of the Australian government to develop oil conservation policies in accordance with the sustainability and precautionary principles or approaches proposed and declared by the Brundtland Commission and the Rio Declaration discussed above. The Australian government addressed the 1987 Brundtland Report by releasing a public discussion paper in 1989 to develop a National Strategy for Ecological Sustainable Development (NSESD).[33] The term adopted in Australia is 'ecologically sustainable development' (ESD) to address the Brundtland Commission's definition of sustainable development.[34] The NSESD was endorsed by the Australian government in 1992 and it stated that ESD 'aims to meet the needs of Australians today, while conserving our ecosystems for the benefit of future generations'. The NSESD established working groups that include energy production and energy use, but the objectives identified under this category focus on harmful emissions rather than conservation of oil.[35]

Australia's commitment to promoting ESD is reflected in the Inter-Governmental Agreement on the Environment (IGAE) between the Commonwealth, States and Territories, providing for a cooperative national approach to the environment.[36] The IGAE provides that all levels of government should be guided by and take into consideration the sustainability and precautionary principles in developing and implementing environmental policy and programmes.[37]

The precautionary principle has also been adopted in the Environment Protection and Biodiversity Conservation Act 1999 (Cth)_(EPBC Act) that aims at protecting national and world heritage places, wetlands, nationally threatened species, marine parks and protects the environment from nuclear actions.[38] Although some Australian Commonwealth and State legislation includes the precautionary principle explicitly or incidentally by providing for ESD as defined in the NSESD or the IGAE,[39] including the preservation of fisheries stocks,[40] it excludes the sustainability of oil even though lack of oil could have a more drastic effect than fisheries resources on the survivability of the Australian population and its livelihood.

The judiciary in Australia has accepted the relevance of the precautionary principle in deciding cases,[41] but this does not include decisions pertaining to the sustainability of oil. In the case of *Leatch v. National Parks and Wildlife Service*, Stein J applied the precautionary principle in the decision even though the National Parks and Wildlife Act 1974 (NSW) did not specifically require the precautionary principle to be taken into account.[42] In *Telstra v. Hornsby*, Preston CJ set out a detailed approach to the application of the precautionary principle. His Honour held that two conditions precedent must be met to trigger the need to take precautionary measures: (1) a threat of serious or irreversible environmental damage; and (2) scientific uncertainty as to the environmental damage. Where both preconditions are satisfied, the precautionary principle is activated.[43] This judgment further elaborates that the precautionary principle invokes preventative action and that the measures should be proportionate to the potential threats.[44]

It is submitted that the Australian oil position requires action under the precautionary principle. As regards oil as an energy source of consumption for Australia, the two factors identified by Preston CJ in *Telstra v. Hornsby* are satisfied. The Australian government is fully aware of Australia's oil vulnerability as stated in the Draft Energy White Paper that was released in December 2011.[45] This should force policymakers in Australia to take preventative measures. It is submitted that a properly designed energy tax can assist in promoting preventative measures for the sustainability of oil, and this is discussed in the next section.

5. HOW THE PRECAUTIONARY PRINCIPLE CAN ASSIST IN DESIGNING ENERGY TAXES IN AUSTRALIA

It can be concluded from the above discussion that there is a call for the Australian government to take precautions and promote the sustainability of oil. However, there is uncertainty about how the precautionary principle should be applied in practice. Various strengths of the precautionary principle can be applied in practice, ranging from weak to strong,[46] as demonstrated in Table 3.1.

The strong version of the precautionary principle was applied in the Earth Charter (2000), which stated: 'When knowledge is limited apply a precautionary approach . . . Place the burden of proof on those who argue that a proposed activity will not cause significant harm, and make them responsible parties liable for environmental harm.'[47] Thus an appropriate energy tax designed using the strong version of the precautionary principle should place the burden on the end user to make appropriate choices of energy products they purchase and use.

The European Union is moving towards the direction of imposing taxation based on the actual energy that a product generates in gigajoules (GJ) and has proposed to change its Energy Taxation Directive. Under the new directive, the European Union will fix minimum rates for member countries at €9.60/GJ for motor fuels and €0.15/GJ for heating fuels.[48] Australia currently imposes Aus $0.38 per litre excise on petrol amounting

Table 3.1 Different forms of the precautionary principle

	Weak	Moderate	Strong
Proof required for policymaker or decision taker	Proof of serious or irreversible damage	Proof of potential damage	No proof of damage required
Need for action	No requirement to justify the need for action	The presence of an uncertain threat is a positive basis for action	Requires action unless there is firm evidence of no harm
Examples	Rio Declaration 1992; United Nations Framework Convention on Climate Change 1992	United Kingdom Biodiversity Action Plan 1994	Earth Charter 2000

Source: New Zealand Treasury Policy Perspectives Paper 06/06.

to Aus $11.54/GJ, which is about €7.8/GJ if the excise rate is converted to show the rate based on energy content of the fuel.[49] Australia's fuel excise has declined over the last decade as the excise rates are not indexed to the consumer price index and the rate has remained at 38.143 cents per litre. The fuel excise in Australia is only imposed to raise revenue with no emphasis on environmental impact. The precautionary principle calls on the Australian government to design an energy tax that reduces the use of fuel and encourages the choice of energy efficient products, for example, a LET designed for passenger motor vehicles to curb both the choice and usage of a motor vehicle with attributes that have the tendency to consume more oil, such as the vehicle weight, engine capacity and engine power.

The weight of a vehicle influences the energy required to move that vehicle. Plotkin notes that the weight of the vehicle affects the inertia required in accelerating the car as well as the rolling resistance from tyre friction.[50] Cheah states that every 100kg of weight reduction will yield a 0.39L/100 kilometre reduction in fuel consumption for the current average gasoline car in the United States.[51]

As regards engine capacity, engines with greater capacities are usually more powerful and provide greater torque at lower revolutions per minute. A bigger engine will also weigh more, creating more rolling resistance. Therefore, an engine that is larger in cubic centimetres has the capacity to increase power and in the process consume more oil.

The framework of the energy taxation should also take into consideration the power generated by a motor vehicle. Engine weight, engine capacity and engine power are interrelated, and omission of one of the factors from the energy tax may encourage policy gaming. Incorporating the engine power within the tax criteria would encourage consumers to seek motor vehicles with engines that do not produce excessive power, and such motor vehicles may drive a little slower, resulting in reduced air drag, leading to a reduction in oil consumption.

To magnify the deterrent effect of the above criteria in the design of an energy tax, they should be incorporated to apply both when purchasing the motor vehicle and when using it. Countries such as Denmark and Norway already impose higher one-off registration taxes to discourage the purchase of larger motor vehicles. Norway's one-off registration tax is based on a combination of the vehicle's unladen weight (kg), the engine output (kW), and either its CO_2 emissions or cylinder volume. The registration tax in Norway is charged on each factor, thereby discouraging heavy, powerful, CO_2-emitting motor vehicles.[52]

The Australian government should impose a high one-off energy tax when the motor vehicle is purchased, based on the vehicle weight, vehicle power and its engine capacity. The reason for this is that Australians are increasingly demanding large and powerful motor vehicles. Reported data shows that new car sales in Australia increased from 458,131 in 1979 to 631,866 in 2008, an increase of 37.9 per cent, whereas the sale of four-wheel drive vehicles in the same period increased from 15,556 to 210,933, an increase of 1255.9 per cent.[53] An OECD 2012 study showed that a US$50,000 four-wheel drive in Australia would cost a consumer US$57,886 after tax, whereas in Norway the same car would cost US$133,330 and in Denmark it would cost US$139,686.[54] Australia could follow the example of some of the OECD countries and impose a one-off energy tax on the purchase of a vehicle in order to reduce the demand for large and heavy vehicles.

An energy tax should also deter the use of large and powerful motor vehicles and, to achieve this, the same criteria that are applied to the one-off energy tax on the purchase of a vehicle should also apply to a recurrent energy tax. Thus, the motor vehicle weight, power and engine capacity should be reflected in fuel cost and annual registration charges. This means that a person who chooses to drive a motor vehicle with greater weight, power and engine capacity should be required to pay greater fuel excise and motor vehicle taxes in comparison with a person who chooses to drive a lighter motor vehicle with smaller engine capacity and less power. Such a system would support the strong version of the precautionary principle as the polluter pays for choosing a motor vehicle that has the potential to consume more oil. Although one could argue that a greater fuel excise is already incorporated in the amount of fuel being used, a greater penalty should be imposed for the potential to use extra fuel that could otherwise be sustained for the next generation. Innovative collection methods would be required in order to collect different rates of fuel for each user. New methods of collection are already being tested in some jurisdictions, such as the Oregon Use Fee Pilot Programme.[55] The author of this chapter has designed an innovative collection method in her PhD thesis, *Using Tax and Regulatory Measures to Reform Choice and Usage of Motor Vehicles for Personal Transportation in Australia for the Sustainability of Oil*,[56] where she proposed a single LET for Australia that could replace all motor vehicle taxes and excise relating to passenger motor vehicles. The LET system involves an allocation of progressive points in accordance with the polluter-pays principle for each motor vehicle characteristic, being the vehicle weight, engine capacity, engine power and CO_2 emissions and then allocating a tax rate per number of LET points at various taxing points.

It is submitted that without an appropriate energy tax for passenger motor vehicles in Australia, the message that energy from oil is a luxury and that it should be used wisely will not penetrate. Moreover, the

Australian government can use the revenues collected from such an energy tax to increase and modernize the public transport infrastructure.

6. CONCLUSION

This chapter reinforces the notion that the precautionary principle places a moral and arguably a legal obligation to apply it to the sustainability of oil, and energy taxes have a role to play in discharging this obligation. In December 2010, the UN General Assembly declared 2012 the International Year of Sustainable Energy for all and called for action on energy issues at the local, national, regional and international levels. The UN Secretary General Ban Ki-moon has made sustainable energy one of the five priorities that will guide his second five year term.[57] If oil that has taken millions of years to form is used up within one or two centuries, what will happen to the needs of future generations in the centuries to come?

NOTES

1. United Nations (1992), Report of the United Nations Conference on Environment and Development, Rio Declaration (3–14 June 1992).
2. United Nations (1987), Report of the World Commission on Environment and Development, Our Common Future.
3. Prafula Pearce (2011), 'Australian Tax Reform for Sustainable Transportation', in L. Kreiser, Julsuchada Sirisom, Hope Ashiabor and Janet E. Milne (eds), *Environmental Taxation in China and Asia-Pacific, Critical Issues in Environmental Taxation, Volume IX*, Cheltenham, UK and Northampton, MA, US: Edward Elgar, pp. 183–97, 195.
4. See Proposal for a Council Directive amending Directive 2003/96/EC Restructuring the Community Framework for the Taxation of Energy Products and Electricity, (COM(2011) 169/3).
5. OECD (2013), *Taxing Energy Use: A Graphical Analysis*, OECD Publishing, p. 21.
6. United Nations (1972), Declaration of the United Nations Conference on the Human Environment, Stockholm, Sweden (5–16 June 1972).
7. Thijs de la Court (1990), *Beyond Brundtland*, Zed Books Ltd, p. 19.
8. United Nations, above n 2, p. 122.
9. *Ibid.*, p. 119.
10. United Nations, above n 1.
11. United Nations (2000), United Nations Millennium Declaration (8 September 2000), para. 21.
12. United Nations (2002), Report of the World Summit on Sustainable Development, Johannesburg (26 August–4 September 2002).
13. United Nations (2012), Report of the United Nations Conference on Sustainable Development, Rio de Janeiro (20–22 June 2012), p. 11.
14. Australian Government Department of Resources Energy and Tourism, Geoscience Australia and ABARE (2010), Australian Energy Resource Assessment, p. 344.
15. *Ibid.*, p. 18.
16. *Ibid.*, p. 4.
17. *Ibid.*, p. 48.

18. *Ibid.*, p.42.
19. There are many prestigious books and refereed articles published on the precautionary principle and the polluter-pays principle, for example, see: Sharon Beder (2006), *Environmental Principles and Policies*, University of New South Wales Press; Nicolas de Sadeleer (2005), *Environmental Principles from Political Slogans to Legal Rules*, Oxford University Press; Richard Moules (2011), *Environmental Judicial Review*, Oxford: Hart Publishing; J. F. de Carvalho, Sonia Seger, P. Mercedes and Ildo L. Sauer (2010), 'Precautionary Principle, Economic and Energy Systems and Social Equity', *Energy Policy* 38 (10), 5399.
20. See Joel Tickner (2003), *The Precautionary Principle in Action*, Science and Environmental Health Network, pp. 20–23.
21. Linda Cameron (2006), 'Environmental Risk Management in New Zealand – Is There Scope to Apply a More Generic Framework?' New Zealand Treasury Policy Perspectives Paper 06/06, p. 11.
22. For a discussion on food supply and oil, see comments in *Karavans*, 'Our Precarious Food Supply', available at http://www.karavans.com/food.html. Also see Ian T. Dunlop (2013), 'Peak Oil, Climate Change & Global Sustainability – the Case for Emergency Action', paper presented at the ASPO Oil Vulnerability Symposium, Brisbane, 4 June 2013.
23. US Joint Forces Command (2010), 'The Joint Operating Environment (JOE)' (Distribution Statement), p. 12.
24. See Australian Bureau of Statistics (2008), Population Projections, Australia (Catalogue No. 3222.0) and Australian Bureau of Statistics (2009), Australian Demographic Statistics (Catalogue No. 3101.0), reported in Australian Government Department of Resources Energy and Tourism, Geoscience Australia and ABARE, above n 14, p. 26.
25. Tickner, above n 20, pp. 20–23.
26. United Nations (2010), 'Sustainable Development From Brundtland to Rio 2012', Background Paper prepared for consideration by the High Level Panel on Global Sustainability at its first meeting, 19 September 2010, p. 20.
27. Australian Government Department of Resources Energy and Tourism, Geoscience Australia and ABARE, above n 14, p. 18. Also see Australian Government National Sustainability Council (2013), Sustainable Australia Report 2013 Conversations with the Future, Canberra: DSEWPaC, p. 204.
28. Australian Government Department of Resources Energy and Tourism, Geoscience Australia and ABARE, above n 14, p. 4.
29. *Ibid.*, p. 52.
30. Australian Government Department of Resources, Energy and Tourism (2013), Energy in Australia 2013, ABARE, Canberra, p. 6.
31. John Blackburn (2013), Australia's Liquid Fuel Security: A Report for NRMA Motoring and Services, 28 February 2013, available at http://www.mynrma.com.au/about/fuel-security.htm, pp. 7, 10. Also see Cameron Stewart (2013), 'Doomsday Warning on Fuel Stock', *The Australian* (Sydney), 28 February 2013.
32. Blackburn, above n 31.
33. Australian Government Department of the Environment, An Overview of the National Strategy for Ecologically Sustainable Development, available at http://www.environment.gov.au/archive/esd/national/nsesd/overview/index.html, accessed 19 September 2013.
34. Productivity Commission (1999), Implementation of Ecologically Sustainable Development by Commonwealth Department and Agencies, Report No. 5, AusInfo, Canberra, p. xviii.
35. Australian Government Department of the Environment, National Strategy for Ecologically Sustainable Development, Energy Use, Energy Production and Transport, available at http://www.environment.gov.au/about/esd/publications/strategy/energy.html, accessed 19 September 2013.
36. Australian Government Department of Environment, National Strategy for Ecologically

Sustainable Development, Appendix A – Summary of the InterGovernmental Agreement on the Environment, available at http://www.environment.gov.au/about/esd/publications/strategy/appndxa.html, accessed 19 September 2013.

37. Intergovernmental Agreement on the Environment 1992 (Cth) ss. 3.5.1, 3.5.2.
38. Environment Protection and Biodiversity Conservation Act 1999 (Cth), s. 391(2).
39. Jacqueline Peel (2005), *The Precautionary Principle in Practice*, The Federation Press, Appendix A.
40. Jon Nevill (2008), 'The Precautionary Principle in Fisheries', available at www.only-oneplanet.com/marinePrecautionBenchmarks.doc, accessed 19 September 2013.
41. See *Leatch v. National Parks and Wildlife Service* (1993) 81 LGERA 270; *Nicholls v. Director-General of National Parks and Wildlife* (1994) 84 LGERA 397; *Telstra Corporation Ltd v. Hornsby Shire Council* (2006) 67 NSWLR 256; *Newcastle and Hunter Valley Speleological Society Inc v. Other Hunter Shire Council and Stoneco Pty Ltd* [2010] NSWLEC 48.
42. Justice Kevin Bell (2010), Supreme Court of Victoria, 'The Precautionary Principle: What is it and How do Courts Use it to Protect the Environment?' Paper presented at the Environment Defenders Office Seminar Series 2010, p. 4.
43. Katherine McGree (2009), 'The Legal Obligation to Consider Greenhouse Gas Emissions in an Application of the Precautionary Principle', *Queensland Law Student Review* 2(1), pp. 46, 48.
44. *Ibid.*
45. Australian Government Department of Resources Energy and Tourism, Geoscience Australia and ABARE (2011), Draft Energy White Paper, p. 31.
46. Cameron, above n 21, p. 12.
47. *Ibid.*, p. 13.
48. See above n 4.
49. OECD, above n 5, Figure 1.1.
50. Stephen E. Plotkin (2009), 'Examining Fuel Economy and Carbon Standards for Light Vehicles', in International Transport Forum Round Tables, *The Cost and Effectiveness of Policies to Reduce Vehicle Emissions*, OECD Publishing, 1st edn., p. 38.
51. Lynette W. Cheah (2010), *Cars on a Diet: The Material and Energy Impacts of Passenger Vehicle Weight Reduction in the US*, Thesis, Doctor of Philosophy in Engineering Systems, Massachusetts Institute of Technology, p. 32.
52. Norway Ministry of Finance (2011), *Budget 2011*, Ministry of Finance, available at http://www.statsbudsjettet.no/english, accessed 12 August 2011, pp. 17–18.
53. Bureau of Infrastructure, Transport and Regional Economics, 'Fuel Consumption by New Passenger Vehicles in Australia 1979–2008', Information Sheet No. 30, August 2009.
54. OECD (2012), *Consumption Tax Trends 2012 VAT/GST and Excise Rates, Trends and Administration Issues*, OECD Publishing, pp. 156–9.
55. See Oregon Department of Transport (2007), Oregon's Mileage Fee Concept and Road User Fee Pilot Program Final Report, available at www.oregon.gov.ODOT/HWY/RUFPP/docs/RUFPP_finalreport.pdf, accessed 3 September 2010.
56. Prafula Pearce (2013), *Using Tax and Regulatory Measures to Reform Choice and Usage of Motor Vehicles for Personal Transportation in Australia for the Sustainability of Oil*, Australian Tax Research Foundation, Research Study 48.
57. United Nations (2012), United Nations International Year of Sustainable Energy for All, available at http://www.unaa.org.au/international-years.html, accessed 15 September 2013.

Section B

The relationship between environmental taxation and trade

4. Inherent logic of EU energy taxes: toward a balance between market protection and environment protection

Álvaro Antón Antón and Marta Villar Ezcurra

1. INTRODUCTION

The road transport sector is excluded from the EU's Emission Trading System (hereinafter, ETS) due to the difficulties of measuring the CO_2 emissions associated with it. Energy taxes could play a complementary role to ETS in that sector to achieve the EU's CO_2 reduction targets.

However, currently, many EU Member States have used different energy taxes on the road transport sector, mainly for revenue-raising purposes. This situation is largely the result of the fact that these taxes must conform to the internal logic of the EU Energy Tax Directive (hereinafter, ETD), which harmonized energy taxation of electricity and energy products used as motor fuels or as heating fuels in the EU. This implies that the underlying purpose of these harmonized taxes is to tax all energy products regardless of their environmental performance. Consequently, it can be stated that the real inherent logic of harmonized energy taxes in the EU, and, thus, their real objective, is not the protection of the environment, but to ensure the proper functioning of the internal market.

Among EU Member States, this situation has prevented a true transition from a general energy taxation system, focused on revenue collection, to a truly environmental energy taxation system based on the carbon content of each energy product.

In light of the various objectives of energy taxation, revenue collection and environmental protection, it is necessary to examine how the ETD should be configured so that taxes introduced under its scope keep the necessary balance between the achievement of the internal market and the protection of the environment. This implies the need to identify clearly the logic that should govern energy taxes introduced by Member States, harmonized or not, and, therefore, define their underlying purpose.

Specifically, this chapter analyses how correctly setting the inherent logic of energy taxation at the EU level could help to determine when tax reliefs constitute State aid within the meaning of Article 107 of the Treaty on the Functioning of the European Union (hereinafter TFEU). In particular, it is important to understand when these aids are introduced to promote renewable energies, to coordinate the ETS and the ETD, and to mitigate the costs of energy intensive industries to avoid carbon leakage. All this would help to better assess the compatibility of such tax measures with the internal market.

2. THE FRAMEWORK OF THE EU FOR ENERGY TAXATION

The role of taxes to reduce CO_2 emissions has been on the political agenda of the EU since the 1990s. Since then, the European Commission began work on the strengthening and consolidation of these instruments through specific Directives aimed at addressing environmental problems through economic instruments.[1]

However, the proposals of the Commission were eventually withdrawn as they did not receive the unanimous support of the Council needed to adopt fiscal measures for environmental protection.[2] Until now, these efforts have been assumed by the Member States – mainly in Northern Europe – that introduced national taxes on CO_2 emissions.

As a consequence of these successive rejections, from 1997 onwards the idea of establishing an EU tax was abandoned and efforts were focused on the protection of the internal market, since it was seen under threat due to the diversity of energy product prices among Member States.[3] In this context, the EU's priority became the creation of a common framework for taxation of energy products and electricity, and not the establishment of a single wide emission tax as a means of protecting the environment.[4]

However, the fear of a loss of competitiveness of European enterprises, due to new taxes, meant that Member States spent nearly six years to reach an agreement. Thus, in order to obtain unanimity, the initial proposal underwent numerous modifications which progressively undermined its environmental content.

On 27 October 2003, the EU finally approved Council Directive 2003/96/EC, restructuring the Community framework for the taxation of energy products and electricity. The environmental aspects of the final Directive were far different from those proposed in 1992 and 1995, including numerous transition periods, and the ability of the Member States to establish exemptions or differentiated tax rates, even below the EU minimum level.[5]

2.1 The Lack of a Truly Environmental Component in the EU'S Energy Tax System

The main goal of the ETD is to ensure the proper functioning of the internal market as regards the taxation of energy products and electricity. Thus, the ETD sets minimum rates for the taxation of energy products used as motor fuel, heating and electricity. This structure makes it a potentially suitable instrument for these products to reflect in their prices the cost to the society of the CO_2 emissions resulting from their use. In particular, the taxation of energy products allows the EU to combine the incentive role of taxes in favour of an energy efficient and environmentally friendly role with the ability also to generate revenue.

However, the ETD sacrificed its environmental pretensions in exchange for a greater role in EU's energy taxation harmonization.[6] Essentially, the current minimum rates based on the volume of energy products consumed do not reflect the energy content or the CO_2 emissions of each energy product, leading to an inefficient energy use and distortions in the internal market. Therefore, it is considered that the current structure of the ETD creates incentives that are in contradiction with the energy and climate objectives of the EU, since, for instance, it promotes the use of coal as heating fuel. In this regard, the Commission has stated that, from the point of view of EU energy policy, the existing ETD does not provide incentives or even price signals to encourage alternative energy or to encourage consumers to save energy.[7] In fact, it may be said that the current approach of the ETD not only does not comply with its main objective (avoiding distortions of the internal market),[8] but also fails in encouraging a more efficient and environmentally friendly energy consumption.[9] This lack of harmonization is due to its flexibility, as it leaves the actual interaction between EU policies on energy, transport and the environment in Member States' hands. Specifically, the Commission has indicated that the ETD, in its current version, presents the following inconsistencies:[10]

1. It does not ensure the desirable degree of consistency in the treatment of the basic fossil energy sources and electricity. According to the Commission, taking into account the energy content of the various products, minimum levels of taxation vary substantially according to the product concerned.

2. The price signal introduced by the ETD through their minimum levels of taxation is not well related to the need of combating climate change. In this regard, the Commission submits that the provisions of the ETD are not well adapted to ensure the proper functioning of the internal market, in particular in circumstances in which Member States use CO_2 related taxation in order to reduce such emissions.
3. Tax treatment of renewable fuels under the ETD is not adapted to their characteristics and any adaptation can only take the form of optional de-taxation subject to a strict State aid assessment. In particular, standard taxation on renewable fuels is based on volume and on the rate applicable to the fossil product replaced by the renewable product concerned.
4. According to the Directive, energy taxes are always applied in the same way regardless of whether, in a particular case, the limitation of CO_2 emissions is guaranteed by the EU ETS.

2.2 The Inherent Logic to the EU's Energy Taxation System

One of the reasons behind the lack of a true environmental character in the current ETD is the fact that minimum tax rates provided in the ETD do not emit a proper price signal to reduce CO_2 emissions. Specifically, minimum tax rates are not high enough to discourage the consumption of fossil energy products and indirectly encouraging renewable ones. With regard to this issue it must be taken into account that the aim to achieve a proper quantification of the tax rate is crucial to not relegating the environmental objective to the background, keeping only the revenue collection purposes of the tax.[11]

However, in the case of energy taxes introduced under the ETD, the lack of a true environmental character is not only a consequence of the problems associated with the current minimum levels of taxation but also of the Directive's objective scope (e.g. renewable energy products are also taxed). In particular, and as regards the objective scope of these taxes, it should be noted that, in accordance with Article 1 and 2 of the ETD, Member States have had to tax the production and import of electricity and energy products for their use as heating fuel or motor fuel regardless of their fossil or renewable origin. Consequently, the inherent logic of the current EU energy tax harmonization of the EU is to include in the scope of the energy taxation system all energy products intended for consumption regardless of their environmental performance.

This means that, under the ETD Member States have to tax all forms of energy regardless of their behaviour in terms of CO_2 emissions. For this reason, we believe that the ETD introduces general taxes on energy products, that is, taxes which have to tax all particular forms of energy regardless of its environmental performance.[12] Therefore, in the EU domain we are actually detecting taxes whose internal logic responds to the primary purpose of tax revenues.

The above problems could be solved if the rest of the elements of the tax were designed in a way that take into consideration the impact that each product has on global warming. Thus, for example, it could be argued that an energy tax has an environmental character if there is a strong link between the tax base and environmental damage, which, moreover, is not the case of the current structure of the ETD.[13]

In this context, it should be noted that in the case of the ETD, it was decided to apply the minimum rates on the volume of each energy product consumed as a general rule. In our view, this option is not the most adequate to provide a real environmental character to the energy taxes introduced by Member States. And this is because, as these taxes take as a parameter the volume of each product consumed, they do not reflect the energy content or the CO_2 emissions of each energy product. According to the Commission, this configuration results in an inefficient use of energy and affects the correct functioning of the internal market.

On the basis of these considerations, it could be argued that what was really introduced by the ETD were broad-based energy taxes.[14] This means that their internal logic is to tax all energy products regardless of their environmental behaviour in terms of CO_2 emissions.[15] As discussed below, this issue becomes important when the Commission declares as State aid, within the meaning of Article 107 TFEU, the tax benefits introduced by Member States on their energy taxes to encourage renewable energies or coordinate the ETS and the ETD.

3. THE ROLE OF EU MEMBER STATES ON 'GREENING' HARMONIZED ENERGY TAXATION

Notwithstanding the foregoing, the ETD provides Member States with the possibility to correct this described situation. Specifically, the Directive has left to their discretion the decision of orienting the EU broad-based energy taxation system towards national energy taxes with greater environmental character. In particular, Member States may either set up their energy taxes so as to take into account the environmental performance of each energy product taxed, or include 'ecological tax elements' in their traditional energy taxes.

With respect to the first option, the ETD, as indicated in its recital (10), specifies that Member States should be permitted to comply with the Community minimum taxation levels by taking into account the total charge levied in respect of all indirect taxes which they have chosen to apply (excluding VAT). This allows some States, such as Sweden and Denmark, to introduce energy taxes based on carbon content or on emissions of each energy product in order to meet the minimum rates set by the ETD. Regarding the second option, some States chose to attempt 'greening' their energy taxes through environmental tax elements in the form of tax exemptions or differentiated tax rates in favour of renewable energies. For example, some States have used the possibility provided by Article 16 of the ETD to apply favourable tax treatment for biofuels and thus offset the costs of producing these products.

Based on the above, it can be deduced that, in the EU context, it is currently not possible to talk about an effective harmonization in the field of energy and environmental taxation especially when States decide unilaterally to resort to CO_2 related taxation to cut their emissions, and, therefore, that the existing structure of the ETD does not guarantee the proper functioning of the internal market. In this regard, the Commission itself has noted that:

> from the point of view of the single market, Member States currently might not tax CO2 emissions as much as they would like because it could put their businesses at a disadvantage or induce consumers to buy their fuel in lower tax Member States leading to revenue losses. Member States are beginning to implement a variety of different approaches to environmental taxation, which may lead to distortions and double taxation within the single market.[16]

Furthermore, the high degree of flexibility of the ETD has brought with it not only a clear lack of environmental efficiency, but also a further problem directly related to the facultative nature of many of the tax measures adopted by Member States to increase the environmental coherence of harmonized energy taxes. Precisely those States that have decided to implement these measures have faced the Commission's decision to initiate the procedure provided for in Article 108 TFEU, as it has understood that the measures are State aids under Article 107 TFEU. As discussed below, in the EU's State aid policy, the fact that, according to the ETD, the internal logic of Member State's energy taxes is to tax all energy products regardless of their environmental behaviour becomes of paramount importance.

4. STATE AID RULES AND ENVIRONMENTAL TAX EXEMPTIONS ADOPTED UNDER THE ETD

As just noted, the logic behind the current version of the ETD is to tax all energy products used as fuel, irrespective of their environmental performance. This means that, in principle, States are required to also tax renewable fuels included in their scope of application. So, Member States are the ones that have to adapt their energy taxes to the peculiarities of renewable fuels or to coordinate the ETS and the ETD, by introducing tax exemptions. This means that, in the EU context, we are facing a State intervention in the economy through measures that may be classified as State aid under EU law. The EU's State aid policy control is an essential component of the competition policy and a necessary safeguard for effective competition and free trade. For this reason, Article 107 (1) TFEU states that:

> save as otherwise provided in the Treaties, any aid granted by a Member State or through State resources in any form whatsoever which distorts or threatens to distort competition by favouring certain undertakings or the production of certain goods shall, in so far as it affects trade between Member States, be incompatible with the internal market.

Under Article 107 (1) State aids are, in principle, incompatible with the common market.

From the point of view of State aid rules, the objective of a tax measure is irrelevant, *a priori*, when categorizing it as State aid. Given that, according to settled case-law, the European Court of Justice (hereinafter, ECJ) considers that, to determine whether a State measure constitutes aid, only the effects of the measure are to be taken into consideration.[17] Therefore, the objectives of the measure are not relevant at the stage of determining the existence of aid.[18] However, according to the ECJ case-law these elements may become relevant at a later stage of the analysis, particularly when assessing the compatibility of the aid from the point of view of the exceptions provided by the Treaty.[19]

4.1 Existence of State Aid

The authors of the Treaty did not suggest that the Commission has to monitor and control all kinds of measures that could affect companies, but only those that meet all the criteria listed in Article 107 TFEU. In accordance with settled ECJ case-law, to be considered State aid, a measure must meet all four conditions set out in Article 107:

(1) there must be an intervention by the State or through State resources;
(2) it must confer a selective advantage on the recipients;
(3) this intervention must distort or threaten to distort competition; and
(4) in order to be caught by the prohibition of Article 107, the aid measure must affect competition and trade:
   (a) Transfer of State resources. It must involve the transfer of State resources. However, the aid does not necessarily need to be granted by the State itself as it may also be granted by a private or public intermediate body controlled by the State.
   In addition, according to the ECJ criteria the financial transfers that constitute an aid can take many forms: not just direct grants but also loan guarantees, accelerated depreciation allowances, capital injections, tax exemptions etc.
   (b) Economic advantage. It must be determined whether the recipient undertaking has received an economic advantage which it would not have received under normal market conditions[20] or has been spared costs which it would normally have had to bear from its own resources.[21]
   (c) Selectivity. The advantage must be specific or selective in the sense that it favours certain enterprises or certain productions.
   (d) Effect on competition and trade. Finally, an aid must have a potential effect on competition and trade between Member States. For the Commission to declare that a given aid affects competition and trade it is enough if it can be shown that the beneficiary is involved in an economic activity and that it operates in a market in which there is trade between Member States.

Consequently, measures that fulfil all the criteria outlined above are, in principle, incompatible with the internal market regardless of its purpose, justification or objective. However, the general principle of incompatibility is not absolute, as Article 107 (2) and (3) TFEU specify a number of cases in which State aid could be considered acceptable. This implies that Member States are obliged to notify the Commission about these measures before implementing them so that the EU institution evaluates their compatibility with the internal market.

4.2 The Influence of the Internal Logic of the ETD When Declaring Exemptions as State Aids

Even though they are pursuing a clear objective of the EU, intervention in the national economy through tax exemptions from energy taxes, such as those promoting biofuels or coordinating the ETD and ETS, are conditioned by the EU regulations on State aid.[22]

This is the case of Article 16 of the ETD, which authorizes Member States to apply, under fiscal control, exemptions or reduced tax rates to biomass-derived energy products, which includes biofuels. In fact, it is a well-established Commission doctrine to conclude that the excise reduction for biofuels fulfils the elements of Article 107(1) TFEU and, thus, have to be regarded as State aid.[23] The Commission concluded that these tax benefits were State aid for the following reasons.[24]

First, because those measures are normally attributable to the public authorities and involve the transfer of State resources. Excise tax reductions are granted from State resources because aid granted in the form of tax exemptions involves State resources as the Member State thereby forgoes fiscal income, or the possibility of fiscal income, that would normally accrue to it.

On the other hand, the selectivity of those measures is not justified by the so-called 'nature of the system' because the Commission considers that the logic behind the energy taxes introduced under ETD is to tax all energy products irrespective of their origin. Consequently, any tax reduction stipulated in energy excise duties to favour biofuels entails a deviation from the general structure of the tax system.

Second, the excise tax reduction for biofuels favours a selective group of firms, such as biofuels producers. The aim of that measure is to compensate the biofuels producers for part of their production costs. By reducing the tax obligation imposed on the products, the measure favours certain undertakings and the production of certain goods. Consequently, the prices for biofuels can be lowered to a level that is competitive with fossil fuels. In relation to this issue, the Commission concluded that, on the one hand, beneficiaries of tax reductions are biofuels producers and not consumers of fuels as it is understood that it is most likely that consumers pay a more or less equivalent price to the fuel prices which compete directly with biofuels.

Finally, the Commission considered that, since biofuels serve as a substitute for fossil fuels, the advantage granted through the excise duty reduction may distort competition in the internal EU-market. As fuels are tradable internationally, the measure is also likely to affect trade between Member States and therefore constitutes State aid.

Another example is when, in order to avoid overlapping regulations, Member States propose to exempt, fully or partially, industrial activities covered by ETS from taxes on energy or CO_2.[25] In these cases, the Commission has taken the view that the measure constitutes State aid. From its perspective, these types of measures are funded by State resources. They are also a selective economic advantage, as they apply only to companies covered by the EU ETS and relieve these companies from costs that they would otherwise bear from their operating budgets. And finally, the Commission considered that the beneficiaries of the measure are active in markets that are open for competition and trade, which may affect the internal market.[26]

In these cases, some national authorities have argued that the selective advantage of the tax relief is justified by the nature and structure of the energy tax system. And this is because they consider that the energy–CO_2 taxes and the ETS have the same objective, i.e., to reduce CO_2 emissions. Therefore, the CO_2 tax no longer serves any environmental purpose from the moment that the ETS was introduced. Thus, for companies covered by the ETS, the CO_2 tax is nothing more than an additional financial burden. However, the Commission has noted that the energy tax system has only partially the same objective as the EU ETS. From the Commission's point of view, the system of reference is the energy tax system and not the ETS. Thus, according to the ETD, the internal logic of that system is to tax electricity and each energy product used as heating or motor fuel. Therefore, the Commission understands that exempting these products from an energy tax is not in line with that logic.[27]

In both considered cases, the fact that the internal logic of the ETD responds to the structure of a broad-based energy tax determines that the tax elements introduced for environmental reasons are likely to be found to be State aid. Notwithstanding the foregoing, Article 107(3)(c) TFEU provides an exemption from the general rule of incompatibility with the internal market, as stated in paragraph (1) of that Article, for aid to facilitate the development of certain economic activities or of certain economic areas, where such aid does not adversely affect trading conditions to an extent contrary to the common interest.[28] Specifically, the aid could be declared compatible with the TFEU if the conditions set by the Commission in its Guidelines on State aid for environmental protection are respected. The risk of those Guidelines is that they give the Commission room for interpretation, as has been seen in some cases.[29] This has led to a high degree of legal uncertainty, further to the distortions in the market already outlined. The best means of avoiding current and future problems with the Commission is removing from its interpretative domain the establishment of these types of measures; for example, by introducing more general measures, such as a refined block exemption regulation for environmental tax exceptions.[30] However, this cannot be done in a proper way while Member States remain responsible for providing energy taxation with an environmental character.

5. CONCLUSIONS: TOWARDS AN ENERGY TAXATION SYSTEM WITH A TRULY ENVIRONMENTAL PURPOSE

In the area of energy taxation, it is common to find that energy taxes being harmonized at the EU level are presented as environmental but are predominantly implemented for tax collection purpose. Among other reasons, this is because the fiscal purpose of energy taxation is older than the interest in environmental protection. Thus, although 80 per cent of the world's energy comes from fossil origin products, energy taxes are not always environmental taxes, as we understand that real environmental taxation should discriminate on the basis of the polluting potential of each energy source. Therefore, it is imperative that the inherent logic of energy taxes is oriented towards an environmental objective. For this purpose, it is necessary that both the objective and the structure of these taxes respond to that internal logic.

In this regard, the Commission itself has noted that energy taxes have been traditionally levied for several reasons, in particular to raise revenue, but also to guide consumer behaviour toward a more efficient use of energy and to cleaner energy sources.[31] Therefore, regardless of their capacity to collect tax revenues, we understand that energy taxation could play an important role that complements the ETS in some sectors such as road transport. As the Commission itself has indicated, this would lead to more responsible, economic and rational energy use as it would discourage the use of fossil fuel energy products in the sectors that the ETS does not cover.

However, for the ETD to play a complementary role it is necessary to refine its environmental aspects. In this sense, the Commission has presented a proposal to revise the ETD.[32] With the revision of the ETD it is pretended, on the one hand, to rebalance the charge between different fuels, including renewable energies, in an objective manner (based on energy content and on CO_2 emissions) and, on the other hand, to provide a framework for CO_2 taxation in the internal market.

Thus, if this proposal is approved, each component into which the ETD would be divided would respond to different inherent logic. This means that, on the one hand, the CO_2-related taxation would complement the ETS by taxing the CO_2 emissions produced in the sectors excluded from its scope of application, such as road transport. On the other hand, the general energy tax would tax all the energy products used in transport irrespective of their origin. In this way, the Member States' goal of continuing to resort to energy taxation for fiscal reasons would be fulfilled. Therefore, if this proposal is accepted the ETD would emerge as, not only an adequate instrument to obtain income through general energy consumption taxation, but also as a system to support renewable energies and to protect the environment. And this is because the CO_2 tax would help to guide consumer behaviour towards a more efficient use of energy and to a greater use of renewable fuels.

From the point of view of State aid policy, a greater legal certainty would be achieved for Member States if the proposals provide a more precise definition of the inherent logic considering each component in which the ETD would be divided, since, in these cases, it would be possible to establish more clearly, *ex ante*, the criteria that State aid has to meet to be declared compatible with the TFEU rules. Moreover, it would help the introduction of general measures both to coordinate the ETS and the ETD and to mitigate the costs of energy intensive industries in order to avoid carbon leakage.

NOTES

1. *A Community Strategy to Limit Carbon Dioxide Emissions and to Improve Energy Efficiency. Communication from the Commission to the Council*, SEC (91) 1744 final, 14 October 1991.
2. *Proposal for a Council Directive Introducing a Tax on Carbon Dioxide Emissions and Energy*, COM (92) 226 final, 30 June 1992 and *Amended proposal for a Council Directive introducing a tax on carbon dioxide emissions and energy*, COM (95) 172 final, 10 May 1995.
3. *Proposal for a Council Directive restructuring the Community framework for the taxation of energy products, Presented by the Commission*, COM (97) 30 final, 12 March 1997.
4. Since 1992 there have been two Community Directives that harmonize the structure and type of special taxes on hydrocarbons (Directive 92/81/EEC and Directive 92/82/EEC). Taking into account that 'the absence of Community provisions imposing a minimum rate of taxation on electricity and energy products other than mineral oils may adversely affect the proper functioning of the internal market', this was an attempt to extend this degree of harmonization to the majority of energy products, including electricity, natural gas and coal. As a result, its utility as a means of combating climate change became a consequence of the taxation of energy products and electricity, rather than being an end in itself.
5. Cornejo Pérez maintains that for those who hoped the EU would establish a harmonized energy tax as an environmental protection policy instrument, Directive 2003/96/EC has been a disappointment, the only positive aspect being the updating of Community minimum tax levels (although below the rate of inflation). A. Cornejo Pérez (2004), 'La nueva directiva sobre fiscalidad de los productos energéticos', *Crónica Tributaria*, 111, 99.
6. Proof of this is that Article 2.4 of the ETD excludes some of the most polluting industries from its scope ambit, such as glass, ceramics and fibreglass production, sectors which are included in the EU ETS.
7. European Commission, *Smarter energy taxation for the EU: proposal for a revision of the Energy Taxation Directive*, COM (2011) 168 final.
8. According to the Commission, the current minima do not create a level playing field for business consumers, because, in practice, economic operators can be better off compared to others depending on the energy source they use.
9. The current minimum rates also discriminate against renewable fuels. In fact, if a tax

exception is not included they would be taxed at the same rate of the conventional fuel which they replace even though their energy content is lower.

10. European Commission, *Proposal for a Council Directive amending Directive 2003/96/ EC, restructuring the Community framework for the taxation of energy products and electricity*, COM (2011) 169.
11. According to economic theory, certain environmental taxes do not lead to corrective behaviours as it can be found by the evolution of the collection that polluters will just pay the tax and continue polluting. This is probably related to the low tax rate used. In fact, electric undertakings (which almost all pay the tax) have suggested that environmental effects are almost nil because it is not profitable for them to introduce remedial technologies, as some authors remind. I. Bilbao Estrada (2009), 'El sistema tributario como complemento de los instrumentos económicos previstos en el protocolo de Kioto', *Seguridad y medio ambiente*, 113, 52–64.
12. According to Milne, 'energy-related taxes are defined by the fact that the tax base (the commodity being taxed) is some form of energy'. J. Milne (2008), 'Carbon Taxes in the United States: The Context for the Future', *Vermont Journal of Environmental Law*, 10, 1–31.
13. The OECD itself has showed that when the link between the tax base and damage to the environment is weak, the tax risks not exercising the desired impact and introduces unnecessary distortions and costly production decisions and consumption. OECD (1993), *Taxation and the Environment Complementary Policies*, Paris: OECD Publishing, p. 58.
14. S. Speck (2008), 'The Design of Carbon and Broad-Based Energy Taxes in European Countries', *Vermont Journal of Environmental Law*, 10, 31–59.
15. As defended in Milne, 'Carbon Taxes in the United States: The Context for the Future', p. 4, 'a classic broad based energy taxed would define the tax base in terms of the energy content of the energy content of the identified range of energy sources'.
16. European Commission, *Smarter energy taxation for the EU: proposal for a revision of the Energy Taxation Directive*, COM (2011) 168 final.
17. According to the ECJ, Article 107 TFEU does not distinguish between causes or objectives but defines state aid in relation to the effects. Case 173/73 *Italy /Commission* [1974]; Case 310/85 *Deufil/Commission* [1987]; and Case C-241/94 *France/Commission* [1996].
18. Case C-142/87 *Belgium/Commission* [1990] and Case 40/85 Belgium/Commission [1986]; Case T-16/96 *Cityflyer Express/Commission* [1998]; Case C-39/94 *SFEI and others* [1996].
19. M. Villar Ezcurra (2013), 'State Aids and Energy Taxes: Towards a Coherent Reference Framework', *Intertax*, 41(6&7), 340–50.
20. Case C-39/94 *SFEI and others* [1996].
21. Case C-301/87 *France/Commission* [1990].
22. In the case at hand, it could be argued that, as these exemptions are contained in the ETD, they cannot be declared State aid. However, the Commission recalls that its competence on State aid issues originates directly from the TFEU. Therefore, any EU legislation cannot possibly impair the Commission's competence in this field (Commission Decision of 11 March 2008 on State aid exemption from mineral oil tax for greenhouse undertakings (Germany), C (2008) 860). Moreover, Article 26 of the ETD expressly states that information provided to the Commission on the basis of the ETD does not release Member States from the notification obligation pursuant Article 108 TFEU.
23. NN 61/2004 Excise duty exemption to biofuels (Spain); N 57/2008 Operating aid for biofuels (Poland) and N 63/2008 Excise duty reduction for biofuels (Italy).
24. A. Antón Antón (2012), 'Promotion of biofuels and EU state aid rules: the case of Spain', in L. Kreiser, A.Y. Sterling, P. Herrera, J.E. Milne and H. Ashiabor (eds), *Critical Issues in Environmental Taxation, Volume XII* (*Green Taxation and Environmental Sustainability*), Cheltenham, UK and Northampton, MA, USA: Edward Elgar, pp. 41–55.

25. A. Antón Antón and I. Bilbao Estrada (2010), 'State aid and the EU Council Directive 2003/96/EC: the case for augmenting the environmental component', in C.D. Soares, J. Milne, H. Ashiabor, L. Kreiser and K. Deketelaere (eds), *Critical Issues in Environmental Taxation: International and Comparative Perspectives*, Oxford: Oxford University Press, pp. 448–63.
26. Joint State aid cases C 44/04 and C 47/04 (Slovenia); State aid case C 41/2006 (Denmark) and State aid case N 22/08 (Sweden).
27. Commission Decision C (2009) 4517, *on aid scheme C 41/06 (ex N 318/A/04) which Denmark is planning to implement for refunding the CO2 tax on quota-regulated fuel consumption in industry*.
28. Commission Guidelines on State aid for Environmental Protection, [2008] OJ C 82/01.
29. For example, in Commission Decision C (2009) 4517, above n 27.
30. C. Dias Soares (2007), 'Energy tax treatment of undertakings covered by emissions trading', *EC Tax Review*, 17, 184 and following.
31. European Commission, *Proposal for a Council Directive amending Directive 2003/96/ EC, restructuring the Community framework for the taxation of energy products and electricity*, COM (2011) 169.
32. European Commission, *Proposal for a Council Directive amending Directive 2003/96/ EC, restructuring the Community framework for the taxation of energy products and electricity*, COM (2011) 169.

5. WTO open trade rules and domestic environmental protection policies: a balancing approach

Bill Butcher

1. INTRODUCTION

A fundamental principle of the World Trade Organization (WTO) is a commitment to the protection of the environment. However, difficulties arise due to the competition between that commitment and the WTO's perceived overarching mission of preserving and promoting trade liberalization. WTO dispute panels periodically confront cases where the will to combat trade restrictions and the promotion of environmental protection come into direct conflict. While there are mechanisms in WTO rules to excuse certain trade restrictions on the basis of their environmental protection intent and effect, these are typically subject to an overriding requirement that the impugned policy is not trade protectionism in disguise.[1] This is a legitimate condition, given the WTO's role as an open trade body and not a conservationist agency, but the fact remains that the WTO has some obligation to the environment and yet its rules, by proscribing or constraining domestic measures, may hinder progress in environmental protection.[2]

The literature in this area focuses in large part on legal critique of WTO Panel and Appellate Body (AB) reports and on the extent to which WTO rules constrain domestic policy initiatives.[3] This chapter takes a different approach. With a particular focus on Article XX of the General Agreement on Tariffs and Trade (GATT), and consideration of the interplay between Article XX and paragraph 11.3 of China's WTO Accession Protocol the chapter proposes a reconsideration of the rules themselves to permit policies that clearly produce positive environmental outcomes. A current WTO dispute highlighting the benefits of such an approach is *China – Rare Earths*, a challenge brought by the United States, the European Union and Japan in respect to China's export policies on rare earths elements.[4] In recent years, China, which has a practical monopoly in the mining and treatment of rare earths, has imposed sharply rising export restrictions in the form of quotas, export taxes and the non-refund of VAT on those minerals – with a consequential increase in prices on world markets and growing concerns about shortages and disruptions to critical supply lines.[5] China's policy in many respects improves the situation for the environment, but its implementation lies on shaky legal ground because of its apparent protectionist motives and the attendant economic and trade implications.

The chapter proposes that instead of necessarily prohibiting domestic measures identified as disguised protectionism, an approach of balancing recognized outcomes should be adopted. This would entail a comparative analysis between the environmental and health benefits that a domestic measure brings with any negative trade and economic impact it may have. The comparison would examine outcomes at both the global and the individual WTO Member level. Any regulation whose environmental benefits clearly outweigh the economic and trade costs should be considered compliant with WTO obligations.

2. THE INTERSECTION OF TRADE RULES AND ENVIRONMENTAL PROTECTION POLICY

Membership of the WTO constrains a government's freedom to make policy decisions and its capacity to make domestic regulation. These restrictions are manifold and include limits on the granting of subsidies to domestic producers,[6] on treating one country's exports more favorably than another's,[7] on the imposition of anti-dumping duties[8] and on imposing restrictions on foreign investment.[9] In this chapter, the focus is on a member government's acceptance of limits on its capacity to restrict exports of its natural resources.

Consider this scenario: Country X has an effective monopoly on Product Y. Product Y is a finite resource and its extraction and processing involve substantial damage to health and to the natural environment. Product Y is an essential component worldwide of an extensive range of consumer and strategic products. The government of Country X wishes to preserve its natural resources and protect the environment and health of its citizens by limiting the extraction and processing of Product Y. Country X introduces a range of measures towards these ends, including tighter domestic limits on production and emissions, together with restrictions on exports of Product Y through the imposition of export duties and quotas, while still maintaining domestic supply. Foreign governments are concerned the export measures will cause shortages and price rises for Product Y globally, while increasing supply and reducing prices in Country X. Some of those governments raise objections to the WTO that Country X's primary motivation is not environmental protection but the promotion of its domestic industries, a planned move to drive up prices on international markets and to compel foreign end-users of Product Y to shift their operations to Country X in order to maintain supply. As such, the foreign governments contend that this constitutes a breach by Country X of its obligations under WTO rules. The WTO finds in favor of the complainants, thereby removing this arrangement from Country X's arsenal of potential responses to the environmental and health concerns associated with Product Y.

While considerably more complex and nuanced, the background to the *China – Rare Earths* dispute is essentially the situation described in the scenario immediately above.

The concern expressed in this chapter is that a ruling for the complainants in *China –Rare Earths* limits an approach which has already proved effective in achieving a number of positive environmental outcomes – including industry consolidation and improvement in the mining and processing of rare earths within China, a shift to mining in countries with higher environmental standards, a more efficient use of rare earths in manufacturing processes and the development of less damaging substitutes.[10]

The chapter is not concerned with any sovereignty issues that might arise. China contended in its first written submission on the rare earths dispute that the principle of sovereignty over natural resources entitles states to 'husband the use of the resources to promote the production of more sophisticated processed products'.[11] As expressed in the Third Party Oral Statement of Australia on the rare earths dispute: 'Whilst Australia agrees that States have sovereign rights over their natural resources, Members have also exercised their sovereign rights in becoming party to the WTO Agreements. Members have thus agreed to exercise their sovereign rights in a manner that is consistent with their obligations under the WTO Agreements'.[12]

In short, it is not open to WTO Members to assert that their traditional sovereign rights 'trump' their agreed WTO obligations. It is, however, open to Members to seek interpretations of those obligations that better serve their own policy objectives.

3. EXPORT RESTRAINTS AND THE CHINA – RAW MATERIALS DISPUTE

To date, there have been only five WTO disputes dealing with export restrictions: *Canada – Herring and Salmon* (1988),[13] *Japan – Semiconductors*

(1988),[14] *Argentina – Hides and Leather* (2001),[15] *US – Measures Treating Export Restrictions as Subsidies* (2001),[16] *China – Raw Materials* (2011)[17] and *China – Rare Earths* (2013).[18] Apart from *US – Export Restrictions*[19] all involved alleged breaches of GATT Article XI's requirement that Members broadly eliminate prohibitions and quantitative restrictions on exports.[20] Of the other four disputes, the circumstances of *China – Raw Materials* and *China – Rare Earths* have the greatest relevance to the theme of this chapter.[21]

The *China – Raw Materials* dispute examined a range of restraints imposed by China on the export of nine types of raw materials. The complainants (the European Union, Mexico and the United States) challenged those restraints alleging that they constituted export duties, export quotas, export licensing, and minimum export price requirements, in breach of China's commitments under China's Accession Protocol, paragraph 11.3[22] and GATT Articles VIII:1(a), VIII:4, X:1, X:3(a) and XI:1. The complainants argued that the export restraints created scarcity and forced up prices of raw materials in global markets; as a result, Chinese domestic industries gained a significant advantage through sufficient supply and lower and more stable prices.[23] China sought to defend the measures by resort to, *inter alia*, the general exceptions permitted under GATT Article XX.[24] The AB released its report on the case on January 31, 2012. In ruling that China's measures were inconsistent with its WTO obligations, the AB addressed several important aspects of the application of GATT Article XX which are also critical to the determination of the more recent *China – Rare Earths* case and to the view expressed in this chapter that a more open interpretation would lead to better environmental outcomes, while still preserving fair trade.[25]

The apposite part of Article XX provides as follows:

> Subject to the requirement that such measures are not applied in a manner which would constitute a means of arbitrary or unjustifiable discrimination between countries where the same conditions prevail, or a disguised restriction on international trade, nothing in this Agreement shall be construed to prevent the adoption or enforcement by any contracting party of measures:
> (*b*) necessary to protect human, animal or plant life or health; . . .
> (*g*) relating to the conservation of exhaustible natural resources if such measures are made effective in conjunction with restrictions on domestic production or consumption. . ..

Except for questioning the finding that Article XX is not available for breaches of paragraph 11.3 of China's Accession Protocol, discussed immediately below, this chapter makes no assertion that the reasoning in *China – Raw Materials* was legally unsound or contradicted previous WTO decisions. Nor does it suggest that the rulings were unfounded in policy terms: In the circumstances of the case the finding against China's export restraints was appropriate. The chapter does, however, contend that a broader view be taken of Article XX or that it be renegotiated to better foster domestic environmental regulation.

The first question open to the AB in *China – Raw Materials* was whether Article XX is available as a defense to measures which would otherwise contravene paragraph 11.3 of China's Accession Protocol.

In a 2009 case, *China – Publications and Audiovisual Products*,[26] the AB had ruled that China could rely on Article XX as a defense for breaches of paragraph 5.1 of the Protocol. While that finding opened the door to Article XX exceptions in China's Accession Protocol disputes, the AB in *China – Raw Materials* ruled that the *China – Publications and Audiovisual Products* decision applied only to paragraph 5.1 cases. The opening words of paragraph 5.1 are: 'Without prejudice to China's right to regulate trade in a manner consistent with the WTO Agreement . . .', which was seen as an effective cross reference to the GATT, meaning that defenses under Article XX were available. Paragraph 11.3 contains no similar phrase; an absence the AB deemed reflected an intention by the negotiators of China's accession to exclude Article XX as a defense for violations of that commitment.[27]

At first sight, the conclusion accords with general principles of interpretation[28] but examination of its consequences suggests it may be misplaced. Its effect is to allow China resort to the Article XX defense for the imposition of quantitative export restraints, proscribed in Article XI of GATT, but not for the imposition of tariffs, proscribed in paragraph 11.3 of the Protocol. Thus China has an incentive to impose export quotas in preference to export tariffs.[29] Such an outcome runs counter to the WTO's strong preference for tariff barriers over less-distorting non-tariff barriers, and it is most unlikely that the negotiators would have wished to contradict that preference in China's Accession Protocol.[30]

The AB then concluded that even if Article XX was available as a defense, China had not met its requirements. The AB agreed with the Panel's view on Article XX(b) that China had not established a sufficient link between the export restrictions and its objective of protecting public health and the environment. On Article XX(g), the AB upheld China's appeal that the Panel erred in holding that the phrase 'made effective in conjunction with restrictions on domestic production or consumption' imposed a requirement that the export restraints ensure the effectiveness of associated domestic restrictions[31] but did not overturn the Panel's finding that China could not rely on Article XX(g) because China's measures lacked the requisite 'even-handedness' of treatment between domestic and export supplies.[32]

China also raised an unsuccessful defense under Article XI:2(a) in respect of one of the raw materials under consideration, refractory-grade bauxite. China argued that since bauxite is an exhaustible resource[33] of considerable importance to the Chinese economy, the restrictions applied to it were justified as ‘temporarily applied to prevent or relieve critical shortages of foodstuffs or other products’.[34] That aspect of the ruling will not be considered in this chapter since the redrafting or reinterpretation of Article XX suggested here will provide effective protection without the need for the Article XI:2(a) defense.[35]

4. THE *CHINA – RARE EARTHS* DISPUTE

The current dispute over China’s rare earth export restrictions has clear echoes of *China – Raw Materials*. It entails a similar near-monopoly supply position, similar environmental damage from mining and processing, and similar export restraints. Where it differs is that, firstly, rare earths present more opportunity for production efficiencies and substitutes than the elements considered in *China – Raw Materials* and secondly, the rare earths export restraints are part of a broader package of measures which include extensive regulation at a domestic level.

Rare earths are neither rare nor earths. They are a group of 17 different metals[36] whose properties make them critical to the manufacture of a substantial range of consumer electronics (such as iPads, smart phones, DVD players and hard drives), green technologies (wind turbines, hybrid car batteries and magnetic levitation trains) and high-tech military equipment (navigation systems, submarine engines and missile guidance systems).[37]

Their characterization as ‘rare’ derives from the difficulties in mining, separating and refining of rare earths and not from any scarcity in the earth’s crust.[38] Rare earth elements do not exist in their elemental state, so they need to be separated from the other minerals in which they occur, a process which is further complicated because mineral deposits often contain several rare earth elements.[39]

Given their environmental protection benefits, it is a sad irony that the major drawback of rare earths is that their extraction and processing entail significant damage to public health and to the environment. The consequences include loss of surface vegetation, water loss, soil erosion, pollution, acidification, reduced or even eliminated food crop output, landslides and clogged rivers.[40]

There are five steps in the rare earth element processing supply chain (see Figure 5.1): (1) mining, (2) separating the rare earth ore into oxides, (3) refining the oxides into metals, (4) forming the metals into alloys and

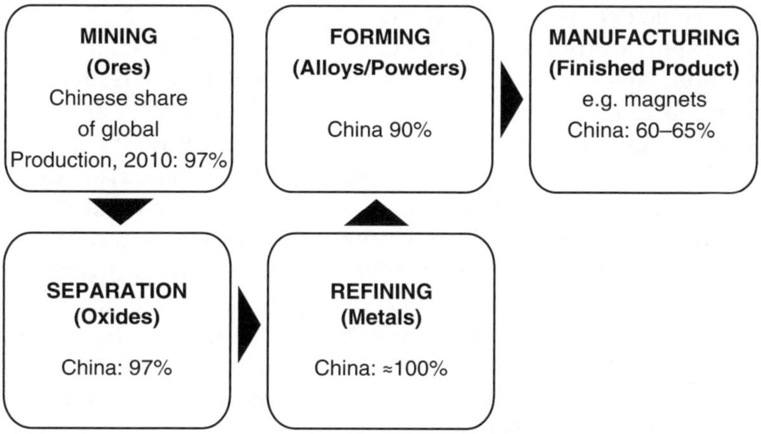

Note: The figures for China's share of each level are based on 2010 statistics. The United States and Australia have increased mining of rare earths but China still controls about 95% of production.

Source: 'Rare Earth Metals in the Defense [sic] Supply Chain', United States Government Accountability Office, Washington DC, 2010 (Jepson, 'A 21st century scramble', p. 8).

Figure 5.1 Main stages of the rare earth production process

(5) manufacturing the alloys into applications. While the United States and Australia have in recent years increased their mining activities China maintains a dominant position in all levels of the supply chain worldwide.

China has evidently been aware of the political and economic value of rare earths for decades. Deng Xiaoping recognized the importance of rare earths in 1992 when he observed, 'as there is oil in the Middle East, there is rare earth in China'. By contrast, importing countries, most notably the United States and major economies in Europe, seem to have had less sense of the fragility of their supply or of the need to prepare for disruptions to supply.[41] A growing urgency came when China began actively to constrain exports in recent years through various forms of export restriction and, on one occasion in September 2010, temporarily cut off all supplies to Japan, possibly in retaliation for perceived Japanese aggression over the disputed Diaoyu or Senkaku Islands.[42] In response to the export restrictions, the United States, the European Union and Japan instituted the *China – Rare Earths* dispute, relying on the arguments successfully raised in *China – Raw Materials*.

However, there were important differences between the circumstances of the two disputes. In contrast to the heavily oriented slant against exports seen in the raw materials case, the rare earths restraints were part of a consolidated policy which saw significant domestic tightening as well as export restrictions. At the domestic level, China imposed tighter production caps, stricter emission standards and higher resource taxes, all designed to protect the environment, preserve resources and promote sustainable development of the rare earths sector.[43] With one eye on the impending Panel report in *China – Rare Earths*, China also released a White Paper on rare earths[44] addressing global concerns at its export restrictions by setting out the environmental damage caused by its rare earths industry and pointing to its rapidly declining rare earths reserves.[45]

At the time of writing, the *China – Rare Earths* Panel's interim report has been provided to the parties involved in the dispute, but not publically released. This is apparently due to opposition from China to a more widespread release. It has been widely reported,[46] however, that the interim report's findings are in favor of the complainants, indicating that its conclusions endorse those presented in the Panel and AB reports in *China – Raw Materials*.[47]

5. THE CASE FOR REVISITING ARTICLE XX

The export restrictions impugned in *China – Rare Earths* have already resulted in improved outcomes for the environment and the world economy at large. They have alerted previously sanguine rare earth users to the dangers of shortages and to the need to take positive steps to ensure availability and to mitigate the effects of any supply challenges. As a result other countries, most notably the United States and Australia, have revived long-suspended local rare earths mining operations whose environmental impacts are less than China's. Manufacturers around the world have actively sought out alternative supplies and made progress on demand destruction through efficiencies in the use of rare earth elements and the development of substitutes.[48]

At a time when broad top-down measures to address carbon emissions through international agreements are stalling (such as the Durban climate conference of December 2011, which produced little concrete progress), narrower, ground-up approaches of the type undertaken taken by China on rare earths may present a more productive way forward.[49] With some exceptions, such as the European Union, there is strong global resistance to 'going it alone' on climate change mitigation. As part of a transition to an elusive comprehensive global agreement on environmental protection, it may be time for the WTO to accept a new paradigm. This paradigm would see a more lenient treatment for those restrictive trade measures which come with considerable attendant environmental dividends. A balancing test could be applied where export measures otherwise in breach of a Member's WTO obligations would be permitted, provided their environmental benefits clearly outweigh the economic and other costs. A measure need not qualify under any of the Article XX exceptions as currently applied or be matched by parallel restrictions on domestic production and consumption, as required by Article XI:2(a) of GATT. Looking to the rare earths case, it may be that even under this more lenient approach the restrictions imposed there might still be found non-compliant, but such an approach would provide governments everywhere with opportunities to advance their domestic economies while preserving the environment and with less political risk than introducing purely domestically applied regulation such as carbon pricing.

The WTO decision process would involve a complex balancing of the values involved but is not beyond the resources of WTO panels or the AB and could be achieved by recourse to a revisited Article XX.

It can be argued that WTO rulings are becoming 'greener',[50] but it remains the case in environment-related WTO disputes that a win for the complainant is often a loss for the environment.[51] *China – Rare Earths* may be seen as no exception. While the actual decision in the case is less significant in achieving positive environmental impacts than the fact of the dispute itself, a successful outcome for the complainants produces a less favorable outcome for the environment. China can be expected to appeal the Panel decision but if it is obliged to terminate its export restraints, there is no certainty that they will be replaced by any other measures of equivalent environmental benefit. Indeed, it is even possible that China's response could include some reduction in the broader components of its overall policy moves to curb the environmental degradation associated with rare earths. On the other hand, a finding in China's favor would oblige the complainants and other rare earth elements importers to further expedite their own exploration, treatment and conservation measures, with a greater emphasis on cooperation, while the Chinese government would be free to continue its policies of consolidation and greater supervision of illegal mining without undue impact on its domestic economy.

6. CONCLUSION

Progress can happen in environmental protection, as in many situations, in unexpected ways. The 'crisis' in relation to rare earth supplies exemplifies this. When opportunities for positive environmental outcomes present themselves, in whatever form, international rules and dispute mechanisms should be loath to strike them down.

The Preamble of the WTO Agreement, which pervades all the covered agreements, including GATT and China's Accession Protocol, states that:

> relations in the field of trade and economic endeavour should be conducted with a view to raising standards of living, ensuring full employment and a large and steadily growing volume of real income and effective demand, and expanding the production of and trade in goods and services, *while allowing for the optimal use of the world's resources in accordance with the objective of sustainable development, seeking both to protect and preserve the environment* and to enhance the means for doing so in a manner consistent with their respective needs and concerns at different levels of economic development (emphasis added).[52]

Thus, trade liberalization is not to be pursued as an end in itself but rather as a means to desired ends, one of which is environmental protection.

The proposal in this chapter does not contend that on current WTO rules and their interpretation the Panel came to the wrong conclusion in *China – Raw Materials* or even in *China – Rare Earths*, where China has a somewhat stronger defense. Neither is it arguing that the rule changes or interpretation proposed here would necessarily have produced a different result in either case. It may well be that even with the loosening of WTO rules and the balancing of environmental benefits versus economic and trade detriments advocated here, the rare earths decision would have been the same. Certainly the raw materials decision would have been. What the chapter does suggest is that WTO rules as currently applied unduly constrain domestic environmental policy and should be revisited to give proper weight to environmental protection as an *outcome* rather than disregarding it in cases where it appears to be a pretext for trade distortion.

NOTES

1. The most significant being Article XX of the General Agreement on Tariffs and Trade (GATT), discussed throughout this chapter.
2. For example, Article XI of the GATT, which proscribes a range of export restrictions, including some which could produce improved environmental outcomes.
3. For example, J. McDonald (2005), 'Environmental Taxes and International Competitiveness: Do WTO Border Adjustment Rules Constrain Policy Choices', *Volume II Critical Issues in Environmental Taxation* (Hope Ashiabor, Kurt Deketelaere, Larry Kreiser and Janet Milne, eds.), UK: Richmond Law & Tax Ltd; E. Baroncini (2012), 'The China-Rare Earths WTO Dispute: A precious chance to revise the China-Raw Materials conclusions on the applicability of GATT Article XX to China's WTO Accession Protocol', *Cuadernos de Derecho Transnacional* (October 2012), Vol. 4, No. 2, 49.
4. WTO Dispute Settlement, *China – Measures Related to the Exportation of Rare Earths,*

Tungsten and Molybdenum, (*China – Rare Earths*), WT/DS431, WT/DS432, WT/DS433, available at http://www.wto.org/english/tratop_e/dispu_e/cases_e/ds431_e.htm (last accessed November 30, 2013).
5. Chuin-Wei Yap (October 30, 2013) 'Beijing Says WTO Rules Against China in Rare Earth Dispute', *WSJ.com*, available at http://online.wsj.com/news/articles/SB10001424052702304527504579167132115793314 (last accessed November 4, 2013).
6. The WTO Agreement on Subsidies and Countervailing Measures.
7. The famous Most Favoured Nation principle enshrined in Article I of GATT.
8. The WTO Anti-Dumping Agreement.
9. The WTO Agreement on Trade-Related Investment Measures.
10. Sonja Elmquist (2011), 'Rare Earths Fall as Toyota Develops Alternatives: Commodities', *Bloomberg News*, September 29, 2011, available at http://www.bloomberg.com/news/2011–09–28/rare-earths-fall-as-toyota-develops-alternatives-commodities.html (last accessed October 10, 2013).
11. *China – Rare Earths*, note 4 above, China's first written submission, para. 58.
12. *China – Rare Earths*, note 4 above, *Third Party Oral Statement of Australia*, February 27, 2013, para. 7.
13. GATT Dispute Settlement Report (1988), *Canada – Measures Affecting Exports of Unprocessed Herring and Salmon* (*Canada – Herring and Salmon*), L/6268 - 35S/98, adopted March 22, 1988, available at http://www.wto.org/english/tratop_e/dispu_e/87hersal.pdf (last accessed November 20, 2013).
14. GATT Dispute Settlement Report (1988), *Japan – Trade in Semi-Conductors* (*Japan – Semiconductors*), L/6309 - 35S/116, adopted 4 May 1988, available at http://www.wto.org/english/tratop_e/dispu_e/87semcdr.pdf (last accessed November 18, 2013).
15. WTO Panel Report (2001), *Argentina – Measures Affecting the Export of Bovine Hides and the Import of Finished Leather* (*Argentina – Hides and Leather*), WT/DS155/R, adopted February 16, 2001, available at http://www.wto.org/english/tratop_e/dispu_e/cases_e/ds155_e.htm (last accessed November 18, 2013).
16. WTO Panel Report (2001), *US – Measures Treating Export Restrictions as Subsidies*, (*US – Export Restrictions*) WT/DS194/R, adopted June 29, 2001, available at http://www.wto.org/english/tratop_e/dispu_e/194r_a_e.pdf (last accessed November 18, 2013).
17. WTO Dispute Settlement, *China – Measures Related to the Exportation of Various Raw Materials* (*China – Raw Materials*), DS394, 395, 398, available at http://www.wto.org/english/tratop_e/dispu_e/cases_e/ds394_e.htm (last accessed October 10, 2013).
18. *China – Rare Earths*, note 4, above.
19. *US – Export Restrictions* examined whether export restrictions applied to raw materials could be considered 'subsidies' to downstream users of those materials, for the purposes of the WTO Agreement on Subsidies and Countervailing Measures. The Panel determined that such restrictions do not constitute subsidies.
20. That part of the text of Article XI relating to export restraints provides: '1. No prohibitions or restrictions other than duties, taxes or other charges, whether made effective through quotas, import or export licences or other measures, shall be instituted or maintained by any contracting party on the importation of any product of the territory of any other contracting party or on the exportation or sale for export of any product destined for the territory of any other contracting party. 2. The provisions of paragraph 1 of this Article shall not extend to the following: (*a*) Export prohibitions or restrictions temporarily applied to prevent or relieve critical shortages of foodstuffs or other products essential to the exporting contracting party; (*b*) Import and export prohibitions or restrictions necessary to the application of standards or regulations for the classification, grading or marketing of commodities in international trade.'
21. For further analysis of the first four disputes listed, see B. Karapinar (2012), 'Defining the Legal Boundaries of Export Restrictions: A case analysis', *Journal of International Economic Law* 15(2) 443.
22. Paragraph 11.3 provides that 'China shall *eliminate all taxes and charges* applied to exports unless specifically provided for in Annex 6 of this Protocol or applied in

conformity with the provisions of Article VIII of the GATT 1994' (emphasis added – note that this requirement contrasts with GATT Article XI.1, which prohibits only quantitative restrictions and specifically excludes 'duties, taxes or other charges' from its purview). China's export duties in *China – Raw Materials* were applied to some minerals not listed in Annex 6, and in other cases exceeded the maximum rates permitted under Annex 6.

23. Office of the United States Trade Representative, Executive Office of the President, *Fact Sheet*, *WTO Case Challenging China's Export Restraints on Raw Material Inputs*, June 2009.
24. WTO Dispute Settlement, *China – Raw Materials*, note 17 above, para. 3.5.
25. *Ibid.*
26. WTO Appellate Body Report, *China – Measures Affecting Trading Rights and Distribution Services for Certain Publications and Audiovisual Entertainment Products* (*China – Publications and Audiovisual Products*), adopted December 21, 2009, para. 415(a), available at http://www.wto.org/english/tratop_e/dispu_e/cases_e/ds363_e.htm (last accessed October 10, 2013).
27. WTO Appellate Body Report, *China – Raw Materials*, note 17 above, para. 293.
28. Notably *expressio unius est exclusio alterius* ('the express mention of one thing excludes all others').
29. Baroncini, note 3 above, at para. 23. See also J. Qin (2012) 'The Predicament of China's "WTO-Plus" Obligation to Eliminate Export Duties: A commentary on the China-Raw Materials Case', *Chinese Journal of International Law*, 11, 237–46.
30. B. Gu (2012), 'Applicability of GATT Article XX in China-Raw Materials: A clash within the WTO Agreement', *Journal of International Economic Law*, 15(4), 1007.
31. WTO Appellate Body Report, *China – Raw Materials*, note 17 above, para. 361.
32. *China – Raw Materials*, note 17 above, para. 7.466.
33. For example, China claimed that its reserves of refractory-grade bauxite had an estimated lifespan of 16 years at the time of the dispute.
34. *China – Raw Materials*, note 17 above, para 7.239.
35. For a detailed examination of China's arguments under Article XI:2(a) and the Panel's conclusions, see Karapinar, note 21 above, at 449–56.
36. 15 are within the chemical group called lanthanides: lanthanum, cerium, praseodymium, neodymium, promethium, samarium, europium, gadolinium, terbium, dysprosium, holmium, erbium, thulium, ytterbium and lutetium, plus yttrium and scandium.
37. A particular advantage of rare earths over potential substitutes is their capacity to produce the strongest magnetic fields currently possible, hence enhancing design. An oft-cited example is that in the absence of rare earths, laptop computers would be 50% larger and twice as heavy as current units: K. Gschneider (2011), 'The Rare Earth Crisis – the Supply/Demand Situation for 2010–2015', *Material Matters*, 6 (2) Milwaukee, available at http://www.sigmaaldrich.com/technical-documents/articles/material-matters/the-rare-earth-crisis.html; N. Jepson (2012), 'A 21st Century Scramble: South Africa, China and the rare earths metals industry', Centre for Chinese Studies and SAIIA, available via, http://www.saiia.org.za/occasional-papers/a-21st-century-scramble-south-africa-china-and-the-rare-earth-metals-industry, at p.12.
38. G. Haxel, J. Hedrick and J. Orris (2002), 'Rare Earth Elements Critical Resources for High Technology', Reston (VA): United States Geological Survey. USGS Fact Sheet: 087–02, available at http://pubs.usgs.gov/fs/2002/fs087–02/fs087–02.pdf (last accessed November 10, 2013).
39. G. P. Hatch (2011), 'Critical Rare Earths: Global supply and demand projections and the leading contenders for new sources of supply', available at http://www.criticalrareearthsreport.com/downloads/cre-0811.pdf (last accessed September 10, 2013).
40. Information Office of the State Council, The People's Republic of China (2012), 'Situation and Policies of China's Rare Earth Industry', *Foreign Language Press*, available at http://www.miit.gov.cn/n11293472/n11293832/n12771663/n14676956.files/n14675980.pdf (last accessed June 10, 2013).

41. Japan appears to have better anticipated the supply risks, particularly through accumulating stockpiles of rare earth elements: K. Bradsher (2010), 'China Said to Resume Shipments of Rare Earth Materials', *The NYTimes.com*, October 28, 2010, available at http://www.nytimes.com/2010/10/29/business/energy-environment/29rare.html?pagewanted=all&_r=0 (last accessed July 1, 2013).
42. These are a group of territorially disputed islands in the South China Sea, known to China as Diaoyu and to Japan as Senkaku. See A. Showstack (March 27, 2012), *Eos, American Geophysical Union*, Vol. 93, No. 13. China has also, on other occasions, briefly suspended all supplies of rare earths to the United States and the European Union.
43. D. Stanway (2012), 'China Says to Tighten Regulation of Rare Earth despite WTO Probe' (July 25, 2012), *Thomas Reuters Online*, available at http://in.reuters.com/article/2012/07/25/us-china-rareearth-wto-idINBRE86O08T20120725 (last accessed July 3, 2013).
44. Information Office of the State Council, note 40 above.
45. China asserts that if exports were not constrained, its identified reserves of rare earths would be exhausted within 15 to 20 years.
46. L. Hornby and S. Donnan (October 29, 2013), 'WTO Rules Against China on Rare Earths Export Quotas', *FT.com*, available at http://www.ft.com/intl/cms/s/0/486d5c68–40b5–11e3-ae19–00144feabdc0.html#axzz2mI3rqGe8 (last accessed October 30, 2013); Yap, note 5 above.
47. *China – Raw Materials*, note 17 above.
48. STRATFOR Global Intelligence, Special Report: China and the Future of Rare Earth Elements, October 12, 2010, available at http://ec.europa.eu/digital-agenda/futurium/sites/futurium/files/futurium/library/Global,%20Corporation,%20Funds%20-%202010%20-%20SPECIAL%20REPORT%20China%20and%20the%20Future%20of%20Rare%20Earth%20Elements.pdf (last accessed February 11, 2013).
49. P. Huck (2012), 'Climate for Worldwide Change', *NZ Herald*, May 11, 2012, available at http://www.nzherald.co.nz/world/news/article.cfm?c_id=2&objectid=10804986 (last accessed May 12, 2012). Other examples include Scotland's investment in wave energy; *see* http://blueandgreentomorrow.com/2013/10/22/scottish-wave-power-could-create-hundreds-of-long-term-jobs/ (last accessed July 1, 2013) and, most notably, the EU Aviation Directive, which, while currently postponed, appears to have spurred moves by the International Civil Aviation Organization towards the use of market based mechanisms for international aviation emissions; *see* http://ictsd.org/i/news/bioresreview/178622/ (last accessed July 1, 2013) There have been some unsuccessful initiatives as well, such as Ecuador's recently abandoned proposal to preserve a major rainforest by having wealthy donors pay it to leave a large oil reserve untouched; *see* http://www.washingtonpost.com/blogs/wonkblog/wp/2013/08/16/ecuador-asked-the-world-to-pay-it-not-to-drill-for-oil-the-world-said-no/ (last accessed July 1, 2013).
50. However, it has also been observed that 'the WTO Appellate Body has expanded the scope of WTO environmental jurisprudence by addressing many of the criticisms voiced by moderate environmentalists': R. Jebe, D. Mayer and Y. Lee (2012), 'China's Export Restrictions of Raw Materials and Rare Earths: A new balance between free trade and environmental protection?', *The George Washington International Law Review*, Vol. 44, No. 4, 579 at 625.
51. Most famously, *Report of the Panel, United States – Restrictions on Imports of Tuna* (*Tuna/Dolphin I*), DS21/R (August 16, 1991). Also, Appellate Body Report, *United States – Standards for Reformulated and Conventional Gasoline* (*US – Gasoline*), WT/DS2/AB/R, adopted May 20, 1996.
52. Marrakesh Agreement Establishing the World Trade Organization, Preamble, available at http://www.wto.org/english/res_e/booksp_e/analytic_index_e/wto_agree_01_e.htm (last accessed February 10, 2013).

6. Addressing the inequality issue under border carbon adjustment

Xin Zhou, Takashi Yano and Mustafa Moinuddin

1. INTRODUCTION

Border carbon adjustment (BCA) aims to address the competitiveness and carbon leakage concerns caused by the asymmetric requirements for developed and developing countries regarding their domestic mitigation under the Kyoto Protocol. Depending on the nature of domestic carbon pricing policy, BCA measures can take two different forms. One is border tax adjustment (BTA), under which a carbon tariff is levied on imported products. Another form requires importers to surrender allowances under a cap-and-trade system.

As a trade measure, BCA has received political attention and was included in several legislative proposals for domestic climate policy. The 2009 American Clean Energy and Security Act passed by the House includes a provision on border adjustment measures. In January 2012, the European Commission decided to include emissions from international aviation to and from EU 27 countries in the EU Emissions Trading System, which gave further momentum to the global discussions over BCA.

In this chapter, we argue that although BCA measures can level up the playing field of foreign producers to the same level as domestic producers, these measures cause another form of inequity in favour of the BCA-implementing countries because they charge the carbon costs of imports but do not issue corresponding emission credits to offset the emissions from the exporting countries. We propose a solution and use a multi-region computable general equilibrium (CGE) analysis to support our proposal.

2. THE ISSUE

Domestically, under a carbon tax system, emitters pay the carbon tax for their emissions. Under an emissions trading system, emitters pay to buy the emission permits. In both cases, emitters pay for the carbon costs in exchange for the right to emit (see the two-directional arrows within the boundary of Country A under Scheme A in Figure 6.1). Because BCA is essentially an extension of domestic climate policy to imports, if the same

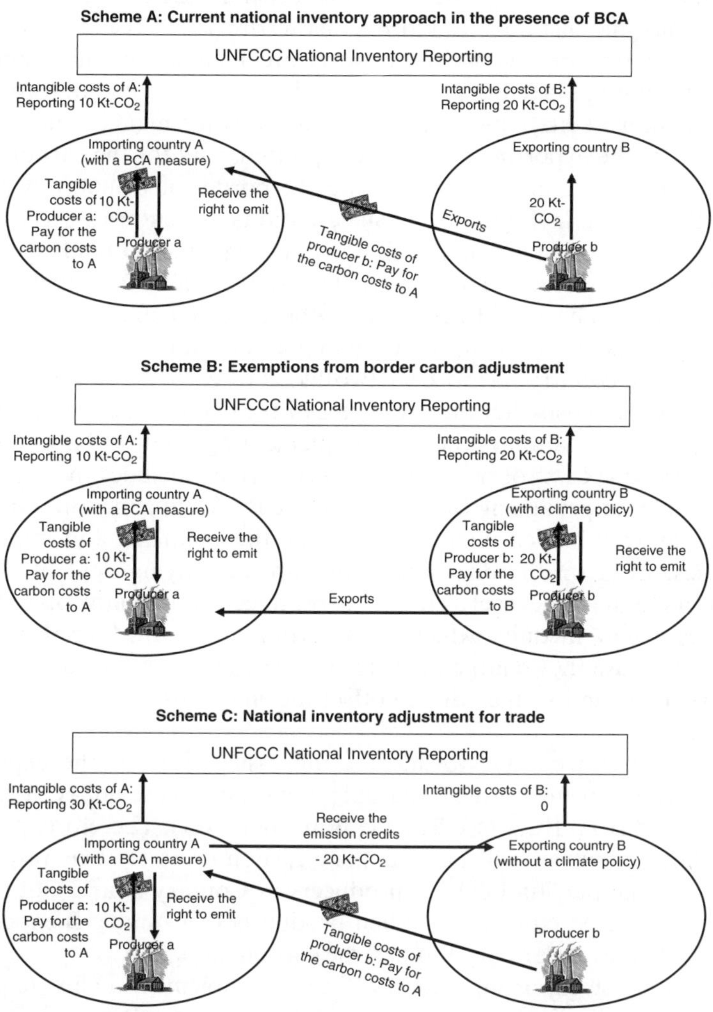

Figure 6.1 The inequality issue under border carbon adjustment

rationale is applied to BCA, exporting countries pay for the carbon costs to the importing country and in return they can receive emission credits. Therefore exporting countries can deduct export-related emissions from their national inventory and the deducted emissions need to be added to the national inventory of the importing country. However, none of the existing BCA proposals provide such a mechanism.

The current national inventory approach of the Kyoto Protocol requires that countries report 'emissions and removals taking place within national (including administered) territories and offshore areas over which the country has jurisdiction'.[1] Based on this territorial emissions approach, emissions corresponding to the exports are included in the exporting country's national inventory. If the BCA-implementing country does not issue emission credits, export-related emissions will remain in the national inventory of the exporting country though they paid for the carbon costs (see the one-directional arrow crossing the border of Country A and B under Scheme A in Figure 6.1). Since national inventories are used as reference for ranking national emissions, setting national binding targets and assessing historical and accumulated contributions to global climate change, they can be considered as intangible costs to countries. Following current national inventory approach and policy arrangements under BCA, the exporting country has to bear two kinds of carbon costs. One is the tangible carbon costs that the producers of the exporting country pay for entering into the market of the BCA-implementing country. The other one is the intangible costs of national inventory, which includes the emissions accountable for producing the exports to the BCA-implementing country.

This causes a hidden inequality between the exporting and importing countries. BCA on the one hand levels up the playing field of foreign producers to the same level as domestic producers; but, on the other hand, it causes a new inequity which is in favour of the BCA-implementing country because they charge the carbon costs of imports but do not issue corresponding emission credits to offset the emissions from the exporting country.

We propose two ways to address this issue. First, if the exporting country also implements a comparable domestic climate policy, it should be exempted from BCA (see Scheme B in Figure 6.1). Therefore, producers in both countries will pay for their carbon costs to their respective countries. The playing field for producers in Country A and Country B can be considered equivalent. When producers of Country B exports to Country A, they do not need to pay the carbon costs to A.

Second, if the exporting country does not implement a climate policy or a comparable climate policy, producers of Country B will pay for the carbon costs to Country A but at the same time Country B will receive emission credits from Country A (see the two-directional arrows for cross-border transactions under Scheme C in Figure 6.1). The national greenhouse gas (GHG) inventories of both countries should be adjusted accordingly. The emissions related to trade should be added to the national inventory of Country A and deducted from that of Country B, keeping the global GHG emissions at the same level. We call this National Inventory Adjustment for Trade (NIAfT). Following the NIAfT, producers from both countries are placed at the same level of the playing field and both countries have an equitable responsibility for their national GHG emissions.

To examine the inequality issue, we applied a multi-region CGE model to assess the economic and environmental effectiveness of the existing BCA proposal versus our proposal. Two practical issues related to the implementation of a BCA measure, the comparability of domestic climate policies across countries and World Trade Organization (WTO) compatibility of BCA, are discussed.

Our focus country is Japan. In October 2012, Japan started a carbon tax on fossil fuels to help achieve domestic targets of 25 per cent GHG reductions from the 1990 level by 2020 and 80 per cent reductions by 2050.[2] There have been great concerns over the impacts on industrial competitiveness in domestic policy debates, in particular over energy-intensive and trade-exposed (EITE) industries, and BCA measures have been discussed in this regard.[3]

3. ANALYSIS

3.1 Model Description

A multi-region CGE model, GTAP6inGAMS,[4] is applied to assess the economic and environmental impacts of a carbon tax on fossil fuels and the BTA in Japan. A Leontief-constant elasticity of substitution (CES) nested function is employed as a production function. Intermediate goods and a composite of value added are defined by Leontief production function. Value added is aggregated by a CES function of production factors including unskilled labour, skilled labour, capital stock, land and natural resources. Allocation between domestic and imported intermediate goods follows the Armington approach.[5]

A representative household maximizes her utility, expressed in a CES function of energy and non-energy commodities. Energy and non-energy commodities are aggregated by the Cobb–Douglas function. Their allocations follow the Armington approach. Different from the GTAP6inGAMS model, household behaviour is formulated by using per capita variables. Government behaviour is presented by the Leontief function. Revenues from carbon tax and border carbon tariffs will become governmental revenue and are not transferred to households. Investment is treated as an exogenous variable. Thus, the exogenous paths for production factors and population growth determine the dynamics of the model.

3.2 Data and Assumptions

For the construction of the multi-region CGE model, GTAP Database Version 7 (base year of 2004) is employed.[6] We categorized the regions in the world into seven and sectors into 39. Except for Japan, the United States, Republic of Korea, China, India and the Association of South East Asian Nations (ASEAN) are considered as major trading partners of Japan in Asia and the Pacific. Other countries are grouped into the rest of the world (ROW).

There are three energy sectors (petroleum and coal products, electricity, and gas manufacture and distribution) and 36 non-energy sectors, of which six are defined as EITE sectors. Based on other studies,[7] we define paper products and printing, chemical, rubber and plastic products, non-metallic minerals, iron and steel, non-ferrous metals and fabricated metal products as EITE sectors in Japan. For emissions data, we use the GTAP-E database, which is included in the package of GTAP Database Version 7.

3.3 Simulation Scenarios

Carbon tax rate is added to the output prices and import prices of fossil fuels, which include coal, gas and oil. Carbon tax is set to be introduced from 2012 onwards at a fixed rate of JPY289/t-CO_2.

For policy simulation, we set four scenarios. Under a business-as-usual (BAU) case, Japan does not charge a carbon tax. Under CTax_J, Japan levies a domestic carbon tax on fossil fuels. Under BTA_J, Japan adopts a carbon tax system with a BTA measure under which imports of EITE sectors from other regions are subject to a carbon tariff at the same rate as Japan's domestic carbon tax, i.e. JPY289/t-CO_2. The carbon content of imports is determined by the direct emissions from the production of imported products, calculated as total sectoral emissions divided by total sectoral outputs. Reference year is 2004 with projections up to 2020.

Under NIAfT_J, national inventories of Japan as an importing country and other regions as exporting countries will be adjusted. Direct emissions in other regions from the production of the products exported to Japan will be added to Japan's national GHG inventory (see Equation 1) and deducted from the account of other regions (see Equation 2).

$$e^{J}_{NIAfT\_J} = e^{J}_{BTA\_J} + \sum_{R(-J)} \sum_{EITE} e(EITE)^{R(-J)J}_{BTA\_J} \quad (1)$$

$$e^{R(-J)}_{NIAfT\_J} = e^{R(-J)}_{BTA\_J} - \sum_{EITE} e(EITE)^{R(-J)J}_{BTA\_J} \quad (2)$$

where $e^{J}_{BTA\_J}$, $e^{R(-J)}_{BTA\_J}$, $e^{J}_{NIAfT\_J}$ and $e^{R(-J)}_{NIAfT\_J}$ represent the national inventories of Japan and other regions under the cases of BTA_J and NIAfT_J, respectively. $e(EITE)^{R(-J)J}_{BTA\_J}$ represents the emissions from the production of the exports of EITE sectors to Japan from other regions *R*(-*J*).

4. RESULTS

4.1 Impacts on International Competitiveness

International competitiveness of EITE sectors is measured by output change. Table 6.1 presents the output change of EITE sectors in Japan under CTax_J and BTA_J. Output change is evaluated in terms of both value change and percentage change. We compare the differences between (1) CTax_J and BAU and (2) BTA_J and CTax_J. Table 6.1 indicates that under CTax_J, the outputs of EITE sectors will be impacted negatively; however, the impacts are trivial, ranging from -0.03 per cent to -0.0002 per cent. The sector of chemical, rubber and plastic products will be influenced the most and paper products and the printing sector will be influenced the least in six EITE sectors. Except for fabricated metal products, the BTA measure in most cases is effective to help reduce competitiveness loss and, in many cases, it can even help EITE sectors gain more competitiveness compared with BAU. For fabricated metal products, the BTA measure will worsen the competitiveness of the sector in terms of outputs.

4.2 Carbon Leakage Effect

To test the carbon leakage effects of different climate policies of CTax_J and BTA_J, we compared the changes in the national emissions of seven regions based on the Kyoto Protocol's inventory approach. Under NIAfT_J, the national inventories of Japan as an importing country and other regions as exporting countries are adjusted based on our proposal (Equation 2).

Comparing the cases of CTax_J and BAU_J (Table 6.2) we find that CTax_J can reduce domestic emissions in Japan; however, at the same

Table 6.1 Output changes of EITE sectors under CTax_J and BTA_J

	ppp[1]				crp			
	Change in value[2] (billion USD)		Change in percentage[3] (%)		Change in value (billion USD)		Change in percentage (%)	
	CTax_J	BTA_J	CTax_J	BTA_J	CTax_J	BTA_J	CTax_J	BTA_J
2012	−0.0002	0.0028	−0.0001	0.0014	−0.0023	0.0172	−0.0005	0.0039
2015	−0.0006	0.0052	−0.0003	0.0026	−0.0090	0.0344	−0.0019	0.0074
2020	−0.0023	0.0067	−0.0011	0.0032	−0.0304	0.0515	−0.0060	0.0102
	nmm				i_s			
	Change in value (billion USD)		Change in percentage (%)		Change in value (billion USD)		Change in percentage (%)	
	CTax_J	BTA_J	CTax_J	BTA_J	CTax_J	BTA_J	CTax_J	BTA_J
2012	−0.0003	0.0135	−0.0003	0.0164	−0.0015	0.0042	−0.0008	0.0022
2015	−0.0012	0.0170	−0.0013	0.0191	−0.0060	0.0075	−0.0029	0.0036
2020	−0.0048	0.0135	−0.0046	0.0129	−0.0220	0.0096	−0.0089	0.0039
	nfm				fmp			
	Change in value (billion USD)		Change in percentage (%)		Change in value (billion USD)		Change in percentage (%)	
	CTax_J	BTA_J	CTax_J	BTA_J	CTax_J	BTA_J	CTax_J	BTA_J
2012	−0.0007	0.0020	−0.0010	0.0029	−0.0005	−0.0018	−0.0004	−0.0014
2015	−0.0031	0.0019	−0.0039	0.0024	−0.0022	−0.0033	−0.0016	−0.0024
2020	−0.0141	−0.0021	−0.0124	−0.0019	−0.0082	−0.0053	−0.0056	−0.0036

Notes:

1. ppp: Paper products and publishing; crp: Chemical, rubber and plastic products; nmm: Non-metallic minerals; i_s: Iron and steel; nfm: Non-ferrous metals; fmp: Fabricated metal products.
2. For the output changes in value, CTax_J is calculated as Output (CTax_J) - Output (BAU); BTA_J is calculated as Output (BTA_J) - Output (CTax_J).
3. For the output changes in percentage, CTax_J is calculated as [Output (CTax_J) - Output (BAU)] / Output (BAU); BTA_J is calculated as [Output (BTA_J) - Output (CTax_J)] / Output (CTax_J).

Table 6.2 National emissions changes under CTax_J, BTA_J and NIAfT_J

	Japan						Korea					
	Change in amount[1] (Mt CO_2)			Change in percentage[2] (%)			Change in amount (Mt CO_2)			Change in percentage (%)		
	CTax_J	BTA_J	NIAfT_J	CTax_J	BTA_J	NIAfT _J	CTax_J	BTA_J	NIAfT _J	CTax_J	BTA_J	NIAfT _J
2012	−0.0015	0.0107	26.4694	−0.0001	0.0010	2.5672	0.0000	0.0014	−0.7782	0.0000	0.0003	−0.1743
2015	−0.0056	0.0169	22.8445	−0.0005	0.0016	2.1214	0.0002	0.0023	−0.8133	0.0000	0.0005	−0.1688
2020	−0.0188	0.0186	20.0067	−0.0016	0.0016	1.7488	0.0008	0.0018	−0.8535	0.0001	0.0003	−0.1593
	China						India					
	Change in amount (Mt CO_2)			Change in percentage (%)			Change in amount (Mt CO_2)			Change in percentage (%)		
	Ctax_J	BTA_J	NIAfT _J	Ctax_J	BTA_J	NIAfT _J	Ctax_J	BTA_J	NIAfT _J	Ctax_J	BTA_J	NIAfT _J
2012	0.0013	−0.0451	−8.7628	0.0000	−0.0008	−0.1609	0.0003	0.0017	−0.3744	0.0000	0.0001	−0.0312
2015	0.0038	−0.0308	−4.8803	0.0001	−0.0006	−0.0882	0.0008	0.0035	−0.3009	0.0001	0.0003	−0.0246
2020	0.0116	−0.0090	−1.7713	0.0002	−0.0002	−0.0332	0.0015	0.0008	−0.1603	0.0001	0.0001	−0.0136
	ASEAN						USA					
	Change in amount (Mt CO_2)			Change in percentage (%)			Change in amount (Mt CO_2)			Change in percentage (%)		
	CTax_J	BTA_J	NIAfT _J	CTax_J	BTA_J	NIAfT _J	CTax_J	BTA_J	NIAfT _J	CTax_J	BTA_J	NIAfT _J
2012	0.0001	−0.0141	−4.4231	0.0000	−0.0014	−0.4297	0.0003	0.0071	−3.6203	0.0000	0.0001	−0.0625
2015	0.0003	−0.0199	−4.2516	0.0000	−0.0018	−0.3851	0.0007	0.0103	−3.8777	0.0000	0.0002	−0.0649
2020	0.0013	−0.0202	−4.4352	0.0001	−0.0017	−0.3632	0.0018	0.0013	−3.9340	0.0000	0.0000	−0.0633

Table 6.2 (continued)

	ROW						Total of Regions Other than Japan					
	Change in amount (Mt CO_2)			Change in percentage (%)			Change in amount (Mt CO_2)			Change in percentage (%)		
	CTax_J	BTA_J	NIAfT _J	CTax_J	BTA_J	NIAfT _J	CTax_J	BTA_J	NIAfT _J	CTax_J	BTA_J	NIAfT _J
2012	0.0007	−0.0017	−8.5507	0.0000	0.0000	−0.0771	0.0026	−0.0507	−26.5095	0.0000	−0.0002	−0.1060
2015	0.0032	−0.0023	−8.7407	0.0000	0.0000	−0.0762	0.0089	−0.0368	−22.8644	0.0000	−0.0001	−0.0887
2020	0.0125	−0.0085	−8.8676	0.0001	−0.0001	−0.0746	0.0294	−0.0338	−20.0219	0.0001	−0.0001	−0.0759

Notes:

1. For the changes in amount, CTax_J is calculated as National Emissions (CTax_J) - National Emissions (BAU); BTA_J is calculated as National Emissions (BTA) - National Emissions (CTax_J); NIAfT_J is calculated as National Emissions (NIAfT_J) - National Emissions (CTax_J).
2. For the changes in percentage, CTax_J is calculated as [National Emissions (CTax_J) - National Emissions (BAU)] / National Emissions (BAU); BTA_J is calculated as [National Emissions (BTA_J) - National Emissions (CTax_J)] / National Emissions (CTax); NIAfT_J is calculated as [National Emissions (NIAfT_J) - National Emissions (CTax_J)] / National Emissions (CTax_J).

time triggers the mechanisms of carbon leakage in other regions. Domestic reduction effects are very small, less than 0.002 per cent decrease compared with the BAU case. Though the carbon leakage rate (the amount of total increase of emissions in other regions divided by the amount of emissions reductions) is as high as 1.8, the scale of carbon leakage is very small, less than 0.0001 per cent increase of the total emissions in other regions compared with the BAU case. Carbon will leak mainly to China and ROW; however, the levels are very low, around 0.0002 per cent increase in China's total emissions compared with the BAU case. This indicates that the carbon tax policy implemented in Japan has little effect on either domestic reductions or carbon leakage.

The BTA_J case can generate negative carbon leakage at the global level. In most cases in China, ASEAN and the ROW, negative leakage will occur. However, the positive effects of the BTA measure on preventing global carbon leakage are also very small. Unexpectedly, a carbon tax policy with a BTA measure cannot achieve any reductions in Japan but oppositely increases domestic emissions compared with the BAU case. Furthermore, emissions from Korea, India and the United States will also increase though very lightly.

Based on our proposal of NIAfT_J, the emissions related to the imports of EITE sectors from other regions to Japan are added to Japan's national inventory, which makes Japan's total national emissions increase dramatically, around 2 per cent. This is partly because in most of the cases the carbon intensities of EITE sectors in other countries, in particular China, India and ASEAN, are several times higher than in Japan. In contrast to Japan, the national inventories of all other regions will decrease, particularly in China and the ROW, indicating significant negative carbon leakage.

5. DISCUSSIONS AND CONCLUSIONS

In this chapter we presented the inequality issue in accounting for the emissions related to the bilateral trade when BCA is introduced as part of national climate policies. The problem is due to lacking the proper crediting mechanism regarding trade-related emissions. To address this inequality, we proposed two ways. One is to exempt the exporting country from the BCA coverage when a comparable climate policy is in place in the country. Another is the NIAfT, by which the exporting country pays for the carbon costs of their exports and receives emission credits in return. As a result, the national inventories of both exporting and importing countries should be adjusted accordingly.

Two issues are worth further discussions. One is how to implement NIAfT when Country B implements a domestic climate policy which is not comparable with the one implemented in Country A. Another is about whether a BCA measure with NIAfT can be compatible with WTO rules.

5.1 Comparability of Domestic Climate Policies

If Country B implements a domestic climate policy which is considered incomparable with the one implemented in Country A – for example, B implements a carbon tax with the rate much lower than the tax levied in A – the carbon prices in the two countries, pc_A and pc_B, will be different and $pc_A > pc_B$. Given other conditions equal, the carbon costs of the same products produced in B will then be lower than the carbon costs in A. Due to these differences in the strictness of climate policies, producers facing different carbon costs in different countries will be placed on an unequal playing field. The competitiveness and carbon leakage concerns still remain unsolved under this situation. How to define the comparability of domestic climate policies among participating countries is a practical challenge in designing a BCA and has been discussed in many BCA proposals.[8] Currently, the post-Kyoto arrangement for global mitigation is under negotiations under the UNFCCC. Expanding the coverage of participation to include all major emitters can be expected; however, allowing long-term differences in the strictness of setting national mitigation targets might be a compromised outcome of international negotiations. Against this background, how to address the compatibility issue will be very relevant to the design of BCA.

To address this situation, we discuss several options. We use the case of a BTA measure to explain these options. First, use the carbon price in A as the criteria to determine the level of border adjustment. To equalize the carbon prices, it is rational to use the difference of the carbon prices in the two countries, i.e. $pc_A - pc_B$, to determine the carbon tariff rate of BTA. Based on our proposal, as B pays for the additional carbon costs to A, B should be given emissions credits from A and therefore the national inventories of both countries should be adjusted accordingly. It is then rational to use the ratio $(pc_A - pc_B)/pc_A$ to determine the emissions credits that A gives to B, i.e. $[(pc_A - pc_B)/pc_A] \times e(EITE)^{BA}$ amount of emissions will be added to A's national inventory and deducted from that of B. However, in practice it may be a big challenge to determine pc_B and therefore $pc_A - pc_B$ if the climate policy implemented in B does not provide a definite price on carbon emissions, such as under a regulatory measure. As an alternative way, if pc_B is much lower than pc_A, we can consider B the same as a party which does not implement domestic carbon pricing policy.

In such a case, pc_A can be used to determine the carbon tariff rate for the exports from B to A and the national inventories of both A and B will be adjusted based on our NIAfT proposal. If $pc_A - pc_B$ is very small, we can consider B the same as a party which implements a comparable domestic climate policy. Therefore, B will be exempted from the list of country coverage of the BTA implemented in A.

Second, use a universal reference carbon price, pc_u, as the criteria to determine the level of border adjustment. The reference carbon price can be determined based on global average marginal abatement costs or through international negotiations under the UNFCCC. There are two cases: (1) When $pc_A > pc_u > pc_B$, $pc_u - pc_B$ can be used as the criteria. However, different from the discussions in the case of using pc_A as the criteria, the price difference, $pc_A - pc_u$, cannot be properly addressed. If $pc_A - pc_u$ is large, the competitiveness concern and carbon leakage concern will remain. (2) When $pc_A > pc_B > pc_u$, based on our proposal, B should be exempted from the BTA implemented in A. However, similar to the previous case, the price difference, $pc_A - pc_B$, cannot be properly addressed. If $pc_A - pc_B$ is large, the competitiveness concern and carbon leakage concern will remain. In addition, using the universal reference carbon price as criteria can address fairness and respect national diversity; however, it cannot encourage countries to adopt stricter climate policies.

5.2 WTO Compatibility

Our proposed BTA measure with exemption and NIAfT can potentially address the hidden inequality between the exporting and importing countries. However, as a trade policy measure, BTAs are subject to WTO rules and regulations. These measures have to be either compatible with member country's market access commitments and applied in a non-discriminatory manner, or must be otherwise justified by the general exceptions provided under General Agreement on Tariffs and Trade (GATT). This section explores the questions whether and how the proposed BTA with exemption and NIAfT can be implemented in a WTO-compatible manner.

For market access, the first issue is whether the imported carbon-intensive and domestic low-carbon products are 'like' or not. The Appellate Body has explained that the criteria for likeness test typically include the products' end-uses, consumer preferences, physical properties and tariff classification.[9] Additionally, WTO jurisprudence on several occasions have confirmed that the likeness test is related to products, not inputs,[10] and that the term 'like' products does not apply to processes and production methods (PPM).[11] Since the difference between low-carbon and carbon-intensive products is concerning their PPM, these products will most certainly be considered as 'like' products following the criteria set forth by the WTO.

For 'like' products, the BTA with exemption and NIAfT must be consistent with GATT's national treatment and most-favoured nation (MFN) principles. Pursuant to GATT Article III.2 on national treatment, internal charges applied to imported products must not be 'in excess of those applied . . . to like domestic products'. Since the BTA without NIAfT applies a carbon tariff at the same rate as the importing country's domestic carbon rates, the measure is not inconsistent with Article III.2. Additionally, the BTA with exemption and NIAfT either exempts carbon tax for countries with a comparable carbon policy, or applies an adjusted national inventory on countries without a comparable carbon policy or without a policy at all. Thus, with exemption and NIAfT, the internal charges do not exceed the charges applied on like domestic products. Therefore, we argue that the BTA with exemption and NIAfT is also consistent with national treatment obligations.

For the MFN clause, GATT Article I requires that there is no discrimination among 'like' products based on their country of origin. The BTA without NIAfT is origin-neutral since it does not differentiate between countries with and without (or non-comparable) carbon policies. On the other hand, the proposed BTA with an exemption to countries which implement a comparable carbon pricing policy and the NIAfT to countries which do not implement a comparable domestic policy or do not have a climate policy at all may cause MFN inconsistency because it applies to certain WTO members and not to all the members, which will breach the 'unconditionality' requirement under Article I.1.

However, a GATT-inconsistent measure can still be justified under the exceptions of GATT Article XX. For carbon taxes, Article XX(g), which applies to measures 'relating to the conservation of exhaustible natural resources', is most relevant.

We argue that the BTAs with and without NIAfT are justified under Article XX(g) for the following reasons:

1. A low-carbon atmosphere for the planet is an 'exhaustible natural resource'. This is consistent with the ruling in *US – Gasoline*, which found clean air to be an 'exhaustible natural resource'.[12]
2. The BTAs are 'related to' conserving the planet's atmosphere because there is a substantial relationship between domestic climate policy and the conservation of the atmosphere. Our modelling results show that although Japan's domestic emissions increase under BTA_J and NIAfT_J cases, both BTAs can contribute to global emissions reduction. Though the reduction effect is small, the very presence of

the effect is sufficient to justify that the measures are 'related to' the environmental objective. The Appellate Body in *US – Shrimp* only assessed whether there would be an effect of the measure at stake, not the magnitude of the effect.[13]

3. The measures also apply to domestic production and consumption in the importing country.

However, if the BTA is applied without exemption and the NIAfT, it may not be justified under the introductory clause of Article XX, which requires that the measure does not create arbitrary or unjustifiable discrimination, or act as a disguised restriction. If the BTA without exemption applies an equal tax rate to those exporting countries which apply the same degree of carbon policies, 'other specific policies and measures that an exporting country may have adopted for the protection and conservation' of the atmosphere, a requirement of the WTO,[14] are not taken into account. The BTA without NIAfT creates a *de facto* unequal playing field which can be considered as disguised trade restriction that is in favour of domestic like products. The BTA with NIAfT, on the other hand, applies adjusted tax rates considering the levels of carbon restrictions in other countries. Thus, the BTA with NIAfT does not cause arbitrary or unjustifiable discrimination, whereas such discrimination is present in the BTA without NIAfT. However, according to WTO jurisprudence, prior to the implementation of the BTA with NIAfT, the importing country must have 'serious, across-the-board negotiations with the objective of concluding bilateral or multilateral agreements' for addressing climate change.[15]

We conclude that our proposed BTA with exemption and NIAfT, which addresses the hidden inequality of BTA measures, can be implemented consistently with WTO rules as an exception under GATT Article XX.

5.3 Conclusions

Existing BCA proposals can address the inequality issue in the playing field between domestic and foreign producers but at the same time create another inequality issue related to a proper emissions crediting mechanism and national inventory accounting. To address the latter inequality issue, we proposed a BTA with exemption and NIAfT. By assessing different climate policy scenarios for Japan, i.e. the carbon tax policy, the BTA and the BTA with exemption and NIAfT, we draw several conclusions as follows:

1. On the one hand, the carbon tax policy implemented unilaterally in Japan can reduce domestic emissions but at the same time triggers the

carbon leakage mechanisms which result in an increase in the global emissions. However, both domestic mitigation effects and the carbon leakage effects are very small. On the other hand, Japan's carbon tax policy will impact the competitiveness of domestic industries adversely, in particular the EITE sectors. However, the impacts are trivial. Therefore, Japan's domestic carbon pricing policy cannot be considered effective to address domestic mitigation nor as a real risk of carbon leakage or as a threat to the competitiveness of domestic industries.

2. By introducing BTA, the competitiveness loss of EITE sectors can be prevented; however, Japan's domestic emissions will increase, contradicting the objective aiming to address domestic mitigation. On the other hand, Japan's carbon tax policy with a BTA measure will reduce emissions in other countries which do not have a comparable climate policy in place and contribute to global emissions reduction.
3. To testify WTO compatibility, we argue that imported carbon-intensive and domestic low-carbon products are 'like' products and the BTA with exemption and NIAfT is consistent with WTO's national treatment obligations but very likely to be questioned by the 'unconditionality' requirement of the MFN clause. However, our proposed BTA with exemption and NIAfT, which addresses the hidden inequality of BTA measures, can be implemented consistently with WTO rules as an exception under GATT Article XX.
4. The inequality issue that we discussed is based on the experience of Japan. For countries which are not parties to the Kyoto Protocol but implement a strict domestic climate policy, the competitiveness and carbon leakage concerns, and the introduction of BCA and the related inequality issue will be similar to the case of Japan.

NOTES

1. UNFCCC (1998), *Kyoto Protocol to the United Nations Framework Convention on Climate Change*, *Technical Report*, United Nations Framework Convention on Climate Change (UNFCCC), Bonn: UNFCCC.
2. Ministry of the Environment of Japan (2012), 'Introduction of Carbon Tax to Combat Global Climate Change', available at http://www.env.go.jp/policy/tax/about.html, accessed 12 November 2012.
3. Council on the Global Warming Issue (2008), 'Proposal of the Council on the Global Warming Issue: In Pursuit of Japan as a Low-carbon Society', available at http://www.kantei.go.jp/foreign/hukudaphoto/2008/06/16proposal.pdf, accessed 12 November 2012; Research Group on Environment and Tariff Policy (2010), 'Summary of Discussions by the Research Group on Environment and Tariff Policy', available

at http://www.mof.go.jp/english/customs_tariff/information/Report.pdf, accessed 12 November 2012.

4. Thomas Rutherford (2005), 'GTAP6inGAMS: The Dataset and Static Model', available at http://www.mpsge.org/gtap6/, accessed 20 August 2012.
5. P. Armington (1969), 'A Theory of Demand for Products Distinguished by Place of Production', *IMF Staff Papers*, 16(1), 159–78.
6. Narayanan Badri and Terrie Walmsley (ed.) (2008), *Global Trade, Assistance, and Production: The GTAP 7 Data Base*, Indiana: Purdue University Center for Global Trade Analysis.
7. Trevor Houser, Rob Bradley, Britt Childs, Jacob Werksman and Robert Heilmayr (2008), *Leveling the Carbon Playing Field: International Competition and US Climate Policy Design*, US: Peterson Institute for International Economics and World Resources Institute; Stéphanie Monjon and Philippe Quirion (2010), 'Addressing Leakage in the EU ETS: Results from the CASE II Model', available at http://www.kth.se/polopoly_fs/1.61926!A2_Monjon.pdf, accessed 15 September 2010; Julia Reinaud (2005), 'Issues behind Competitiveness and Carbon Leakage: Focus on Heavy Industry', IEA Information Paper, Paris: International Energy Agency; S. Takeda, H. Tetsuya and T. Arimura (2012), 'A Computable General Equilibrium Analysis of Border Adjustments under the Cap-and-trade System: A Case Study of the Japanese Economy', *Climate Change Economics*, 3(1).
8. H. van Asselt and T. Brewer (2010), 'Addressing Competitiveness and Leakage Concerns in Climate Policy: An Analysis of Border Adjustment Measures in the US and the EU', *Energy Policy* 38, 42–51.
9. WTO (2001), Appellate Body Report, *European Communities – Measures Affecting Asbestos and Asbestos-Containing Products*, WT/DS135/AB/R, DSR 2001: VII, 3243, para. 101.
10. WTO (2012), Appellate Body Report, *Philippines – Taxes on Distilled Spirits*, WT/DS396/AB/R/WT/DS403/AB/R. paras. 125–8.
11. GATT (1992), *GATT Panel Report, United States – Restrictions on Imports of Tuna*, DS21/R, BISD 39S/155.
12. WTO (1996), Appellate Body Report, *United States – Standards for Reformulated and Conventional Gasoline*, WT/DS2/AB/R, DSR 1996:I, 3, pp. 14–15.
13. WTO (1998), Appellate Body Report, *United States – Import Prohibition of Certain Shrimp and Shrimp Products*, WT/DS58/AB/R, DSR 1998:VII, 2755, paras. 135–42.
14. WTO (1998), Appellate Body Report, *United States – Import Prohibition of Certain Shrimp and Shrimp Products*, WT/DS58/AB/R, DSR 1998:VII, 2755, paras. 161–2.
15. WTO (1998), Appellate Body Report, *United States – Import Prohibition of Certain Shrimp and Shrimp Products*, WT/DS58/AB/R, DSR 1998:VII, 2755, para. 166.

7. Toward green transfer pricing: including environmental parameters in transfer pricing rules

Alice Pirlot[1]

1. INTRODUCTION

Environmental taxation is based on the idea that tax law may be supportive of environmental policies. At the national level, the relationship between tax and environmental law has been widely studied, proving that tax law can be a useful tool to foster environmental goals. At the international level, however, the question of how international taxation – and more specifically transfer pricing rules – interacts with environmental policies and environmental standards has not been much discussed so far. This chapter analyses one specific subject of international law – the multinational – from an environmental and tax perspective. In environmental as well as in tax law, the legislator faces the same challenges associated with regulating the activities of multinationals that operate cross-border. In tax law, the differences in tax regimes between jurisdictions may lead to profit shifting to low-tax countries, commonly called 'tax havens'. The recent action plan on Base Erosion and Profit Shifting published by the Organization for Economic Cooperation and Development (OECD) illustrates the importance of this issue today.[2] In environmental law, international differences in environmental standards may lead to the relocation of enterprises to 'pollution havens'.

Aside from the parallels that can be drawn between environmental and tax issues, environmental and tax policies may interact and eventually support each other in regulating the activities of multinationals.[3] For example, the international emissions trading regime is one legal field where tax law may influence the efficiency of climate change policies. In October 2012, the UN Committee of Experts on International Cooperation in Tax Matters issued a note on the 'tax treaty issues arising from the granting and trading of emissions permits and emissions credits under the UN Model Tax Convention'.[4] This note analyses the fiscal challenges related to the market-based mechanisms of the Kyoto Protocol and provides guidelines as to the fiscal treatment of the income arising from the granting and trading of emissions permits and credits. A similar note was also published by the OECD on the 'tax treaty issues related to emissions permits and credits'.[5]

In this chapter, the objective is not to study the relationship between specific environmental policies (such as the international emissions trading regimes) and transfer pricing rules. Nor is it to analyse how transfer pricing rules may strengthen the efficiency of specific environmental policies. Rather, this chapter approaches the issue from the other way around. It aims at defining how environmental policies may affect the implementation of transfer pricing rules. More specifically, this chapter will study the international tax regime of multinationals from an environmental perspective, focusing on the legal aspects of transfer pricing. Though interesting, the economic dimension will be left aside. The ultimate objective is to serve as a basis for further research in order to assess the relevance of 'green' transfer pricing rules.

Five main sections will structure this analysis. Section 2 will clarify the meaning of the concept of 'multinational' under environmental and tax law. Section 3 will examine the *ratio legis* of transfer pricing so as to determine the potential impact of environmental policies on the implementation of transfer pricing rules. In the next two sections, the analysis will be refined to touch upon allocation methods. Section 4 will discuss the arm's length principle. On the basis of the *ratio legis* of the arm's length principle, this section will explain how environmental criteria may affect the allocation of profits under this method. In Section 5, the focus will shift to formulary apportionment in an attempt to determine whether this method interacts with environmental factors in a different way to the arm's length principle. Finally, Section 6 will conclude with general comments on the feasibility of 'greening' allocation rules.

2. MULTINATIONALS UNDER TAX AND ENVIRONMENTAL LAW

2.1 Multinationals under Tax Law

The location of multinationals in different countries makes the taxation of their profits complicated. On the one hand, multinationals face the risk of double taxation: two or more countries could tax the same profits. On the other hand, governments face the risk that multinational enterprises could shift their profits to low-tax jurisdictions.

In order to reduce the risk of double taxation and profit shifting, bilateral conventions have been established in order to help define how profits should be allocated in cross-border situations. Those conventions are usually based on the OECD Model Tax Convention on Income and on Capital.[6] Under the OECD Model, no specific provision addresses the tax treatment of 'multinationals'. However, articles 7 and 9 deal with the case of enterprises carrying out business in different countries, either through permanent establishments (article 7) or associated enterprises (article 9). According to article 7 of the Model Convention, profits should in principle be taxable in the state of residence of the enterprise. However, when the enterprise carries out business through permanent establishments in other states, the profits may be taxed there. Article 9 of the OECD Model Convention allows governments to adjust economic transactions between associated enterprises when those transactions do not reflect normal market conditions.[7] The idea is that economic transactions between associated enterprises should be priced the same way as between independent enterprises.[8] This principle is called the 'arm's length principle'.

Although the principles of the OECD Model Convention are still prevalent among countries, more and more authors are now questioning the adequacy of the arm's length principle in allocating the profits of multinationals.[9] Alternatively, authors are suggesting a switch towards a new method called 'formulary apportionment', which allocates the profits of multinational enterprises on the basis of a predetermined formula usually defined by three criteria: sales, assets and labour.[10]

2.2 Multinationals under Environmental Law

Multinational enterprises are not only important subjects of international taxation; they also play a growing role in environmental law.[11] As in tax law, the diverse geographic locations of multinational enterprises pose a significant challenge to environmental law. The fact that multinationals operate all over the globe falling within different jurisdictions makes it difficult (if not impossible) for states to completely regulate their activities.[12] Moreover, in addition to the complexity for states to address the behaviour of multinational corporations, domestic environmental policies may have an impact on the location of multinational entities. Pollution havens may emerge, leading to the relocation of polluting enterprises to countries with low environmental standards.[13] Finally, though environmental law is often seen as a cost for multinationals, it could actually be a useful tool to protect them. Indeed, multinationals will be more and more affected by environmental degradation.[14]

Initiatives have emerged that are designed to control the activities of multinationals at the international level. For example, the United Nations (UN) and the OECD have issued guidelines for 'responsible business conduct'.[15] However, no clear legal framework regulates multinationals' activities as far as environmental issues are concerned. Moreover, the concept of 'multinational enterprises' has not been clearly defined.[16] A definition is often considered 'unnecessary' for the purpose of non-binding guidelines.[17]

2.3 Between Environmental and Tax Law: the Approach of this Chapter

This chapter analyses transfer pricing rules from an environmental perspective, as one of the potential interactions between tax and environmental law. Hence, the approach is grounded in tax law while environmental law is used as one factor to test the extent to which environmental parameters affect the implementation of allocation methods. The concepts of 'environmental parameters', 'environmental criteria' and 'environmental factors' are used interchangeably to refer to 'environmental policies' (understood as policies imposing environmental obligations onto multinationals), except when another meaning is explicitly indicated.

3. THE RATIO LEGIS OF TRANSFER PRICING RULES

Of course, the primary purpose of transfer pricing rules is not to achieve environmental goals. Yet, this chapter explores the rationale behind current transfer pricing rules in an effort to evaluate the place given to environmental factors in transfer pricing.

The central question here touches upon the reasons that explain the preference of legislators for certain types of allocation methods. Should transfer pricing rules ensure that the allocation of profits reflect the 'real' economic activity of each enterprise? Or are transfer pricing rules rather aimed at distributing profits according to the public 'benefits' enjoyed by the enterprise? When transfer pricing rules are grounded in a pure economic approach, environmental parameters will usually be considered as far as they represent a cost for the enterprise. On the contrary, when the allocation of profits attempts to reflect the public 'benefits' that the enterprise avails itself of, environmental parameters will eventually affect allocation rules in proportion to the domestic 'natural services' used by the enterprise. Hence, the impact of environmental criteria on transfer pricing rules will highly depend on the definition of their *ratio legis*.

In what follows, three general approaches to allocation rules are described.[18] For each of them, an explanation is given about how the *ratio legis* will influence the role played by environmental parameters in transfer pricing regimes.

3.1 The Approach of the 'True Allocation of Income'

The approach of the 'true allocation of income' is based on the belief that income should be allocated according to where it originates in opposition to the 'false' allocation of income resulting from profit shifting.[19] Under this approach, environmental factors will not play a direct role in identifying where the income originates. Usually, as for independent enterprises, environmental policies will be considered a cost. Indeed, a high level of environmental protection often implies expenses for the enterprises. In other words, all others things being equal, an enterprise normally generates more profits in a country with a low level of environmental regulation.

3.2 The 'Equal Capacity to Earn Income Approach'

This second approach considers that the cross-border character of multinationals' activities makes it illusionary to try determining the exact geographic location where the profits originate.[20]

Instead of striving to locate the 'true' source of income, allocation rules should better seek to allocate profits according to income-producing factors.[21] As its name indicates, this method relies on the idea that the allocation of profits should reflect the ability of each enterprise to generate profits.[22] Therefore, the allocation of profits should be based on benchmarks related to income-generating factors. Under this approach, environmental policies will usually be considered a cost. Indeed, environmental policies generally limit the capacity of enterprises to generate profits. Nevertheless, environmental 'parameters' such as eco labels could also be considered part of an enterprise's income-generating factors in so far as they can effectively participate in the increase of profits.

3.3 The 'Benefit Principle' Approach

This third approach also rejects the idea that allocation methods should help determine the 'true' geographic source of income.[23] However, instead of focusing on the capacity of each enterprise to earn income, the 'benefit principle' approach is founded on the belief that profits should be divided according to the benefits provided by governments to companies.[24] This approach is based on the observation that companies benefit from various public services when operating within a country: infrastructures, legal protection, natural resources, an appropriate marketing environment, etc.[25] Under the 'benefit principle' approach, allocation methods should be based on benchmarks of the public services which multinational entities benefit from. Though 'nature' is rarely considered a 'public service' in today's industrial economy, the environment is sometimes given an 'economic value' through the internalization of environmental costs.[26] From this perspective, an allocation method based on the 'benefit principle' approach could include benchmarks inspired by environmental parameters. When an enterprise operates in a country, its activities often pollute and damage its natural environment, which could be compared to the use of 'natural capital'.[27] In the same way as a company benefits from a country's infrastructure or educated employees, it can also be considered that it benefits from its natural resources.[28] Hence, under the 'benefit principle' approach, the method of allocating profits could take into account environmental benchmarks. Those environmental criteria should reflect the 'environmental benefit' of the enterprise. This could be evaluated by the pollution generated by the enterprise's activities, the 'expenses' involved in protecting the environment for the country, etc.

4. THE ARM'S LENGTH PRINCIPLE AND THE ENVIRONMENT

The arm's length principle is the most common principle used to allocate profits among associated enterprises.[29] The idea underlying this allocation method is that transactions between related entities should be valued 'at arm's length', meaning 'as if they were independent entities'.[30]

According to Rectenwald:

> the implementation of ALS [the arms-length standard] was justified at the outset only in terms of its function as a tool for the preservation of the corporate tax base, without any further theoretical focus on ALS per se. However, as ALS developed into a global standard, governments and international institutions developed a clear set of policy justifications for its continued use.[31]

One of the main justifications of the arm's length principle is grounded in the approach of the 'true allocation of income': as the prices of transactions between associated enterprises may differ from 'natural prices', the arm's length principle is aimed at adjusting those prices to – what is considered to be – the economic reality.[32] As already mentioned, the 'true allocation of income' approach does not give much room to environmental considerations in the allocation of profits. Yet, environmental policies may interact with the arm's length principle in two different ways.

First, environmental parameters may have an impact on the comparability analysis. Since the arm's length principle requires valuing transactions between associated enterprises in the same way as between independent enterprises, the conditions for controlled transactions and transactions between unrelated parties should be made comparable.[33] In other words, all differences that can affect the comparison between the transactions should be taken into account in order to ensure the comparability of the transactions and their correct valuation.[34] The OECD guidelines provide for five factors to guide the comparability analysis: the characteristics of the property and services transferred, the contractual terms, the economic circumstances of the parties, the functions they perform and their business strategies.[35] Indirectly, environmental parameters can be included in those factors. For example, the property transferred may be more or less environmentally friendly. Similarly, the fact that an enterprise performs research activities in green products is a function that should be considered for the comparability analysis. Environmental regulations – as far as they may have an impact on the market comparability – may also need to be considered as affecting the economic circumstances between the parties.

Second, another type of potential interaction between environmental policies and the arm's length principle exists when the purpose of the transaction valued at arm's length is aimed at allowing one of the associated enterprises to comply with its environmental obligations. One example is given by Fischer in her article entitled 'Multinational taxation and international emissions trading'. [36] In this article, Fischer studies the impact of the tax treatment of emissions abatement costs incurred by subsidiaries so as to allow their parent companies to meet their emissions goals.[37] She writes: 'all else equal, the desire to keep profits in lower-tax countries would make multinational firms more reluctant to incur more abatement costs in those countries, unless they are compensated with higher transfer prices'.[38] In other words, the fiscal regime applied to the carbon offset activities undertaken by a subsidiary to meet its parent's emissions obligations will potentially influence the location of abatement costs and the efficiency of international abatement mechanisms.[39] The more similar market-based mechanisms will be used at the international level for environmental purposes, the more interactions of this type there will be.

5. FORMULARY APPORTIONMENT AND THE ENVIRONMENT

While the allocation of profits is based on a comparability analysis between associated and independent enterprises under the arm's length principle, formulary apportionment allocates the profits of multinationals on the basis of a 'predetermined and mechanistic formula'.[40] Depending on the criteria used in the formula, environmental parameters will more or less interact with formulary apportionment.

The most common formula – called the Massachusetts formula – relies on three factors: sales, payroll and property.[41] The choice of those factors can be explained by reference to the objectives that formulary apportionment is supposed to pursue. Usually, sales, payroll and property are considered to be proxies of the ability of a company to earn income, which matches the 'equal capacity to earn income' approach.[42] Though formulary apportionment is often assimilated to the Massachusetts formula, other formulas could be envisaged depending on the approach favoured by the legislator.[43]

In the case of a formula based on sales, payroll and property, the interaction between formulary apportionment and environmental policies will be mostly indirect. Indeed, environmental parameters will potentially influence the valuation of sales, payroll and assets. For example, it is likely that 'green' assets will be evaluated at a higher value. Aside from this indirect influence, environmental parameters could also play a more direct role in the implementation of formulary apportionment. Under the 'benefit principle' approach, environmental parameters could become one of the factors of the formula since, as mentioned earlier, enterprises benefit from 'natural resources' in a similar way as they benefit from infrastructure, legal protection, etc. However, the question of how to define such environmental factors would be highly complex.[44] As developed in the next section, the definition of an 'environmental factor' is a sensitive issue, facing many challenges.

6. THE LIMITS OF A 'GREEN' FORMULA

One general criticism against formulary apportionment is related to the challenge of providing a precise definition of the factors of the formula. When looking at the opportunity to add an environmental factor to the formula, the challenge is even bigger.

A first challenge concerns the difficulty in measuring 'the environmental benefit' that was provided to an enterprise. As Mayer points out, 'the application of a benefits view on apportionment cannot imply measuring benefits received and costs incurred in each jurisdiction. Rather, the apportionment factors located in the different jurisdictions constitute the quantifiable geographic link between the income of a multinational enterprise and those benefits and costs.'[45] On which parameters should the factor representing the 'environmental benefit' be based? Should it depend on the pollution emitted by the enterprises? Or should it be based on the level of environmental policies in the country where the enterprise is located? How are we to ensure that the definition of the 'environmental factor' reflects the 'natural services' used by an enterprise? Though difficult, these questions are not impossible to answer: it is certainly feasible to find proxies for the 'environmental benefit'.[46]

Related to this first challenge, a second – and more important – criticism limits the opportunities for establishing a 'green' formula. Indeed, it is far from certain that 'greening' transfer pricing rules would be beneficial for the environment. In other words, including an environmental parameter in formulary apportionment may be consistent with the 'benefit principle' approach without having a positive impact on the protection of the environment. According to the 'benefit principle', the more an enterprise benefits from 'natural services', the more profits should be allocated to the state providing those 'services'. Such an approach could lead to a higher allocation of profits to states where enterprises pollute the most. Hence, countries with low levels of environmental protection would not be encouraged to improve their environmental policy framework. Such a consequence puts into question the opportunity to include environmental factors in allocation rules. Indeed, under a strict interpretation of the 'benefit principle' approach, the inclusion of an environmental factor will not necessarily lead to the 'greening' of transfer pricing rules.[47] Therefore, a new *ratio legis* may be necessary to justify including an environmental factor in the apportionment formula.

Finally, a third challenge is related to the risk of abuse and manipulation of the 'environmental factor' by multinationals. Indeed, a formula including an environmental factor may encourage multinationals to relocate their polluting activities to low-tax countries. However, this criticism can be tempered. Generally, the factors used in formulary apportionment (such as sales, property and payroll) are considered difficult to shift from one place to another.[48] This is one of the advantages of formulary apportionment: multinationals cannot easily circumvent the formula in order to reduce their tax liability.[49] The 'environmental factor' should therefore be defined so as to ensure that multinationals cannot manipulate it to shift their profits from one country to another. Once more, this last challenge proves that a definition of the 'environmental factor' is an essential element for the success of a 'green' formula.

7. CONCLUSION

This chapter has discussed the different approaches guiding the allocation of profits between multinational enterprises in an attempt to highlight the interactions between environmental policies and transfer pricing rules. It has illustrated that environmental parameters may influence each of the three general approaches to allocation rules. On the one hand, the approach of the 'true allocation of income' and the approach of the 'equal capacity to earn income' generally view environmental policies as a cost. On the other hand, the 'benefit principle' approach may offer an opportunity to include environmental parameters in the benchmarks used to allocate the profits of multinational enterprises located in different tax jurisdictions.

As to the arm's length principle, its foundation in the approach of the 'true allocation of profits' prevents a real interaction between environmental policies and transfer pricing rules. Indeed, the arm's length principle is primarily based on the comparison of transactions between related and unrelated enterprises, which barely allows the taking into account of differences in the legal frameworks of the countries where the entities of a multinational are located.

While the 'greening' of transfer pricing rules seems difficult to realize through the arm's length principle, the analysis of formulary apportionment indicates that the adoption of 'green' allocation rules is theoretically possible. However, many challenges put into question the relevance of including an environmental factor in formulary apportionment. Further research should examine how environmental factors could effectively and efficiently help to foster environmental goals through allocation rules. One of the most central and essential challenges will be to find a suitable definition for the environmental factor.

NOTES

1. The author would like to thank her supervisor Prof. Dr. Edoardo Traversa, her colleagues Arnaud Lecocq, Luke Kemp, Miguel Nicolas, César Alejandro Ruiz Tatiana Falcão, Romain Su and the reviewers for their comments that help improve this chapter.
2. OECD, *Action Plan on Base Erosion and Profit Shifting* (OECD Publishing, 2013).
3. *See* Michael Ewing-Chow and Darryl Soh, 'Pain, Gain, or Shame: The Evolution of Environmental Law and the Role of Multinational Corporations' (2009) 16 *Indiana Journal of Global Legal Studies* 195, 209; Carolyn Fischer, 'Multinational taxation and international emissions trading' (2006) 28(2) *Resource and Energy Economics* 139.
4. UN Committee of Experts on International Cooperation in Tax Matters, 'Note on Tax Treaty Issues Arising from the Granting and Trading of Emissions Permits and Emissions Credits under the UN Model Tax Convention', 15–19 October 2012, E/C.18/2012/CRP.6. This document has been updated in October 2013 (E/C/18/2013/CRP.6, in particular §§ 130–3).

5. OECD, 'OECD Model Tax Convention: Revised Discussion Draft on Tax Treaty Issues Related to Emissions Permits and Credits', 19 October 2012 to 15 January 2013.
6. OECD, *Model Tax Convention on Income and on Capital 2010* (OECD Publishing, 2012). *See also* United Nations Model Double Taxation Convention between Developed and Developing Countries.
7. *See* OECD, *OECD Transfer Pricing Guidelines for Multinational Enterprises and Tax Administrators 2010* (OECD Publishing, 2010).
8. *Ibid.*, 31.
9. *See* Sol Picciotto, 'Towards Unitary Taxation of Transnational Corporations' (2012) *Tax and Justice Network*; Reuven S. Avi-Yonah and Ilan Benshalom, 'Formulary Apportionment: Myths and Prospects – Promoting Better International Policy and Utilizing the Misunderstood and Under-Theorized Formulary Alternative' (2011) 3(3) *World Tax Journal* (*WTJ*) 371; Kerrie Sadiq, 'Unitary Taxation – The Case for Global Formulary Apportionment' (2001) 55(7) *Bulletin for International Taxation* (*BIT*) 275.
10. *See* the references cited in note 9 above. *See* also OECD, *Transfer Pricing Guidelines*, above n 7, 26; Eric J. Coffill, 'Differences in Productivity and Profitability: A Response to Allegations of the Misattribution of Income in the Application of California's Worldwide Unitary Method' (1987) 5(2) *Berkeley J. Int'l L.* 246; Walter Hellerstein, 'International Income Allocation in the Twenty-first Century: The Case for Formulary Apportionment' (2005) *International Transfer Pricing Journal* 103; Glen Rectenwald, 'A Proposed Framework for Resolving the Transfer Pricing Problem: Allocating the Tax Base of Multinational Entities based on Real Economic Indicators of Benefit and Burden' (2012) 23 *J. Comp. & Int'l L* 425; Joann Martens Weiner, 'Formulary Apportionment and Group Taxation in the European Union: Insights From the United States and Canada' (2005) 8 European Commission Working Paper 11.
11. Ewing-Chow and Soh, above n 3, 200.
12. *Ibid.*, 209; Nitin Desai, 'Symposium: The Road from Johannesburg' (2002–2003) 15 *Geo. Int'l Envtl. L. Rev.* 809, 820.
13. Gunnar S. Eskeland and Ann E. Harrison, 'Moving to Greener Pastures? Multinationals and the Pollution Haven Hypothesis' (2003) 70(1) *J. Dev. Econ.* 1; Beata K. Smarzynska and Shang-Jin Wei, 'Pollution Havens and Foreign Direct Investment: Dirty Secret or Popular Myth?' (2001) 8465 National Bureau of Economic Research (NBER) Research Working Paper; Mariana Spatareanu, 'Searching for Pollution Havens: The Impact of Environmental Regulations on Foreign Direct Investment' (2007) 16 *J. Env. Dev.* 161.
14. On the issue of how climate change will affect multinationals, *see inter alia* Ans Kolk and Jonatan Pinkse, 'Multinational Enterprises and Climate Change Strategies' in Alan Verbeke and Hermant Merchant (eds), *Handbook of Research on International Strategic Management* (Cheltenham, UK and Northampton, MA, USA: Edward Elgar, 2012).
15. OECD, *OECD Guidelines for Multinational Enterprises* (OECD Publishing, 2011); UN Sub-Commission on the Promotion and Protection of Human Rights, *Norms on the Responsibilities of Transnational Corporations and other Business Enterprises with Regards to Human Rights*, 26 August 2003, E/CN.4/Sub.2/2003/12/Rev.2; United Nations Human Rights Office of the High Commissioner, *Guiding Principles on Business and Human Rights*, 2011. *See also* Elisa Morgera, 'Multinational Corporations and International Environmental Law' in Shawkat Alam, Jahid Hossain Bhuiyan, Tareq M.R. Chowdhury and Erika J. Techera (eds), *Routledge Handbook of International Environmental Law* (Abingdon: Routledge, 2012), 204; Neil Gunningham, 'Corporate Environmental Responsibility: Law and the Limits of Voluntarism' in Doreen McBarnet, Aurora Voiculescu and Tom Campbell (eds), *The New Corporate Accountability: Corporate Social Responsibility and the Law* (Cambridge University Press, 2007), 476.
16. *See* e.g. the very general definition of 'transnational corporations' in the UN *Norms on the Responsibilities of Transnational Corporations*, para 20, above n 15.
17. *See* OECD, *OECD Guidelines for Multinational Enterprises*, above n 15, 17: 'A precise definition of multinational enterprises is not required for the purposes of the *Guidelines*.

These enterprises operate in all sectors of the economy. They usually comprise companies or other entities established in more than one country and so linked that they may coordinate their operations in various ways. While one or more of these entities may be able to exercise a significant influence over the activities of others, their degree of autonomy within the enterprise may vary widely from one multinational enterprise to another. Ownership may be private, State or mixed.'

18. This division has been inspired by the approach of Ana Agúndez-Garcia in a working paper on the EU Consolidated Tax Base (Ana Agúndez-Garcia, 'The Delineation and Apportionment of an EU Consolidated Tax Base for Multi-jurisdictional Corporate Income Taxation: a Review of Issues and Options' (2006) 9 European Commission Working Paper, 32–7).
19. *See* Rectenwald above n 10, 430, 434–6. *See also* Charles E. McLure, 'Replacing Separate Entity Accounting and the Arm's Length Principle with Formulary Apportionment' (2002) *BIT* 586, 592 and 598; Walter Hellerstein and Charles E. McLure, 'The European Commission's Report on Company Income Taxation: What the EU Can Learn from the Experience of the US States' (2004) 11 *Int. Tax Public Finance* 199, 208; Stefan Mayer, *Formulary Apportionment for the Internal Market* (Doctoral Series, 17, IBFD 2009), 24–9.
20. Hellerstein, above n 10, 104 (quoted by Agúndez-Garcia, above n 18, 34 and 36).
21. *See* Agúndez-Garcia, above n 18, 35–6.
22. *Ibid.*
23. Hellerstein, above n 10, 104.
24. Agúndez-Garcia, above n 18, 36–7. *See also* David G. Duff, 'Tax Fairness and the Tax Mix' (2008) *Foundation for Law, Justice and Society* 4; Nancy H. Kaufman, 'Fairness and the Taxation of International Income' (1998) *L. & Pol'y Int'l Bus.* 145, 152–3, 157; Mayer, above n 19, 27 and 30–7; Wolfgang Schön, 'International Tax Coordination for a Second-Best World (Part I)' (2009) 1(1) *WTJ* 67, 75–7.
25. Agúndez-Garcia, above n 18, 36–7; Mayer, above n 19, 31–2.
26. *See* the work of the economist Arthur Cecil Pigou, *The Economics of Welfare* (4th edn., London, Macmillan and Co, 1932). *See also* Clóvis Cavalcanti, 'Conceptions of Ecological Economics: its Relationship with Mainstream and Environmental Economics' (2010) 24(68) *Estudos Avançados* 53.
27. *See inter alia* Paul Hawken, Amory B. Lovins and L. Hunter Lovins, *Natural Capitalism: Creating the Next Industrial Revolution* (New York, NY: Little, Brown and Company, 1999).
28. *See* Mayer, above n 19, 31.
29. OECD, *Transfer Pricing Guidelines*, above n 7, 31.
30. *Ibid.*
31. Rectenwald, above n 10, 434.
32. *Ibid.*, 435. *See also* Sadiq, above n 9, 275; Wolfgang Schön, 'International Tax Coordination for a Second-Best World (Part 3)' (2010) 2(3) *WTJ* 227, 231–3.
33. OECD, *Transfer Pricing Guidelines*, above n 7, 41–2.
34. *Ibid.*, 41–3.
35. *Ibid.*, 43–51 (para. 1.36).
36. Fischer, above n 3.
37. *Ibid.*, 141.
38. *Ibid.*, 155.
39. *Ibid.*, 140. *See also* Sigurd Naess-Schmidt, Ulrik Møller, Eske S. Hansen and Jonatan Tops, 'Tax Treatment of ETS Allowances: Options for Improving Transparency and Efficiency' (2010) Copenhagen Economics Report ordered by DG Taxud, available at http://ec.europa.eu/taxation_customs/resources/documents/common/publications/studies/ets-report.pdf, accessed 15 August 2013, 51–2.
40. OECD, *Transfer Pricing Guidelines*, above n 7, 37.
41. *See* International Bureau of Fiscal Documentation, International Tax Glossary.
42. *See inter alia* Agúndez-Garcia, above n 18, 5; Hellerstein, above n 10, 105; Michael

Kobetsky, 'The Case for Unitary Taxation of International Enterprises' (2008) *BIT* 201, 202; McLure, above n 19, 587; Schön, above n 32, 234. Please note that other conceptions exist (*see* Agúndez-Garcia, above n 18, 36–7 and 59; Joann Martens Weiner, *Company Tax Reform in the European Union* (New York, NY: Springer, 2006), 48–9; McLure, above n 19, 592).

43. McLure, above n 19, 592; Agúndez-Garcia, above n 18.
44. See Mayer, above n 19, 37.
45. *Ibid.*, 37.
46. *See* e.g. Christian Layke, 'Measuring Nature's Benefits: A Preliminary Roadmap for Improving Ecosystem Service Indicators' (2009) *World Resources Institute*, available at http://pdf.wri.org/measuring_natures_benefits.pdf, accessed 11 August 2013.
47. This challenge is related to the dichotomy between the 'international' value of the natural capital (i.e. the protection of the environment is a 'global' issue) and the national objective of transfer pricing (i.e. the allocation of profits between associated enterprises located in different countries for tax purposes).
48. *See* Reuven S. Avi-Yonah and Ilan Benshalom, above n 9, 371, 382, 385, 391, 395–6; Reuven S. Avi-Yonah, Kimberly A. Clausing and Michael C. Durst, 'Allocating Business Profits for Tax Purposes: A Proposal to Adopt a Formulary Profit Split' (2008) 138 Public Law and Legal Theory Working Paper Series, 18.
49. *Ibid.*

Section C

Permit trading and price stability

8. The EU Emission Trading Scheme: is there a need for price stabilization?

Claudia Kettner, Daniela Kletzan-Slamanig and Angela Köppl

1. INTRODUCTION

2005 marked the start of the EU Emission Trading System (EU ETS). It is the largest cap-and-trade system worldwide and represents the key instrument of EU climate policy. Several years of experience and various adaptations of the regulatory framework have been accompanied by discussions whether an institutional setting is needed that helps stabilize carbon markets and allowance prices.

Prior to the introduction of the EU ETS a number of papers theoretically and empirically addressed the issue of environmental effectiveness and economic efficiency of emission trading systems (see e.g. Vesterdala and Tinggaard Svendsen (2004) and the literature cited therein). These arguments were re-emphasized as advantages of the market-based instrument by the European Commission and economists when the EU ETS came into force: Once the emissions cap is determined, the allowance price is formed on the market and the desired reduction target is achieved at least cost, providing flexibility for regulated entities. Evidence from the first two trading phases, however, sheds doubts on this assumption and a too strong reliance on market forces. The implementation of the instrument was faced with market failures, which undermined its optimal functioning. The regulating bodies' uncertainty about emissions and abatement options led to an overly generous allocation in Phase 1, resulting in a substantial price drop and a loss of abatement incentives. In Phase 2 the exogenous shock of the global financial and economic crisis had more or less the same effect despite the tightening of the cap.

In this chapter, we argue that – contrary to theoretical assumptions – imperfections in market forces may undermine abatement incentives of emission trading schemes. In order to underpin our arguments we provide empirical evidence from the first two EU ETS phases. This is followed by a discussion of two central price stabilization mechanisms, liquidity management and direct price control, which could strengthen the role of carbon prices in investment decisions. The last section concludes.

2. ECONOMIC THEORY OF EMISSIONS TRADING

There has been an extensive scientific discussion regarding the optimal instrument choice to control emissions. In economic theory, market-based instruments like taxes or emissions trading are preferred over command-and-control regulation as they not only ensure environmental effectiveness but also economic efficiency, which means that emission reductions are achieved at lowest costs. Abatement activities will be carried out as long as the price of an emission allowance or the tax rate is higher than marginal abatement costs. In addition, compared to, for example, a fixed technological standard, flexibility in the choice of abatement measures is provided for.

In the case of a carbon tax, the price of CO_2 emissions is determined by the regulator whereas the quantity of emissions follows from abatement activities, given firms' adjustments to the regulation and their respective marginal abatement costs.[1]

In the case of tradable emission permits, the quantity of emissions, i.e. the cap, is determined by the regulator, while the price for emissions is formed on the market by demand and supply of emission permits. Supply is determined by the overall cap on emissions while demand depends on the firms' respective marginal abatement cost functions (Metcalf 2009).

According to economic theory, a carbon tax and an emission trading scheme would deliver the same outcome. This rationale would presuppose a world without externalities and uncertainty, i.e. perfect information, rational agents and the absence of market failures (McKibbin and Wilcoxen 2002; Hepburn 2006).

In the real world, however, numerous uncertainties affect the efficiency and effectiveness of emission control instruments. These include asymmetries of information between regulator and firms regarding abatement costs and technological options, uncertainties regarding the development of energy prices, technology costs, innovation and economic growth, as well as regarding the stability of regulation.

Weitzman (1974) showed that under uncertainty the outcomes of taxes and permits are not equivalent, and that the relative slopes of the curves determine the ultimate outcome of the policy[2]. Therefore, both market-based instruments have advantages and disadvantages depending on the respective market characteristics and uncertainties; policy-makers have to decide whether the uncertainty about prices or about quantities represents the greater burden to society (Murray, Newell and Pizer 2009).

3. A RATIONALE FOR PRICE-STABILIZING PROVISIONS

The EU and other countries like the United States or New Zealand opted for or discussed emission trading systems because of certainty regarding the emission limit and political feasibility. However, emissions trading schemes always bear the risk of price volatility, which poses a problem for firms' decision-making on investments in abatement measures. Hence, price stabilization measures are an issue in scientific literature (Hepburn 2006; Frankhauser and Hepburn 2010; Murray, Newell and Pizer 2009; Philbert 2009) as well as in the political debate (Point Carbon 2011). In order to illustrate the argument for price stabilization the development carbon prices in the EU ETS as well as causes of price fluctuations are discussed in the following.

3.1 Development of EU ETS Carbon Prices

Stabilizing carbon prices is often discussed as a prerequisite for providing investment and innovation incentives for low carbon technologies. Experience in the EU ETS shows a high variability in the price for allowances (European Unit Amounts, or EUAs) in particular in the first trading phase. Various drivers for these price fluctuations can be distinguished and have been analyzed in a number of papers (Kettner, Köppl and Schleicher 2010): the stringency of the cap; economic business cycles; fuel prices; fuel switching and other abatement options; weather conditions; market conditions and speculation as well as regulatory decisions. These factors have influenced price development for EUAs to a varying degree in the period 2005–2013 as illustrated in Figure 8.1.

The analysis of price development in the EU ETS between 2005 and 2013 indicates that in Phase 1 fluctuations were mainly caused by incomplete information at the beginning, adjustments after the publication of verified emission data and regulatory decisions (no banking between Phase 1 and Phase 2).

However, the price development in Phase 2 reveals the strong influence of economic fundamentals exogenous to the CO_2 market on emission prices. This includes the effects of high fossil energy prices as well as the impacts of unpredictable shocks like the economic crisis and restrained

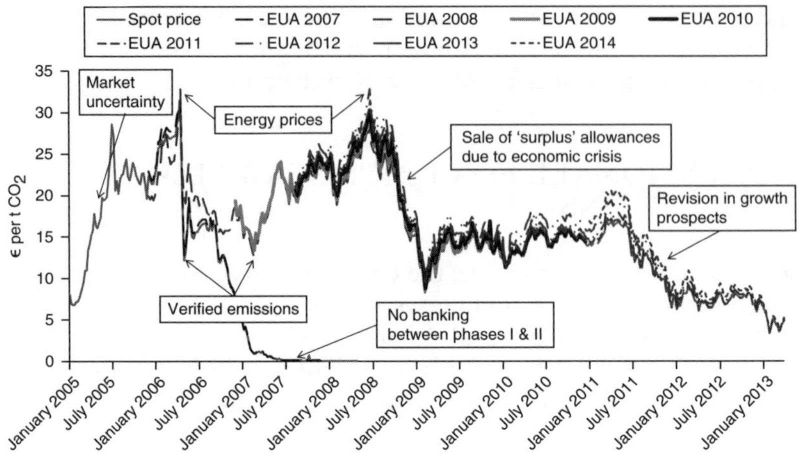

Source: Kettner et al. (2011).

Figure 8.1 Development of OTC closing prices in the EU ETS (2005–2013)

growth prospects that effectively loosen the (ex-ante defined) emissions cap. All these influences, however, have to be seen in light of a different regulatory regime compared to Phase 1, as banking of allowances between Phase 2 and 3 was allowed.

3.2 Allocation, Emissions and their Impact on Prices

In Phases 1 and 2, the overall cap of the EU ETS was the result of the national emission caps set by Member States in their National Allocation Plans (NAPs). In the pilot phase (2005–2007), substantial over-allocation of emission allowances was observed in most EU Member States and the overall EU emission cap was not stringent in any year, i.e. allocated allowances exceeded verified emissions (see Figure 8.2).

For Phase 2 (2008–2012), the European Commission took more influence in the Member States' NAPs. Most of the proposed national caps had to be adjusted downwards by the Member States after the European Commission's review process. For 2008, total allocated allowances were reduced by 244 Mt (11 per cent) compared to Phase 1 (from 2,153 Mt to 1,907 Mt). EU ETS emissions, in contrast, only declined by 4.3 per cent between 2007 and Phase 2 (from 2,126 Mt to 2,061 Mt). For 2008, the overall EU cap was binding, with verified emissions exceeding allocated allowances on aggregate by 7.2 per cent. Under the prospect of a regular

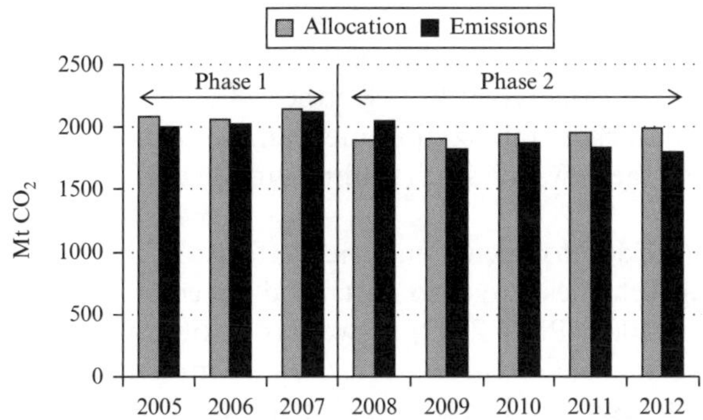

Sources: European Union Transaction Log (EUTL) (2013); own illustration. Data includes the EU-27 except Bulgaria due to data inconsistencies.

Figure 8.2 Allocation and verified emissions in Phase 1 and Phase 2 of the EU ETS

development of economic activities this would suggest an increased incentive for emission abatement resulting from the cap and rising allowance prices. For 2009, however, the unexpected exogenous shock of the economic crisis translated into a sharp drop in verified emissions. The overall allocation again exceeded verified emissions; the total surplus of allowances amounting to 5.6 per cent. Although in 2010 the economy started to recover, leading to a modest rise in emissions, the EU-wide emission cap was still not binding. For 2011 and 2012, the surplus of allowances further increased due to the warm winter and continued modest economic growth. Thus, allowance prices remained rather low, dropping further with the Greek crisis in 2011. As the excess allowances could be banked for Phase 3, a substantial additional amount of allowances is available in the market, dampening the price signal that could be expected from the continuous tightening of the emission cap until 2020 and the increasing role of auctioning as an allocation mechanism.

4. PRICE MANAGEMENT INSTRUMENTS

The EU ETS is an instrument to tackle the environmental externality of greenhouse gas (GHG) emissions. Given the substantial emission reduction targets for 2050 radical technological innovation is required. A stable carbon price can provide an incentive for stimulating respective R&D activities and is thus a rationale for price management in the EU ETS.

The strong variability in allowance prices was also discussed intensively during the negotiations of the EU Climate and Energy Package (European Commission 2008). Several Member States suggested actions for preventing excessive price volatility (Kettner, Köppl and Schleicher 2010). Fundamental market stabilization mechanisms have, however, not been integrated into the new emissions trading directive (European Commission 2009).

Carbon price developments and their effects on the efficiency of emissions trading schemes are also discussed in economic theory (Grubb 2008; Philbert 2009; Pizer 2002) as well as flexibility provisions in order to strengthen the role of carbon prices as an investment and innovation signal (Frankhauser and Hepburn 2010; Hood 2011).

There is a trade-off between a cap-and-trade scheme's main advantage, the certainty of the emission limit, and the likelihood of price volatility. Strongly fluctuating prices are counterproductive to abatement and long-term investment decisions as no clear signal regarding compliance costs is delivered.

Fluctuating prices thus bear the risk of reducing or eliminating abatement incentives and may even lead to investment delay or technological lock-in investments in fossil technologies if carbon prices are low. Various instruments can be integrated in a cap-and-trade scheme in order to reduce price volatility. These approaches include liquidity management and combinations of price and quantity mechanisms that are usually termed hybrid schemes as well as provisions for banking and borrowing. The latter option is already provided for under the EU ETS. In order to ensure a stabilization of carbon prices through banking and borrowing it would be required that firms act rationally and have adequate foresight. This assumption is, however, not given in a real world setting (Kettner et al. 2011). In the next sections we therefore focus on the options for liquidity management and direct price control.

4.1 Liquidity Management by an Independent Carbon Authority

In summer 2011, requests for a carbon authority[3] for the EU ETS intensified (Point Carbon 2011; IDEAcarbon 2011; de Perthuis 2011). The mandate for such an institution would be to ensure the achievement of the EU 20–20 targets (European Commission 2008) via liquidity management, i.e. the carbon authority would decide on the timing of auctions and the quantity of allowances to be auctioned. The proven sensitivity of carbon prices to various endogenous and exogenous influences and the resulting lack of stable investment incentives for market participants were arguments put forward for an independent carbon authority.

De Perthuis (2011) accentuated the need for an independent carbon authority given the major disruptions and regulatory failures of the EU ETS. VAT frauds, CER recycling and organized theft of allowances from national registries showed that the existing system was vulnerable from different angles (Nield and Pereira 2011; Aatola, Ollikainen and Toppinen 2013).[4] De Perthuis (2011) took up the idea of a carbon authority similar to a central bank for the monetary system as already discussed in Helm, Hepburn and Mash (2003) and mentioned in Brunner and Jakob (2011). The main arguments by Helm, Hepburn and Mash (2003) for an independent carbon authority were time inconsistency problems[5], pertaining uncertainty with respect to climate change issues and political risk. These problems could be restricted by an independent agency that could improve credibility of carbon policy in analogy to the role of central banks for monetary policy. Helm, Hepburn and Mash (2003) emphasized two differences to central banks: first, the trade-off between energy prices and emissions is long-term (compared to the trade-off between inflation and growth targets), and second, expectations about carbon prices influence investments with a lifetime of several decades and may result in a carbon intensive technological lock-in. The long-term aspect even aggravates the problem of policy credibility that could be overcome by institutional design and delegation to an independent agency.

De Perthuis (2011) sees similarities between central banks and a carbon authority, as CO_2 allowances could be thought of as new currency to pay for emissions that is created by public authority through the allocation process. The currency, however, loses its value once it is surrendered for compliance. In contrast to central banks, which regulate overall money supply, an independent carbon authority would not control the overall cap and thus the overall supply of allowances; its mandate would only comprise the management of the supply of allowances in the primary market and the potential to intervene in the secondary market by withdrawing or adding allowances in order to reduce price variability. This would contribute to stabilizing investors' expectations and support investment decisions into low carbon technologies.

The constraint for a carbon authority of not being able to create new allowances in a tight market situation could be overcome by the right to auction borrowed allowances from future periods that need to be paid back in consecutive periods. This would ensure the long-term environmental effectiveness of the emissions trading scheme.

4.2 Direct Price Control

Even with the introduction of price stabilization provisions in cap-and-trade schemes such as banking and borrowing, cost concerns can at best be alleviated but not removed, since cost certainty is not provided for, as the allowance price is determined in the market and is not only affected by currently available (technological) abatement options but also by (long-term) expectations about innovation, energy prices, policy interventions etc. Therefore, a key alternative, initially suggested by Roberts and Spence (1976), is to establish a hybrid policy which is characterized by elements of both a cap-and-trade scheme and a carbon tax. The options include the establishment of a price ceiling, a price floor or a price corridor.

4.2.1 Price ceiling

A price ceiling, i.e. an upper limit for the price of emission allowances, is one option to prevent an excessive cost burden for regulated entities in the case that emission abatement is more costly than expected. This approach offers more certainty regarding compliance cost and a protection against the upside price risk of a cap-and-trade scheme.

One way to implement a price ceiling is a 'safety valve' provision (Metcalf 2009; Murray, Newell and Pizer 2009; Pizer 2002). If allowance prices reach a predefined threshold (maximum price), firms can buy allowances directly from the government, providing cost containment (Tatsutani and Pizer 2008). However, an unlimited additional supply of allowances at the ceiling price eliminates quantitative certainty and thus environmental effectiveness. In order to preserve a certain degree of environmental integrity the amount of allowances that can be purchased at the safety valve price can be constrained as proposed by Murray, Newell and Pizer (2009) under the title of strategic allowance reserve.[6] A restriction of the additional amount of allowances is of particular importance in schemes with unlimited banking. If future allowance prices are expected to increase, a conventional safety valve would encourage firms to buy as many allowances as possible at the current ceiling price for later use. The crucial task for the regulator is the definition of the appropriate amount of additional allowances in the reserve, which will depend on the stringency of the emissions cap, the ceiling price, and the acceptable extent of price (Murray, Newell and Pizer 2009; Stavins 2008).[7] If paying a penalty is an alternative to compliance, the penalty will effectively constitute a ceiling price.[8]

4.2.2 Price floor

The mirror instrument to a price ceiling is the definition of a minimum price for allowances, a price floor. A price floor ensures emission reductions also in the case when allowance prices are lower than expected without the requirement to adjust the emission target (Wood and Jotzo 2011). This provides more certainty and a minimum rate of return for firms that invest in abatement technologies and is especially important when abatement costs turn out to be lower than expected. As summarized in Burtraw, Palmer and Kahn (2010) costs have been overestimated rather than underestimated in implemented cap-and-trade schemes,[9] which emphasizes the importance to price floors since too low costs and thus reduced incentives for abatement seem to be a greater concern than overshooting prices.

As with a price ceiling, there are various mechanisms to introduce a minimum price in a cap-and-trade scheme (Wood and Jotzo 2011; Grüll and Taschini 2011):

1. The regulator guarantees to buy back allowances at the floor price or to subsidise sellers when the price drops below the threshold level. This approach would, however, create an unpredictable financial burden for the regulator as *ex-ante* the amount of allowances that will have to be bought back or subsidised is not known.
2. A reserve price is determined for the auctions of allowances.[10] In this case, though, the market price could still fall below the minimum price. To what extent the auction reserve price determines an effective floor price depends on the share of permits that is auctioned. If the major part of allowances is allocated via grandfathering the market price could likely drop below the reserve price. In addition, if offsets can be used for compliance, they might also lower the price level. A reserve price will therefore limit the downward price risk but will most likely not determine a strict price floor (Wood and Jotzo 2011).
3. Emitters have to pay an extra fee for each ton of emissions in addition to having to surrender allowances.[11] The fee could be either fixed or variable. In the first case, the floor price equals the fee, which has to be paid in addition to the market price for allowances. In the second case, the fee is only levied if the market price falls below the predefined minimum level. The fee would then amount to the difference between market price and floor price. In terms of budgetary effects a fixed fee would result in a predictable revenue stream while with a variable fee revenues accrue only when allowance prices are too low and revenues are thus unpredictable.

A price floor represents insurance for firms investing in low carbon technologies and abatement measures, guaranteeing a minimum return on investment and increasing planning security. It can help stimulate innovation and investment by reducing the firms' price risk (Hepburn 2006). This is especially important when the price drops drastically due to unexpected exogenous shocks (e.g. an over-supply of allowances due to an economic crisis). Nevertheless, a price floor also entails disadvantages:

first, its introduction may increase the complexity and transaction costs of a trading scheme. Second, a price floor could lead to higher overall abatement costs. If the floor price is exercised, abatement could have been achieved at a lower price. Finally, in case of buying back allowances at the minimum price or subsidising firms that hold excess allowances if the market price drops below the threshold, the budgetary effects are unpredictable and might be substantial.

4.2.3 Price collar for GHG cap-and-trade programmes

A price collar or price corridor[12] for GHG cap-and-trade schemes is a combination of a floor and a ceiling price as described above. It aims at decreasing the permit price uncertainty on the high and low side and '*create[s] a more flexible response to the threat of climate change in the context of uncertain costs*' (Philbert 2009, emphasis added). The allowance price would move within a predefined band between the fixed floor and ceiling. The setting of a price band combines the properties of quantity- and price-based approaches. The narrower the corridor, the more the scheme resembles a carbon tax, the wider it is the more it corresponds to pure trading. The main advantages of a hybrid scheme are limiting price volatility and compliance costs[13] on the one hand and ensuring abatement incentives and a certain reliability of the emission limit on the other. However, the disadvantages of price floors and ceilings described above are also of concern in a hybrid scheme. These include above all potential budgetary effects of a floor price and the loosening of the environmental target.

In addition, the market intervention may affect the regulated firms' trading strategies (Grüll and Taschini 2011). When the market price is close to the price ceiling, firms short of allowances will wait to see if prices fall before the end of the compliance period as they would never have to pay more than the set maximum price. In contrast, firms that hold more allowances than they need to cover their emissions would be interested to sell at a high price as they cannot expect higher revenues. Vice versa – i.e. with prices close to the floor – firms in permit excess would not be interested to sell, since they can expect revenues to rise, while firms in a short position would be willing to buy, thus minimizing their expenditures for allowance purchases. Such strategic behaviour would automatically prevent the permit price from moving outside the price collar.

5. CONCLUSIONS

The EU ETS is the key instrument of European climate policy and was also intended to be a beacon project for international climate policy.

However, evidence from the first two trading phases shows that despite all good intentions information asymmetries and exogenous shocks have led to significant price variability and undermined the desired abatement and innovation incentives of the scheme. The EU ETS so far illustrates that the theoretical assumptions on emissions trading are not matched by a real world setting in which market failures exist and market participants do not act fully rationally nor possess perfect information.

Several attempts were made to integrate stronger price control mechanisms in the EU ETS and experience especially in the pilot phase led to various improvements in the policy design for Phase 3. But, although the necessity of price stabilization was recognized and potential mechanisms were discussed, conflicting policy interests especially in the direction of reviving growth and employment in Europe and ensuring international competitiveness have prevented stricter provisions.

NOTES

1. Emissions are adjusted until the tax rate is equal to marginal abatement costs.
2. A quantity instrument is preferable only if the marginal benefit curve is steeper than the marginal cost curve; in case the marginal cost curve is steeper than the marginal benefit curve, a carbon tax is preferable.
3. Sometimes also referred to as carbon central bank (de Perthuis 2011).
4. The European Commission has already reacted to some of these problems with regulatory changes that aim to restore confidence in the system (e.g. introduction of a European emission registry).
5. In short, the time inconsistency problem refers to the sequence of decision making: Firms make irreversible investment decisions according to their expectations about future policy developments before policy-makers act. Time inconsistency in this context means that policy-makers with conflicting objectives (e.g. emission reduction targets and the provision of cheap energy) may have different incentives before and after the investment decisions of the firms and may hence act differently (Helm, Hepburn and Mash 2003).
6. A similar provision has been included in the EU's Emission Trading Directive (European Commission 2009) in Article 29a to deal with excessive price fluctuations. In the case that the allowance price is more than three times the average price of allowances during the two preceding years for more than six months, and the price does not correspond to changing market fundamentals, Member States may either bring forward their auctions or auction up to 25% of the remaining allowances in the new entrants reserve.
7. Stavins (2008) suggests setting the safety valve price at the highest socially acceptable level, such that only drastic price spikes are mitigated. In addition, revenues from selling the reserve allowances should be earmarked for financing abatement measures in non-ETS sectors, thus preserving environmental integrity.
8. In the EU ETS, the penalty for each tonne of CO_2 emitted, for which the operator has not surrendered allowances, amounts to €100 since the beginning of Phase 2. However, in addition to paying this penalty firms are also obliged to surrender the missing number of certificates.
9. This may be due to overestimated baseline emissions as well as asymmetric information between polluters and regulators.

10. This approach was proposed in the Waxman–Markey Bill (http://www.opencongress.org/bill/111-h2454/actions_votes) and is used in the RGGI scheme (http://www.rggi.org/).
11. The UK government introduced a price floor for installations from the power sector in the EU ETS from April 2013 on. The floor price started at around £16 (€18.4) per ton of CO_2; until 2020 it will be linearly increased to £30 per ton of CO_2 (€35; both in 2009 prices) (Kettner et al. 2011). For the Australian Carbon Pricing Mechanism, that started in 2012 as a carbon tax and was to be transformed into a trading scheme, initially a floor price of AUD 15 was planned from 2015 on. However, trading will not become effective as, after a change in government in 2013, the scheme will be abolished by mid-2014 (http://www.climatechange.gov.au/reducing-carbon/carbon-pricing-policy/carbon-pricing-issues-timeline).
12. Also named a symmetric safety valve by Burtraw, Palmer and Kahn (2010).
13. Modelling results indicating more efficient outcomes of hybrid systems compared to taxes or conventional emissions trading can be found in Pizer (2002); Burtraw, Palmer and Kahn (2010); Fell and Morgenstern (2010) and Philibert (2009).

REFERENCES

Aatola, P., M. Ollikainen and A. Toppinen (2013), 'Price determination in the EU ETS market: Theory and econometric analysis with market fundamentals', *Energy Economics*, 36, 380–95.

Brunner, S. and M. Jakob (2011), Optimal commitment under uncertainty: adjustment rules for climate policy, Working paper, Potsdam Institute for Climate Impact Research, Potsdam.

Burtraw, D., K. Palmer and D. Kahn (2010), 'A symmetric safety valve', *Energy Policy*, 38(9), 4921–32.

de Perthuis, C. (2011), Carbon markets regulation: the case for a CO_2 Central Bank, Les Cahiers de la Chaire Economie du Climat, Information and Debates Series, Paris.

European Commission (2008), 2020 by 2020 – Europe's climate change opportunity (COM (2008) 30).

European Commission (2009), Council Directive 2009/29/EC to improve and extend the greenhouse gas emission allowance trading scheme.

European Union Transaction Log (EUTL) (2013), available at http://ec.europa.eu/environment/ets/.

Fell, H. and R. Morgenstern (2010), 'Alternative approaches to cost containment in a cap-and-trade-system', *Environmental and Resource Economics*, 47(2), 275–97.

Frankhauser, S. and C. Hepburn (2010), 'Designing carbon markets. Part I: Carbon markets in time', *Energy Policy*, 38(8), 4363–70.

Grubb, M. (2008), Carbon prices in Phase III of the EU ETS, Climate Strategies Briefing Note.

Grüll, G. and L. Taschini (2011), 'Cap-and-trade properties under different hybrid scheme designs', *Journal of Environmental Economics and Management*, 61(1), 107–18.

Helm, D., C. Hepburn and R. Mash (2003), 'Credible Carbon Policy', *Oxford Review of Economic Policy*, 19(3), 438–50.

Hepburn, C. (2006), 'Regulation by prices, quantities, or both: a review of instrument choice', *Oxford Review of Economic Policy*, 22(2), 226–47.

Hood, C. (2011), Summing Up The Parts, Combining Policy Instruments for Least-Cost Climate Mitigation Strategies, IEA Information Paper, Paris.
IDEAcarbon (2011), Controlling Oversupply in Emissions Trading Systems: Introducing the Carbon Central Bank, available at http://www.ideacarbon.com/resources/recent-features.htm/jdwjkbbdbj.
Kettner, C., D. Kletzan-Slamanig, A. Köppl, T. Schinko and A. Türk (2011), Price volatility in carbon markets – Why it matters and how it can be managed, WIFO Working Papers, 409/2011.
Kettner, C., A. Köppl and S. Schleicher (2010), 'The EU Emission Trading Scheme: Insights from the first trading years with a focus on price volatility', in Dias Soares, Janet Milne, Hope Ashiabor, Larry Kreiser and Kurt Deketelaere (eds) *Critical Issues in Environmental Taxation VIII*, Oxford: Oxford University Press, pp. 187–225.
McKibbin, W.J. and P.J. Wilcoxen (2002), 'The role of economics in climate change policy', *Journal of Economic Perspectives*, 16(2), 107–29.
Metcalf, G. (2009), Cost Containment in Climate Change Policy: Alternative approaches to mitigate price volatility, Working Papers 15125, National Bureau of Economic Research, Cambridge, 2009.
Murray, B.C., R.G. Newell and W.A. Pizer (2009), 'Balancing cost and emissions certainty: an allowance reserve for cap-and-trade', *Review of Environmental Economics and Policy*, 3(1), 84–103.
Nield, K. and R. Pereira (2011), 'Fraud on the European Union emissions trading scheme: effects, vulnerabilities and regulatory reform, *European Energy and Environmental Law Review*, 20(6), 255–89.
Philibert, C. (2009), 'Assessing the value of price caps and floors', *Climate Policy*, 9(6), 612–33.
Pizer, W.A. (2002), 'Combining price and quantity controls to mitigate global climate change', *Journal of Public Economics*, 85(3), 409–34.
Point Carbon (2011), 'Calls for "carbon central bank" grow louder', available at http://www.pointcarbon.com/news/1.1555690.
Roberts, M.J. and M. Spence (1976), 'Effluent charges and licenses under uncertainty', *Journal of Public Economics*, 5(3–4), 193–208.
Stavins, R. (2008), 'Addressing climate change with a comprehensive US cap-and-trade system', *Oxford Review of Economic Policy*, 24(2), 298–321.
Tatsutani, M. and W.A. Pizer (2008), Managing Costs in a U.S. Greenhouse Gas Trading Program, A Workshop Summary, Resources for the future discussion paper RFF DP 08–23.
Vesterdala, M. and G. Tinggaard Svendsen (2004), 'How should greenhouse gas permits be allocated in the EU?', *Energy Policy*, 32(8), 961–8.
Weitzman, M. (1974), Is the Price System or Rationing More Effective in Getting a Commodity to Those Who Need It Most?, Working papers 140, Massachusetts Institute of Technology (MIT), Department of Economics.
Wood, P.J. and F. Jotzo (2011), 'Price floors for emissions trading', *Energy Policy*, 39(3), 1746–53.

9. Incentivizing technologic change in emissions trading systems: the case of excess supply

Stefan E. Weishaar

1. INTRODUCTION

Economic activity is associated with greenhouse gas emissions and therefore affects climate change. One can address climate change by targeting energy production (e.g. renewable energy or shale gas), by reducing the emission intensity of the industry (e.g. through emissions trading or carbon taxes) and by inducing behavioural changes of consumers (e.g. building regulation, smart energy meters).

While addressing all factors contributing to climate change makes intuitive sense, the policy instruments mutually affect each other. A high CO_2 allowance price for example makes investments in renewable energy sources more attractive and, incentivizes home owners to invest in better insulation. In addition to supporting other climate change policy instruments, a high emission allowances price incentivizes companies to invest in technological innovation, research and development. It is this transformation of the economy that is expected to stem from emissions trading systems and is a declared objective of the European Emissions Trading System (EU ETS).[1]

Emissions trading systems are appealing because they reduce greenhouse gas emissions at the lowest cost. Covered entities with the lowest abatement cost invest in abatement technology. These 'saved' emissions can be sold to entities that have higher abatement costs. Investment in abatement technology is thus an integral part of emissions trading. A mismatch between supply and demand in a cap-and-trade emissions trading system is not a problem for reaching the determined environmental target – its environmental effectiveness is not harmed. It is only a problem if one strives to incentivize green investments.

Whether incentivizing investment is indeed a policy objective of the emissions trading system must of course be assessed within the legal framework of every emissions trading system.[2] Incentivizing environmentally friendly production technology allows for economic growth of covered sectors and future competitiveness. It prevents lock-in in existing technology and helps to align marginal abatement costs across various policy areas.

While innovation is expected to 'automatically' follow from an emissions trading system, the European experience shows that this is not the case. After over-allocation in the first trading period (2005–2007), an economic downturn led to a contraction in the demand for emission allowances and to allowance prices that were too low to incentivize investments in the second trading period (2008–2012). Prices are also expected to remain low during the third trading period (2013–2020). European policymakers currently examine solutions to this over-supply situation.

This chapter examines how investments can be supported by addressing excess supply situations in an efficient manner and how existing emissions trading systems address this threat. The structure of the chapter is as follows.

Section 2 presents Europe's experience with the emissions trading market (background). Section 3 reviews the market determinants of emission trading markets, investment incentives and describes the problem of excess supply. Subsequently, section 4 develops criteria to be observed to incentivize investment (price effects, price predictability, structural solution and efficiency). On the basis of these criteria the best policy choices to address over-supply are evaluated. In selecting policy choices due note of the consultation discussions held by the European Commission in March and April 2013 is taken. Section 5 places the European experience into an international context by examining solutions found in other emissions trading systems and concludes.

2. THE EU EXPERIENCE (BACKGROUND)

The EU ETS constitutes a multi-jurisdictional attempt of 31 countries to reduce CO_2 emissions from several broad sectors: (1) energy (electric power, oil refineries, etc.), (2) the production and processing of ferrous metals (iron and steel), (3) minerals (cement, glass, ceramics), (4) pulp and paper and (5) aviation. It caps approximately 40 per cent of the European Union's greenhouse gas emissions.

The EU ETS was implemented in several trading phases (phase 1 ranging from 2005–2007, phase 2 from 2008–2012, and phase 3 from 2013–2020). The first trading period was described as a 'learning by doing' phase. The system suffered from over-allocation, which – when it became public knowledge – led to a crash in the emission allowance price from 28 euros to ultimately 10 euro cents in 2007. Over-allocation is in part attributable to data problems and to over-optimistic company growth expectations.

Before the start of the second trading period the European Commission required Member States to reduce emission allocations. The cap was set 6.5 per cent lower than for phase 1 and was considered ambitious when it was set.[3] Contrasting expectations, a significant amount of over-supply arose during this period that spills over to the third trading phase.

The over-supply of emission allowances in the EU ETS has various causes. It is predominantly attributable to the economic contraction of the European economy in 2009 and slow economic growth ever since. Associated with the lower industrial production carbon emissions also declined and so did demand for carbon emission allowances. In addition to the lower demand there was a second reason: increases in supply. Additional sources of emission allowances are believed to stem from several sources (see Table 9.1):

- the sale of emission allowances contained in national new entrance reserves (around 100 million);
- the sale of emission allowances from the New Entry Reserve (NER) 300 (200 million in 2012 and 100 million in 2013) programme run by the European Investment Bank to incentivize Carbon Capture and Storage and Renewable Energy demonstration projects;[4]
- early auction of 2013 emission allowances to facilitate the transition to the third trading phase and to mitigate allowance price increases due to hedging demand (120 million allowances);
- offsets from Clean Development Projects (CDM).

The above-listed first three sources of supply are 'internal' to the EU ETS. The last one is an 'external' source and therefore needs additional explanation. Only relatively few offsets were used in the first trading period in the EU ETS but imports rose quickly in the second trading period. The legislator has responded to limit the sources from which offsets can be derived. These more stringent rules exclude offsets from HFC_{23} reduction projects and N_2O decomposition projects.[5] They are expected to reduce the current availability of CERs[6] but are unlikely to prevent the use of offsets in the EU ETS.

The cumulative over-supply of EU ETS allowances at the end of the second trading phase is estimated to be around 1826 million allowances. This suggests an over-supply of around 19 per cent above the total actual emissions in the second trading phase.[7] In terms of the third trading phase

Table 9.1 Demand and supply of emission allowances (in million tons of CO_2 equivalent)

	2008	2009	2010	2011	2012
Verified emissions	2100	1860	1919	1886	1886*
EU ETS allowances issued	1994	2024	2070	2084	2084*
International credits	82	81	134	252	252*
NER 300					200
Early auction of phase 3					120
Left over of MS auctions					100
Yearly over-supply	−24	245	285	450	870
Cumulative over-supply	−24	221	506	956	1826

Note: * Data assumed to be the same as in the preceding year.

Source: Commission Staff Working Document (2012).

this amounts to around 12 per cent.[8] Estimates of allowance allocation in the third trading period are presented in Table 9.2.

Because banking was allowed during the second and third trading phase of the EU ETS, it is expected that the over-supply will persist beyond 2020,[9] thus into the fourth trading period, implying that no additional reduction efforts are required in the third trading period.[10] Banking is also the reason why the price level of the European Union Allowances (EUAs) in the second trading period has not fallen to 10 euro cents (as in the first trading period) but why prices remained between 4 and 5 Euros. Allowance prices are too low to incentivize investment in abatement technology and innovation. For the period 2013–2015 the price signal is projected to fall around 5.40 euros. Price differences between forecasts for 2020 differ. Barclays projects around 10 euros, Point Carbon 12 euros, PBL 19 euros and Bloomberg as much as 29 euros.[11]

Against this backdrop, the Commission is pursuing a three-pronged approach to address the mismatch between supply and demand in the EU ETS.

- Firstly, it sought the clarification on the legal right of the European Commission to change the timing of auctioning allowances.[12] This is commonly referred to as the 'backloading' decision. The draft proposal of this decision designed by the Commission was referred back to the Parliamentary Committee for amendments and accepted on 3 July 2013. The parliamentary acceptance was taking the form of a parliamentary position, rather than the form of a first

Table 9.2 Allowance allocation estimates, trading period 3 (in million tons of CO_2 equivalent)

Year	2013	2014	2015	2016	2017	2018	2019	2020
Auctioning	1116	1104	1092	1080	1067	1055	1043	1031
Free allocation	862	837	813	789	765	741	717	693
NER	104	102	100	98	96	95	93	91
Estimated auctioning reduction due to transitional free allocation for electricity	−153	−136	−120	−103	−85	−65	−43	0
Offset estimates	112	112	112	112	112	112	112	112
Total	2041	2019	1997	1976	1955	1938	1922	1927

Source: Commission Staff Working Document (2012), section 6.4.2 and following. These estimates do not include the impact on actual auctioning volumes of the NER 300 nor the early auctioning of 120 million phase 3 allowances in 2012 or aviation. The Estimated volumes of transitional free allocation for electricity production are based on the volumes requested by the Member States.

reading. Once COREPER endorsed the parliamentary position without any changes (on 8 November 2013) Parliament accepted the backloading proposal in its first reading (10 December 2013) and the Council followed suit on the 16 December 2013 with signatures placed the following day. With this amendment of Art. 10(4) of Directive 2003/87/EC, the Commission is allowed to adapt the auction timetable once to backload up to 900 million allowances in exceptional circumstances to ensure the orderly functioning of the market.[13]

- Secondly, based on the above amendment of Directive 2003/87/EC, the Commission has recently proposed Commission Regulation 176/2014 to amend the auctioning regulation (Commission Regulation 1031/2010). It proposed to time-shift the auctioning of 400, 300 and 200 million allowances in the years 2014–2016 respectively. These allowances will be auctioned off in 2019 (300 million) and 2020 (600 million) allowances.[14]
- Thirdly, the Commission reviews EU ETS structural reform proposals to address over-supply. The Commission invited responses to its report on the state of the European carbon market,[15] in which it

> proposed structural reform options, held a consultation round and two stakeholder meetings on structural options to strengthen the EU Emissions Trading System in March and April 2013.

The options for a structural reform outlined by the Commission are examined in section 4. Before this, section 3 examines the relation between investment in abatement technology and innovation, and excess supply, paying attention to investment behaviour and market fundamentals.

3. INVESTMENT AND THE PROBLEM OF EXCESS SUPPLY

The treatment below is based on the EU ETS but other cap-and-trade schemes are expected to face similar challenges.

In order to present the relation between investment and excess supply it is important to first examine the idiosyncrasies of the EU ETS market. Subsequently the investment behaviour of entrepreneurs is described. In a third step, challenges for investment in abatement technology and innovation posed by excess supply are presented.

3.1 Emission Market

Allowance markets follow the forces of demand and supply. Prices of emission allowances respond sharply to small changes in the market supply, implying that the demand for allowances is inelastic. Sizable price changes are thus an inherent feature of the EU ETS market.

What appears to distinguish an ETS market from other markets is how supply responds to demand. Firstly, there is no immediate increase in supply when demand increases; supply only stems from investment in abatement or stems from offset projects. Both supply responses may not be immediate and only occur after a period of time. Secondly, in case market prices decline market supply does not contract; there are no 'producers' of emission rights that can go bankrupt. Even if covered entities go bankrupt their emission rights remain on the market.

The properties of the ETS market make it function as an automatic economic stabilizer: at times of economic prosperity of the covered sectors, prices for emissions increase to prevent an overheating of the economy. When allowance demand is low, the low allowance prices do not unduly burden the covered sectors. The environmental integrity of the EU ETS is not impaired.[16]

It can therefore be concluded that the EU ETS market can be expected to have strong price fluctuations and that prices will follow the production patterns of the covered entities. Because the quantity supplied in the EU ETS is fixed and does not respond to the actual demand, it can be expected that the prices of emission allowances will continue to be low for a period of time even when covered industries have started to grow again. The duration of this lagged price increase will depend on the magnitude of the excess supply in the EU ETS.

3.2 Investment Behaviour

Before investing in abatement technology and innovation, companies consider the return on investment and the associated risks. In order to determine the return on investment entrepreneurs have to predict (industrial) production levels and emission allowance prices. We are only concerned with the latter.

Predicting EU allowance prices is difficult, particularly in the context of long term investments that require substantial capital outlays. In contrast to legislator's price predictions of 20 to 33 euros[17] for the first and second trading period, allowance prices strongly declined in the course of the trading periods. Also the price predictions for the third trading phase of 30 euros for 2020[18] will not materialize in the absence of an ETS reform. Presently, allowance prices are around 4.48 euros.[19] Given the current over-supply the EUA market is projected to remain long well into the fourth trading period.[20]

Given the repeated crashes of the EUA market prices, prospects of high allowances prices alone may not be enough to induce investors to take investment risks. Investors relying on legislator's projections have been let down in the first, the second and again in the third trading period. Investors may therefore demand a 'risk premium' to overcome the legislator's credibility deficit. This risk premium could take the form of very high profit opportunities or a measure of market predictability.

Investment in abatement technology will thus take place if emission allowance prices are sufficiently high and predictable. Policy measures addressing over-supply to incentivize investment must produce higher and predictable prices.

3.3 The Problem of Excess Supply

Excess supply of emission allowances describes a mismatch between demand and supply that depresses allowance prices. In the presence of excess supply, allowance prices are too low to incentivize investments in abatement technology.

Excess supply can be caused by over-allocation that stems from too optimistic industry growth projections, from a higher than anticipated influx of offsets into an emissions trading system or from supply sources internal to the system. Excess demand can, however, also be the result of a contraction of demand. Such situations can arise at times of an economic crisis or a business cycle downturn.

While small scale (*ex-post*) corrections of allowances are discussed in the literature, little attention is devoted to the correction of large scale excess supply. This is disappointing since economic downturns – either in the form of a crisis or a business cycle contraction – are a well-noted phenomenon.

Economic cycles have been identified for time periods lasting between 3–5 years, 7–11 years, 15–25 or 45–60 years. Examples include the Kitchin inventory cycle, the Juglar fixed investment cycle, the Kuznets infrastructural investment cycle and the Kondratiev waves. While their predictive value has frequently been challenged, it is beyond doubt that economic development is characterized by ups and downs. Thus, even though the study of economic fluctuations is arguably not *en vogue* anymore, economic downturns prevent emissions trading system to incentivize investments. Emissions trading systems must take excess supply into account.

Policy measure targeting over-supply must adequately address future economic downturns, particularly when long term policy goals are set. It is very possible that until the year 2050, when the EU wants to reduce its greenhouse gas emissions by 80 or 95 per cent below 1990 levels, we will encounter another economic downturn. Since the economic downturn of 2009 would entail that the EU ETS would be oversupplied till probably 2023, it is easy to see that reform measures must structurally take over-supply situations into account. Policy measures that are not structural will not provide for long term business certainty and not trigger economic transition.

It can therefore be concluded that policy measures addressing excess supply situations to incentivize green investments must therefore produce: 1) higher prices (price effect), 2) price predictability, and contain 3) structural safeguards that addresses future economic downturns. The next section applies these criteria to the structural reform policy measures.

4. EVALUATION OF STRUCTURAL REFORM MECHANISMS

This section examines mechanisms that can be used to address over-supply within the context of the EU ETS. Before addressing each policy option, the three criteria discussed above as well as efficiency are revisited from a methodological perspective.

Price effect

Any instrument addressing over-supply must give rise to a price effect on the emissions trading market to incentivize investment. Basic microeconomics teaches us that scarcity drives prices up. When examining the price effect we therefore examine scarcity.

Price predictability

Predictable market prices enable operators to take long term investment decisions. To evaluate this criterion we examine how the measures affect price formation in the future.

Structural safeguards

This criterion examines if the instrument is an ad hoc (i.e. one time only) measure, or if it is structural in the sense that it offers a solution in case another over-supply situation should arise.

Efficiency

The efficiency implications of the respective policy measures are based upon administrative costs and financing costs. Administrative costs are thought to be higher if the measure requires additional work from companies or bureaucrats or if the measure is financed through taxes. Taxation is costly for society since taxes distort the general price level so that too little of the taxed good is being produced.

The following policy options are assessed in turn:

i) Permanently Retiring Allowances,
ii) Adjusting the Linear Reduction Factor,
iii) Adding Sectors,
iv) Limiting Offsets,
v) Scarcity Management,
vi) Price Support, and
vii) Auction Reserve Prices.

i) Permanently Retiring Allowances

Cancellation of allowances reduces the overall quantity of allowances on the market. This leads to more scarcity and a higher allowance price during the third and subsequent trading periods since allowances that could have been banked are taken off the market.

Price effect
The cancelling of allowances will have an immediate price effect. All else equal, the future price level of allowances will shift upwards in a parallel fashion.

Price predictability
Price levels will be higher, but no guidance is offered to investors what the prices will be in the future. It does not constitute a good investment guide.

Structural safeguards
Permanently cancelling allowances constitutes an ad hoc response to over-supply. It thus does not signal to investors that in case of future excess supply situations allowances will again be cancelled.

Efficiency
Taking allowances from the market is easily and cost-effectively achieved by taking allowances out of the auction reserve. Transaction costs are low. Reducing the overall level of allowances, however, will also increase abatement costs at times when allowance prices are high.

ii) Adjusting the Linear Reduction Factor

Adjusting the annual linear reduction factor (currently set at −1.74 per cent) increases scarcity. The reduction factor can be set to align the current EU ETS with future policy ambitions.

Price effect
There will be an immediate price effect of this measure because adjusting the linear reduction factor to −2 per cent, for example, will increase the long term scarcity of the EU ETS.

Price predictability
This measure alters the slope of the price curve to make it rise more strongly but does not prevent prices falling in the future. There is thus no price predictability associated with this measure, yet increased scarcity will make low prices less likely.

Structural safeguards
Increased long term scarcity of the allowance market makes low future prices less likely. It does not, however, constitute a solution to future economic downturns.

Efficiency

Administrative costs will be low if allowances are taken from the auctioning reserve. Reducing the overall level of allowances also increases abatement cost when prices are high, entailing higher societal costs of fighting climate change.

iii) Adding Sectors

Extending the EU ETS to other sectors (e.g. maritime shipping) could increase scarcity, provided these sectors are allocated fewer allowances than need.

Price effect

The price effect is difficult to predict for market participants as it depends on the additional degree of scarcity deriving from additional sectors.

Price predictability

Prices may become more volatile and hence less predictable if sectors are added to the ETS that move in the same business cycle of sectors that are already covered.

Structural safeguards

Adding sectors will not prevent future price drops and thus does not constitute a structural solution.

Efficiency

Adding sectors is time consuming because accurate data on actual emissions may not be available. Administrative costs are high since sectors enjoying low administrative costs have already been included in the EU ETS.

iv) Limiting Offsets

Offsets constitute a significant source of supply. Limiting the use of offsets increases scarcity and hence the price.

Price effect

Limiting overall supply by limiting offsets increases scarcity and increases prices. Given the recent measures to limit offsets, the price effect of additional measures in this area may be limited.[21]

Price predictability

Further limiting offsets may not strongly affect supply and hence market price. Price predictability does not therefore seem to be supported. Moreover, as demand from European covered entities shifts towards specific offset types, production may follow suit over time. It could therefore imply that price predictability in the long run cannot easily be safeguarded.

Structural safeguards

Restricting offsets does not provide a structural over-supply solution because it does not reduce existing over-supply, though it can limit additional supply and thereby support a more timely recovery of the market price.

Efficiency

Administrative costs of limiting offsets are likely to be low. Yet limiting offsets deprives European operators from cost-effective abatement opportunities abroad. Hence, the overall costs of the EU ETS will increase. In addition, investments into offset projects that would now be forbidden to be sold to the EU ETS (by far the largest market for offsets) could turn out to be bad investments (stranded costs).

v) Scarcity Management

Scarcity management allows the Commission to withhold or buy back allowances from the market when the market is oversupplied. Allowances are accumulated. When allowances are scarce, the accumulated allowances are released back onto the market. The system has been proposed by industry within the forum dedicated towards 'discretionary pricing mechanisms' even though it is a quantity based scheme.[22]

Price effect

This scheme directly addresses the prevailing quantity that is available on the market and hence has an immediate price effect.

Predictable price

Because this scheme springs into action as a scarcity threshold level is reached, it allows investors to design business plans based upon the projected level of scarcity. It may not be easy to determine the price level based solely upon a scarcity level, but it nevertheless offers entrepreneurs some form of abstract guidance.

Structural safeguards
Also in the eventuality of another future economic downturn, the scarcity management system provides a positive market price. Once the threshold level is triggered, the available quantity of allowances will be restricted so as to support the profitability of green investments.

Efficiency
This system suffers from high administration costs and data availability problems. Determining when a company is 'long' or 'short' of allowances is very difficult. It does not only depend on operators' actual allowances and derivative holdings but also on their future allowance needs based on their order books and market prospects. Civil servants may lack the required information to assess the degree of market scarcity in an accurate and timely fashion. In addition, it will be difficult to determine an optimal degree of scarcity that should trigger policy intervention.

vi) Price Support

Price support schemes can be designed in several ways. A levy can, for example, be placed on every offset entering the emissions trading scheme whenever the market price falls below a minimum price that is required to incentivize investments in green technology. This incentivizes investments provided there is an allowance scarcity on the domestic market and the levy for offsets is set high enough – if domestic demand is lacking, prices could be supported by government purchases.

Price effect
In a situation where the government pledges to buy allowances at a particular market price, there will be an immediate and positive price effect.

Predictable price
The price level triggering price support is known to investors. Provided that the government's pledge is credible (little policy risk, sufficient funds), investors are incentivized to invest into green technology.

Structural safeguards
Since the safety-net of the price support scheme is also available for future economic downturns, such a price support scheme is structural.

Efficiency
The execution of market purchases via exchanges is not costly, yet there are efficiency concerns. Firstly, if the funds used for buying back allow-

ances would derive from taxes rather than from auction proceeds, costs to society could be large. Secondly, the floor price must be set correctly. Setting an optimal price is inherently difficult since ETS designers will not have enough knowledge on the marginal abatement costs of covered entities. Thirdly, the floor price will effectively set the overall minimum market price and exchanges between market participants below the floor price will not take place.

vii) Auction Reserve Prices

A pre-announced reserve price can be set at a long term price trajectory to incentivize investments. Allowances are not auctioned at prices below reserve price and these unsold allowances are cancelled. This price prevents the 'flooding' of an oversupplied market with allowances. It does not impede the price setting and allows operators with different abatement costs to trade at all times, both above and below the auction reserve price. For secondary market prices below the auction reserve price, negotiating power, however, shifts towards sellers. Unless in extreme circumstances the secondary market price during economic downturns will at least be at the level of the auction reserve price since any over-supply is contained by preventing the inflow of auctioned allowances.

Price effect

Because the auction reserve price works to restrict the supply of allowances at times the market prices is below the set reserve price, there is no additional supply stemming from auctions. Since in the EU ETS a sizable and increasing number of allowances are auctioned, this measure will impact the price.

Price predictability

An auction reserve price sets a clear price signal and is therefore capable of incentivizing investments. Since prices are prevented from falling to levels that endanger investments, the business risk of investing in carbon abatement technology is reduced. Determining the correct auction reserve price to incentivize investments is, however, difficult. It requires a good understanding of the current and future price levels capable of incentivizing investment in abatement technology. If the reserve price is set poorly, the effectiveness of the reserve price is undermined.

Structural safeguards

A benefit of the auction reserve price is that it provides a price floor for auctioned allowances at any time market prices are low. It therefore constitutes a structural response to future economic downturns.

Table 9.3 Policy instrument properties

	Price effect	Price predictability	Structural solution	Efficiency
Permanently retiring quantity	+	–	–	+/–
Linear reduction factor	+	–	–	+/–
Adding sectors	+	–	–	–
Limiting offsets	+	–	–	–
Scarcity management	+	+/–	+	–
Price support	+	+	+	+/–
Auction reserve price	+	+	+	+

Efficiency

Auction reserve prices are also attractive from an efficiency perspective. Setting a reserve price is not complicated and costs will be very low. Determining the right level of the reserve price may, however, be more complicated and hence costly. The benefit of the reserve price is that it does not increase the overall compliance cost of the emissions trading system at times that the economy is growing. In addition transactions between market participants can take place both above and below the actual auction reserve price.

Summary

Seven policy instruments have been evaluated. The findings are summarized in Table 9.3.

Based on the criteria of price effect, price predictability and structural component, three policy instruments appear to be suitable to address over-supply situations. These instruments are scarcity management, price support schemes and auction reserve prices. They differ, however, with regard to their efficiency evaluation. It appears that price support schemes and in particular auction reserve prices do come out on top.

5. EXCESS SUPPLY: EUROPEAN AND INTERNATIONAL APPROACHES

This section of the chapter contains a number of findings, observations and critiques highlighting the different approaches and treatment of the over-supply problems in various emissions trading systems. It also offers explanations for the bias perceived in the EU ETS context.

The first, policy measures considered by the European Commission is biased against pricing mechanisms as evidenced by the use of the term 'discretionary price instrument'.[23] It is therefore not surprising that in the consultation meeting on these pricing mechanisms actual pricing instruments have not been discussed. Evidently, stakeholders know better than to lobby for something that the Commission is unwilling to accept. From a methodological perspective it is wrong to exclude potentially effective and efficient instruments from evaluation.

Secondly, while the Commission appears to exclude pricing mechanisms from scrutiny, other jurisdictions recognize the importance of over-supply and the necessity to incorporate price support measures. In the Californian emissions trading system a reserve price auction is used. It is set at US$ 10 in 2012 and increases by 5 per cent plus the rate of inflation as measured by the most recently available 12 months of the Consumer Price Index for All Urban Consumers.[24] Also in the Quebec system a reserve price was set at CAD$ 10 in 2012. The reserve price here will rise by 5 per cent per annum above the prevailing inflation level.[25] Similarly, the Regional Greenhouse Gas Initiative (RGGI) employs a reserve price auction system. The current auction floor price is currently set at US$ 1.98 per ton of CO_2.[26] The Australian Carbon Pricing Mechanism (CPM) was originally envisaged to operate as a price collar system. The price of emission allowances would have been fluctuating within the bandwidth of a price floor and a price ceiling. The price floor was set at AU$ 15 and would have been linearly increasing by 4 per cent in real terms per annum. But, as a result of the linking negotiations between the Australian CPM and the EU ETS, the price floor was abolished.[27] Jurisdictions that do not have an over-supply response are the EU ETS, the Swiss ETS, several Chinese pilots and the Tokyo cap-and-trade programme. It is interesting to notice that jurisdictions that embrace shale gas and are hence likely to face declining allowance prices are among those jurisdictions that have introduced mechanisms to address over-supply situations.

Explanations for why the European legislator has decided to refrain from adequately addressing over-supply problems can be two-fold. It may be that the Commission regards the objective of 'incentivizing technological innovation' to be of lesser importance and hence is not willing to change the current design to address this objective. In the alternative, it could be attempted to be explained by reference to exposure to criticism that the introduction of a pricing mechanism such as an auction reserve price would transform the ETS into a tax measure. Tax measures are to be decided upon by the European Council by unanimity rather than by qualified majority. Opposition in the Council could then endanger EU climate policy. It appears, however, more than questionable that an auction reserve price system for allowances would qualify as a tax measure.

Whatever the underlying reason of the Commission to *a priori* exclude capable measures to address over-supply situations, it seems doubtful that the structural reform process will be optimally incentivizing investment in green technology and be capable of avoiding the impacts of future economic downturns.

NOTES

1. *See* Recital 8 of Directive 2009/29/EC.
2. For the EU ETS objectives *see* Weishaar and Tiche (2013).
3. *See* http://ec.europa.eu/clima/policies/ets/reform/index_en.htm (last accessed 11 September 2013.
4. *See* Commission Staff Working Document (2012).
5. *See* Commission Regulation (EU) 550/2011.
6. Around 80% of the CDM credits that were surrendered in 2010 are banned as of 1 May 2013. *See* Commission Staff Working Document (2012) and Commission Regulation (EU) 550/2011.
7. According to Commission data the total number of verified emissions in the second trading phase was 9,651 million tons of CO_2 equivalents (assuming that the numbers for 2012 are the same as for 2011), while total supply was 11,477 million tons of CO_2 equivalents (assuming that the number of offsets used for compliance in 2012 was the same as for 2011) (see Commission Staff Working Document (2012)). Dividing total supply by total verified emissions and subtracting 1 yields an oversupply of 18.92%.
8. The estimated total amount of emission allowances that will be available during the third trading period is 15,775 million tons. 1826/15775 = 11.57%.
9. *See* PBL (2013), p. 30.
10. *See* on this Egenhofer, Marcu and Georgiev (2012) and PBL (2013), p. 29.
11. *See* Commission Staff Working Document (2012), pp. 22–3 and PBL (2013), p. 30.
12. COM(2012) 416 final.
13. European Parliament legislative resolution of 10 December 2013 on the proposal for a decision of the European Parliament and of the Council amending Directive 2003/87/EC clarifying provisions on the timing of auctions of greenhouse gas allowances (COM(2012)0416 – C7–0203/2012 – 2012/0202(COD)) available at http://www.europarl.europa.eu/sides/getDoc.do?type=TA&language=EN&reference=P7-TA-2013-0543#BKMD-44 (last accessed on 18 November 2013).
14. *See* http://ec.europa.eu/clima/policies/ets/reform/docs/com_2014_xxx_en.pdf.
15. COM(2012) 652 final.
16. Under a cap-and-trade scheme the environmental effectiveness is automatically achieved in a static context.
17. COM(2001) 581 final, p. 47.
18. Commission Staff Working Document (2012), p. 16.
19. *See* http://www.eex.com/en/ (last accessed 2 December 2013).
20. This will change if backloading would indeed be introduced in 2014 and in addition lead to a cancelling of course allowances.
21. *See* Commission Regulation (EU) 1123/2013 and Commission Regulation (EU) 550/2011.

22. *See* http://ec.europa.eu/clima/events/articles/0070_en.htm, contribution by David Hone.
23. COM(2012) 652 final.
24. *See* California Air Resource Board (2012), § 95911(b).
25. Environmental Quality Act, Art. 49.
26. *See* http://www.rggi.org/docs/Auctions/21/Auction_21_Webinar_Jul_11_2013.pdf, slide 63.
27. *See* the Parliamentary amendment bill of 26 November 2012, available at: http://parlinfo.aph.gov.au/parlInfo/download/legislation/bills/r4895_aspassed/toc_pdf/12167b01.pdf;fileType=application%2Fpdf (last accessed 29 April 2013).

REFERENCES

California Air Resources Board (2012), 'California cap on greenhouse gas emissions and market-based compliance mechanisms', 1 September 2012, available at: http://www.arb.ca.gov/cc/capandtrade/september_2012_regulation.pdf (last accessed 15 September 2013).

COM(2012) 416 final, 2012/0202 (COD), Proposal for a Decision of the European Parliament and of the Council amending Directive 2003/87/EC clarifying provisions on the timing of auctions of greenhouse gas allowances, Brussels, 25 July 2012.

COM(2001) 581 final, Proposal for a Directive of the European Parliament and of the Council establishing a scheme for greenhouse gas emission allowances trading within the Community and amending Council Directive 96/61/EC 2001/0245 (COD), Brussels, 23 October 2001.

COM(2012) 652 final, Report from the Commission to the European Parliament and the Council, 'The state of the European carbon market in 2012', Brussels, 14 November 2012.

Commission Regulation (EU) 550/2011 of 7 June 2011 on determining, pursuant to Directive 2003/87/EC of the European Parliament and of the Council, certain restrictions applicable to the use of international credits from projects involving industrial gases, OJ L 149/1, 8 June 2011.

Commission Regulation (EU) 1123/2013 of 8 November 2013 on determining international credit entitlements pursuant to Directives 2003/87/EC of the European Parliament and of the Council, OJ L 299/32, 9 November 2013.

Commission Staff Working Document (2012), 'Information provided on the functioning of the EU Emissions Trading System, the volumes of greenhouse gas emission allowances auctioned and freely allocated and the impact on the surplus of allowances in the period up to 2020', Brussels, 25 July 2012, SWD(2012) final, available at: http://ec.europa.eu/clima/policies/ets/cap/auctioning/docs/swd_2012_234_en.pdf (last accessed 24 September 2013).

Directive 2009/29/EC of the European Parliament and of the Council of 23 April 2009 amending Directive 2003/87/EC so as to improve and extend the greenhouse gas emission allowance trading scheme of the Community, OJ L 140/63, 5 June 2009.

Egenhofer, C., A. Marcu and A. Georgiev (2012), Reviewing the EU ETS Review? Report of the CEPS Task Force, Centre for European Policy Studies (CEPS), Brussels.

Environmental Quality Act, Regulation respecting a cap-and-trade system for greenhouse gas emission allowances, Quebec, Chapter Q-2, r. 46.1 (Chapter Q-2, s. 31, 1st para., subparas b, c, d, e.1, η and h.1, ss. 46.1, 46.5, 46.6, 46.8 to 46.16, 115.27 and 115.34), as of 1 November 2013, available at: http://www2.publicationsduquebec.gouv.qc.ca/dynamicSearch/telecharge.php?type=3&file=/Q_2/Q2R46_1_A.HTM (last accessed 5 October 2013).

PBL (Planbureau voor de Leefomgeving) (2013), 'Evaluatie van opties om het Europese emissiehandelssysteem te hervormen', available at http://www.pbl.nl/publicaties/evaluatie-van-opties-om-het-europese-emissiehandelssysteem-te-hervormen (last accessed 5 October 2013).

Weishaar, S. and F.G. Tiche (2013), 'Hybrid emissions trading systems: what about efficiency?' in Michael Faure and Guandong Xu (eds) *Using Economics to Improve Regulation: The Case of China*, Abingdon: Routledge.

Section D

Political economy

10. The political economy of subsidy reform: which factors are game-changers?

Jacqueline Cottrell

1. INTRODUCTION

Over the past thirty years, a great deal of progress has been made on identifying and quantifying environmentally harmful subsidies in terms of volume and their impact on the environment, as well as on analysing the political economy of their reform, as exemplified by the work of the Organisation for Economic Cooperation and Development (OECD), the International Energy Agency (IEA), the World Bank, the International Monetary Fund (IMF), the European Commission and the European Environment Agency (EEA). The fiscal, economic and environmental benefits of subsidy reform are well known and understood (see the work of the IEA, the Organisation of Petroleum Exporting Countries (OPEC), the World Bank and the OECD, e.g. IEA et al. 2010).

In part as a result of the research and awareness-raising efforts on the part of these international organisations, subsidy reform has entered mainstream political, fiscal and economic policy dialogue. In addition, since it began in 2008, the global economic crisis has unbalanced budgets in many countries, and has created considerable pressure on governments to spend scarce revenues more carefully. Thus, at the G20 summit in Pittsburgh in 2009, G20 members were prepared to agree, in principle at least, to phase out 'inefficient' fossil fuel subsidies (G20 2009). In the same year, Asia-Pacific Economic Cooperation (APEC) member countries were content to sign up to a similar declaration, while flagging up the importance of providing essential energy services for those in need (APEC 2009). At the time of writing, in early 2014, efficient spending and long-term fiscal sustainability remains a driving force behind economic and fiscal policy, and austerity remains a primary focus of many finance ministers.

Nonetheless, subsidy reform remains a difficult process, with positive beginnings often ending in policy turnarounds, as a result of ultimately political barriers, such as concerns for vulnerable groups in society – which can be alleviated by timely and targeted compensation measures – or political responses to fierce lobbying on the part of beneficiaries. Particularly if subsidies are presented in political discourse as a benefit, which can be lost should reform be successful – rather than focusing on the benefits of reform for all – politicians can lose their nerve and reverse unpopular policies, in the hope of optimising their chances of re-election.

Against this background, this chapter attempts to extract some lessons from past successes and failures of subsidy reform in a range of different countries, from all over the world, and to identify those factors which tend to be the key drivers of successful reform.[1] While it is always dangerous to make generalisations based on particular cases, some commonalities between reform processes are discernible, and it is possible that such lessons, if adapted to a particular country's policy landscape and implementation culture, can help to identify possible strategies for driving forward subsidy phase-out.

2. ENABLING FACTORS VERSUS KEY DRIVERS

Clearly, for subsidies to be reformed a number of enabling factors should already be in place. Transparency is, for example, a key element in paving the way to subsidy phase-out. Knowledge of harmful subsidies can spur on the political debate, and keep a reform debate alive. Similarly, accurate quantification of subsidies, and a clear understanding of the winners and losers under the status quo, can highlight a number of strong arguments in favour of reform.

In the European Union (EU), for example, state aid – including explicit state subsidies harmful to the environment – is generally prohibited. All new state aid policies must be notified to the European Commission, which can accept or reject such measures. Also very important in the context of this chapter is the State Aid Scoreboard, which contains information on all explicit subsidies in each of the EU Member States (MS). This can facilitate the identification of existing subsidies, highlighting inefficiencies and bringing harmful subsidies to the attention of the EU MS and the EU Commission – which can itself act as a catalyst for reform (see section 6 below on coal subsidies in Germany).

The International Institute for Sustainable Development (IISD) has identified 'be prepared' as one of the single most important things a government should do in the run-up to subsidy reform. This means not only identifying environmentally harmful subsidies, quantifying them, and understanding what the impacts on winners and losers will be once they are reformed, but also drawing up phase-out proposals that take into account the underlying reasons why subsidies are in place (IISD 2013). Such proposals can then be 'taken out of the drawer' when a window of opportunity – perhaps a crisis, or a new pro-reform government – presents itself. Nonetheless, a detailed analysis of numerous cases of subsidy reform reveals that the development of policies alone is rarely sufficient to ensure the elimination of subsidies, as administrative, economic and political obstacles often prove to be insurmountable (IISD 2012a).

Careful planning of subsidy phase-out also entails the development and communication of relatively comprehensive compensatory measures. In the case of households, it is important that these are targeted at vulnerable groups, well-publicised and easily accessible – otherwise, policy-makers run the risk of hitting vulnerable sectors of the population hard when subsidies are reformed. As key stakeholders, it can be helpful to consult citizens during policy development, so that policy-makers know which kinds of compensation measures will be most useful for – and most welcomed by – vulnerable households. Such approaches lend a greater degree of legitimacy to reform, facilitate the development of appropriate policies and help create the political space necessary to make reform possible (IISD 2013).

For business, support measures should aim to foster a transition away from subsidy dependence and facilitate adaptation to the new subsidy-free business environment. All compensation measures – new subsidies – should be carefully targeted and regularly reviewed, in line with OECD guidelines, to ensure that different dependencies do not result from reform (see e.g. OECD 2006). Compensation measures are essential to foster support for reform and are a key factor in smoothing a transition towards a subsidy-free economy. In some cases they may, if well-designed, targeted and effective, be sufficient to bring business and citizens on side and thus to drive a reform process forward.

Attempts to reform fossil fuel subsidies, particularly in resource-rich countries, have shown that for reform to be sustainable, it is absolutely essential that energy prices are depoliticised (see e.g. IISD 2013). Citizens have to come around to the belief that energy prices are beyond the control of governments, who must make a great effort in their policy communications to make clear that this is indeed the case. If not, governments will repeatedly come under pressure to intervene and control domestic energy prices. This can result in protests, riots and even bring down the government – as in Indonesia in 1998, when fuel price hikes were a significant factor in the fall of the Suharto government. Similarly, in Nigeria in 2012 and Bolivia in 2010, fossil fuel subsidy removal provoked mass strikes and demonstrations, which led to subsidies being rapidly reinstated, in part or in full. This problem is by no means exclusive to industrialising countries. In the UK in 2013, for example, environmental taxes on domestic energy were reduced following a prolonged period of political and media attention portraying high energy taxes as a political issue, rather than one related to high wholesale energy prices.[2]

In all cases, the situation might have been averted had policy measures been better and more clearly communicated. If fossil fuel subsidies are to be reformed, governments need to make it absolutely clear that fuel prices are dependent on global energy prices and not on political decision-makers, and that subsidies are fiscally and economically unsustainable. A higher degree of transparency, which should result in greater trust in government, should also foster support for reform (World Economic Forum 2013).

However, in the majority of cases, while the factors mentioned above are necessary for reform, they are rarely sufficient in isolation. Ultimately, for subsidy reform to be successful, it also requires key drivers and/or catalysts to initiate and, crucially, sustain the reform process. This might mean a policy champion with the political will to sustain a policy process, or an economic or fiscal crisis which draws attention away from a particular subsidy reform measure, or creates sufficient urgency to drive through unpopular measures. This chapter will try to identify some of these, in the hope that identifying such drivers can help facilitate more effective reform in the future.

3. NEVER LET A GOOD CRISIS GO TO WASTE: SUBSIDY REFORM IN IRELAND, GERMANY AND IRAN

The three cases below have been deliberately drawn from three very different economies to demonstrate how a crisis, in three very different political, economic and social contexts, can act as a driver of reform. All three examples show how a sense of urgency can enhance the willingness – or indeed force the hand – of governments to introduce measures which, in less pressured circumstances, they would probably not have implemented. However, while never letting a good crisis go to waste might be good advice, the sustainability of measures introduced in such circumstances may be at risk, particularly if policy-makers do not make an effort to establish them in the policy landscape as an accepted policy measure, e.g. by raising awareness of the medium- and long-term benefits of the measure.

3.1. Ireland's National Recovery Plan 2011–2014

The response to the fiscal and economic crisis in Ireland from 2008–2010 was a combination of cuts in government expenditure and increases in taxation to raise and/or save a total of between €10 and €15 billion over a four year period (EEA 2010). The resulting 2011–2014 National Recovery Plan included a number of measures to reduce (explicit or implicit) environmentally harmful subsidies: increases in carbon taxation, to a rate of €30 per tonne by 2014, making up 22–26 per cent of total tax increases within the recovery package; the phase-out of carbon tax exemptions; a site-value tax on land; and the introduction of domestic water metering and consumption-related charging (Irish Government 2011).

A major factor which smoothed the introduction of these policies was the economic and fiscal crisis in Ireland. Without it, reform would have been far more debated. Under the circumstances, a traumatised public was willing to accept water charging and the carbon tax rise as 'just a little more noise in a cacophony of bad news' (Convery, Dunne and Joyce 2013: 33). The importance of the crisis context should not be underestimated, however, and the two are closely associated in the minds of the public and policy-makers. Once the crisis subsides, there is a very great risk that the carbon tax may be 'unwound' (Convery, Dunne and Joyce 2013).

This risk is probably far lower in relation to water charging. Although the fiscal crisis was an enabling factor in the rapid and radical action taken to reform domestic water charging, in 2010, Ireland was the only OECD country not to have cost coverage in the domestic water sector. Thus, the government could cite convincing economic and environmental reasons for charging, including estimated savings of €500 million per annum on operating costs once water charges came into effect (Irish Government 2011). As in the case of the carbon tax, water charging initially faced little political resistance, as it was common knowledge that savings had to be made, and government revenues increased, if Ireland was not to face bankruptcy. Resistance did increase by 2012, when a fixed standing charge for all households was proposed (water meter installation was not yet complete). In contrast to carbon taxation, however, the underlying reasons for water charging, and the exceptional case of Ireland prior to the reform, make it less likely that water charging will be reversed once the economic crisis abates.

3.2 The 2010 Economic Stimulus Package, Germany

Germany's 2010 stimulus package introduced several measures to reduce environmentally harmful subsidies. Most notably, a controversial nuclear fuels tax of €145 per gram of nuclear fuel was introduced and was initially expected to raise €2.3 billion in revenues from 2011–2016 – which would balance out at least some of the explicit and implicit subsidies to the nuclear industry in the country, estimated to amount to about €7 billion, or 0.25 per cent of German gross domestic product (GDP) in 2010 (Meyer and Küchler 2010a). The package also included reduced Ecotax rates for industry and a new air ticket tax on all flights departing from Germany.

The central catalyst for introducing these measures was the urgent need felt to tackle the economic crisis, and the election of a new coalition government of conservative CDU/CSU parties and the economically liberal FDP party in 2009. The coalition came under considerable pressure to take decisive and effective action to meet the crisis and consolidate the budget, which led to the economically liberal FDP party rapidly reneging on its election promise to cut taxes. Thus, unforeseen policy measures, which the government would not have implemented in different circumstances, were seized upon by the legislators.

Perceptions of the crisis were such that when a nuclear fuels tax was announced in June 2010, the government adopted an uncompromising position, with the ruling parties noting in draft legislation that there was simply no alternative to the tax ['Alternativen: keine'] (Bundestag 2010: 1). Amendments to energy tax privileges for industry and an air ticket tax were also introduced quickly and decisively. Additional enabling factors smoothed the way, but without the fiscal and economic crisis acting as a key driver for the implementation of subsidy reform, the status quo would almost undoubtedly have been maintained.

As in the case of Ireland, these measures swiftly came under attack once Germany recovered from the crisis. Air ticket tax, for example, was fiercely politically debated in the run-up to the 2013 elections, although it was upheld in the 2013 coalition agreement.

3.3 Economic and Political Crisis in Iran in 2010

In Iran in 2008, the need to reform price controls on domestic energy had become increasingly obvious. Free on-board gasoline prices[3] had reached about US$2/litre, while domestic prices were set at 10 US cents. To meet domestic demand, Iran was importing ever more gasoline at this higher price, and Iranian oil energy companies were starved of funds for investment, due to low profit margins as a result of the low domestic price (Guillaume, Zytek and Farzin 2011). Thus, maintaining price controls simply became politically and economically unsustainable. Widespread acknowledgement of this fact in public and political discourse meant that the impending economic crisis if reform did not take place could be used to good effect by policy-makers to justify their policy choices and, in a well-planned policy process, energy subsidies were phased out in 2010.[4]

Clearly, many additional factors initially smoothed the reform process in Iran, all of which can provide valuable lessons in how to manage subsidy reform. These include: high visibility of the reform as a whole, and of the compensation measures available to all (although the rich were discouraged from applying); monetary policy to stabilise inflation; widespread awareness of the environmental, economic and fiscal unsustainability of price controls, and the social inequity resulting from cheap energy; acceptance by business due to targeted assistance programmes; and the use of multi-tier tariffs on electricity, water and natural gas (Guillaume, Zytek and Farzin 2011). Nonetheless, if politicians had not been spurred on by the crisis and the realisation that change was both urgent and inevitable, it is unlikely that the reform process would have gone as far as it did.

Since the reform was introduced, however, international sanctions, high rates of inflation – officially 23 per cent in July and August 2012, but according to a field study on average 63 per cent between May and July 2012 – and currency depreciation have undermined the reform process (IISD 2012b). A new crisis has overwhelmed the old.

3.4 Subsidy Reform as an Integral Part of Economic and Political Transformations

As shown above, an economic crisis, or a period of radical political change, can usher in subsidy reform by creating a window of opportunity for change. The sections above look in detail at three specific responses to fiscal, economic and political crisis – but they are by no means isolated examples. Responses to the 1997 Asian financial crisis, or dramatic price hikes in the former Soviet Union in the 1990s, are also examples of subsidy reform being swept in on a tide of political or economic transformation (IISD 2013).

In the Czech Republic, full cost recovery for water services was introduced in 1991 as part of the transition from a planned economy to a market economy. In spite of the fact that for some households, water prices went up by as much as 626 per cent, and even though the reform was introduced at a time of economic recession, the reform was not opposed and has been successful – both in reducing water consumption by 40 per cent and in achieving full cost coverage for the sector (Withana et al. 2012: Annexes). Even in a relatively short time, fundamental improvements in water quality and management were achieved. In such crisis moments, where change comes to be regarded as inevitable and irreversible, reforms tend to be opposed much less than they would be at other times.

To safeguard the longevity of reform, however, policy-makers must act to ensure the stability of changes made, making clear that reforms introduced in a crisis context are permanent and have been introduced for sound, long-term economic, fiscal, environmental and social reasons – which will remain valid once the crisis has passed. Similarly, where governments phase-out price-setting mechanisms, it is essential that fuel prices become and remain completely non-politicised in the future, if possible either by removing all price management mechanisms, or by putting fuel prices in the hands of an independent body. Otherwise, the temptation to reduce fuel prices and boost political popularity is too high for many governments to resist (IISD 2010).

4. COMPREHENSIVE APPROACHES

The cases of Ireland and Germany both exemplify reforms introduced as part of a broader policy package – on the one hand, reducing attention paid to reforms, and on the other, enabling compensatory measures to be introduced at the same time. Similarly, the case of Iran shows that a reform package with the facility to redistribute a large proportion of revenues previously used to subsidise energy prices was well received.

4.1 A Package of Reform in the Netherlands

In the Netherlands, a clear need for a broad income tax reform, and a long-standing focus on fostering green commuter behaviour, facilitated the reform of environmentally harmful tax treatment of company cars as one element of a broad tax reform package in 2001 (Potter et al. 2006). Including reform of company car taxation within a general reform gave legislators the chance to ensure that income tax distribution would not be affected overall, and that there would be no short-term losses for particular socio-economic groups (Withana et al. 2012: Annexes). In this way resistance was reduced, as transport tax 'sticks' were linked to income tax reform 'carrots' to smooth the path of reform (Potter et al. 2006).

This approach to reform packages in the Netherlands was repeated in the crisis context of the 2013 emergency budget, where reduced excise taxes for diesel used in agricultural machinery worth an estimated €250 million per year were reformed within a raft of measures geared towards reducing the budget deficit in the Netherlands (Withana et al. 2012: Annexes).

4.2 Linking a Falling Tax Burden to Subsidy Reform in Sweden

In the case of Sweden, energy price changes were implemented as part of a broad tax reform package. Against a backdrop of a high tax burden in the late 1980s, in 1991 'the tax reform of the century' was implemented, introducing a carbon tax and reducing both corporate and labour taxes, reducing the overall tax burden. As a proportion of GDP, tax revenues fell from 55.6 per cent in 1989 to 52.7 per cent in 1991 (Forstop 2013). This approach of incorporating subsidy reform – in the form of a move towards full cost pricing of fossil fuels – in a programme to reduce the tax burden took a great deal of the heat out of the political discourse (Åkerfeldt 2011).

For a variety of reasons, the Swedish tax reform survived the economic crisis of the early 1990s, as well as several general elections. Exemptions for industry and the volume of revenues raised by the tax were both useful incentives in preserving the tax under different governments, while a broad-based sense of duty to protect the environment in Sweden meant that many strongly supported the CO_2 tax in principle (Forstop 2013). But in addition, a major point appears to have been the consistent approach of linking increased CO_2 taxation to a more general tax reform, resulting in reduced labour costs, e.g. in reforms from 2001–2006 and 2007–2010 (Åkerfeldt 2011).

Sweden today has the most robust and politically long-lasting carbon tax in the world. Certainly one reason for its survival has been its association with the implementation of a tax policy package, giving policymakers the possibility to compensate those hit by the reform elsewhere in the tax system.

4.3 The Many Advantages of Comprehensive Approaches

Implementing a raft of reforms within a broad-based policy package has a number of advantages. Policy packages can implement broad-based solutions to a range of policy issues and can introduce several policy elements to address the multi-aspect nature of many environmental problems (OECD 2007). A broader package can also include a number of checks and balances to compensate for a particular aspect of subsidy reform – for example, by introducing a change in a social security system to compensate for increased energy prices.

A raft of policies can combine sticks and carrots to change behaviour and enhance the popularity of an overall package. This is particularly relevant because electorates tend to perceive 'pull' measures (carrots) more favourably than 'push' measures (sticks, such as increasing prices as a result of tax increases or subsidy reform), which tend to be regarded rather negatively as coercive (see e.g. de Groot and Schutema 2012).

5. INVISIBLE REFORM: PHASING OUT SUBSIDIES WHILE THE COST OF LIVING IS FALLING

If policy-makers have reform plans in place, then introducing reform in times of low energy use, at times of falling energy prices, or at times of low inflation, can facilitate relatively 'painless' restructuring by reducing resistance. Many policy-makers have effectively employed this strategy to heighten the chances of success of their reforms.

For example, the 2010 pricing reform in Iran was timed to coincide with December, a time when energy consumption is lowest in the country. In the Philippines, following the introduction of costly ad hoc oil price subsidies in response to the oil price crisis in the 1970s, oil prices were deregulated in 1998, against a backdrop of declining world prices for energy and economic crisis in the region (IISD 2013). In China, the 2008–2009 drop in the oil price created a window of opportunity to switch to formula-based pricing of gasoline and diesel – although the reform has only been moderately successful, with government maintaining the option of not adjusting domestic prices to the international oil price (IISD 2013). Keeping in mind higher prices of food and consumer items at holiday times and at the end of the year, the Indonesian government times fuel price increases to coincide with times of lower inflation and tends to align fuel price adjustments with the revision of the annual state budget (IISD 2012a).

Similarly, in Denmark, environmental tax reforms to gradually introduce full cost pricing of fossil energies – and thus to eliminate fossil fuel subsidies – were also introduced in times of falling global energy prices and as part of a tax reform package.

Thus, taking advantage of relative pricing changes can facilitate policy changes which might otherwise prove impossible. Being able to predict seasonal energy price or energy consumption fluctuations, or simply seizing the moment and implementing reform when global energy or commodity prices are falling, can create space for reform and reduce resistance.

6. SHIFTS IN POLITICAL ALLIANCES

Often, political alliances opposing subsidy reform are very entrenched. Subsidy dependency, fear of change, powerful lobbies in favour of retaining their advantage, and political lethargy can all contribute to maintaining the status quo. In Germany, lobbies in favour of maintaining subsidies to the coal industry were so strong that reform was almost unthinkable, until an unexpected election result turned the political constellation on its head – as discussed in section 6.1.

6.1 Coal Subsidy Reform in Germany

The gradual phase-out of hard coal subsidies in Germany by 2018 exemplifies how shifting political alliances can play a decisive role in driving forward reform processes. At their peak in 1996, coal subsidies amounted to €6.7 billion annually. By 2011, subsidies had fallen to €1.9 billion – nevertheless a substantial sum (OECD 2013). These subsidies were in place largely to prevent job losses in the mining industry in the Ruhr and Saar regions of Germany. However, in 2011, less than 21,000 were employed in the sector, meaning that the subsidy was effectively cost more than €90,000 per job.[5]

In the face of such telling facts, a consensus did come into existence between the OECD, IEA, European Commission,[6] the German Finance Ministry, the Federal Environment Agency, many German policy-makers, and the electorate. These organisations and individuals gradually became convinced that subsidies were neither sustainable nor efficient and had outlived their rationale, and that investment in other sectors could create more jobs at less cost.

In spite of this growing consensus, however, progress remained slow in Germany for many years. Subsidies were fiercely defended by a coalition of vested interests – specifically the Social Democratic Party (SPD), the mining industry, and the coal power sector in North Rhine Westphalia (NRW). The catalyst for reform, which undermined the combined power of these organisations, was a new coalition government of the CDU and the (economically) liberal FDP parties in the state of NRW following elections in 2005. This new NRW government was a driving force for reform, and worked alongside the new federal government, a 'grand coalition' of the SPD and the CDU, to break the deadlock on subsidy reform. A politically favourable constellation was the major catalyst and enabling factor for reform and without the change, progress would have been doubtful. As it was, a timetable for the phase-out of hard coal subsidies to 2018 was agreed first within Germany, and finally negotiated with the European Commission in 2010; as state aid measures, coal subsidies required additional agreement with the Commission, as they are considered to result in distortions within the single market.[7]

7. THE EU AND INTERNATIONAL POLICY PROCESSES AS POSSIBLE DRIVERS OF REFORM

7.1 The European Union

As shown above, in the EU context, one factor which influenced coal subsidy reform in Germany was the state aid process at EU level, which created external pressure to draw up a timetable for subsidy phase-out. This is only one of many policy processes which may open up windows of opportunity for reform in the future at EU level, and has done for many years. For example, one of the most recent documents is the 2011 *Roadmap for a Resource Efficient Europe*, one of the *Europe 2020: A European Strategy for Smart, Sustainable and Inclusive Growth's* 'flagship initiatives'. The *Roadmap* set the following milestone: 'By 2020 Environmentally Harmful Subsidies (EHS) will be phased out, with due regard to the impact on people in need' (European Commission 2011b). While it does not have teeth as such, the *Roadmap* is still an important and influential document and its existence brought subsidies once again to the attention of policy-makers.

However, much more important and in all likelihood, the process with the most potential to act as a real driver of subsidy reform at EU level is the annual European Semester of economic and fiscal policy coordination. The Semester begins with the publication of an Annual Growth Survey (AGS) in November, which includes a series of guidelines for economic and fiscal policy for the following year. Since its inception in 2011, the AGS has consistently called on EU MS to reform environmentally harmful subsidies and to implement green tax shifting (taxing labour less and environmentally harmful behaviours and practices more). The 2014 AGS stated that 'Environmentally harmful subsidies should be reduced' (European Commission 2013c) – a weaker formulation than the 2013 AGS, which stated simply that 'Environmentally harmful subsidies should be phased out' (European Commission 2013a).

The AGS, the subsequent National Reform Programmes (NRPs), submitted by all EU MS to the European Commission, and the Commission's Country-Specific Recommendations (CSRs) – made on the basis of the NRPs – could all serve as drivers of reform in the future. If subsidy reform is included in CSRs for a particular country, for example, then pressure on the government to take action will be increased – and those seeking to influence policy will have strong arguments in favour of action. Regrettably, however, as discussed in (Cottrell 2014), thus far the outcomes of the European Semester process have been rather disappointing, with environmental and social issues taking a back seat.

Nonetheless, a recommendation from the Commission could offer governments a very real window of opportunity to initiate a process of subsidy reform – and, as such recommendations come from outside the country, the credibility and the force of such a proposal might be higher. CSRs have the potential to create greater levels of awareness of subsidies, and thus influence the implementing environment and enhance acceptance of reform. Moreover, the inclusion of a particular policy recommendation in the Commission's CSRs in one year means that the recommendation will be retained in subsequent years, until it has been implemented. Thus, the repetition of a particular recommendation over time may well prove to be a catalyst for its implementation in the future. Hence, the Semester should be regarded as a powerful tool and at least potentially, a significant driver of subsidy reform within the EU's ongoing process of exchange and review of national fiscal policy and policy reforms.

7.2 A Brief Look at Subsidy Reform Internationally

Outside the closer integration of the EU, there are also numerous international policy processes which have been working towards subsidy reform over the years. The 1992 Rio Earth Summit, the Rio +20 summit and the ongoing process of developing Sustainable Development Goals (SDGs); the G20 process and research undertaken by OECD, the IMF, World Bank and the IEA, both in response to requests from the G20 since the Pittsburgh summit in 2009 and independently of the G20 process; declarations made by APEC – to name but a few. However, while much progress has been made in defining, identifying and quantifying subsidies, particularly through the work of the OECD, it seems unlikely that any of these international organisations will act as decisive drivers of reform on a national level. After all, subsidies remain very much a question of national fiscal and economic policy, and international policy processes, while important in terms of raising awareness and feeding into the framework conditions necessary for reform, are unlikely to really act as catalysts for change to the domestic policy.

8. BEHAVIOURAL ECONOMICS AND SUBSIDY REFORM: WORKING WITH HUMAN NATURE TO MAXIMISE SUPPORT AND DESIGN SUSTAINABLE REFORMS

Behavioural economics uses insights from (social) psychology to increase the explanatory power of economics, offering insights into how people interpret and respond to information. It has demonstrated that the behaviour of individuals deviates systematically from what economic models and expectations of rationality would predict (Pollitt and Shaorshadze 2011).

For example, behavioural economics has demonstrated that individuals give extra value to goods they already own or services they already receive and perceive the value of an object higher if they possess it than if they do not – the so-called 'endowment effect' (Knetsch 1989).

8.1 Reform of Fossil Fuel Subsidies in Iran – Successful as a Result of the Endowment Effect?

The timing and design of the subsidy reform process in Iran in 2010 seems to have made good use of the endowment effect, although it is not clear whether this was deliberate. When reform was introduced in December 2010, almost 80 per cent of Iran's population was granted access to compensatory payments which had already been deposited in specially created bank accounts from October of the same year. As a result, energy price increases were welcomed, as the public had been eagerly awaiting the reform so they could finally access bank accounts holding their compensation payments. Thus, the timing of various reform elements worked with, and not against, the endowment effect; individuals valued the compensation which they had already 'owned' prior to the reform more highly than they would otherwise have done.

In addition, the reform was portrayed in the media as a 'switch' of subsidies from products to households – a shift to a more equitable subsidy regime, but by no means as a loss of a subsidy. The endowment effect was thus also implicitly served by this communication strategy.

8.2 Further Research

The impact findings from behavioural economics could have on the structure of subsidy reform processes, as well as on the way such processes are communicated to stakeholders, is yet to be thoroughly investigated. Behavioural economics findings have very real potential to feed into improvements in the design of subsidy reform, in the timing of reform elements, and in the way it is communicated. Research efforts to extract lessons from existing processes of reform, and to develop proposals for improvements, may enable policy-makers to take better advantage of windows of opportunity for reform in the future.

9. CONCLUSIONS AND WAYS FORWARD

As shown above, there are a number of factors which are necessary before environmentally harmful subsidies can be phased out, but which are not in themselves sufficient for this to take place.

What is also needed is a catalyst or a driver of reform, to bring political momentum behind the reform process and overcome resistance. This chapter set out to explore some of these drivers and distil some lessons learned from past subsidy reform processes in very different contexts, both within the EU and beyond it.

Environmentally harmful subsidies face a great deal of resistance, which cannot easily be overcome. Subsidies tend to become 'locked in' to an economy, creating dependency on particular technologies or fuels, and so they also create a great deal of dependence. This can slow down or even prevent reform processes – thus, as a general rule, trying to maintain the status quo is easier for political decision-makers than introducing widespread subsidy reform. It is therefore often the case that a political window of opportunity or some kind of catalyst for reform processes is necessary to bring about change – and that if this additional element comes into play, subsidies may be reformed relatively quickly and unexpectedly.

The above discussion looked at a number of different examples where these catalysts or drivers have been crucial for reform to take place, and tried to identify commonalities between reform processes. It identified crises and periods of political and economic transformations as drivers of reform, which create an environment within which radical change is more likely to be accepted, while drawing attention away from a possible reform and its negative impacts. The chapter also showed that times when the cost of living is falling – for example, due to falling global energy prices, a reduced tax burden, or seasonal variations in consumption of energy – provide a window of opportunity for subsidy reform to be introduced while minimising impacts on vulnerable stakeholders. In addition, unexpected or atypical shifts in entrenched political alliances or political constellations, e.g. as a result of elections on a national or federal level, can also act as a catalyst for reform, enabling seemingly intractable problems to be addressed and reform implemented with the support of new political groupings.

Finally, this chapter has proposed that the timing and design of subsidy reform processes could be improved by taking behavioural economics findings into account – for example, by enhancing the perceived value of compensation measures by distributing revenues before a spike in relative prices as a result of reform. Improving reform approaches in this way might offer a further tool to policy-makers to ensure that reform is implemented smoothly, and is sustained. This is certainly a field that merits further research in the future.

NOTES

1. In this chapter, there is not sufficient space to discuss the history of each case of subsidy reform discussed. Readers are requested to refer to the bibliography for further reading on EU policies relating to reform of environmentally harmful subsidies and for background information on the country cases. See European Commission (2007), (2012), (2013b); European Council (2009), (2010); European Environment Agency (2005); European Environmental Bureau (2013); European Union (2002), (2006); FÖS (Forum Ökologisch-Soziale Marktwirtschaft) (2010); Frondel, Kambeck and Schmidt (2007); 'Gesetze im Internet: Kernbrennstoffsteuer'; Irish Times (2012), (2013); Küchler and Meyer (2012); Meyer and Küchler (2010b); Meyer, Schmidt and Eidems (2010); Potter and Atchulo (2013); ten Brink and Mazza (2013); Valsecchi et al. (2009).
2. See numerous press articles in the UK press, including: http://www.telegraph.co.uk/finance/personalfinance/consumertips/household-bills/10564117/Did-your-energy-firm-pocket-the-50-green-tax-rebate.html and http://www.theguardian.com/commentisfree/2013/oct/27/green-taxes-bills-saving-energy-fossil-fuels (both accessed 20 January 2014).
3. The term 'free on board' price typically refers to the price of oil or natural gas actually charged at the producing country's port of loading. The reported f.o.b. price includes deductions for any rebates and discounts or additions of premiums where applicable and should be the actual price paid to the seller with no adjustment for the cost of ocean freight, insurance, or credit. See http://www.eia.gov/tools/glossary/index.cfm?id=F#free_on_board (accessed 28 November 2013).
4. Although it is of note that, unlike Germany and Ireland, the contribution of reform to fiscal consolidation was expected to be small, as revenues would be redistributed to poorer households and used to support industry to improve its energy efficiency.
5. Statistics from *Gesamtverband Steinkohle e. V.*, available online at: http://www.gvst.de/site/steinkohle/statistik.htm (accessed 11th September 2013).
6. In 2002, new state aid rules came into force which required the European Commission to examine all state aid in relation to its impact on the single market.
7. The timetable agreed with the European Commission (within state aid procedures) also applied to other EU MS still subsidising coal, such as Poland and Spain. Appeals on the part of Spanish regions to depart from the timetable and continue subsidies beyond 2018 were rejected by the European Court of Justice in January 2014.

REFERENCES

Åkerfeldt, S. (2011), 'Swedish Energy and CO2 Taxes: National Design within an EU Framework', Presentation given at a conference on *Environmentally Related Taxes and Fiscal Reform* organised by the Ministry of Economy and Finance in collaboration with the European Environment Agency, Rome December 15, 2011, available online at: http://www.dt.tesoro.it/export/sites/sitodt/modules/documenti_it/eventi/eventi/SESSION_I_-_SUSANNE_AKERFELDT_x6x.pdf (accessed 21 January 2014).

APEC (2009), *Singapore Declaration – Sustaining Growth, Connecting the Region*, Singapore, 14–15 November 2009, available online at: http://www.apec.org/

Meeting-Papers/Leaders-Declarations/2009/2009_aelm.aspx (accessed 20 January 2014).
Bundestag (2010), 'Draft of the Law on Nuclear Fuels Tax', available online (in German) at: http://dip21.bundestag.de/dip21/btd/17/030/1703054.pdf (accessed 21 March 2013).
Convery, F., Dunne, L. and Joyce, D. (2013), 'Ireland's Carbon Tax and the Fiscal Crisis: Issues in Fiscal Adjustment, Environmental Effectiveness, Competitiveness, Leakage and Equity Implications', OECD Environment Working Papers No. 59, OECD, Paris, available online at: http://search.oecd.org/officialdocuments/publicdisplaydocumentpdf/?cote=ENV/WKP%282013%296&docLanguage=En (accessed 28 November 2013).
Cottrell, J. (2014), 'Reforming EHS in Europe: Success Stories, Failures and Agenda Setting' in F. Oosterhuis and P. ten Brinck, *Paying the polluter: Environmentally Harmful Subsidies and their Reform*, Cheltenham, UK and Northampton, MA, USA: Edward Elgar.
de Groot, J. and G. Schutema (2012), 'How to Make the Unpopular Popular? Policy Characteristics, Social Norms and the Acceptability of Environmental Policies', *Environmental Science and Policy* 19–20: 100–07.
European Commission (2007), *Mid-term review of the Sixth Community Environment Action Programme*, COM(2007) 225 final, Brussels, available online at: http://eur-lex.europa.eu/LexUriServ/LexUriServ.do?uri=COM:2007:0225:FIN:EN:PDF.
European Commission (2011a), *Annual Growth Survey: Advancing the EU's comprehensive response to the cri*sis, COM(2011) 11 final, Brussels, 12 January 2010.
European Commission (2011b), *Roadmap to a Resource-Efficient Europe*, COM(2011) 571 final, Brussels, 20 September 2011.
European Commission (2012), *Annual Growth Survey*, Communication from the Commission, COM(2011) 815 final, Brussels, 23 November 2011, VOL. 1/5.
European Commission (2013a), *Annual Growth Survey*, Communication from the Commission, COM(2012) 750 final, Brussels, 28 November 2012.
European Commission (2013b), 'State Aid: An Overview', available online at: http://ec.europa.eu/competition/state_aid/overview/ (accessed 27 July 2013).
European Commission (2013c), *Annual Growth Survey*, Communication from the Commission, COM(2013) 800 final, Brussels, 23 November 2013.
European Council (2009), *Council Conclusions on EU position for the Copenhagen Climate Conference, 2968th Environment Council Meeting*, Brussels, 21 October 2009, available online at: http://www.consilium.europa.eu/uedocs/cms_data/docs/pressdata/en/envir/110634.pdf.
European Council (2010), *Improving Environmental Policy Instruments – Council Conclusions, 3061st Environment Council Meeting*, Brussels, 20 December 2010, available online at: http://www.consilium.europa.eu/uedocs/cms_Data/docs/pressdata/en/envir/118646.pdf.
European Environment Agency (EEA) (2005), *Market-Based Instruments for Environmental Policy in Europe*, EEA Technical Report, No.8 2005, Copenhagen, available online at: http://www.eee2006.org/presentations/EEA_technical_report_8_2005.pdf.
European Environment Agency (EEA) (2010), *Further Environmental Tax Reform – Illustrative Potential in Ireland, EEA Staff Position Note*, SPN 10/01.
European Environmental Bureau (2013), Metamorphosis 69, available online

at: http://www.eeb.org/?LinkServID=7132C7E2–5056-B741-DB00BEB267D3C55B&showMeta=0&aa.

European Union (2002), *Sixth Community Environment Action Programme, 1600/2002/EC 22 July 2002*, available online at: http://eur-lex.europa.eu/LexUriServ/LexUriServ.do?uri=OJ:L:2002:242:0001:0015:EN:PDF.

European Union (2006), *Renewed Sustainable Development Strategy, 10917/06*, Brussels, available online at: http://register.consilium.europa.eu/pdf/en/06/st10/st10917.en06.pdf.

Forstop, M. (2013), *Barriers to change and ways forward for fossil fuel subsidy reform in Sweden*, Master Thesis Series in Environmental Studies and Sustainability Science, No 2013:015, Lund University Centre for Sustainability Studies.

FÖS (Forum Ökologisch-Soziale Marktwirtschaft) (2010), *Themenpapier Dienst- und Firmenwagenbesteuerung – Ökologische und Soziale Fehlanreize Beseitigen*, April 2010, Berlin.

Frondel, M. R. Kambeck and C. Schmidt (2007), 'Hard Coal Subsidies: A never-ending story?', *Energy Policy* 35 (2007) 3807–14.

G20 (2009), *Leaders' statement: The Pittsburgh Summit*, 24–25 September 2009, available online at: https://www.g20.org/sites/default/files/g20_resources/library/Pittsburgh_Declaration_0.pdf (accessed 20 January 2014).

'Gesetze im Internet: Kernbrennstoffsteuer', available online at: http://www.gesetze-im-internet.de/bundesrecht/kernbrstg/gesamt.pdf (accessed 21 March 2013).

Guillaume, D., R. Zytek and M.R. Farzin (2011), *Iran –The Chronicles of the Subsidy Reform*, IMF working paper 11/167, International Monetary Fund.

IEA, OPEC, OECD, World Bank (2010), *Analysis of the Scope of Energy Subsidies and Suggestions for the G20 initiative*, prepared for submission to the G-20 summit meeting, Toronto (Canada), 26–27 June 2010, available online at: http://www.oecd.org/env/45575666.pdf (accessed 20 January 2014).

Irish Government (2011), *The National Recovery Plan 2011–2014*, available online at: http://www.budget.gov.ie/The%20National%20Recovery%20Plan%202011–2014.pdf (accessed 11 March 2013).

Irish Times (2012), 'What's Ireland's Problem with Water Charges?', available online at: http://www.irishtimes.com/news/what-s-ireland-s-problem-with-water-charges-1.506087 (accessed 11 March 2013).

Irish Times (2013), '500m Annual Water Charges due by 2015', available online at: http://www.irishtimes.com/news/500m-annual-water-charges-due-by-2015–1.1255395 (accessed 11 March 2013).

IISD (2010), *Untold Billions: Fossil Fuel Subsidies, their Impacts and the Road to Reform*, IISD, Geneva, available online at: http://www.iisd.org/gsi/sites/default/files/synthesis_ffs.pdf (accessed 28 November 2013).

IISD (2012a), *Reforming fossil-fuel subsidies to reduce waste and limit CO2 emissions while protecting the poor*, APEC Energy Working Group, Singapore, September 2012, available online at: http://www.iisd.org/gsi/sites/default/files/ffs_apec.pdf (accessed 29 November 2013).

IISD (2012b), *Recent Developments in Iran's Energy Subsidy Reforms*, Policy Brief, Geneva, October 2012.

IISD (2013), *A guidebook to fossil fuel subsidy reform for policy-makers in South East Asia*. IISD, Geneva, available online at: http://www.iisd.org/gsi/sites/default/files/ffs_guidebook.pdf (accessed 28 November 2013).

Knetsch, J.L. (1989), 'The Endowment Effect and Evidence of Nonreversible

Indifference Curves', *The American Economic Review*, Vol. 79, No. 5 (December 1989), 1277–84.
Küchler, S. and B. Meyer (2012), *The full costs of power generation: A comparison of subsidies and societal cost of renewable and conventional energy sources*, report commissioned by BWE, the German Wind Energy Association, and Greenpeace Energy, Berlin.
Meyer, B. and S. Küchler (2010a), *Staatliche Förderungen der Atomenergie im Zeitraum 1950–2010*, FÖS-Studie im Auftrag von Greenpeace, Berlin, available online at: http://www.foes.de/pdf/2010_FOES_Foerderungen_Atomenergie_1950–2010.pdf.
Meyer, B. and Küchler, S. (2010b), *Billiger Strom aus Atom und Kohle? Staatliche Förderungen 1970–2008*, Hintergrundpapier im Auftrag von Greenpeace Energy e.G., Berlin, available online at: http://www.foes.de/pdf/2010.10_FOES_Foerderungen_Strom_Atom_Kohle_Vergleich.pdf.
Meyer, B., S. Schmidt and V. Eidems (2010), *An investigation into all forms of state aid for atomic energy 1950 –2008*, Green Budget Germany research report commissioned by Greenpeace FÖS-Studie im Auftrag von Greenpeace, Berlin, available online at: http://www.foes.de/pdf/State%20Aid%20for%20Atomic%20Energy.pdf.
OECD (2006), *Subsidy Reform and Sustainable Development Economic, Environmental and Social Aspects*, Paris: OECD.
OECD (2007), *Instrument Mixes for Environmental Policy*, Paris: OECD.
OECD (2013), *Inventory of estimated budgetary support and tax expenditures for fossil fuels*, Paris: OECD.
Pollitt, M. and I. Shaorshadze (December 2011), *The Role of Behavioural Economics in Energy and Climate Policy*, ESRC Electricity Policy Research Group, University of Cambridge.
Potter, S. and A. Atchulo (2013), 'A Review of Ten Years of CO2-based Company Car Taxation: Impact and Potential', in *Universities Transport Studies Group Annual Conference*, 3–5 January 2013, Oxford.
Potter, S., M. Enoch, T. Rye, C. Black and B. Ubbels (2006), 'Tax Treatment of Employer Commuting Support: An International Review', *Transport Reviews* 26 (2006) No. 2, 221–37.
ten Brink, P. and L. Mazza (2013), 'Reforming Environmental Taxes and Harmful Subsidies: Challenges And Opportunities', Background paper under the IEEP project on Charting Europe's environmental policy future, London/Brussels.
Valsecchi C., P. ten Brink, S. Bassi, S. Withana, M. Lewis, A. Best, F. Oosterhuis, C. Dias Soares, H. Rogers-Ganter and T. Kaphengst (2009), *Environmentally Harmful Subsidies: Identification and Assessment*, Final report for the European Commission's DG Environment, November 2009.
Withana, S., P. ten Brink, L. Franckx, M. Hirchnitz-Garvers, M. Mayeres, I. Oosterhuis and L. Porsch (2012), *Study supporting the phasing out of environmentally harmful subsidies, A report by the Institute for European Environmental Policy* (IEEP), Institute for Environmental Studies – Vrije Universiteit (IVM), Ecologic Institute and VITO for the European Commission – DG Environment, Final Report, Brussels, 2012.
World Economic Forum (2013), *Lessons drawn from reforms of energy subsidies*, Geneva, available online at: http://www3.weforum.org/docs/GAC13/WEF_GAC13_LessonsReformsEnergySubsidies_Report.pdf (accessed 29 November 2013).

11. Decision making for market-based environmental cost allocation: the case of packaging waste policy in Germany

Susumu Kitagawa

1. INTRODUCTION‡

Numerous environmental problems have emerged and worsened during the last half-century, leading to the ever-increasing costs of addressing the consequences. The dilemma facing society today is how to cope with and allocate responsibility for the associated rising environmental costs within a framework acceptable to the involved parties and society. One illustration of a critical environmental issue is that of the increasing volume of packaging waste produced by our consumer society, and the question is how to allocate the cost burden of collecting, sorting, and recycling the refuse, a task that has heretofore been the jurisdiction of local governments. As a means of addressing this problem, countries have explored the use of regulatory mechanisms as well as economic solutions.

Among these pioneering nations, Germany is well known for the Duales System Deutschland (DSD) system[1] – new and highly innovative model for allocation of environmental costs. Established in 1990 by manufacturers and industries related to packaging manufacturing and distribution, the DSD system is designed to collect, sort, and recycle packaging waste. It was devised by the business sector to deflect the intent of the soon-to-be enacted Packaging Ordinance (1991)[2] that would have placed the major responsibility on manufacturers[3] and distributors[4] for the collection, sorting, and recycling of post-consumer packaging waste. The DSD system and Packaging Ordinance demonstrate the world's first practical example of the new environmental principle of Extended Producer Responsibility (EPR) (OECD 2004, p. 120).

With the implementation of the DSD system, the collection and sorting of packaging waste was no longer funded by local government taxes, but instead was assumed by packaging manufacturers and distributors participating in the DSD system. Also, the operation of the DSD system was funded by user charges paid by companies participating in the DSD system. This system, in which participating companies take on the cost burden of collection and sorting, truly embodies the EPR concept. Remarkably, the DSD system, which appears to impose a heavy cost burden on industry, actually was proposed by the German economic sector.

The DSD system has been extensively analyzed to identify its impact on waste reduction rates and its degree of economic efficiency.[5] At the same time, the background of the DSD system, and the Packaging Ordinance that propelled its creation, is surprisingly unclear. Since the conservative coalition's rise to power in 1982, the economic sector and conservative political parties vehemently opposed an increase in the environmental cost burden that would have been imposed by the introduction of the waste tax and the carbon tax. So it is hard to fathom how they came up with the DSD system proposal, even if it was founded on a market-based cost allocation concept.

This chapter focuses on the decision-making process surrounding the establishment of the DSD system and uncovers the reasons that the German economic sector proposed it. Further, it explores the significance of the establishment of the DSD system in the context of the enactment of the Packaging Ordinance and demonstrates, through the use of contemporaneous unpublished primary sources, the basis for policy decisions that were made. In recent years, studies have pointed to the importance of pursuing environmental policy history studies, in the fields of environmental policy studies and environmental history research, to help clarify the historical processes of the establishment and development of environmental policy (Kitagawa 2014). This chapter pinpoints an extremely narrow time frame during 1990 when the debate surrounding the establishment of Germany's DSD system intensified. It is hoped that this case study in environmental policy history will contribute to the growing literature in this field.

2. OVERVIEW OF THE PACKAGING ORDINANCE AND THE DSD SYSTEM

In Germany during the latter half of the 1970s, the increasing volume of packaging waste was becoming a major social problem. At the end of the 1970s, the German federal government – at the time composed of a coalition of the Social Democratic Party (Sozialdemokratische Partei Deutschlands: SPD) and the Free Democratic Party (Freie Demokratische Partei: FDP) – sought to conclude voluntary agreements with various industries, such as the packaging, beverage, and retail industries, with the objective of reducing the volume of one-way (disposable, non-returnable) drinks packaging. However, the main reduction goals in these voluntary agreements were not achieved (Rat von Sächverstandigen für Umweltfragen 1998, p. 199). Even the coalition government led by Helmut Kohl, which arose after the fall of the SPD/FDP coalition government in 1982 and was composed of the Christian Democratic Union (Christlich-Democratische Union: CDU), Christian Social Union (Christlich-Soziale Union: CSU), and the FDP political parties, could not stem the overwhelming tide of packaging waste produced in German society. This spurred the Federal Ministry of the Environment, Nature Conservation and Nuclear Safety (Bundesministerium für Umwelt, Naturschutz und Reaktorsicherheit: BMU) to begin developing an ordinance in 1990 to address packaging waste. And in June 1991, the Packaging Ordinance became law.

It is particularly worth noting that the 1991 Packaging Ordinance imposed the following three responsibilities on businesses. However, these three requirements would be waived if a certain condition, which will be discussed later, could be met. First was the responsibility for distributors to collect used sales packaging[6] from or in the immediate vicinity of the point of sale. This meant that a collection center would be set up to collect used sales packaging from each of the various retail outlets. Second, the responsibility for aggregating and recycling the collected sales packaging from each of the retail outlets would be borne by the sales packaging manufacturers and distributors. Third, the responsibility for the execution of the deposit-refund[7] process would be imposed on distributors of one-way drinks packaging. Accordingly, this required distributors selling beverages in one-way drinks packaging to collect the used beverage containers from the various stores.

In accordance with the sales packaging collection requirement, distributors were forced to absorb the cost associated with installing collection containers at each retail store and maintaining storage space for the collected waste. Not surprisingly, the German retail sector and major business associations strongly opposed the introduction of the deposit-refund system for one-way drinks packaging. According to their reasoning, if the deposit-refund system was imposed, the price of a drink in a one-way container would increase by the amount of the deposit, and the price advantage of a beverage in a returnable container would be lost. In essence, if the deposit-refund system, which motivated consumers to purchase beverages sold in returnable containers, were to be changed, it would make returnable containers less appealing, given the convenience of beverages in disposable containers. Ultimately, manufacturers and distributors, on whom the responsibility for recycling was imposed, had to create a system to collect and sort sales packaging from each of the countless number of stores throughout the country, but this was going to be an enormous financial burden.

In actuality, as mentioned previously, according to the enacted Packaging Ordinance (1991), exemptions from the three responsibilities could be had if the following condition was met. Essentially, if a system developed jointly by sales packaging manufacturers, distributors, and other related businesses to collect, sort, and recycle packaging waste was able to achieve the collection and recycle rates dictated in the 1991 Packaging Ordinance,[8] the responsibilities would be waived. The DSD system was developed to meet these requirements.

After the debut of the DSD system, the system collected, free of charge, the container and packaging portion from the household waste stream, previously for which local governments had charged collection fees. The administration and operation of the DSD system was implemented by the DSD. To carry out its functions, the DSD system developed an administrative strata, including departments specializing in management, human resources, legal affairs and contracts, public relations, and accounting. Also, in the DSD system, the collection and sorting of sales packaging waste from households is not actually performed by DSD. Rather, DSD contracts out the waste processing work to private businesses and local government. Accordingly, DSD pays both parties for these contracted services.

Income from what are called 'Green Dot' fees, paid by participating businesses into the DSD system, goes toward these costs. The Green Dot symbol must be printed on the sales packaging that is collected and sorted by the DSD system. Therefore, businesses seeking to participate in the DSD system must first contract with DSD and become licensed to use the Green Dot symbol. The businesses must then pay DSD the Green Dot fee for collection and sorting of their waste. User charges are usually associated with waste processing in the public sector – however, the DSD system was created by private industry, and the Green Dot fee can be said to also function as a kind of user charge.[9] Although the Green Dot fee has been amended several times since the establishment of the DSD system, it is fundamentally based on the weight of materials classified into the following categories: glass, tinplate, paper, aluminum, plastics, and composite materials.

3. THE DSD SYSTEM CONCEPT PROPOSED BY LAMBSDORFF

The year 1990 marked a major turning point for Germany. To begin with, the Federal Diet (Bundestag) elections were scheduled for 1990 and, as the SPD campaign gathered increasing support, it became apparent that the Kohl government was at a disadvantage. For Kohl, the reunification of Germany was the panacea that would revive his lagging poll numbers and help him maintain his grip on power. He actively worked toward reunification, advancing negotiations with East Germany, the US, the USSR, England, and France during the first half of 1990, and in July of that year, establishing a common currency for East and West Germany. In this political context, in spite of the passage and implementation of The Waste Avoidance and Waste Management Act (Abfallgesetz) of 1986, the packaging waste problem was not only not improving, the situation was in danger of getting much worse because the destination for West Germany's waste in the environmentally lax East Germany could be lost with the unification of the country. At this point, it was Otto Graf Lambsdorff's proposal of the DSD system in January of 1990 that transformed the situation.

Lambsdorff was an FDP politician and expert on economic policy who, since 1988, had towed the neoliberal line as party chief. In early January 1990, all of a sudden, Lambsdorff announced his proposal for Germany's waste processing system in *Handelsblatt*, the leading German business and financial newspaper (Lambsdorff 1990). The essential features of the plan are as follows.

Up until that point, household waste was collected, for a fee, by local governments. However, the massive increase in waste collection costs would soon squeeze local government finances and become a political problem. What was needed was a 'dual waste management (Duale Abfallwirtschaft)' strategy in which a new private system for collecting recyclable waste would be jointly funded by the relevant industries, and the public sector would continue, as before, to be responsible for processing wastes that had to be disposed of in landfills or by incineration. The cost of building the new collection system would be covered by the relevant industries. Following the announcement of the plan, on 6 February 1990 Lambsdorff sent a letter to Klaus Töpfer, the German environment minister, in which he informed him that the economic sector was ready to quickly establish a DSD system.[10]

In reality, the two-dimensional waste processing concept, i.e., the DSD system, was being promoted by the major business associations – the Federation of German Industries (Bundesverband der Deutschen Industrie: BDI) and the Association of German Chambers of Industry and Commerce (Deutscher Industrie und Handelstag: DIHT) – in collaboration with the packaging industry lobbying group, The Task Force on Packaging and Environment (Arbeitsgemeinschaft Verpackung und Umwelt: AGVU). Accordingly, Lambsdorff, known as an indefatigable industry lawyer,[11] took it upon himself to sell the DSD system concept to the political and finance sectors. As was revealed subsequently, Lambsdorff played an important role through his participation in behind-the-scenes negotiations with the BMU, which had formulated a draft of the Packaging Ordinance, and by succeeding in aligning the Packaging Ordinance with the interests of the economic sector.

4. BACKGROUND OF LAMBSDORFF'S PROPOSAL

At the end of the 1980s, in the face of an unrelenting rise in the volume of packaging waste, which had begun in the 1970s, the BMU was considering measures to reduce packaging waste, including a deposit-refund system for one-way drinks packaging – a plan which was opposed by business. The German business sector was put on the defensive by these developments, so what led it to propose the operationally as well as financially burdensome DSD system? The answer lies in the privatization of packaging waste collection and sorting operations, the viability of the cost allocation scheme, and the opportunity for expansion of new waste collection and recycling businesses to other European countries. These factors will be explored below.

4.1 Privatization of Services for Collecting and Sorting Packaging Waste

At the time, according to The Waste Avoidance and Waste Management Act of 1986, the responsibility for waste processing of household waste lay with local government, and aside from a portion of this task contracted to private companies, local government conducted the collection and sorting of waste. Therefore, the shift in the locus of responsibility for collection and sorting of waste containers and packaging from local government to the DSD system would demonstrate that the EPR concept had indeed become reality and waste processing services had been privatized. This is why the Public Service, Transport and Traffic Union (Gewerkschaft Öffentliche Dienste, Transport und Verkehr: ÖTV), which was the government labor union, was critical of the DSD system concept and felt that it was an attack on public sector waste processing operations and would endanger jobs and destroy the then current local government recycling system.[12]

Lambsdorff expressed the view that to make such an extraordinarily large investment in a system for collection, sorting, and reuse of valuable waste resources, private investment was indispensable, and so the FDP political party was calling for the privatization of the waste management sector (FDP 1990a). This perspective was in line with the policy of privatization advanced by the Kohl government.

4.2 Feasibility of the Cost Allocation Structure

Accompanying the operation of the DSD system, a new cost allocation arrangement would emerge for businesses engaging in packaging manufacturing and sales. On this point, in April 1990, Lambsdorff thought that operating costs of the DSD system could be passed on to the consumer and that the profits from recycling collected wastes would support the system.[13] Therefore, we can assume that Lambsdorff planned to pass on the operating costs of the DSD system to consumers and to have businesses bear a large part of the initial investment. The opportunity was coming to expand the waste management sector through privatization, and Lambsdorff's idea undoubtedly held a certain persuasive power for the related business sectors. Also, from 1983 to 1990, the German economy experienced an unprecedented historic economic expansion, and this provided the impetus for approval of the initial investments in the DSD system.

4.3 New Developments in the Recycling Business

Lambsdorff pointed out that the DSD system could become a model for the rest of Europe (FDP 1990b). It is conceivable that he was aiming to expand the new DSD system business model of waste collection, sorting, and recycling throughout Europe. Also, we can surmise that within his sights was the expansion of the waste management business into post-unification East Germany.

4.4 Attitude Change in the Economic Sector

In his declaration of 17 May 1990, Lambsdorff sought federal government action to facilitate the rapid development of a sound legal framework to fully guarantee the large investment by the relevant industries in the valuable resource recovery system (FDP 1990a). This reveals an attitudinal change on the part of the German economic sector and the FDP, including Lambsdorff, who had long opposed the introduction of regulatory measures in the packaging waste processing sector. What was behind this attitudinal change?

Many different kinds of businesses were involved in the distribution of, as well as manufacture of materials for, glass, paper, metal, and plastic containers and packaging – materials that ended up as packaging waste. Likewise, businesses held widely differing stakes. For example, thanks to advanced technologies, the glass and paper industries benefited from low recycling costs for glass and paper containers and packaging. However, technologies for sorting and recycling plastics lagged behind, and the cost-benefits were not as compelling.

If, as before, the collection, sorting, and recycling of packaging wastes were conducted voluntarily with no legal requirement, it would be difficult to balance the interests of the various industries and realize full business participation in the DSD system. As a result, even if the DSD system were to be established, it would likely not become a large-scale system able to cover the entire country or be able to achieve the sufficient volume of collection and recycling that would be needed to maintain the system. If that were to happen, the government and the public would probably criticize the system for its insignificant contribution to environmental improvement, and this would perhaps lead to the collapse of the entire system. Then the investment of the economic sector would have been for naught. Furthermore, the economic sector would be discredited and forced to accept government-mandated measures, such as the deposit-refund system for dealing with one-way drinks packaging.

The FDP and Lambsdorff, who had taken a leading role in spreading the party's neoliberal economic agenda, had hoped to shrink government and reduce the role of the public sector in the waste processing arena. However, the outcome was the adoption of the DSD system, which had no precedent anywhere in the world, and participating businesses were required to take on the risk of a considerable initial investment. It was the Packaging Ordinance that provided the legal framework that the economic sector needed to mitigate this risk.

5. THE PROCESS BY WHICH THE BMU ACCEPTED THE DSD SYSTEM

The economic sector's DSD system proposal was accepted by the BMU, and the draft of the Packaging Ordinance soon became the presumed basis for the establishment of the DSD system. The then German environment minister Klaus Töpfer played a central role. Töpfer was a politician affiliated with the CDU party and previously had been a researcher in the field of regional development policy. This section will consider how, as a requirement for the early establishment of the DSD system, Töpfer ensured that the Packaging Ordinance would be acceptable to the economic sector.

5.1 The BMU's Fundamental Policy

In March 1990, as the BMU began formulating the basic principles for the Packaging Ordinance, it considered imposing on businesses the duty of collecting packaging waste.[14] By imposing on the private sector the responsibility for the collection of packaging waste, which was part of household waste streams collected by local government, the BMU would be simultaneously endorsing the privatization of packaging waste processing as well as executing an extreme measure to immediately reduce the volume of waste collected by the public sector.

5.2 Closed-door Negotiations between Töpfer and Lambsdorff

In April 1990, the BMU started drafting the Packaging Ordinance. Subsequently, closed-door negotiations on the BMU-authored Packaging Ordinance draft commenced between the BMU, represented primarily by Töpfer, and the FDP political party, which was represented mainly by Lambsdorff.[15] The negotiations identified the following two matters of concern in the draft.

First was the issue of whether distributor responsibility for collection of sales packaging from or in the vicinity of the point of sale would be waived if the distributor contracted with the DSD system to do the collecting. If distributors could not receive an exemption by contracting the DSD system, then the establishment of the DSD system would be meaningless for the economic sector. Another concern was whether an exemption from the deposit-refund duty for one-way drinks packaging could be obtained by using the DSD system. Up until that point, the retail sector and the major business associations had opposed the introduction of the deposit-refund duty for one-way drinks packaging.

5.2.1 Debate on exemption from the duty to collect sales packaging

In BMU's draft Packaging Ordinance, dated 20 April 1990,[16] it was not certain whether distributors would be exempted from the duty of collecting sales packaging by contracting the DSD system. This same draft also mentioned the responsibility of bottlers and distributors of one-way drinks packaging to collect from purchasers a deposit of 0.50 German marks per container, but there was no mention of an exemption from this obligation.

Negotiations on these two concerns occurred within the FDP on 3 May 1990.[17] Four parties participated in these negotiations: Töpfer,

Lambsdorff, the director of the BMU, and an FDP environmental policy expert. They all agreed that if a collection system as broad and wide ranging as the DSD system was established, it must exempt distributors from the responsibility of collecting sales packaging at or in the vicinity of stores.

5.2.2 Exemption from deposit-refund duty for one-way drinks packaging

In Töpfer's letter to Lambsdorff sent in mid-May 1990, progress was made in the discussion of the mandatory deposit-refund duty for one-way drinks packaging.[18] In his letter, Töpfer first of all pointed out that without the introduction of the deposit-refund system for one-way containers, their volume would increase exponentially and become unmanageable. Töpfer also noted that establishing the DSD system without introducing the deposit-refund system for one-way containers would create a crisis for the existing deposit-refund system for returnable containers and for small-to-medium size beer companies that use returnable containers.

In light of these points, Töpfer offered the following proposal. While acknowledging that these crises may occur, but also that potential major profits would be accompanied by minimal risk, Töpfer suggested that if the DSD system were to be established in each county and city by a certain date and confirmed by the relevant governing agencies, it would be worth considering suspension of the implementation of the deposit-refund system for one-way drinks packaging dictated in the Packaging Ordinance. Töpfer's proposal indicated that if there were other appropriate means of recycling used drinks packaging, largely collected from consumers, then he would not necessarily insist on the introduction of the deposit-refund system and would be open to discussions with the relevant industries. Töpfer's statement was reiterated in an article in the *Die Welt* newspaper.[19]

5.2.3 The urgency of establishing the DSD system

Why did Töpfer and the BMU camp not only easily accept the first matter of concern, which was the exemption from responsibility for collection of sales packaging, but would have even tolerated a detrimental influence on the existing deposit-refund system for returnable drinks packaging, all for the sake of an expedited establishment of the DSD system?

Actually, as he explained in his letter to Lambsdorff, Töpfer could not ignore popular demand for materials recycling and a curb on the continuous increase in the volume of packaging waste in household trash, and he speculated that the problem of packaging waste would become a major issue in the upcoming Bavarian Assembly and Federal Diet elections.[20] Indeed, the issue did become a point of controversy during the elections at that time.

The CDU political party met with successive defeats in the 1990 state assembly elections. Most notably, on 13 May, around the time of the correspondence between Lambsdorff and Töpfer, not only was the CDU beaten in the North Rhine-Westphalia state assembly (Land Diet) election by Johannes Rau, who led the SPD – but the fall to the opposition party in the Lower Saxony state assembly elections allowed a coalition government to form, composed of Gerhard Schröder's SPD and the Green Party. As a result, the balance of power between the ruling and opposition parties was overturned in the Federal Council (Bundesrat), which was composed of representatives from the states. At the federal level also, the Kohl government was expected to make a poor showing in the Federal Diet election held in the same year, and it seemed likely that power would be turned over to the SPD. Oskar Lafontaine, the SPD candidate for prime minister in the 1990 Federal Diet election, reversed previous SPD policy and formed a coalition with the Green Party, threatening the conservative coalition government. Lafontaine had previously focused on environmental policy (Lafontaine 1985), and we may assume that the Kohl government was desperate for an election strategy that included an environmental policy with demonstrably successful outcomes.

Furthermore, enacting legislation on packaging waste policy, which had long been an issue for the federal government, was a golden opportunity for Töpfer to restore his honor. The public had high expectations for Töpfer, especially considering that he had been a regional development policy researcher and was an authority on environmental issues. However, in April 1989, two years after his appointment as Germany's Minister of the Environment, Töpfer's political stature was diminished by the impression that he was more talk than action, and his critics claimed that he had not produced any noteworthy achievements. His career as a politician had hit a crossroads.[21]

Accordingly, as the packaging waste problem was clearly becoming a political issue impossible to ignore, enacting the Packaging Ordinance before the upcoming Federal Diet election in the fall of 1990 was thought to be a way to avoid defeat for the conservative coalition government and a way for Töpfer to redeem his reputation. These political motives were the reasons that Töpfer sought to quickly establish the DSD system. At the time, the SPD political party and the Greens planned to introduce a waste tax and prohibit certain containers such as the one-way PET bottle.[22] Precisely because the conservative coalition government would not implement these kinds of policies, it was perhaps all the more important for it to promote the packaging waste policy, with its emphasis on the DSD recycling system. In addition, amid the looming prospect of a regime change after the Federal Diet election, the successful introduction of the packaging waste policy, achieved while the conservative coalition government was still in power, was seen as extremely favorable for the economic sector because it would stop not only the imposition of a waste tax and prohibition of the PET bottle, but also the implementation of a deposit-refund system for one-way drinks packaging.

6. SUBSEQUENT DEVELOPMENTS

Töpfer's 17 May 1990 press conference first introducing the Packaging Ordinance draft set off a flurry of criticism in the pages of the major newspapers.[23] The newspaper reporting of the time claimed that Töpfer's goal was to introduce the deposit-refund system for one-way drinks packaging,[24] but as we have seen, by that time, Töpfer and Lambsdorff had already struck an agreement for exemptions to the two outstanding issues raised by the draft.

By the end of May 1990, provisions had been included in the draft that exempted distributors from collecting sales packaging from or in the vicinity of stores and from having to adopt the deposit-refund system for one-way drinks packaging. The economic sector responded by formalizing the DSD system concept, and by the end of September 1990, the DSD management organization had been established through joint funding by the business associations and related businesses. As a result, the discussion of the draft in the various agencies and legislature necessarily was based on the assumption that the DSD system, as conceived in the draft, would become reality. In subsequent deliberations of the Federal Council, minor revisions were made to the Packaging Ordinance, but its general framework, centering on exemptions to the two major concerns, was adopted, and the Packaging Ordinance became law in 1991.

7. CONCLUSION

Normally, we see many cases in which the implementation of environmental policies is obstructed by political and economic interests, but the German example shows that the advancement of environmental policies can be furthered not only by a commitment to environmental preservation, but also by political and economic motives. In other words, established political parties do not usually behave like the Green Party, which strives to advance all policy issues related to the environment. Rather, they tend to choose the most feasible environmental policy that benefits their political or economic interests, or a combination thereof. In the German case, the factor that spurred this choice was, for the economic sector, the threat of even more severe policies, such as the deposit-refund system for one-way drinks packaging and a waste tax imposed on businesses – and for the conservative party, it was the specter of political defeat. It was in this context that the German business sector's intense opposition to the waste tax and deposit-refund system led the BMU, the German Federal Ministry for the Environment, to call for the establishment of the DSD system with its associated user charges.

The environmental tax, the deposit-refund system, and the DSD system were similar in the sense that they all required business to shoulder environmental costs. However, the DSD system had advantages for the business sector that the waste tax and the deposit-refund policies lacked. Also, an additional benefit was the anticipated generation of new markets related to the collection, sorting, and recycling of container and packaging waste. It follows therefore that the design of the user charge system, referred to as the Green Dot, was left to the business sector, and government participation was largely sidelined. Despite this, however, the creation of the DSD system was extremely desirable for the BMU. Namely, the alternative, i.e., introduction of an environmental tax, which would encompass a waste tax, would precipitate an undoubtedly contentious public debate and time-consuming negotiations among the relevant governmental jurisdictions. Politically speaking therefore, given the urgency to show positive accomplishments on this issue before the soon-to-be-held general election, pursuing the waste tax was not a realistic option. Ultimately, the DSD system was established, rather than the waste tax or the deposit-refund system, under the auspices of the BMU.

NOTES

‡ I am grateful to Soocheol Lee and two anonymous reviewers for their comments and suggestions on this manuscript. This study was supported by the Mitsui & Co., Ltd. Environment Fund and the Ministry of Education, Culture, Sports, Science and Technology of Japan, Grant-in-Aid for Scientific Research C (22510042).

1. The DSD System is also called the 'Dual System.' In this chapter, as is mentioned later, the collection, sorting, and recycling of packaging waste operated by the DSD will be called the DSD system to distinguish it from other dual systems operated by businesses.
2. Verordnung über die Vermeidung von Verpackungsabfällen vom 12 Juni 1991, in: *Bundesgesetzblatt I*, p. 1234.
3. 'Manufacturer,' as defined in the Packaging Ordinance, is anyone who manufactures packaging or products from which packaging is directly manufactured.

4. 'Distributor,' as defined in the Packaging Ordinance, is anyone who puts into circulation packaging, materials or products from which packaging can be directly manufactured, and packaged products, at any commercial level. This definition also includes entities involved in the mail-order trade.
5. *See*, for example, Michaelis (1993).
6. In the Packaging Ordinance, sales packaging – consisting of glass, paper, tinplate, plastic, aluminum, etc. – refers to used containers and packaging that have reached the end of their functional life and are thrown away by the end consumer.
7. A deposit-refund system is one in which a deposit is added to the sales price of a product, the product is consumed, and then the container is returned to a designated place, upon which the deposit amount is returned to the purchaser. Before the enactment of the Packaging Ordinance, Germany had a deposit-refund system for what was called returnable beverage containers, which, after use, could be collected, sanitized, and refilled. Accordingly, it must be pointed out that in the debate prior to enacting the Packaging Ordinance, the pros and cons of introducing the deposit-refund system for one-way packaging were discussed.
8. An essential requirement for the exemption of one-way beverage containers was matching the rate of returnable beverage container recycling, which was over 72% of the volume of domestic beverage container recycling at the time.
9. 'User charge' as it is used here conforms to the OECD concept, which states: 'User charges are payments for the costs of collective or public treatment of effluents' (OECD 1989, p. 15).
10. Refer to Reference Material 1. For bibliographic information on primary sources used in this Chapter, please refer to the section on primary sources.
11. *Der Spiegel*, No. 8, February 17, 1986, p. 27.
12. *Frankfurter Rundschau*, August 7, 1990.
13. *Frankfurter Allgemeine Zeitung*, April 17, 1990.
14. Refer to Reference Material 2.
15. Based on a review of this set of preserved BMU documents, it can be concluded that the debate surrounding the two matters of concern in the Packaging Ordinance draft took place between only two camps – the BMU and the FDP political party. There was no evidence of perspectives from any person or group outside the coalition government or the business sector, such as the SPD political party, the Greens, or environmental organizations, which did not have a political or financial interest in the Packaging Ordinance. In this respect also, the BMU public documents are useful in clarifying the nature of the debate surrounding the Packaging Ordinance draft.
16. Refer to Reference Material 3.
17. Refer to Reference Material 4.
18. Refer to Reference Material 5. For details on the deposit-refund system in the 1991 Packaging Ordinance, *see* Section 2.
19. *Die Welt*, May 18, 1990.
20. Refer to Reference Material 5.
21. *Der Spiegel*, No. 15, April 10, 1989, pp. 36–56. After overseeing the successful enactment of the Packaging Ordinance and upon leaving his post as Germany's environment minister, Töpfer was appointed Executive Director of the United Nations Environment Programme.
22. Refer to SPD (1990) and Deutscher Bundestag, Drucksache 11/1927 (neu), June 1, 1988.
23. *See*, for example, the May 18, 1990 issues of major newspapers, such as *Frankfurter Allgemeine Zeitung*, *Süddeutsche Zeitung*, and *Die Welt*.
24. *Frankfurter Rundschau*, May 18, 1990.

REFERENCES

Primary Sources

Documents from Germany's Federal Archives (the Bundesarchiv Koblenz [BA Koblenz]), for example, are customarily cited indicating only the call number, as follows. Bundesarchiv Koblenz Bestände des Bundesinnenministeriums: B 106/21969. However, the BMU materials used in this chapter are the original documents, which may be eventually destroyed. Therefore, while somewhat cumbersome, references to the documents used here also include the document title. Reference materials 1 through 4 are located in files 'B295/53545, 30 114–1/3 SB, vom 02/90 bis 06/90, Band 1' in the custody of the Federal Archives. Reference material 5 is located in file 'WA II 4, 30114–1/3, Entwurf bis Kabinettsbeschluß, vom Okt.1990 bis 10.1990, Band 2,' which is in the custody of the BMU.

Reference Material 1. Letter from Lambsdorff to Töpfer, February 6, 1990.

Reference Material 2. Referat WA II 3, WA II 3 - 530 114 – 0, Refl.: MR Kreft, Betr.: Vermeidung des Verpackungsabfalls, hier: Strategieüberlegungen, Bonn, March 1, 1990.

Reference Material 3. Bundesminister für Umwelt, Naturschutz und Reaktorsicherheit, Entwurf einer Verordnung über die Rücknahme und Verwertung von Verpackungen (AbfVRückV) vom . . . 1990, April 20,1990.

Reference Material 4. Abteilungsleiter WA, Vermerk.:Betr.: Entwurf einer Rechtsverordnung nach §14 zur Vermeidung von Verpackungsabfällen; hier: Besprechung mit FDP-Fraktionsführer Dr. Graf Lambsdorff, Bonn, May 3, 1990.

Reference Material 5. Referat WA II 3, WA II 3 - 530 114 – 1/7, Refl.:MR Kreft, Schreiben des Herrn Ministers, Bonn, May 11, 1990.

Secondary Sources

FDP (Freie Demokratische Partei) (1990a), 'Duale Abfallwirtschaft gegen ÖTV-Interessen,' FDP – Bundestagsfraktion informiert. Fachinfo Abfall, Nr. 2928, September 28,1990.

FDP (Freie Demokratische Partei) (1990b), 'Lambsdorff: 20 grosse Müllverbrennungsanlagen überflüssig,' fdk tagesdienst, May 17,, 1990.

Kitagawa, Susumu (2014), 'Vision and Significance in Environmental Policy History,' in Ts'ui-jung Liu (ed.), *Environmental History in East Asia: Interdisciplinary Perspectives*, London: Routledge, pp. 64–90.

Lafontaine, Oskar (1985), *Der Andere Fortschritt: Verantwortung statt Verweigerung*, Hamburg: Hoffmann und Campe.

Lambsdorff, Otto Graf (1990), 'Duale Abfallwirtschaft statt Markteingriffe,' *Handelsblatt*, January 5/6, 1990.

Michaelis, Peter (1993), *Ökonomische Aspekte der Abfallgesetzgebung*, Tübingen: J.C.B. Mohr.

OECD (1989), *Economic Instruments for Environmental Protection*, Paris: OECD.

OECD (2004), *Economic Aspects of Extended Producer Responsibility*, Paris: OECD.

Rat von Sachverständigen für Umweltfragen (1998), *Umweltgutachten 1998: Umweltschutz: Erreichtes sichern – Neue Wege gehen*, Stuttgart: Metzler-Poeschel.
SPD (Sozialdemokratiche Partei Deutschlands) (1990), 'Wir lassen uns nicht entwickeln – Kampf dem Verpackungswahn!,' *Die SPD im Deutschen Bundestag*, April 20, 1990.

PART II

Impact

Section A

Environmental taxes

12. Environmental taxes – definitional analysis: behavioural change or revenue raising

Sally-Ann Joseph*

1. INTRODUCTION

When the Organisation for Economic Cooperation and Development (OECD) first reviewed the use of environmental economic instruments in 1987, it identified about 150 instruments.[1] The database now contains approximately 375 such taxes with an additional 250 environmentally related fees and charges.[2] These can be levied on the input to, the production of, or the output of environmental services. In fact, anything affecting the environment can be considered, such as congestion charges, waste levies, park entrance fees and landfill taxes. In other words, environmental taxes can take on a multiplicity of forms and perform divergent functions.

This chapter first discusses the purpose of environmental taxation, from its traditional roots as a motivator for behavioural change to its more modern recognition as a revenue raising tool. The definitions and characterisations of environmental taxes are then canvassed, commencing with a discussion of the international definition, followed by an analysis of how environmental taxes are defined, and hence classified, in Australia and the United Kingdom. This has implications for what is considered to be an 'environmental tax'. The scope of this discussion, and hence of this chapter, is restricted to the characterisation of environmental taxation. It is not the author's intention to critique the political and fiscal budgetary implications.

2. PURPOSE OF ENVIRONMENTAL TAXATION

The origin of environmental taxation is closely tied to the polluter pays principle and Pigouvian theory. The polluter pays principle states that those who damage the environment should bear the costs of it.[3] This makes the act of polluting financially costly, encouraging more non-polluting behaviour.

Pigouvian theory, on the other hand, attempts to internalise externalities by embodying them in the costs of production and hence in prices.[4] Here the purpose of environmental taxes is to encourage consumers and producers to adjust their consumption and production patterns to achieve environmental outcomes.

Thus the purpose of environmental taxation has traditionally been to influence a change in behaviour.

However, there is increasing acknowledgment that environmental taxes raise revenue. Originally perceived as producing a ‘double dividend’, the implementation of environmental taxes was advocated as a means of reducing distorting taxes on labour, investment or consumption.[5] However, the discussion has now progressed to using environmental taxes to raise revenue in their own right.

There are two particular environmental taxes that could make a significant contribution to revenues. These are energy and transport taxes. This is because they both have broad tax bases and high tax rates which can be justified by the environmental externalities. A fuel tax, introduced for the stated purpose of reducing emissions, could have the same effect as a fuel tax introduced for fiscal reasons. This is because the environmental impact of the tax comes mainly through its effect on relative prices. The more inelastic demand is, the greater this effect. Indeed, this is often the defining mark between an environmental purpose (or discouraging environmentally detrimental behaviour) and a revenue raising purpose: the more elastic demand is, the more revenue will be eroded by behavioural responses. This has raised concerns over the stability and predictability of environmental tax revenues. However, it is now being questioned whether this problem has been ‘greatly overstated’.[6]

While revenue from a tax can be estimated with a degree of accuracy, an environmental response to an environmental tax is more difficult to quantify. Certain behavioural responses may also be more difficult to predict.

3. ENVIRONMENTAL TAXES

3.1 International Definition

In 2012 the United Nations, the International Monetary Fund, the World Bank, the OECD, the European Commission and the Food and Agricultural Organisation jointly issued the System of Environmental-Economic Accounting (SEEA) Central Framework. Through this they reindorsed the definition of 'environmental tax' as 'a tax whose tax base is a physical unit (or a proxy of it) of something that has a proven, specific, negative impact on the environment'.[7]

The tax base was viewed as the only objective basis for identifying environmental taxes. The name of the tax, the purpose stated by the legislator and the use or earmarking of the revenue derived for environmental purposes were considered to be impractical as identifiers. What defines (or characterises) a measure as an environmental tax is the impact it has on the cost of activities, and the prices of services and products, that have a negative effect on the environment. As noted above, this effect is also influenced by price elasticities.[8]

The emphasis on the effect of the tax is also what differentiates the SEEA definition from economics literature. In the latter, environmental taxes are defined with reference to taxing negative externalities, that is, Pigouvian theory. Pigouvian taxes do not include taxes collected for revenue raising purposes.[9]

Since the purpose of the tax (that is, the reason for enacting the tax) is not considered in the SEEA definition, it has been suggested that a more precise term is 'environmentally related taxes'.[10] The OECD, together with the International Energy Agency and the European Commission, agreed to define this term as any compulsory, unrequited payment to general government levied on tax bases deemed to be of particular environmental relevance.[11]

The definition of 'environmentally related taxes' is narrower than that of the SEEA. This term is also used by the European Union in its regulations but, confusingly, is defined in the same way as the SEEA definition.[12]

Under the SEEA definition, a tax can have a negative impact on the environment without necessarily the tax itself having a particular environmental relevance as its purpose. The focus is on the effects of taxes rather than the aims behind their introduction. As such, a tax introduced to raise revenue rather than reduce environmental degradation can nevertheless be defined as an environmental tax if it has the effect of reducing environmental degradation (as with the example of fuel taxes above). This definition therefore reflects the increasing acknowledgement that environmental taxes do raise revenue.

Having a definition that has evolved through international consensus between member states means that inter-country comparative studies, in terms of tax structure, tax base and tax revenues, are possible. As the endorsers of the SEEA definition include the United Nations, the OECD and the European Commission, it would be expected that member countries of these organisations would conform and adopt the same definition. This is the case in Australia with both Treasury and the Australian Bureau of Statistics adopting this definition. In the United Kingdom this is the definition used by the Office for National Statistics (ONS) but not by HM Treasury (HMT).

3.2 Environmental Taxes in Australia

Under the SEEA definition, there are four categories of environmental taxes: energy, transport, pollution and resource taxes. Energy taxes include taxes on energy products used for both transport (such as petrol and diesel) and stationary purposes (such as natural gas, coal and electricity). Carbon dioxide (CO_2) taxes are included under energy taxes rather than under pollution taxes. Transport taxes include taxes relating to ownership and use of motor vehicles and may be one-off purchase taxes or recurrent taxes. Pollution taxes include taxes on emissions to air and water as well as the generation of solid waste. The last category, resource taxes, includes taxes levied on the commercial exploitation of natural resources such as water, minerals (excluding oil and gas) and forestry.

Of these four categories, Australia only legislates under energy and transport. Taxes on energy include taxes on fossil fuels for transport, carbon taxes and renewable energy certificates while taxes on transport include vehicle stamp duty, the luxury car tax and registration taxes. The resource rent taxes are classified as corporate income taxes.

The revenue raised by environmental taxes has generally increased, some incrementally while others have had exponential growth. For example, over the ten year period 2000–2001 to 2010–2011 revenue from crude oil, LPG, gas and petroleum products increased by nearly 30 per cent. However, over the same period both the luxury car tax and road and registration charges increased over 100 per cent. The carbon pricing mechanism commenced on 1 July 2012. On its introduction it was forecasted to raise AU$4,020 million in its first year, increasing to AU$6,750 million in 2015–2016.[13] However, it is slated to be repealed following a change in government.

Environmental taxes in total have grown by 5.5 per cent per annum over the last decade. They account for around 7 per cent of total tax revenue and approximately 2 per cent of gross domestic product (GDP) for each period. It must be remembered that these ratios result from the tax mix and are influenced by the level of traditional taxes such as income tax and the goods and services tax. These traditional taxes are more sensitive to economic conditions such as the global financial crisis.

More difficult to assess are the environmental effects attributable to these environmental taxes. Traditional thought supported an inverse relationship between the effects of an environmental tax and revenue.[14] That is, an environmental tax was deemed effective if its tax revenues decreased. In other words, to be effective the environmental tax would have to erode its own tax base. However, given the acknowledgment that environmental taxes can raise revenue, decreased revenue cannot be viewed as an indicator of environmental improvement. Other means of assessment must be found.

One way to judge the effectiveness of pollution taxes is by a corresponding decrease in pollution emissions. When ratifying the Kyoto Protocol in 2008, Australia's goal was to limit net greenhouse gas emissions to 8 per cent above 1990 levels (threshold) across the period 2008–2012. On a gross basis (that is, excluding net emissions from land use, land use change and forestry), the change between the threshold and 2009 was substantially higher at 31 per cent.[15] Around 90 per cent of Australia's CO_2 emissions occur as the result of fuel combustion. While constituting nearly a quarter of fuel combustion emissions, transport CO_2 emissions have increased by 34.6 per cent over the period 1990 to 2009 and are 'one of the strongest sources of emissions growth in Australia'.[16] Indeed, road transport accounted for 86.3 per cent of 2009 transport emissions, which was also an increase of 32.8 per cent above threshold levels. Of this, 17.6 per cent is attributable to passenger vehicles. While more information is needed categorically to reach a conclusion, there is little to indicate that pollution taxes are having any behavioural effect.

Another example is the luxury car tax, where it would be expected that the imposition of a tax would result in a corresponding decrease in sales. This is a 33 per cent tax on new and demonstrator cars on that portion of the price[17] that exceeds the luxury car tax threshold. For the 2013–2014 financial year, the threshold is AU$60,316, or AU$75,375 in the case of 'fuel efficient cars'.[18]

Originally introduced with a single threshold to ensure equity when the goods and services tax was introduced,[19] it was also viewed as a redistribution of wealth.[20] An amendment to the luxury car tax, effective 1 July 2008, provided for the additional, increased threshold for fuel-efficient cars. However, while the threshold for non-fuel-efficient cars has increased by AU$3,136 since 2008, the fuel-efficient threshold has only increased AU$375.[21]

For luxury car tax purposes, 'luxury' relates to price. However, according to the CommSec Luxury Car Index that reports on data from the Federal Chamber of Automotive Industries, what defines a 'luxury car' is brand.[22] While acknowledging that other car manufacturers also produce vehicles in the luxury class, the index only contains the top 14 brands.[23] However, the two top selling vehicles that exceed the luxury car tax threshold are both Toyotas,[24] which does not feature on the CommSec Luxury Car Index.

It is perhaps ironic that the luxury car tax applies to fuel-efficient cars as these generally cost more due to the expense of developing fuel-efficient technology. Indeed, the luxury car range is generally the first to benefit from technological advances, as that is where the research and development dollars are spent.[25] Another factor that adds significant cost to a vehicle are safety features.[26] A consumer may well decide that safety features are to be preferred over cost when considering what car to purchase.

In June 2011 there were 16.4 million motor vehicles registered in Australia. The annual average growth in new vehicle sales for the past five years has been 2.7 per cent.[27] However, six of the top ten selling brands in 2012 exceeding 15 per cent growth on 2011 numbers.[28] Luxury car sales are also increasing, comprising 4.37 per cent (or 7.1 per cent if Audi is included as a luxury car brand) of all car sales compared with 1.3 per cent two decades ago.[29] Most growth in vehicle sales has been in the sports utility vehicle category.[30]

Again there is no indication that the luxury car tax is having any behavioural effect. This also calls into question whether the other transport taxes such as registration fees, road user charges and stamp duty on motor vehicles are having any behavioural effect. Indeed, it was noted above that the revenue from the luxury car tax and road and registration charges continues to increase significantly.

3.3 Environmental Taxes in the United Kingdom

As noted above, HMT and ONS adopt different definitions. HMT's definition is based on the primary intention or policy intent of the particular tax. That is, to be classified as environmental taxes, they must be primarily structured to change environmental behaviour. This is in contrast to the SEEA and ONS definition, which is based more on the effect of the particular tax. However, HMT's definition is synonymous with the economic definition, Pigouvian theory that precludes revenue raising and the definition of environmentally related taxes.

According to HMT, an environmental tax must meet three criteria, or 'principles'.[31] First it must be explicitly linked to the government's environmental objectives. Second its primary objective must be to encourage environmentally positive behaviour change. Lastly, the tax must be structured in relation to environmental objectives. Thus, the more polluting the behaviour, the greater the tax levied.

The six taxes deemed to be environmental taxes by HMT are the landfill tax, aggregates levy, the climate change levy, the European Union emissions trading scheme (EU ETS), the CRC energy efficiency scheme (previously known as the carbon reduction commitment) and the carbon price floor. The latter two were introduced effective April 2010 and April 2013, respectively.

Taxes deemed to be environmental taxes by the ONS are more numerous. Energy taxes include taxes on fossil fuels for transport, the climate change levy and renewable energy obligations. There are two road vehicle taxes, namely vehicle excise duty and the Northern Ireland Driver Vehicle Agency. Other environmental taxes are the air passenger duty, landfill tax, aggregates levy, the rail franchise premiums and boat and fishing licences. The Northern Ireland Driver Vehicle Agency, the rail franchise premiums and the boat and fishing licences were added in 2012.[32]

Thus, there are only three taxes common to both the ONS and the HMT: the landfill tax, aggregates levy and climate change levy.

In the Coalition Agreement of 2010,[33] the government pledged 'to increase the proportion of tax revenue accounted for by environmental taxes' (the 'Pledge').[34] This was to be achieved by modifying the definition of 'environmental taxes'. In this way certain taxes with declining revenue could be precluded.

Since 1998 and 1999 when environmental tax revenue accounted for 9.7 per cent of total tax revenue and 3.5 per cent of GDP, both statistics have been falling.[35] In the 2010–2011 financial year, revenue from (ONS) environmental taxes accounted for 8.1 per cent of total tax revenue and 2.9 per cent of GDP.[36] Under the HMT definition, however, the percentage of environmental tax to total tax revenue was only 0.5 per cent.[37] Yet the proportion of revenue from these (HMT) taxes is forecast to double by 2015–2016,[38] in line with the Pledge, while the proportion of ONS-defined environmental taxes is forecast to fall. For example, the RAC Foundation (a motoring charity) predicted that continuing increases to fuel efficiency means that future revenue from fuel taxes would fall by £13 billion despite forecasts of traffic growing by 44 per cent.[39]

In the 2011 Budget, the EU ETS, the Carbon Floor Price and the CRC were the primary sources of the increase in the proportion of (HMT) environmental taxes.[40] These taxes were forecast to raise £1.7 billion in 2011–2012, rising to £5.3 billion in 2015–2016. Later forecasts had the 2015–2016 revenue at £6.6 billion.[41] However, this revenue may be in doubt.

No income has been recorded for the CRC. Not only were the first allowance sales deferred to the 2012 financial year, but the scheme was also originally designed to be revenue neutral. With the decision to end revenue recycling, the scheme is now expected to deliver £3 billion over the financial years 2011–2012 to 2014–2015.[42] When announced, the carbon floor price was to start at £16 per tonne, with a target of £30 per tonne by 2020. However, at January 2013 the trading price was under £4 per tonne.[43] Its target of raising £2.8 billion over the three financial years 2013–2014 to 2015–2016[44] is looking unlikely.

The revenue raised by the EU ETS is not recorded in the National Accounts. This is because the ONS, who compiles the National Accounts, has not yet formally announced a classification decision.[45] However, according to HMT, the revenue raised by the EU ETS in 2010–2011 was £0.4 billion.[46]

While recognising that other taxes can deliver environmental benefits, HMT excludes them if their aim is to raise revenue. Thus, fuel duty, vehicle excise duty and air passenger duty are excluded from the HMT definition, as they were not primarily structured to change environmental behaviour. The Pledge, and the reasons for the change in the definition, rests on the idea of proportion rather than value. Thus, while fuel duty is expected to increase by 12 per cent to over £30 billion in 2015–16, as a percentage of total revenue it will fall from 5.1 per cent to 4.5 per cent.[47] However, a proportional approach is highly dependent on the tax mix. An increase in the proportion of revenue raised through environmental taxes may rather be the result of a decrease in revenue from income and company taxes.

Thus, while the ratio or proportion of environmental taxes to total tax revenue has been decreasing, the actual tax revenue has increased over 35 per cent over the period 1998–1999 to 2010–2011.[48] Around 60 per cent of total environmental tax receipts come from fuel duty; tax revenue from road vehicles is now the highest on record since records began in 1993.[49]

But has there been a change in behaviour? Consider the landfill tax, an environmental tax under both definitions. Introduced in October 1996, its objectives were to properly price landfill waste disposal and to encourage sustainable waste disposal.[50] But it was also seen as able to raise revenue.[51]

There are predominantly two ways to measure a behavioural effect: increasing recycling and reuse activities or decreasing volumes of waste disposal. Independent studies have had mixed results. For example, a study by the European Environment Agency in 2000 found the UK landfill tax effective.[52] Other studies have concluded low impacts generally.[53] A 2001 European Commission study found that, while the overall impacts on landfill waste disposal have been limited, commercial and industrial waste producers have decreased their landfill waste. However, this was a combination of reduced waste disposal to landfill sites and the result of new packaging regulations, tempered with increasing dumping of waste at home and/or civic amenity sites to avoid the tax. Indeed, an increase in fly-tipping and a diversion of waste to unlicensed sites has been a 'substantial and additional burden to local authorities as a result of the tax'.[54]

In the 2005 Budget, the government stated that the total volume of waste disposed to landfill had fallen nearly 20 per cent over the period 1997–1998 and 2003–2004, with a corresponding decrease in inert or inactive waste of 60 per cent.[55] Data collated by HM Revenue and Customs from taxpayer declarations shows a consistent decrease in total volumes of waste sent to landfills. This trend is consistent with data collated by the Environment Agency. However, Environment Agency data, notwithstanding it is a government agency, only relates to England and Wales, thereby excluding Scotland and Northern Ireland.[56]

Independent verification of waste disposal volumes is difficult due to a lack of consistent data. A lack of clear and consistent data prevents a thorough assessment being made. Nevertheless business rates the landfill tax highly. Three reasons given are that the tax has a clear purpose and is compatible with other waste reduction policy measures, the determination of the rate provides certainty when making long-term investment decisions and it is designed to complement their target industries operations.[57]

Another environmental tax where an effect should be easily ascertainable is the air passenger duty which is charged on the number of passenger flights from UK airports. It has had a chequered history. Introduced in 1994 to compensate for the aviation industry's exemption from VAT and from fuel duty, it has been restructured repeatedly. In 2001 airports in the Scottish Highlands and Islands were granted duty free status and the rate was halved; in 2007 the rate was substantially increased; in 2009 it was restructured to levy higher duties on longer distances; and in 2013 it was extended to smaller aircraft and business jets.

The justification for the tax has been variously portrayed as being for equity, revenue and environmental reasons. For example the 2007 rate increases were based on environmental impacts. At that time the transport industry was responsible for 30 per cent of all carbon emissions with the aviation sector accounting for one fifth of that.[58] Even though not a HMT environmental tax, the government has acknowledged that the air passenger duty would have some environmental impact by reducing demand by 'perhaps 5 million passengers out of 140 million a year by 2010', equivalent to between 0.2 and 0.5 million tonnes of CO_2 a year.[59]

However, it appears to have had little impact, with passenger numbers increasing from nearly 60,000 in 1998 to over 100,000 by 2007. As a result of the global financial crisis numbers decreased but in 2013 are again approaching 100,000.[60] Air travel is an inelastic service, meaning that its environmental impact is generally small proportionate to its cost.

4. TENTATIVE CONCLUSIONS AND SUMMARY OF ISSUES

Can an assessment be made as to how effective environmental taxes have been from an environmental perspective? At this point in time it would appear unlikely and more research is required. What impedes this are issues relating to both the classification of, and the characteristics of, environmental taxes. These are discussed in turn before an assessment is made as to whether it matters.

4.1 Classification

Some taxes have been designed specifically to meet environmental goals. Examples include the United Kingdom landfill tax and climate change levy and, in Australia, the carbon pricing mechanism. Some existing taxes have been restructured to reflect environmental aims. The luxury car tax in Australia and various road vehicle and fuel taxes in both Australia and the United Kingdom could fall within this category. Lastly, some taxes have an environmental impact even though they were not introduced for environmental reasons. In the United Kingdom the air passenger duty as well as boat and fishing licences are examples, while in Australia some of the transport taxes would be possible contenders.

HMT's definition requires adherence to three principles. From a definitional perspective, it is the first that is contentious. Namely, 'the tax must be explicitly linked to the Government's environmental objectives'.[61] It raises questions as to what is deemed an environmental tax as these can change with a change of government. This makes it subjective and defined by government-of-the-day objectives.

It would also appear to be politically motivated. The government needs to uphold its Pledge to increase the proportion of revenues from environmental taxes. With pressure to reduce motoring costs[62] this commitment would be difficult to meet if motor vehicle taxes were deemed environmental taxes. Indeed changes to motoring taxes and air passenger duty announced in the Budget 2011 will reduce forecast revenues.[63] By excluding fuel duty and air passenger duty from HMT's definition, there will be no incentive to increase them as part of the commitment to increase the proportion of environmental taxes. This could be politically astute.

However, it is interesting to note that all HMT-defined environmental taxes were introduced as being revenue neutral. That is, they were all accompanied by a decrease in contributions to National Insurance. This was under the slogan of shifting from taxing 'goods' to taxing 'bads'.

But it is not only the United Kingdom that has definitional issues. How a tax is defined affects its classification. In Australia, excise on crude oil, LPG, gas and petroleum products is classified as an environmental tax; the petroleum resource rent tax (PRRT) is not. However, the scope of the excise was narrowed when the scope of the PRRT was broadened to include production from Bass Strait, a large petroleum precinct. As they essentially cover the same commodity, why is the PRRT not classified as an environmental tax?

Then it is difficult to see why the luxury car tax is an environmental tax. Adopting the SEEA definition, to be an environmental tax it must have the effect of reducing environmental degradation. All cars have a negative effect on the environment. Indeed, older cars produce a disproportionate share of total emissions.[64] Yet only those costing more are penalised.

4.2 Characteristics

Traditionally an environmental tax was deemed to be successful environmentally if the revenue raised by the tax declined. That can no longer be the measure. What is clear from the above discussion is that, while their revenue raising ability can be readily determined, their environmental performance is more difficult to assess. The difficulty in collecting and collating data can be attributable to the characteristics of environmental taxes.

Their scope has expanded, from an almost exclusive focus on transport and fossil fuel taxes, to cover waste disposal, quarrying and energy efficiency. The nature of these taxes has also expanded from specifically targeted taxes to broad-based revenue raising instruments. But environmental taxes are nonetheless characteristically fragmented. Of the approximately 375 taxes deemed environmental taxes (as noted in the opening paragraph), 150 are levied on energy products, 125 relate to motor vehicles and 50 address various forms of waste. The range includes taxes on batteries, logging, tyres, plastic bags, pesticides, beverage containers, water pollution, groundwater extraction, ozone depletion, among others.

The rapid growth of environmental tax measures has not been accompanied by a clear strategy. Indeed, there is no coherent landscape in which business can invest with confidence. What has necessarily resulted is a piecemeal or fragmented approach.

A problem with environmental taxes is that it is difficult to evaluate their efficacy as the actual environmental impact is often uncertain. It is difficult to identify the extent to which taxation, rather than some other factor or policy, is responsible for behavioural change. For example, can a reduction in emissions be directly attributed to a particular tax? Often the tax is part of a broader policy package making a tax-only assessment not only extremely difficult but also not necessarily useful.

4.3 Does it Really Matter?

HM Treasury argues that environmental taxes are designed to change behaviour. And, because they may change behaviour to such an extent that little or no revenue is generated at all, they are distinguishable from those taxes where there is certainty of demand. An example of the former is the Welsh plastic bag tax where usage has decreased by over 95 per cent in less than a year.[65] In contrast, a tax on fuel may curtail usage but it will nevertheless remain a permanent revenue base.

It is submitted that the difference between the revenue of the two types of taxes has nothing to do with how to define an environmental tax but everything to do with its elasticity of demand. A good or service is considered to be highly elastic if a slight increase in price (due to a tax, for example) leads to a sharp decrease in the quantity demanded or supplied. The more substitutes there are the less the revenue will be. Goods or services seen as necessities (such as the use of a motor vehicle) are more insensitive to price changes. Indeed, inelastic demand provides one important reason for taxing them for fiscal reasons. Yet the most important measure of the success of an environmental tax, however defined or classified, is not the revenue it raises but the change in behaviour it achieves.

Assessing their effectiveness does matter. It has policy, design and application implications. For example, does the current environmental tax regime provide enough incentive to develop, say, the renewable energy industry? And it has implications for the entire tax system. Determining whether environmental taxes are more effective than, say, income tax expenditures, requires being able to assess the effectiveness of both.

Much research is needed in this area. However, without relevant and appropriate data and without unambiguous classification, it is difficult to determine where the behavioural change is.

NOTES

* I would like to thank the anonymous reviewers for their helpful comments and suggestions.

1. OECD (1994), *Managing the Environment: The Role of Economic Instruments*, Paris: OECD, 22.
2. OECD (2006), *The Political Economy of Environmentally Related Taxes*, Paris: OECD, 10.
3. *See*, for example, D. Pearce and P.K. Turner (1992), 'Packaging waste and the polluter pays principle: a taxation solution', *Journal of Environmental Planning and Management*, 35 (1), 5–15.
4. *See*, for example, C.E. Ciocirlan and B. Yandle (2003), 'The Political Economy of Green Taxation in OEGD Countries', *European Journal of Law and Economics*, 15,

203–18; W.J. Baumol and W.E. Oates (1988), *Theory of Environmental Policy*, 2nd edn., Cambridge: Cambridge University Press.

5. *See*, for example, A.L. Bovenberg and L.H. Goulder (2002), 'Environmental Taxation and Regulation', in A.J. Auerbach and M. Feldstein (eds) *Handbook of Public Economics, Volume 3*, Amsterdam: North Holland Elsevie; D. Pearce (1991), 'The Role of Carbon Taxes in Adjusting to Global Warming', *The Economic Journal* 101 (407), 938–48.
6. D. Fullerton, A. Leicester and S. Smith (2008), 'Environmental Taxes', Report prepared for the Commission on Reforming the Tax System for the 21st Century, The Institute for Fiscal Studies, Oxford University Press.
7. United Nations and others (2012), *System of Environmental-Economic Accounting: Central Framework*, 4.150.
8. Price elasticities measure the responsiveness of the quantity demanded of a good to a change in its price. The more substitutes there are available, the higher the elasticity of demand. That is, a small price increase will result in a large decrease in demand.
9. United Nations and others, above n 7, 4.154.
10. European Commission and Eurostat (2001), *Environmental Taxes – a Statistical Guide*, Luxembourg: European Communities, 9.
11. OECD (2006), above n 2.
12. European Union (2011), 'Regulation (EU) No 691/2011 of the European Parliament and of the Council', *Official Journal of the European Union*, L192, Volume 54, 22 July 2011, Article 2.
13. Treasury (2013), 'Appendix C: Revenue and Receipts History and Forecasts', *Pocket Guide to the Australian Tax System*, Canberra: Commonwealth of Australia.
14. C. Heady (2010), 'Directions in Overseas Tax Policy', *Australia's Future Tax and Transfer Policy Conference: Proceedings of a Conference*, Melbourne: Melbourne Institute, 15.
15. ABS (2012), 'Environment', *Year Book Australia 2012*, Canberra: Australian Bureau of Statistics, 118.
16. Department of Climate Change and Energy Efficiency (2011), 'National Greenhouse Gas Inventory Accounting for the Kyoto Target', *Australian National Greenhouse Gas Accounts*, Canberra: Commonwealth of Australia, 10.
17. Including goods and services tax (GST) but excluding government fees and charges such as stamp duty, registration and compulsory third party insurance.
18. To be classified as 'fuel efficient' the vehicle must have a combined cycle fuel consumption of no more than 7.0 litres per 100 kilometres. Australian Taxation Office (2013), 'Luxury Car Tax: What is the Luxury Car Tax Threshold and the Fuel-efficient Car Limit for the 2013–14 Financial Year?' *Luxury Car Tax Determination*, LCTD 2013/1, 22 May 2013.
19. Explanatory Memorandum, *A New Tax System (Luxury Car Tax) Bill 1999*.
20. Australia's Future Tax System (2010), *Report to the Treasurer*, Canberra: Commonwealth of Australia. ('Henry Review').
21. The 2008–2009 luxury car tax threshold for cars and fuel-efficient cars was AU$57,180 and AU$75,000 respectively: Australian Customs and Border Protection Service (2008), 'Amendments to Luxury Car Tax Legislation – Fuel Efficient Luxury Cars', Australian Customs Notice No. 2008/51.
22. C. James (2007), 'The CommSec Luxury Car Index: Spending & Wealth Perspectives', *Economic Insights*, CommSec, 21 March 2007.
23. These are Aston Martin, BMW, Bentley, Ferrari, Jaguar, Lamborghini, Lexus, Lotus, Maserati, Maybach, Mercedes Benz, Morgan, Porsche and Rolls Royce. A notable absentee is Audi.
24. T. Beissmann (2011), 'Toyota Australia Calls for Luxury Car Tax to be Abolished', available at www.caradvice.com.au/124059/toyota-australia-calls-for-luxury-car-tax-to-be-abolished/, accessed 14 November 2013.
25. B. Park (2012), 'Tax Breaks Favour Fuel Guzzlers', available at www.news.drive.com.

au/drive/motor-news/tax-breaks-favour-fuel-guzzlers-20120704–21grm.html, accessed 14 November 2013.
26. R.B. Carson, W.L. Thomas and J. Hecht (2005), *Economic Issues Today: Alternative Approaches*, 8th edn., New York: M.E. Sharpe, Inc.
27. ABS (2012), *Motor Vehicle Census, Australia*, Canberra: Australian Bureau of Statistics.
28. ABS (2013), *Sales of New Motor Vehicles, Australia*, Canberra: Australian Bureau of Statistics.
29. C. Gillett (2012), 'Luxury Car Sales on the Rise in Australia', available at www.news.com.au/money/cost-of-living/luxury-car-sales-on-the-rise-in-australia/story-fnagkbpv-1226476013834, accessed 14 November 2013.
30. ABS (2012), above n 27.
31. HM Treasury (2012), 'Definition of Environmental Tax Published', Press Notices 60/12, 16 July 2012.
32. ONS (2013), 'UK Environmental Accounts, 2013', *Statistical Bulletin* 26 June 2013, London: HMSO.
33. Also called *The Coalition: Our Programme for Government*. It is the policy document that forms the terms of reference governing the Cameron Ministry as a result of a hung parliament following the 2010 general elections.
34. HM Treasury (2011), *Budget 2011* HC 836, 1.111.
35. Environmental Audit Committee (2011), Budget 2011 and Environmental Taxes, 7; ONS (2013), above n 32.
36. ONS (2013), above n 32.
37. HM Treasury (2012), above n 31.
38. Ibid.
39. House of Commons Environmental Audit Committee (2012), 'Autumn Statement 2012: Environmental Issues', Fourth Report of Session 2012–2013, 13 November 2012.
40. Environmental Audit Committee (2011), 'Budget 2011 and Environmental Taxes'.
41. HM Treasury (2012), above n 31.
42. M. Fallon (2013), 'Energy and Climate Change Committee', Supplementary written evidence, House of Commons Select Committee.
43. E. Ares (2013), 'Carbon Price Floor', Standard Note SN/SC/5927, Science and Environment Section, House of Commons Library, 15 March 2013.
44. HM Treasury (2012), above n 31.
45. ONS, 'FOI request: National Accounts Classification', available at www.ons.gov.uk/ons/about-ons/what-we-do/FOI/foi-requests/government/national-accounts-classification-committee--nacc-/index.html?format=print, accessed 31 July 2013.
46. HM Treasury (2012), above n 31.
47. ICAEW Communities, 'Environmental Taxes – A New Definition', available at www.ion.icaew.com/TaxFaculty/25005, accessed 31 July 2013.
48. ONS (2013), above n 32.
49. Ibid.
50. A. Martin and I. Scott (2003), 'The Effectiveness of the UK Landfill Tax', *Journal of Environmental Planning and Management*, 46 (5), 673–89; Ecotec (2001), 'Study on the Economic and Environmental Implications of the Use of Environmental Taxes and Charges in the European Union and its Member States', *Final Report*, Brussels/Birmingham: European Commission.
51. Ecotec, above n 50.
52. EES (2000), 'Environmental Taxes: Recent Developments in Tools for Integration', *Environmental Issues Series No. 18*, Brussels: European Environment Agency, 50.
53. Ecotec, above n 50; Martin and Scott, above n 50.
54. H. Bartelings, P. van Beukering, O. Kuik, V. Linderhof and F. Oosterhuis (2005), *Effectiveness of Landfill Taxation*, Amsterdam: Institute of Environmental Studies, Amsterdam, 10.
55. Ibid.

56. Environment Agency, 'Waste Data and Information', available at www.environmentagency.gov.uk/research/library/data/34169.aspx, accessed 17 September 2013.
57. S. Mayne and L. Ringer (2012), *Solving a Taxing Puzzle*: *Making Environmental Taxes Work for Business*, London: CBI.
58. House of Commons Deb, 6 December 2006, c310.
59. House of Commons Treasury Committee (2008), 'Climate Change and the Stern Review: The Implications for Treasury Policy'. Fourth Report of Session 2007–08, HC 231, 5 February 2008, 110.
60. HM Revenue and Customs (2013), 'Air Passenger Duty (APD) Bulletin – June 2013', available at www.hmrc.gov.uk/statistics/air-pass.htm#1, accessed 20 September 2013.
61. HM Treasury (2012), above n 31.
62. *See*, for example, G. Osborne (2011), 'Autumn Statement', Press Release, HM Treasury, 29 November 2011.
63. G. Osborne (2011), *Budget 2011*, London: HM Treasury.
64. US Congress, Office of Technology Assessment (1992), *Retiring Old Cars*: *Programs to Save Gasoline and Reduce Emissions*, Washington, DC, US Government Printing Office.
65. A. Vaughan (2012), 'Plastic Bag Use in Wales Plummets Due to 5p Charge, Figures Show', *The Guardian*, 4 July 2012.

13. Abatement of emissions for a sustainable future: revisiting the carbon tax in China

Yuhong Zhao

1. INTRODUCTION

Prior to the Copenhagen Conference in 2009, China had announced its voluntary national target to reduce carbon intensity, measured by CO_2 emissions per unit of gross domestic product (GDP), by 40–45 per cent by the year 2020 compared with the 2005 level.[1] The 12th Five-Year Plan for Social and Economic Development (2011–2015) (12th FYP) sets the domestically binding target of a 17 per cent cut of carbon intensity by 2015 as compared to the 2010 level.[2] Also in 2009, France proposed a carbon tariff imposed at EU borders on imports from countries not subject to greenhouse gas (GHG) emissions control (mainly emerging economies of China, India and Brazil). The US House of Representatives passed the *American Clean Energy and Security Act* in the same year to apply border tax adjustments (BTA) against imports of carbon-intensive products effective from 2020. Although the French proposal was not adopted by the EU for fear of the outbreak of a trade war, and the US Bill was defeated in the Senate, the idea of carbon pricing and border adjustments continue to be on the agenda of China's major trading partners.

There is immense pressure on China, the world's largest CO_2 emitter, to take immediate actions to curb fast-growing carbon emissions. Carbon tax is seen as a potentially effective market mechanism to supplement the conventional command-and-control approach to abatement of emissions in China[3] and perhaps a workable solution to counteract potential BTA proposed by developed countries.[4] As a market instrument, carbon tax has been tried and tested by other countries. Scandinavian countries adopted carbon taxes in the 1990s, but they differ considerably in terms of tax base and tax rate (Ekins and Barker 2001, 341; also *see* Andersen and Ekins 2009). The United Kingdom (UK) introduced the climate change levy (CCL) in 2001. CCL is imposed on industrial and commercial use of energy, excluding transportation and residential use. Taxpayers can enter into agreements with the government to reduce emissions in exchange for a significantly reduced tax rate, effectively converting CCL into a command-and-control regulation.[5]

As for the potential application of BTA, the World Trade Organization (WTO) in principle allows importing countries to impose differentiated customs duties on products from countries with weaker environmental constraints under the so-called 'environmental exception', that is, trade restrictions are allowed if needed to protect 'human, animal, or plant life or health' or if they relate 'to the conservation of exhaustible natural resources' and 'such measures are made effective in conjunction with restrictions on domestic production or consumption'.[6] Yet all proposed BTA only target products not subject to GHG or carbon emission control in the country of origin. Introduction of the carbon tax could arguably avoid the carbon tariffs imposed at the border.

Researchers affiliated with the Ministry of Finance (MOF) published its study on carbon tax in 2009 and recommended the introduction of the new tax in 2012–2013 as an important market tool to abate carbon emissions. It proposed a low tax rate of 10 yuan/tC at the initial stage with steady increase so as to avoid strong objection from the relevant industries (Su et al. 2009; also *see* Shi 2009). Simultaneously, another research team affiliated with the Ministry of Environmental Protection (MEP) also studied carbon tax and made policy recommendations (Wang et al. 2009). Yet, by the end of 2013, carbon tax still remains a subject of research rather than implementation.

This chapter revisits carbon tax and argues that despite the short-term burden on enterprises, industrial sectors and the domestic economy in general, it should be a burden that China is able and willing to bear now for the long-term best interest of the nation and the much wider international community. Section 2 briefly discusses the carbon tax proposals put forward by the two research teams affiliated with the MOF and MEP respectively, noting the slightly different priorities given their missions and responsibilities. Section 3 examines the causes for the delay in the introduction of carbon tax and major concerns from different sectors. Section 4 explores measures and strategies to address the concerns over introducing carbon tax in China.

2. CARBON TAX: MARKET TOOL FOR ABATEMENT OF EMISSIONS

Carbon tax has been introduced as a market tool to internalize externalities associated with anthropogenic GHG emissions. It aims to abate carbon emissions through price signal. The burning of fossil fuels (coal, petroleum and natural gas) contributes to 65–85 per cent of the total CO_2 emission. By increasing the cost of fossil fuels, carbon tax aims to encourage investment and technological advancement in energy efficiency, energy conservation and switch to cleaner alternatives of wind, solar and hydro-power. Of the three fossil fuels, coal has the highest carbon content per unit of energy, followed by petroleum and natural gas.[7] If carbon tax is set at the right level so that energy-intensive enterprises and industrial sectors respond positively to improve energy efficiency and make more use of clean and renewable energies, China's heavy reliance on coal, which accounts for roughly 70 per cent of primary energy consumption currently, can be alleviated in the foreseeable future. Control of the growth in coal production and consumption will not only lead to abatement of carbon emissions, but also substantial cut in SO_2 and NOx associated with coal-burning.

2.1 The Tax Base

Theoretically an ideal carbon tax system should cover all activities that produce climate externalities including GHG emissions from energy use, agriculture, forestry and industrial emissions. In practice, law and policy makers are bound to consider administrative, enforcement and political costs of implementing the tax regime. Many sources are very small contributors and hard to measure and tax. As a compromise, a carbon tax is normally levied on the basis of carbon content of fossil fuels including coal, petroleum and natural gas (Hoeller and Wallin 1991, 92), major sources of GHG emissions.[8] The collection and enforcement costs for a tax on emissions from fossil fuels are relatively low. A unit of fossil fuel will emit the same amount of carbon regardless of when or where it is burned. For carbon emissions from fossil fuel combustion, there is an almost perfect correspondence between input and output. Therefore, it is possible to tax the input – the fossil fuels – rather than the output – the emissions. The exception to this is fossil fuel permanently sequestered such as fuel used for tar or carbon that is captured and stored (Metcalf and Weisbach 2009, 523).

The four major uses of fossil fuels are industrial, transportation, residential and commercial. Electricity acts as an intermediate source of emissions – emissions result from the generation of electricity. In general, items likely to offer low-cost abatement and monitoring should be included in the tax base. This is, however, subject to the specific tax system already in existence and the political reality of each country. For example, the UK CCL excludes transportation and residential energy use.

Both proposals recommend that the carbon tax base should cover anyone who emits CO_2 in the process of production or operation powered by fossil fuels of coal, petroleum and natural gas. Considering foreign experience in implementing carbon tax and China's technological and regulatory capacity in monitoring the actual CO_2 emissions, the carbon tax should be calculated on the basis of respective carbon contents of coal, petroleum and natural gas rather than actual CO_2 emissions (Su et al. 2009, 15–16; Wang et al. 2009, 103). However, taxing input (production or consumption of fossil fuels) instead of output (emissions) has one drawback. It creates no incentive for carbon sequestration through carbon capture and storage (CCS), a new technology to capture CO_2 emissions from coal combustion in electricity generators and permanently sequester carbon. By CCS, the CO_2 is compressed, liquefied and transported to a geologically desirable location where it is stored underground. Special allowance or credits have to be offered to those who apply CCS in the design of carbon tax to encourage carbon sequestration.

2.2 The Tax Rate

According to Pigou, the optimal tax rate is where the marginal benefit of abatement equals the marginal cost of abatement.[9] However, it is tremendously difficult to calculate or estimate the optimal tax rate as a result of scientific uncertainty relating to climate change. Prediction of the local effects of climate change combined with prediction of economic and technological developments in the distant future renders accurate calculation a mission impossible. An alternative is to determine a set of taxes over time that would result in meeting a target for emissions reductions or total carbon concentrations in the atmosphere (Metcalf and Weisbach 2009, 511–12). The tax rate shall be re-examined at appropriate intervals (Metcalf and Weisbach 2009, 501), and adjusted over time as new information becomes available about the costs and benefits of reducing emissions.

Studies have found that the higher the carbon tax rate, the more significant an impact on emission cut. At the rate of 20 yuan/tC, China can achieve abatement of 90 million tons of CO_2 emission, or 4.5 per cent of total carbon emission; at the rate of 50 yuan/tC, an abatement of 190 million tons of CO_2 emission, or 9.5 per cent of total carbon emissions; at the rate of 100 yuan/tC, China can achieve an 18.6 per cent cut in total carbon emissions.[10] There is also direct correlation between tax rate and energy saving. Compared to a baseline scenario without carbon tax, China can achieve energy saving of over 20 per cent at a tax rate of 200 yuan/tC, or close to 3 per cent at a tax rate of 20 yuan/tC (Wang et al. 2009, 102).

Determining the tax rate is also a process of setting priority among the goals of carbon tax and various social, economic and political considerations in implementing the tax regime. Researchers affiliated with MOF agree in principle that carbon tax rate should reflect the cost of emissions abatement so that tax payers will react to the tax positively. However, taking into account the political reality of introducing a new tax and its impact on the macro-economy and industrial competitiveness, they recommended a low tax rate of 10 yuan/tC in 2012 with steady increase to 40 yuan/tC in 2020 (Su et al. 2009, 16–17). In contrast, the research team affiliated with MEP proposed an initial tax rate of 20 yuan/tC in 2012, with steady increase to 50 yuan/tC in 2020 and 100 yuan/tC in 2030, even though they accepted the strategy of low tax rate at the initial stage with gradual increase to an optimal level (Wang et al. 2009, 104). Clearly, the latter proposal gives more weight to the effectiveness of carbon tax in emissions abatement.

2.3 Collection of Carbon Tax

A further issue to be decided is whether to tax GHGs on the basis of where the products giving rise to emissions are produced (an origin basis) or where the products are consumed (a destination basis). In deciding where to impose the tax, one should focus on minimizing collection and monitoring costs while ensuring maximum coverage. Collecting the tax upstream, i.e., at the earliest point in the production process, will achieve these goals because there are far fewer upstream producers than there are downstream consumers. The cost will be lower per unit of tax due to economies of scale in tax administration.

Foreign experience and study show that natural gas is the most carbon-efficient fossil fuel in the sense that it produces the largest amount of energy for a given quantity of CO_2 emitted. The collection point for the tax on natural gas needs to minimize administrative costs while maximizing coverage. The two most likely places to do this are at the operator level or at the processing plant (plus imports and coal-bed methane) (Metcalf and Weisbach 2009, 525). Coal can be taxed at the production level (mines and import points) or at the consumption level (electric utilities and industry) (Metcalf and Weisbach 2009, 526). The two potential places to tax petroleum products are at the source (the well or import point) or at the refinery. The advantage of taxing refineries is that they could pay a separate tax on each distillate depending on the carbon content. Distillates, such as tar, that would not be burned would not be subject to tax. Imports of crude oil from countries without a carbon pricing system would be subject to the tax at the refinery without any special provision, while imports of refined products can be taxed at the border if they are from a country without a carbon pricing system (Metcalf and Weisbach 2009, 527).

In China, there is debate as to whether to collect carbon tax imposed on fossil fuels at the stage of production or consumption. The former, collecting tax from those in the business of production, refinery or reprocessing of fossil fuels, is more conducive to the control at source and effective collection at lower transaction cost, while the latter, collecting tax from wholesalers or retailers, will send clearer price signals to consumers to deter use. This is where the two proposals diverge. The one from MOF proposed collection of tax at the production point to achieve maximum efficiency while the one from MEP preferred collection from consumers of fossil fuel to encourage conservation (Su et al. 2009, 17; Wang et al. 2009, 104).

2.4 Use of Carbon Tax Revenue

The use of carbon tax revenue is also subject to debate in China. Should it become part of the general revenue (shared by central and local governments) or special revenue earmarked for designated use (also known as special fund for special use)? The proposal of MEP advocated for the establishment of a special State Fund with the carbon tax revenue used for promotion of energy efficiency, energy conservation, renewable energy, low-carbon technologies and carbon sinks (Wang et al. 2009, 104). MOF preferred the general revenue approach as it will address the regressive nature of carbon tax in the long term, even though it agreed with MEP that China has realistic short-term needs to invest more resources to support energy efficiency, promote energy conservation, develop clean and renewable energy and expand carbon sinks (Su et al. 2009, 18). Revenue from carbon tax should be best used to help China transform from high-speed growth to low-carbon development.

3. OBSTACLES TO IMPLEMENTING CARBON TAX

Resistance to carbon tax has exceeded expectation, which explains years of deliberation after policy recommendations were made by researchers affiliated with MOF and MEP. Concerns range from the adverse economic impact on GDP growth and international competitiveness to social implications relating to the gap between the rich and the poor, as carbon tax is likely to generate substantially different impacts on different industrial sectors, different geographical regions and different income groups.

3.1 Detrimental Impact on Domestic Economy and Regional Development

China is still undergoing the process of industrialization and its economic growth has largely relied on heavy industry powered by fossil fuels. Carbon tax has significant impact on energy-intensive industries. Levying carbon tax will likely affect national economic growth negatively at least in the short to medium term. It is difficult, if not impossible, to predict with certainty how long the transition will take, how much it will cost in both productivity and growth terms, and whether the public supports carbon tax in the longer term.

The impact of carbon tax on economic growth will vary geographically, further widening the gap in development between the East and the West. In China, energy consumption and carbon emissions vary regionally due to different economic structures. Poor provinces in the West and Southwest with abundant natural resources mainly engage in the manufacturing of primary products and high-carbon products. Carbon tax will increase the production cost of local firms and slow down local economic development. Provinces in the East coastal region are more involved in deep processing and high-tech industries with low-carbon emissions. Carbon tax may offer new opportunities to stimulate low-carbon growth in the economically advanced East China. They are technologically capable of taking advantage to benefit from the incentives offered by the tax, whereas the Central and Western provinces more reliant on energy-intensive industries will end up paying more and suffer the pain.

3.2 International Competitiveness

Carbon tax increases the marginal production costs and potentially weakens the international competitiveness of Chinese enterprises. At the firm level, competitiveness is the ability of a firm to maintain or increase international or domestic market share and profitability. It can be affected by carbon tax through increased production costs. Potential losers strongly oppose the levy of carbon tax and even threaten to relocate to countries without carbon tax. At the sector level, electricity and heat supply sectors are likely to be the most affected industrial activities out of the 36 sectors, due to their high reliance on fossil fuels. But, the incremental carbon cost could be passed on to downstream users. In the absence of foreign competitors, the competitiveness impact on this sector is slight. The same is true for the gas production and supply sector. Among the manufacturing sectors, the ferrous metal production sector is potentially most affected by carbon tax because of the high fossil fuel intensity, in particular, the high coal dependency of the sector (Wang, Li and Zhang 2011).

Researchers concluded that if a carbon tax is introduced at low initial rate of 10 yuan/tC, no significant competitiveness impacts at the sector level are found. If at a higher rate of 50 yuan/tC or 100 yuan/tC, certain compensatory measures become necessary for those significantly affected (Wang, Li and Zhang 2011, 4150).

3.3 Social and Income Distribution Concerns

Carbon tax reduces carbon emissions mainly through price signals. It raises the energy price to deter use and encourage conservation. But studies found that carbon tax is likely to be regressive. That is, it generates a heavier burden on low-income households (Metcalf and Weisbach 2009, 513). Energy consumption is a basic need which cannot be displaced. Low-income households have to spend a much higher percentage of their income on energy consumption, e.g. electricity, than high-income households do. Thus, the concern that carbon tax will inevitably further enlarge the gap between the rich and the poor (Xue 2011, 79).

3.4 Interaction with Existing Environment-Related Taxes

In China, resource tax levied on coal, crude oil and natural gas indirectly relates to carbon emissions, although it neither distinguishes the carbon content of different fossil fuels nor reflects the external carbon costs of coal, gas or oil. In addition, consumption tax imposed on gasoline and diesel, vehicle and vessel usage tax, and vehicle purchase tax all relate to emissions resulting from combustion of fossil fuels to a certain extent. The newly proposed carbon tax levied on fossil fuels may result in overlaps of taxation.

4. STRATEGIES TO EASE THE RESISTANCE TO CARBON TAX

Despite the objections to carbon tax and concerns over its social and economic impacts, abandoning the idea is not a viable alternative. As the world's largest GHG emitter, China has an obligation to control and mitigate carbon emissions even though that obligation is not legally binding under the current international climate regime. In order to successfully extend the Kyoto Protocol to its second implementation period (2012–2020), China agreed to negotiate control of total carbon emissions beyond

2020. Carbon tax is one of the market instruments that have been tried and tested by many countries as an effective economic tool with limited negative impacts on domestic economy and international competitiveness (Andersen and Ekins 2009). Given that China is still a developing country with top priority being economic growth, a politically feasible carbon tax policy has to address all valid concerns adequately in order to gain public acceptance and support.

4.1 Low Initial Tax Rate with Progressive Increase

The research team affiliated with MEP found that carbon tax will have negative impact on GDP growth, but it is very limited. At the rate of 20 yuan/tC, a potential loss of 0.1 per cent GDP is possible compared to no carbon tax scenario. Even imposing a carbon tax of 100–200 yuan/tC from 2010 to 2030, the maximum loss of GDP is 0.45 per cent. Note that such projection has not taken into account the positive growth driven by development in clean energy and technology innovation (Wang et al. 2009, 102). Chances are that the loss of dirty GDP can be well compensated by green GDP growth. The team recommended an initial tax of 20 yuan/tC imposed in 2012, with gradual increase to 50 yuan/tC in 2020 and 100 yuan/tC in 2030 (Wang et al. 2009, 104). Meanwhile, the think tank affiliated with MOF proposed an even lower initial rate of 10 yuan/tC in 2012 with steady increase to 40 yuan/tC in 2020 (Su et al. 2009, 17), hoping to allow the Chinese economy to adjust without too much pain and minimize the detrimental impact on China's international competitiveness and the welfare of its people. Despite the differences in the rate, there is no dispute that tax rates must be adjusted to reflect new information about the marginal cost and benefit of abatement. New information is likely to arise all the time as the science of climate change progresses and as abatement technologies are discovered and developed.

To address the concern over disproportional adverse impacts on regional development, options include lower carbon tax rates for the inland provinces and redistribution of carbon tax revenue to inland regions to support local economies (Zhang and Ya 2011). If carbon tax is introduced without the simultaneous adoption of an effective redistribution policy, it will likely aggravate regional economic imbalance in China.

As to the competitiveness argument from the energy-intensive industries such as steel and cement producers, they face the potential challenge of carbon tax imposed at the border by China's major trading partners if they continue to produce high-carbon products for export. Carbon tax imposed domestically will not only help traditional energy-intensive industry to embrace the concept of low-carbon production through technology innovation but also avoid BTA sooner or later imposed by other countries.

4.2 Maintain Overall Tax Burden: Tax Neutral Approach

A further strategy to ease the political resistance of introducing new carbon tax is to take a tax neutral approach, i.e., lower other taxes such as profit tax, income tax and social security tax to maintain the overall tax burden. By way of tax shifting, there is no sudden and substantial increase in the overall tax burden for each tax payer, which can effectively soften their objection to a new tax.

4.3 Special Tax Relief to Energy-Intensive Industries Subject to Conditions

While carbon tax at a low rate of 10 yuan/tC does not generate significant competitiveness impact at the sector level, a high tax rate of 100 yuan/tC necessitates certain compensatory measures to keep the negative impacts to the minimum. Measures include a tax cut or a redistribution of carbon tax revenue to sectors where competitiveness is significantly affected (Wang, Li and Zhang 2011).

Carbon tax will have disproportionate impacts on certain industries such as the coal industry. Due to the very high carbon content of coal, it cannot be exempted from an effective carbon tax regime. But transitional assistance is needed. To ease the adverse effect of carbon tax, the government may offer tax reduction or exemption to the especially affected energy-intensive industrial sectors or enterprises during the transition period. As these tax relief measures will weaken the very function of carbon tax, that is, to increase the cost of carbon-intensive fossil fuels and abate emissions, their use has to be temporary and subject to strict conditions conducive to long-term sustainable development. Such conditions can be emissions abatement agreements signed between government and enterprise to achieve specific targets or to invest in the new technology of CCS.

4.4 Tax Relief and Subsistence for Low-Income Households

The design of carbon tax has to take care of low-income households and alleviate the regressive distributional impacts of carbon tax. There are different approaches to address these special needs. One way is to set a tax-free allowance for essential use of energy by imposing tax on energy only above a certain floor. Another solution is to offer financial subsistence to help alleviate the burden of increased costs of daily energy consumption on low-income households.

5. CONCLUSION

Abatement of emissions from the burning of fossil fuels is of crucial importance for China's long-term sustainable development. Over three decades of economic growth, industrialization and urbanization have been powered by fossil fuels. Large-scale expansion of heavy industry such as cement, aluminium, iron and steel production have substantially driven up energy demand in a country that is 'coal-rich, oil-short and gas-less' (Zhang, Wang and Huang 2011, 1101).[11] Coal, the most carbon-intensive fossil fuel, makes up roughly 70 per cent of China's primary energy consumption. China became the world's largest producer and consumer of coal in the 1990s (Andrews-Speed 2009), and the use of coal is on the rise. From now to 2020, China has to develop effective measures to abate carbon emissions and be prepared for legally binding obligations beyond 2020. Carbon tax as an effective market instrument should be implemented to supplement cap-and-trade and command-and-control regulatory approaches.

NOTES

1. The voluntary target of cutting carbon intensity by 40–45 per cent by 2020 compared with the 2005 level was set at the Executive Meeting of the State Council chaired by Premier Wen Jiabao on 25 November 2009. For more details, *see* http://www.gov.cn/ldhd/2009-11/26/content_1474016.htm, accessed 15 January 2014. The commitment was clearly made to the international community by Premier Wen at the Copenhagen Conference. *See* 'Speech by Wen Jiabao on Building Consensus and Strengthening Cooperation' (18 December 2009), at Xinhua Net http://news.xinhuanet.com/world/2009-12/19/content_12668033.htm, accessed 15 January 2014.
2. The 12th FYP, Chapter 3 Major Targets. These targets are expressly specified by the 12th FYP and approved by the National People's Congress (NPC). They are binding on the central and local governments. Using the 11th FYP as an example, pressure was intense on local officials responsible for delivering both GDP growth and energy-efficiency improvements. In order to meet the targets of 20 per cent cut in energy intensity, the last-minute rush in the end of 2010 took the form of blackouts and forced factory closures that caused serious social and economic disruption.
3. *China's National Plan on Climate Change* was promulgated in June 2007 to take a range of legal, economic, administrative and technological measures to mitigate GHG emissions and enhance its adaptation capacities. In December 2007, CCP Central Committee at its meeting on economic issues expressly demanded 'speeding up the implementation of fiscal, tax, pricing and financial policies to promote energy conservation and emissions abatement'.

4. Proposed BTA for carbon tax imposes tax at border on imports from countries without adequate carbon pricing and offers rebates to exports to such countries.
5. For more details about the climate change levy, *see* http://www.hmrc.gov.uk/climate-change-levy/, accessed 15 January 2014; *see* also comments by Richardson and Chanwai (2003) 39–58.
6. GATT, art. XX.
7. *See* Energy Information Administration, US Department of Energy, *Voluntary Reporting of Greenhouse Gases Program: Emission Factors and Global Warming Potentials, Fuel Emission Factors*, available at http://www.eia.gov/oiaf/1605/emission_factors.html, accessed 15 January 2014.
8. They made up approximately 80 per cent of all US emissions. *See* US EPA (2008), *Inventory of US Greenhouse Gas Emissions and Sinks*: *1990–2006*.
9. At any level of emissions, the correct tax rate should equal the social marginal damages from producing an additional unit of emissions or, more or less equivalently, the social marginal benefit from abating a unit of emissions. *See* Pigou (1932).
10. Wang et al. (2009), at 103. Another study found that a levy of 100, 150 and 200 yuan per ton of standard coal from 2012 will decrease the consumption of coal by 4.88 per cent, 7.31 per cent and 9.75 per cent respectively in 2020, which will lead to the decrease of CO_2 emissions by 8.69 per cent, 13.02 per cent and 17.36 per cent respectively in the same year. *See* Zhang et al. (2011), at 1106.
11. According to Carbon Dioxide Information Analysis Center (CDIAC), coal burning takes up 66–84 per cent of total CO_2 emissions from energy consumption. *See* http://cdiac.ornl.gov/, accessed 15 January 2014.

REFERENCES

Andersen, Mikael Skou and Paul Ekins (eds) (2009), *Carbon-Energy Taxation: Lessons from Europe*, Oxford: Oxford University Press.

Andrews-Speed, Philip (2009), 'China's Ongoing Energy Efficiency Drive: Origins, Progress and Prospects', *Energy Policy*, 37, 1331–44.

Ekins, Paul and Terry Barker (2001), 'Carbon Taxes and Carbon Emissions Trading', 15 *Journal of Economic Survey*, 15, 325–76.

Hoeller, Peter and Markku Wallin (1991), 'Energy Prices, Taxes and Carbon Dioxide Emissions', *OECD Economic Studies*, 17, 91–105, at 92, available at http://www.oecd.org/eco/greeneco/34258255.pdf, accessed 15 January 2014.

Metcalf, Gilbert E. and David Weisbach (2009), 'The Design of a Carbon Tax', *Harvard Environmental Law Review*, 33, 499–556.

Pigou, A.C. (1932), *The Economics of Welfare*, London: Macmillan.

Richardson, Benjamin J. and Kiri L. Chanwai (2003), 'The UK's Climate Change Levy: Is It Working?' *Journal of Environmental Law*, 15, 39–58.

Shi, Jiangtao (2009), 'Think Tank Calls for Carbon Tax by 2013', *South China Morning Post*, 24 September 2009, at 4.

Su, Ming, Zhihua Fu, Wen Xu, Zhigang Wang, Xin Li and Qiang Liang (2009), 'China's Roadmap to Carbon Tax', *Environmental Economy*, (9) 10–22.

Wang, Jinnan, Gang Yan, Kejuan Jiang, Lancui Liu, Jintian Yang and Chazhong Ge (2009), 'China's Carbon Tax Policy in Response to Climate Change', *China Environmental Science*, 29(1), 101–05.

Wang, Xin, Ji Feng Li and Ya Xiong Zhang (2011), 'An Analysis on the Short-term Sectoral Competitiveness Impact of Carbon Tax in China', *Energy Policy*, 39, 4144–52.

Xue, Gang (2011), 'Conflict and Coordination Problem of Carbon Tax's Diversity Targets in China – Based on the Tax Optimization Theory', *Chinese Journal of Population, Resources and Environment*, 9(2), 76–83.

Zhang, Kezhong, Juan Wang and Yongming Huang (2011), 'Estimating the Effect of Carbon Tax on CO_2 Emissions of Coal in China', *Journal of Environmental Protection*, (2) 1101–07.

Zhang, Zhixin and Li Ya (2011), 'The Impact of Carbon Tax on Economic Growth in China', *Energy Procedia*, 5, 1757–61.

14. Effects and issues of the 2010 resource tax reform in Xinjiang

Yanmin He

1. INTRODUCTION

Resource taxation has received wide attention in recent years.[1] Government intervention through tax policy instruments is well recognized as essential for optimal exploration of mineral reserves, the maximization of mineral rents, the maintenance of environmental standards, and the creation of incentives for reinvestment of mineral rents. Some industrialized countries have already imposed various kinds of resource tax on natural resources, such as a severance tax in the United States, a mining tax in Canada, and a mine products tax in Japan.

China's resource tax system was implemented in 1984 under the Draft Regulations on the Resource Tax. This system levies and collects a tax on enterprises and individuals in China engaged in the extraction of crude oil, natural gas, coal, and metallic and non-metallic products. However, systemic deficiencies in the resource tax system have become apparent as China has pursued its reform and opening-up policy and its economic conditions have changed (Zhang 2007; An & Jiang 2008; Fu 2012; Li and Du 2008; Wang 2010). Although the system was previously reformed in 1993 under the Provisional Regulations on the Resource Tax, the tax system has not been modified again during the past 20 years. Beginning in 2010, the government began a resource tax reform pilot program centered in the Xinjiang Uygur Autonomous Region (hereinafter, 'Xinjiang' or 'autonomous region').

Compared with other areas in China, the western regions possess more abundant resources but have relatively underdeveloped economies and weak financial bases. In particular, Xinjiang has the most abundant crude oil and natural gas reserves in China.[2] The pilot resource tax reforms were rolled out in Xinjiang and then expanded to 12 more areas in the western region.[3] Through this pilot program, a draft revision of the Provisional Regulations on the Resource Tax was enacted on November 1, 2011, as the new resource tax system. The new system transitioned from an amount-on-volume system based on sales volume to a fixed-rate ad valorem system based on sales revenue from crude oil and natural gas. At the same time, the system also substantially raised the tax rate on coal and certain other resources.

The Chinese government said that the main objectives of the Xinjiang resource tax reform are (1) to increase tax revenue in proportion to revenue obtained by companies engaged in resource development by raising resource prices and (2) to increase fiscal revenue in rural regions, and to thereby improve regional social security and public services.[4] However, at present, only two years have passed since the launch of the new resource tax system, and only a few studies on Xinxiang's resource tax reform have been conducted. Previous studies mainly analyzed the impacts of resource tax reform from a national perspective (Xi 2010; Cao, Han and Qi 2011; Fu 2012; Zhen 2012). In addition, the existing literature on Xinxiang's resource tax reform has focused mainly on quantitatively estimating its degree of influence and qualitatively analyzing its mechanism of influence (Zhang et al. 2013). Although the reforms have had a direct and significant impact on resource conservation and local revenue in western provinces, there have been few attempts at active empirical research.[5]

In this chapter, the existing statistical data and materials from the period 2000–2012, before and after reform, are used to analyze the reform's inhibitory effects on resource extraction and the impacts on tax revenue. Through this, we discuss the goals and challenges of the Xinjiang resource tax reform and offer suggestions regarding the evaluation and results of the 2011 nationwide resource tax reform.

2. GOALS AND CHALLENGES IN XINJIANG RESOURCE TAX REFORM

2.1 Substance of Xinjiang Resource Tax Reform

Xinjiang, located in far western China, contains within its jurisdiction two prefecture-level cities (Ürümqi and Kelamayi), seven districts (Turpan, Kumul, Aksu, Kashgar, Hotan, Altai and Tarbagatai), and five autonomous prefectures (Ili Kazak, Bortala Mongol, Kizilsu Kirghiz, Bayingolin Mongol and Changji Hui). Through resource tax reforms, the taxation system on crude oil and natural gas in Xinjiang was changed from the previous amount-on-volume system to a fixed-rate ad valorem system. The resource tax rates before and after reforms are shown in Table 14.1. Based on the new tax rate, the amount of resource taxes on crude oil and natural gas is calculated by multiplying sales revenue by the tax rate.

Table 14.1 Resource tax rates before and after the Xinjiang resource tax reform

	Before June 2010	After June 2010
Crude oil	30 yuan/ton	5% of sales volume
Natural gas	9 yuan/1,000 m^3	5% of sales volume
Coal coke	8 yuan/ton	8 yuan/ton
Other coal	3 yuan/ton	3 yuan/ton
Other non-metallic raw ore	0.5–20 yuan/ton	0.5–20 yuan/ton
Ferrous raw ore	2–30 yuan/ton	2–30 yuan/ton
Non-ferrous raw ore	0.4–30 yuan/ton	0.4–30 yuan/ton
Solid salt	10–60 yuan/ton	10–60 yuan/ton
Brine	2–10 yuan/ton	2–10 yuan/ton

Sources: Circular on Adjusting the Standard for Resource Taxes on Crude Oil and Natural Gas; Provisional Regulations on Some Issues with Reform of Resource Taxes on Crude Oil and Natural Gas in Xinjiang; Provisional Regulations on Resource Tax; Rules for the Implementation of the Provisional Regulations on Resource Tax; Circular on Adjusting the Standard for Resource Taxes on Coking Coal; Circular on Adjusting the Standard for Resource Taxes on Coal in Xinjiang.

2.2 Effects of Xinjiang Resource Tax Reform

Hereafter, we will discuss the effects of the Xinjiang resource tax reform from two angles: (1) its inhibitory effect on total crude oil and natural gas extraction and (2) its reinforcing effect on the local fiscal base.

2.2.1 Inhibitory effect on total resource extraction

Figure 14.1 shows changes in total extraction of crude oil and natural gas in Xinjiang from 2000 to 2012.[6] There has been no significant change in the actual extracted amount of crude oil and natural gas since 2010. Total crude oil extraction from 2009 to 2012 has gradually increased from 25.1 million tons to 25.6 million tons, 26.15 million tons and 26.7 million tons. Total natural gas was nearly level at 24.5 billion m^3 and 25 billion m^3 extracted in 2009 and 2012, respectively. After falling slightly to 23.5 billion m^3 in 2011, it once again recovered to 25 billion m^3 in 2012.

Meanwhile, predicted total crude oil extraction levels in FY2010, FY2011 and FY2012, based on the assumption that total crude oil and natural gas extraction would increase at the same average rate as it did from 2000 to 2009 had resource tax reform not been carried out, are 25.99 million tons, 26.91 million tons and 27.87 million tons, respectively, while predicted total natural gas extraction levels are 31.3 billion m^3, 39.9 billion m^3 and 50.8 billion m^3 for these years. In other words, predicted total mining,

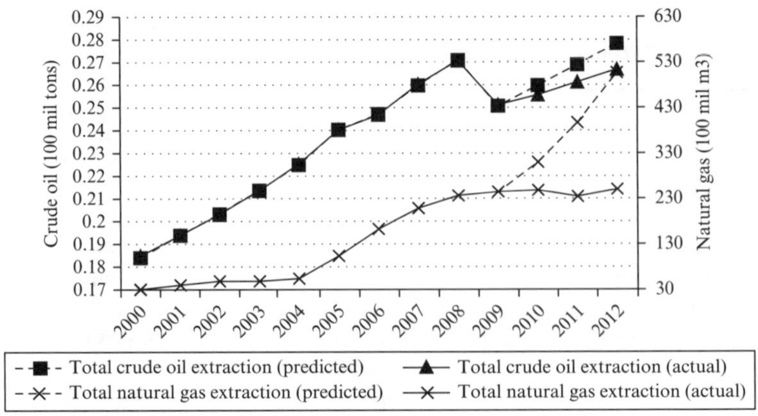

Source: Compiled with data from the 2012 Xinjiang Statistical Yearbook.

Figure 14.1 Changes in total crude oil and natural gas extraction (2000 to 2012)

had resource tax reform not been carried out, greatly exceeds actual total mining, and so resource tax reform played a certain role in inhibiting total resource extraction.

Changing the resource tax on crude oil and natural gas from amount-on-volume to an ad valorem tax, increasing the per ton tax (standard coal equivalent, or SCE) burden and providing mining companies with an incentive to reduce mining, was the likely reason why total resource extraction was inhibited. Based on the resource tax rate prior to Xinjiang resource tax reform, 99.6 billion yuan of resource taxes on crude oil and natural gas were collected according to the amount-on-volume method in 2011.[7] The tax burden of crude oil and natural gas per ton (SCE) is approximately 15 yuan.[8]

Meanwhile, the actual total amount of resource tax on crude oil and natural gas collected according to the ad valorem method in 2011 was 5.577 billion yuan, resulting in a tax burden of approximately 81 yuan/ton (SCE). There is a clear increase in the tax burden following the tax reform.[9]

2.2.2 Reinforcing effect on the local fiscal base

We will examine the reinforcing effect of resource tax system reform on local fiscal revenue from two perspectives: changes in resource tax revenue and changes in local fiscal revenue. The average rates of increase of resource tax revenue and the local fiscal base in Xinjiang from 2000 to 2009

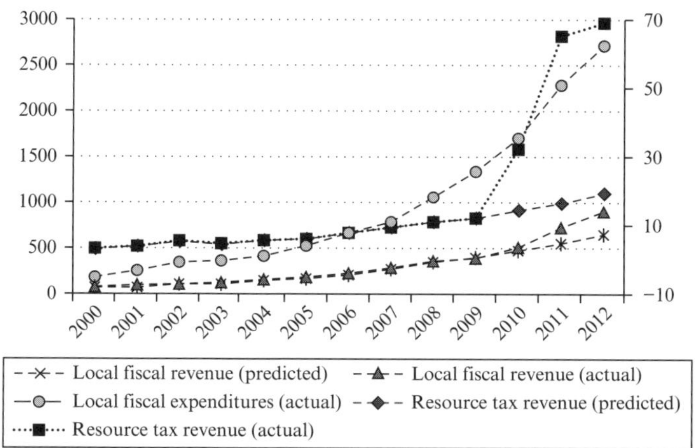

Notes: (1) FY2012 resource tax revenue data according to Xinjiang Daily (March 2, 2013, ed. 4); (2) FY2012 fiscal income and expenditure data based on Report on Xinjiang FY2012 Budget Implementation Status and the FY2013 Draft Budget; (3) does not include funded budget income or expenditures.

Source: Compiled by the author using data from the 2012 Xinjiang Statistical Yearbook.

Figure 14.2 Changes in resource tax revenue and local fiscal budget revenue and expenditures in Xinjiang (2000 to 2012)

were 17.44 percent and 19.56 percent, respectively. Predicted resource tax revenues for FY2010, FY2011 and FY2012, based on the assumption that resource tax revenue and local fiscal revenue would increase at the same average rate as they did from 2010 to 2012, are 1.433 billion yuan, 1.677 billion yuan and 1.962 billion yuan, while predicted local fiscal revenue would be 46.654 billion yuan, 55.985 billion yuan and 67.182 billion yuan.

Using these predicted values as the baseline, Figure 14.2 shows that actual resource tax revenue in FY2010 more than doubled compared to the baseline, while revenue in FY2011 and FY2012 nearly quadrupled versus the baseline. In FY2012, resource tax revenue reached 6.899 billion yuan, becoming the fourth largest tax item in Xinjiang behind business tax, personal income tax and corporate income tax.[10]

Similarly, as shown in Figure 14.2, we can discern an increase in local fiscal revenue in Xinjiang following the resource tax reform, and can see that the gap between fiscal income and expenditures has decreased. Resource tax revenue as a percentage of the total local budget income significantly increased from 3.2 percent to 7.0 percent between 2009 and 2012,[11] indicating that the proportion of resource tax revenue in local internal revenue sources increases due to resource tax reform. This suggests that resource tax reform directly contributed to the shrinking of local budget gaps. In particular, the recent resource tax reform focused on revising the crude oil and natural gas resource tax system, prompting a significant post-reform increase in resource tax revenue from crude oil and natural gas, which increased from a meager 0.766 billion yuan in FY2009 prior to reform, to 2.537 billion yuan in FY2010, 5.577 billion yuan in FY2011, and then to 5.749 billion yuan in FY2012.[12] Even the percentage of total resource tax revenue accounted for by crude oil and natural gas resource tax revenue increased, from 62.53 percent in FY2009 to 83.33 percent in FY2012.

Although the increase in resource tax revenue did serve to reduce the gap between the region's fiscal income and expenditures, this impact requires careful examination. As shown in Table 14.2, the year-over-year growth rates of fiscal revenue in resource-producing autonomous prefectures and districts in Xinjiang averaged 33 percent and 45 percent, respectively, exceeding that of the autonomous region as a whole following resource tax reform. Because statistical data on the resource tax revenue of each autonomous prefecture and district are not released, the extent of the direct contribution of resource tax revenue on local fiscal bases in these regions is unknown. However, the rate of increase in fiscal revenue in the five areas of Aksu, Bayingolin Mongol, Hotan, Kashgar and Kizilsu Kirghiz, collectively known as the Southern Xinjiang Area and having abundant crude oil and natural gas resources, was higher following the reform compared to other regions. Therefore, it is likely that resource tax reform contributes directly to strengthening the fiscal base of these areas.

2.3 Issues With Resource Tax Reform in Xinjiang

As is evident from the above analysis, altering the taxation of crude oil and natural gas has had a discernible inhibitory effect on total resource extraction and a reinforcing effect on the local fiscal base. In FY2009, prior to the reform, coal accounted for around half of total energy produced in Xinjiang, while total crude oil and natural gas production accounted for around a quarter.

If coal extraction were to continue from 2010 to 2012 at the same average rate of increase as from 2000 to 2009, as shown in Figure 14.3, predicted total coal extraction in FY2010, FY2011 and FY2012 would be approximately 71 million tons, 80 million tons and 90 million tons, respectively. But actual total coal extraction significantly outpaced the predicted values. As a result, total energy extraction also increased from

Table 14.2 Local fiscal revenue in Xinjiang autonomous prefectures and districts (units: yuan, %)

	Autonomous region		Ürümqi		Karamay		Turpan		Kumul		Changji		Bortala Mongol		Bayingolin Mongol	
	R	G	R	G	R	G	R	G	R	G	R	G	R	G	R	G
2005	180.3		51.4		23.3		5.8		3.8		11.7		3.4		12.8	
2006	219.5	22	57.0	11	28.8	24	7.7	34	4.7	25	13.9	19	3.8	13	16.2	26
2007	285.9	30	73.4	29	36.5	27	9.3	21	6.1	30	13.8	−1	4.8	26	19.6	22
2008	361.1	26	101.0	38	39.1	7	11.9	28	8.1	33	19.1	38	5.7	18	25.6	30
2009	388.8	8	113.5	12	33.3	−15	12.2	3	10.5	29	24.1	26	4.9	−15	26.6	4
2010	500.6	29	148.0	30	42.4	28	14.6	19	15.0	44	32.7	36	6.3	30	35.2	32
2011	720.4	44	206.2	39	51.0	20	20.4	39	23.5	56	48.2	47	8.2	30	49.1	40
	Kizilsu irghiz		Kashgar		Hotan		Ili Kazak		Tarbagatai		Altay		Aksu		Averages	
	R	G	R	G	R	G	R	G	R	G	R	G	R	G	R	G
2005	0.8		5.6		2.3		9.5		7.0		2.9		13.4		11.0	
2006	0.9	21	6.7	19	2.7	16	12.4	30	10.2	46	3.9	36	18.6	39	13.4	26
2007	1.2	31	8.1	22	3.2	17	14.7	19	12.6	24	6.2	59	25.6	38	16.8	26
2008	1.8	50	10.8	33	3.8	20	19.5	32	14.9	19	9.2	48	34.8	36	21.8	31
2009	2.3	23	14.7	37	4.5	18	23.9	23	13.7	−8	11.8	28	29.6	−15	23.3	11
2010	3.3	44	19.6	33	6.3	40	31.2	31	18.3	34	13.5	15	42.7	44	30.7	33
2011	5.5	70	28.8	46	9.3	48	44.7	43	25.8	41	20.0	48	62.1	45	46.3	45

Note: R represents annual fiscal revenue; G represents year-over-year growth rate.

Source: Calculated from the State Government Finance CEIC. Some data are revised based on statistical annual reports from Xinjiang districts.

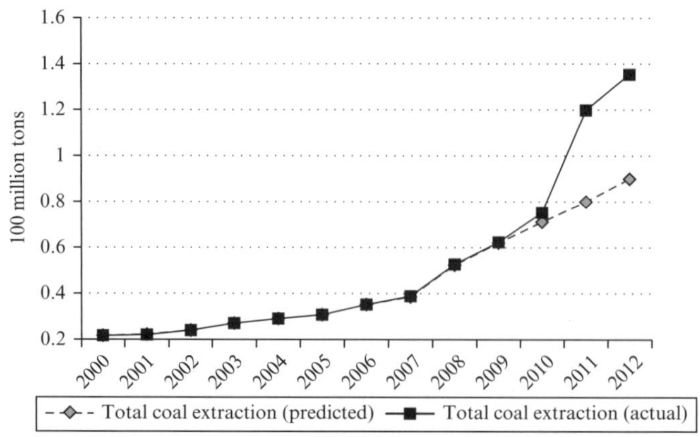

Source: Compiled by the author using data from the 2012 Xinjiang Statistical Yearbook.

Figure 14.3 Changes in total coal extraction (2000 to 2012)

131 million tons in 2009 to 200 million tons in 2012 (Xinjiang Statistical Yearbook, 2012).

In short, although the pilot reform did act to reduce total crude oil and natural gas extraction, the significant increase in coal extraction pushed up total energy production. Among the reasons for this, firstly, is that recent reforms were limited to crude oil and natural gas, which effectively promoted coal extraction and failed to inhibit total energy extraction. Secondly, with attention in recent years focused on resource depletion in coal-producing regions such as Shanxi Province and Inner Mongolia, 'Coal Industry Development' in the 11th and 12th Five Year Plans divided China's 31 districts into coal-importing areas, coal-exporting areas and self-sufficient areas. The 12th Five Year Plan classifies Xinjiang as a coal-exporting area and calls for the expansion of the scale of coal production.[13] Accordingly, the new investment productive capacity of coal extraction increased from 7.32 million ton in 2006 to 48.75 million ton in 2010; at the same time, the new investment productive capacity of coke increased from 3.24 million ton to 5.64 million ton.[14] As a result, fixed-asset investment in the coal industry led to an effective increase in coal extraction.

As is shown from the above analysis, the significant increase in resource tax revenue since 2010 in Figure 14.2 accrues from not only the increase in crude oil and natural gas resource tax revenue due to reform but also from the increase in coal extraction associated with the expansion of fixed-asset investment in the coal industry. Furthermore, resource tax reform contributed to bolstering the fiscal base of not only the Xinjiang but also the autonomous prefectures and districts under it. However, resource distribution between autonomous prefectures and districts is inherently unequal, so in regions with rich reserves of crude oil and natural gas, resource tax revenue rapidly increased due to the reform, while the fiscal revenue gap between regions widened in comparison with the past. As a result, prior to resource tax reform in 2009, the difference in per-capita fiscal revenue between Altay, the lowest, and Kumul, the highest, was 1,827 yuan; however, after reforms the difference in per-capita fiscal revenue between Altay, which does not have crude oil and natural gas resources, and Turpan, which has rich oilfields, increased from 2,545 yuan in FY2010 to 3,578 yuan in FY2011.[15] In other words, resource tax reform may have widened the fiscal revenue gap in Xinjiang. Unless authorities do not reallocate a portion of resource tax revenue allocated to the autonomous region through some kind of fiscal adjustment system, there is concern that a public service gap may develop between different areas.

3. CONCLUSIONS

The results of the 2010 resource tax reform in Xinjiang are as follows. Firstly, changing the resource tax on crude oil and natural gas from an amount-on-volume tax to an ad valorem tax increased the tax burden per ton (SCE) and provided extraction companies with an incentive to reduce extraction of the resources subject to the new tax system. Secondly, the reform significantly increased resource tax revenue, raised local fiscal revenue, and reduced the local budget gap at the autonomous region level. Moreover, reforms also contributed to reinforcing the fiscal base of autonomous prefectures and districts in the autonomous region.

However, the experience of resource tax reform in Xinjiang reveals several challenges. Firstly, because the reform was limited to crude oil and natural gas, it promoted coal extraction and failed to inhibit total energy extraction. As a result, the reform indirectly increased the adverse impacts on the environment of resource extraction.[16]

Secondly, although resource tax reform contributes to strengthening the fiscal base, resource distribution is unequal between autonomous prefectures and districts, prompting concern that the resource tax system reform has widened the fiscal revenue gap between areas within the autonomous region.

These issues provide definite clues with regard to the nationwide implementation of the new resource tax system in 2011, because the new system switches from an amount-on-volume tax to an ad valorem tax on only crude oil and natural gas, leaving the amount-on-volume taxation for coal and all other mineral resources the same as before, which is very similar to reform in Xinjiang. In China, township and village mining enterprises have played a large role in the economic development of lagging regions with abundant resources, thus promoting urbanization and creating jobs. Because of this, authorities cannot afford to allow tax hikes to interfere with the development of these companies. This is why authorities first decided, for the time being, to apply the ad valorem resource tax to the crude oil and natural gas sector, before expanding the tax to other sectors.[17]

Through economic growth, China has become the world's largest primary energy consumer. Its consumption of mineral resources such as coal is expected to increase further as per-capita living standards continue to increase, boosting demand for primary energy in the civil sector. Therefore, authorities will need to increase the tax burden of per-unit resources and incentivize mining companies to reduce mining by switching to an ad valorem taxation system that also applies to coal and other mineral resources.

Moreover, there is concern that mineral resources tend to be unevenly distributed, so levying taxes on them can potentially widen the fiscal gap between regions. Because mineral resources come with instability and unpredictability, their prices fluctuate widely in the global market and fiscal revenue from mineral resources also fluctuates greatly. However, a local fiscal base entails many recurring expenses, so sufficient and stable local tax revenue that is free from the vicissitudes of economic conditions is desirable. In this sense, it is difficult to say that resource tax revenue is an ideal source of fiscal revenue for local governments.

NOTES

1. The origin of the resource tax is widely recognized as Harold Hotelling's 1931 paper, 'The Economics of Exhaustible Resources.' In this paper, he treated the effects of a severance tax or a tax on the value of a mine as a non-renewable resource price and output paths.
2. Xinxiang's estimated crude oil and natural gas reserves of approximately 36.5 billion tons account for almost 30% of China's total land reserves. These reserves consist of 22.7 billion tons of crude oil and 13.8 trillion cubic meters of natural gas (Kang 2007).
3. The government promulgated the Circular on Provisions on Several Issues Concerning the Reform of the Resource Tax on Crude Oil and Natural Gas in Xinjiang in June 2010 and the Circular on Issuing the Provisions on Several Issues Concerning the Reform of the Resource Tax on Crude Oil and Natural Gas in Western Regions in December 2010. The western region contains Chongqing, Sichuan, Guizhou, Yunnan, Shaanxi, Gansu, Ningxia, Qinghai, Xinjiang, Inner Mongolia, Guangxi and Hubei provinces.
4. Response from a supervisor at the State Administration of Taxation to a question from a journalist about the future of resource tax reform in Xinjiang, June 7, 2010 (State Administration of Taxation, http://www.chinatax.gov.cn/, accessed July 9, 2013).

5. Zhang and Wang (2012) analyzed the impact of the regional fiscal revenue in Xinjiang based on financial statements of enterprises. However, the analysis was limited to five districts around Tarim Basin.
6. In this study we analyze data on 'total energy production' from the Xinjiang Statistical Yearbook (2012) as no official statistical data on total resource extraction are available.
7. Calculation for crude oil based on 30 yuan/ton; for natural gas, 9 yuan/1,000 m^3.
8. Conversion to SCE tons based on coefficients (10,000 tons of crude oil = 14,300 tons SCE; 1 m^3 of natural gas = 13,300 tons SCE) provided in general principles for calculation of total production energy consumption (GB2589–81).
9. Using statistical data from 2012, the changes in tax burden for crude oil and natural gas before and after reforms was 66 yuan/ton, which also indicates a clear increase.
10. *Xinjiang Daily* (March 2, 2013, ed. 4).
11. Calculated from the 2012 Xinjiang Statistical Yearbook; Report on Xinjiang FY2012 Budget Implementation Status and the FY2013 Draft Budget.
12. *Xinjiang Daily* (June 4, 2013, ed. 12).
13. In 'Coal Industry Development' in the 12th Five-Year Plan, coal produced in Xinjiang is planned for export to Western Gansu, Qinghai, Sichuan and Chongqing.
14. Calculated from Xinjiang Statistical Yearbooks (2008 to 2012).
15. Calculated from the State Government Finance CEIC. Some data are revised based on statistical annual reports from Xinjiang districts.
16. The activities of the coal industry can result in a number of adverse impacts on the environment such as land use, water pollution and air pollution caused by the coal mining. In addition, the burning of coal produces a large amount of solid waste products including fly ash, bottom ash, and flue-gas desulfurization sludge.
17. Response to a journalist from a supervisor at the Ministry of Finance and Administration of Taxation on the revision of three administrative regulations, including 'Provisional Regulations on the Resource Tax' (October 10, 2011); response from the Ministry of Finance and Administration of Taxation on issues related to the revision of 'Provisional Regulations on the Resource Tax' (October 24, 2011) (Chinese Central Government, http://www.gov.cn/, accessed July 9, 2013).

REFERENCES

An, T. F. and Z. Jiang (2008), 'Resource Tax Reform in China: Existing Issues and Further Suggestions', *International Taxation in China*, 5, 10–13.

Cao, A. H., B. T. Han, and A. T. Qi (2011), 'The Policy Research on the Resource Tax Reform in China', *China Population, Resources and Environment*, 21, 158–63.

CEIC Data Company Ltd., China Premium Database (*see* http://www.ceicdata.com/).

Fu, L. (2012), 'China's Resource Tax Reform', *Forestry Economics*, 5, 117–19.

Hotelling, H. (1931), 'The Economics of Exhaustible Resources', *Journal of Political Economy*, 39(2), 137–68.

Kang, Y. Z. (2007), 'Survey and Exploitation Potential of Oil-gas Resources in Xinjiang Area', *Acta Petrolei Sinica*, 28(4).

Li, W. B. and H. Y. Du (2008), 'Research on the Crude Oil and Natural Gas Resource Tax and Fee', *Research of Financial & Accounting*, 2, 24–5.

Xi, X. J. (2010), 'An Analysis on the Economic Effects of Resources Tax in China', *Co-operative Economy & Science*, 399, 92–4.

Xinjiang Statistical Bureau (ed.) (2008–2012), *Xinjiang Statistical Yearbook*, CN: China Statistics Press.

Wang, M. (2010), *Research on Resource Tax*. CN: Economic Science Press.
Zhang, H. J. and H. K. Wang (2012), 'The Local Finance Effects of the Xinjiang Resources Tax Reform', *Tribune of Social Sciences in Xinjiang*, 6, 18–24.
Zhang, J. (2007), 'Resource Tax Reform Design in China', *Taxation Research*, 11, 45–7.
Zhang, Z. K., J. E. Guo, D. Qian, Y. Xue and L. P. Cai (2013), 'Effects and Mechanism of Influence of China's Resource Tax Reform: A Regional Perspective', *Energy Economics*, 36, 676–85.
Zhen, W. (2012), 'An Empirical Analysis on the Impact Factors of Resource Tax', *Financial Supervision*, 11, 69–70.

15. Macroeconomic effects of environmental tax subsidy reform: an evaluation for Italy

Cristina Brandimarte[1]

1. INTRODUCTION

The increasing need to protect the environment and to enhance economic activity and employment, together with the opportunity for a shift from direct to indirect taxation, suggest the implementing of fiscal measures to support economic growth by envisaging levies on polluting consumptions, ensuring the sustainability of public debt.

Theoretical reasons for implementing environmental taxation reforms are well known and have been widely debated. An extensive literature has shown that fiscal instruments often constitute the most effective and efficient policies to improve the quality of the environment, by reducing externalities through the internalization of social costs and the stimulus to correct behavioral responses.

At first, analyses were mainly conducted in a microeconomic and partial-equilibrium perspective, but, since the 1980s, there has been growing awareness that environmental problems cannot be analyzed without considering macroeconomic issues. Many theoretical and empirical studies have therefore dealt with the evaluation of the macroeconomic effects of environmental taxes, highlighting the existence of a possible trade-off between environmental and other economic policy targets, in particular employment and economic and social welfare, mainly due to loss of competitiveness and tax regressiveness.[2]

In the 1990s the literature has analyzed the possibility of obtaining a 'double dividend', that is a reduction of pollution and higher levels of employment, using the additional government revenues from the environmental tax to reduce other taxes or to increase expenditures in order to eliminate existing distortions, to offset negative effects and to support growth and employment (Pearce 1991; Ulph, Ulph and Pezzay 1991; Bovenberg and de Mooij 1994). Many studies have considered, in particular, the effects of environmental fiscal reforms involving on one hand the introduction of environmental taxes and on the other side the reduction of taxes on labor, leaving the budget balance unchanged. These analyses found that the effects of an environmental taxation reform strongly depend, besides specific features of the implemented fiscal measures, from elasticities of economic variables to changes in economic conditions and from the pre-existing level and structure of taxation, pointing out that it is basically impossible to draw generally-valid conclusions.

In the 2000s, the problem of the public budget became particularly relevant. The weight of public debt to gross domestic product (GDP) reached high levels in the world and fiscal sustainability became the most important and urgent economic policy target in many countries, resulting in the need for a strict control on public budgets. In the euro area severe fiscal rules have been adopted, binding member countries to achieve balanced structural budget balances and progressive reductions of the debt to GDP ratio. Moreover, environmental reforms are currently often considered as a useful tool that could help address fiscal problems (Gale, Brown and Saltiel 2013). In this context, a careful evaluation of the consequences on public finances (both direct and indirect ones, also considering interactions between fiscal and macroeconomic variables), becomes particularly important.

In this chapter, short to medium term effects of an environmental tax reform on economic growth and public finance in Italy are evaluated with the support of the ISTAT (Italian National Institute of Statistics) macroeconometric model on the Italian economy,[3] in order to identify the main risks and opportunities arising from the implementation of specific fiscal measures. In particular, the introduction of a duty on petroleum products and five different re-uses of additional revenues are considered. The analysis is carried out with the rough glance of the macroeconomist, as measures and effects are not outlined with fine micro details, exclusively dealing with broader macroeconomic linkages.

The remainder of this chapter is organized as follows. Section 2 briefly discusses why to consider a tax on petroleum products. Section 3 deals with macroeconomic effects and describes the structure of the model's transmission channels. Section 4 describes the hypotheses and presents the results of the simulation exercises. Finally, some conclusions and policy implications follow in section 5.

2. WHY A DUTY ON PETROLEUM PRODUCTS

2.1 Theoretical Indications

Since its early development, theoretical literature on environmental taxes has identified some general principles for an efficient level of reduction of environmental damage. First of all, the direct imposition of taxes on potential environmental damage is recommended (Pigou 1920).

Subsequent literature has shown that, although in principle taxes should be differentiated according to the marginal damage caused by the polluting agent, the imposition of a uniform price (equal to the average marginal damage) minimizes administrative costs and, in this way, generally leads to greater well-being than the one obtainable with differentiated prices (Baumol and Oates 1971; Baumol 1972; Pearce 1991; Muller and Mendelsohn 2007).

The consideration of administrative costs also suggests the levy of environmental taxes upstream, at the point where the source of pollution enters the economic system, to limit the number of checks, to ensure greater coverage and to reduce the risk of political pressure to get reduced rates at the local, sectoral or individual level (Heine, Norregaard and Parry 2012).

Further contributions suggest to carefully evaluate interactions between environmental taxes and other regulations or existing taxes, as they can change the behavioral responses, the optimal level of the tax and the related costs (Conefrey et al. 2008).

2.2 Tax on Petroleum Products

Since one of the most critical factors impacting the environment is currently represented by carbon dioxide (CO_2) emissions and in line with theoretical indications, economists have long recommended specific taxes on fossil energy sources, in particular a tax on carbon dioxide or 'carbon tax' (Metcalf, 2008; Sumner, Bird and Smith 2009). Among these, a duty on petroleum products has many positive aspects.

First of all, it is a corrective, Pigouvian tax that allows for achieving a more efficient allocation of resources by incorporating negative externalities into market prices. Moreover, it ensures costs minimization as it establishes a uniform price on emissions for all sources. Further, as consumption of a given amount of oil produces a fixed amount of CO_2 emissions, an excise tax on petroleum products is directly linked and proportional to the damage caused by emissions.

It is also effective in reducing emissions both in the short and in the long run, providing a stimulus to private research and innovation for technological progress that involves the use of renewable energy sources and promoting energy-saving behaviors, larger use of renewable energy and energy-efficient goods consumption.

It is consistent with the origin principle, which is to tax the pollutant upstream, and involves low administration costs because it is easier to identify the polluting content of raw materials and intermediate goods, such as petroleum products, compared to that of final goods.

Moreover, an excise tax on petroleum products does not overlap with the EU Emission Trading System as CO_2 emissions coming from fossil fuel combustion are largely excluded from this regulation. It has been remarked (Tol 2007; Conefrey et al. 2008) how imposing a domestic tax on sectors subject to EU regulation in a single country would be ineffective at European level and expensive for the country. In fact, each ton of emissions saved in the country would be emitted in other European areas, while the cost of reducing emissions would rise where the tax has been introduced and decrease elsewhere.

Finally, a duty on petroleum products can have further positive effects such as helping to reduce dependence on foreign energy sources, giving the opportunity to reform and simplify other policies (Gale, Brown and Saltiel 2013) and providing resources to improve the tax system, by removing distortionary measures, or to reduce the public deficit (Parry and Williams 2011).

3. MACROECONOMIC EFFECTS AND TRANSMISSION CHANNELS

3.1 Effects of a Carbon Tax

Over the past 20 years, several countries have introduced a carbon tax in Europe: Sweden, Denmark, Norway and Finland in the early 1990s, followed by the Netherlands and Germany at the end of the decade and Turkey in the early 2000s. Its implementation, however, has often been largely hampered and gradually reduced in size due to growing concerns about its negative consequences on the domestic economy (Heine, Norregaard and Parry 2012).

Theoretical and empirical research shows that a carbon tax could have restrictive effects on economic activity and employment both directly, through changes in relative prices, and indirectly through second round effects on prices and competitiveness and on saving and investment decisions.

With regard to public finance, there is a trade-off between environmental effectiveness and fiscal sustainability, since the introduction of the tax causes a reduction in its tax base that will be greater the more the tax is effective in reducing the polluting consumption. But the effects on public finances do not end there, of course, because the changes in macroeconomic conditions deriving from the tax introduction also have an impact on government accounts.

In Italy, the introduction of a carbon tax could present both opportunities and risks. The potential for a carbon tax in Italy turns out to be wide (EEA 2011) and the weight of indirect taxes relatively low. In addition, Italy is a strong net importer of petroleum products and a carbon tax would improve terms of trade and would reduce dependence on foreign products and energy sources. Risks arise instead because the tax burden is already very high and the introduction of environmental taxes can only be favorably viewed if other taxes are reduced. On the other hand, however, when the level of taxation is high, the reduction of more distortionary taxes could produce large benefits. Moreover, public finance conditions, characterized by a high level of public debt and by severe government budget constraints, join low economic growth perspectives, requiring a careful design of a fiscal reform in order to harm neither the economy nor public accounts.

3.2 The Model

This chapter provides a macroeconomic evaluation of the introduction of a carbon tax in Italy with the support of the ISTAT structural macroeconometric model (Memo-It).

In short, Memo-It[4] is based on a New-Keynesian approach, assuming that in the short-run the economic activity is mainly driven by the demand side, while in the long-run the economic system converges to potential output given by the supply side. The adjustment toward equilibrium is driven by price reaction to the output gap.

The public sector is represented according to an institutional approach which allows for the evaluation of both direct and indirect effects of fiscal policies on the economic system and for assessing the impact of macroeconomic changes on government accounts. Main items of the general government accounts are endogenous and broadly defined by accounting identities and algebraic relations describing accounting and normative rules, while instrumental variables are set exogenously.[5] Public finance variables are mainly linked, through estimated econometric relations, to disposable income, demand, prices and labor costs.

Imbalance between supply and demand influences prices, which, in

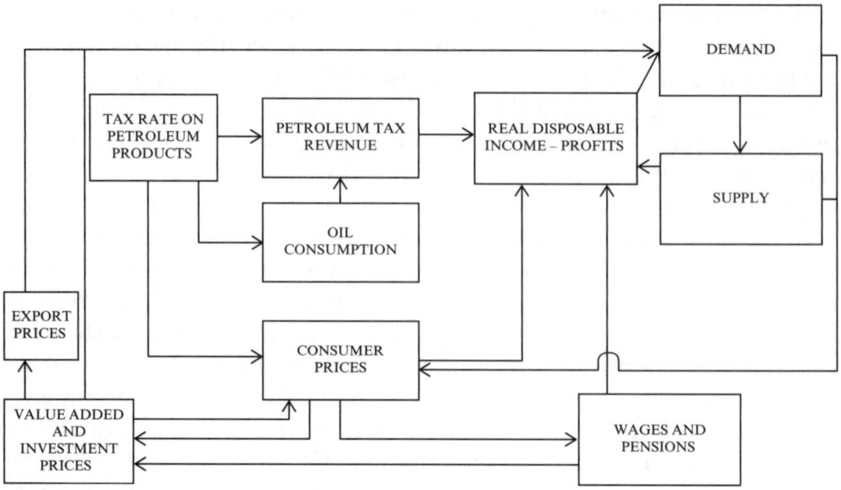

Figure 15.1 Carbon tax transmission channels

turn, feed back to demand variables and affect wages. Demand variables have an impact on employment and supply side variables through capital stock formation. Demand and labor market conditions affect tax bases which, combined with exogenous tax rates, define government revenues.

Labor demand depends on output and, inversely, on real labor costs. Wage determination follows a Phillips curve and depends on unemployment rate and lagged inflation.

3.3 The Transmission Channels

Main transmission channels considered are shown in Figure 15.1. First of all, carbon tax has an impact on consumer prices and the consumption of petroleum products,[6] which, combined with the tax rate itself, determines government revenues.

In turn, these variables affect real disposable income and profits and, in this way, consumption and investment in the demand rectangle and then feed back to consumer prices.

Initially, there is no significant impact on value added, GDP and export deflators, as their estimated impact elasticities to changes in petroleum products prices are low. Subsequently, however, consumer prices affect wages and pensions and, together with higher intermediate goods prices, increase all deflators, with feedbacks to the demand rectangle.

With regard to public finance, the effects of the carbon tax go through the following transmission channels: direct and indirect tax bases are affected by consumption and income; nominal public investment is influenced by changes in investment deflator and the level of private investments affects public subsidies; private wages and inflation affect compensation of employees and pensions; all the above effects and the additional revenues from the carbon tax change public deficit and debt. In turn, public debt influences interest payments and then, together with compensation of employees and pensions, affects disposable income. Then, macroeconomic variable changes feed back again to public finance.

With regard to fiscal measures provided to recycle carbon tax revenues, the effects go through the following transmission channels. A cut in employers' social contribution tax rate affects labor demand and employment, prices and profits and then social contribution revenues. Further, it affects tax bases and other items of the public budget (subsidies to private investment) through changes in consumption, investment and income. The increase in government subsidies to private investment and the expansion of public investment directly affects government expenditures and total investments. Finally, a cut in the personal income tax rate impacts on government revenues and disposable income.

4. SIMULATIONS HYPOTHESES AND RESULTS

4.1 Hypotheses

In this chapter we simulate, over a four-year time horizon, the permanent imposition of a duty on petroleum products in Italy, with five different options for the use of revenues: to reduce public debt; to cut employers' social contribution; to support fixed capital formation through subsidies to private investment or through additional public investments; and to reduce taxation on personal income. All fiscal measures amount to 1 percentage point of GDP in the *ex-ante* evaluation, that is, in the hypothesis that economic agents do not change their behavior in response to the adopted measures, or, in other words, that the tax base remains unchanged.

The *ex-post* effects, accounting for direct and indirect effects, are evaluated with respect to a baseline scenario based on May 2013 ISTAT official forecasts.

All simulation exercises are based on the following hypothesis:

1. nominal interest rates and nominal exchange rates remain unchanged with respect to baseline. These hypotheses are consistent with the assumption of a small open economy belonging to a single currency area and also assume no significant effect on risk premium;

2. no relevant structural change occurs during the time horizon considered;
3. financial markets are functioning normally;
4. in the presence of progressive taxation, increases in nominal incomes are offset through the indexation of income brackets.

Simulation results, expressed in differential terms with respect to the baseline, are shown in Table 15.1.

4.2 Simulation A: Use of Carbon Tax Revenues to Repay Government Debt

In the first exercise we simulate the introduction of a duty on petroleum products that increases government revenues by 1 percentage point of GDP (about 16 billion euros) in the *ex-ante* evaluation.

Two periods can be distinguished: the first two years are characterized by no effect or a slightly positive one on economic activity and by a significant reduction of debt to GDP ratio; in the last two years a strong depressive effect on the economy and a slow reduction of debt to GDP ratio occur.

Regarding the first period, several factors affect economic activity in different ways.
Carbon tax has an impact on consumer prices and reduces real disposable income of households and then consumption, even if this negative effect will gradually be offset by lagged indexation of wages and pensions. Conversely, positive short term effects on economic activity come from:

- terms of trade gains: consumption of petroleum products, largely imported, decreases, and consumption of national products increases, that is imports decrease more than GDP and internal demand;
- reduction in real interest rates.

With regard to exports, negative effects are limited by low elasticities of both a) the value added and export deflators to changes in prices of petroleum products and b) foreign demand of Italian products to export deflator. These results could be explained by several factors: a low dependence of exporting firms' costs on changes in petroleum prices or entrepreneurs' behaviors not oriented towards translating them into final prices; a strong component of no price competitiveness in Italian exported products ('made in Italy'); and the behavior of Italian exporting firms that, in the presence of a weak demand or losses in price competitiveness, endeavor to strengthen their position in foreign markets.

When all the direct and indirect effects are taken into account (see Table 15.1, column A), GDP growth would be reduced by 0.2 percentage points in the first year due to the decline in domestic demand (−0.3%). The fall in demand is, however, largely related to petroleum products and therefore is associated with a stronger reduction in imports (−0.4). Consumer price inflation increases by 2.2 percentage points, more than GDP deflator (+1.6%) while no significant effect on export deflator is detected in the first year.

The government budget balance improves by 0.4 percentage points of GDP (about 6.5 billion) and the debt to GDP ratio falls 2.2 percentage points below the baseline.

In the second year, indexation of wages and pensions to lagged inflation supports household disposable income and domestic demand and, together with a sharp decline in imports, exerts an expansionary effect on GDP growth of 0.2 percentage point. Exports show, for the above reasons, a small reduction (−0.1). General government net borrowing improves by 0.5 percent of GDP and the debt to GDP ratio falls by 4 percentage points below baseline as a result of: the carbon tax; higher inflation, which increases revenues (through the so-called inflation tax) more than expenditures and pushes up the debt to GDP ratio's denominator; and the higher economic growth.

From the third year onward, second round effects on prices and production costs result in a significant loss of competitiveness. Although this does not significantly affect exports, it results in an increase in imports as consumption of domestic goods is reduced in favor of cheaper imported ones. As a result, domestic demand growth rate declines by 0.3 and 0.4 percentage points while growth rate of imports is higher than baseline (0.7 and 0.2% respectively).

In the last two years, GDP growth is lower by 0.6 and 0.5 percentage points respectively. Real disposable income is reduced (−1.6% and −2.2% with respect to baseline) by the increase in prices and the fall in employment.

As a result of higher inflation and of the tax measures adopted and despite the economic growth contraction, public finances continue to improve and debt to GDP ratio at the end of the simulation horizon is 5.3 percentage points lower than baseline.

4.3 Simulation B: Use of Carbon Tax Revenues to Cut Employers' Social Contributions

In this exercise carbon tax revenues are recycled to reduce employers' social contributions, with the additional hypotheses that expectations

Table 15.1 Simulation results

	Debt reduction				Social contribution cut				Increase
	A				B				C
	2013	2014	2015	2016	2013	2014	2015	2016	2013
GDP	−0.2	0.2	−0.6	−0.5	0.1	0.7	−0.3	−0.2	0.5
Imports	−0.4	−1.6	0.7	0.2	−0.1	−1.3	0.6	0.1	0.8
Domestic demand	−0.3	−0.2	−0.3	−0.4	0.1	0.4	0	−0.2	0.7
Households consumption	−0.2	−0.4	−0.1	−0.5	0.1	0.2	0.2	−0.2	−0.1
Investments	0	−0.2	−0.5	−0.5	0.9	0.6	−0.2	−0.3	5.4
Exports	0	−0.1	−0.1	−0.1	0.1	0.1	0	0	0
Employment	−0.1	−0.4	−0.6	−0.5	0.6	0.2	−0.1	−0.1	0.2
Consumer deflator	2.2	0.6	0.5	0.3	1.5	0	0.1	0	2.2
Export deflator	0	0.3	0.3	0.2	−0.4	0	0	0	0
GDP deflator	1.6	0.9	0.7	0.4	0.8	0.2	0.2	0.1	1.6
Real disposable income (*)	−1.2	−0.4	−1.6	−2.2	0.5	1.4	0.5	0.3	−0.8
Net lending (**)	6 527	7 442	14364	15724	−6 679	−4 658	1 294	2 058	−5 702
(in % of GDP)	0.4	0.5	0.8	0.9	−0.4	−0.2	0.1	0.2	−0.3
Gross debt (**)	−6 527	−13890	−28082	−43462	6 679	11255	9 824	7 644	5 702
(in % of GDP)	−2.2	−4	−4.6	−5.3	−0.8	−1.7	−1.5	−1.4	−2.2

Notes:
(*) Percentage difference with respect to baseline.
(**) EUR million-differences with baseline.

about future reductions in pension entitlements do not affect actual behaviors and also that real gross wages are not directly influenced.

Results, shown in Table 15.1 column B, indicate a worsening of government budget balance by 0.4 and 0.2 percentage points of GDP

of contribution to private investment			Expansion of public investment				Income tax reduction			
C			D				E			
2014	2015	2016	2013	2014	2015	2016	2013	2014	2015	2016
0.5	−0.2	−0.3	0.6	0.1	−0.7	−0.6	0	0.4	−0.5	−0.4
−0.9	1.5	0.6	1.2	−1.5	0.7	0.1	−0.1	−1.1	0.9	0.4
0.4	0.4	−0.1	0.9	−0.2	−0.3	−0.5	0	0.2	−0.2	−0.3
−0.2	0	−0.4	−0.1	−0.3	−0.1	−0.5	0.2	0.2	0.1	−0.4
2.8	2.9	1.4	6.2	−0.1	−0.8	−1	0.1	0	−0.4	−0.3
−0.1	−0.1	−0.1	0	−0.1	−0.1	−0.1	0	−0.1	−0.1	−0.1
−0.2	−0.4	−0.4	0.2	−0.4	−0.6	−0.6	0	−0.4	−0.4	−0.5
0.6	0.6	0.4	2.2	0.7	0.6	0.4	2.2	0.6	0.5	0.4
0.4	0.3	0.3	0	0.4	0.3	0.3	0	0.3	0.3	0.2
1	0.8	0.6	1.6	1	0.8	0.6	1.6	0.9	0.7	0.5
0.2	−0.8	−1.2	−0.7	0.1	−1.2	−1.8	0.7	1.6	0.4	−0.1
−5 532	1 707	2 008	−5 714	−4 648	2 236	4 177	−8 495	−7 172	−7 96	−139
−0.3	0.1	0.2	−0.3	−0.2	0.2	0.3	−0.5	−0.4	0	0
11 163	9 320	7 197	5 715	10 292	7 930	3 655	8 495	15 563	16 168	16 108
−3.8	−4.3	−4.6	−2.4	−3.6	−3.6	−3.6	−1.4	−2.7	−2.6	−2.6

respectively in the first two years. In the same period, GDP growth increases by 0.1 and 0.7 percent. Regarding prices, the reduction in labor costs offsets the upward pressure resulting from the carbon tax. An increase in exports joins the improvements in the terms of trade, positively affecting domestic production and employment. With respect to the previous exercise, the lower inflation and the deterioration in government budget balance slow the reduction in debt to GDP ratio: at the end of the second year, debt to GDP ratio is 1.7 percentage points below baseline.

In the last two years, however, depressive effects on the economy also occur in this scenario. Second round effects on price competitiveness of national products, in fact, still cancel out the positive effects on exports and boost imports, which increase more than domestic demand. As a result, GDP is reduced by 0.3 and 0.2 percentage points with respect to baseline. As regards public finance, inflation moderately improves government budget (by about 0.1 of GDP) and debt to GDP ratio, which at the end of the period lies 1.4 percentage points below baseline.

4.4 Simulations C and D: Use of Carbon Tax Revenues to Support Investments

In the third and fourth exercises carbon tax revenues are recycled to enhance investment by, respectively: a) increasing the government contribution rate to private investment (Table 15.1, column C); and b) increasing public investment (Table 15.1, column D). No direct effect on productivity and competitiveness from the additional investment occurs during the short period considered. In both simulations, in the first two years, an expansionary effect on GDP happens, government net lending increases while debt to GDP ratio improves. In the last two years, economic growth slows significantly while government budget balance improves and debt to GDP ratio reduction slows. In the third simulation, the stronger increase in government expenditures[7] does not harm government accounts significantly because they are favorably affected by a higher real economic growth.

4.5 Simulation E: Use of Carbon Tax Revenues to Finance Income Tax Reduction

In the last simulation (Table 15.1, column E) we assume that carbon tax revenues are recycled to reduce income taxes. This measure can be seen as aimed to offset the negative effects of the carbon tax on real disposable income of households.

Results indicate that an expansionary effect on GDP occurs in the first two years, but to a lesser extent than if employers' social contributions are cut (Table 15.1, column B). This happens because no compensation of negative effects on competitiveness occurs[8] and the increased domestic demand is widely directed to foreign goods. In fact, prices rise as in the first simulation, where revenues are used to repay debt, and reduction in the imports of petroleum products is offset by higher imports of other, cheaper, foreign goods.

15. CONCLUDING REMARKS AND POLICY IMPLICATIONS

In this chapter, the macroeconomic effects of the imposition of an excise tax on the consumption of petroleum products in Italy are evaluated with the support of the ISTAT macroeconometric model.

Five different options to recycle carbon tax revenues are considered: to repay public debt; to cut employers social contributions; to subsidize private investment; to increase public investment and to cut direct taxes on personal income.

The analysis contributes to highlight how difficult it is to provide a general assessment of the effects of tax reforms and that they should be individually evaluated, given the specific characteristics and the specific context in which they are implemented, as a large number of factors and assumptions may affect the results.

Nevertheless, some general conclusions can be drawn:

1. A double dividend from the imposition of a carbon tax in Italy may exist in the short term, even if it is implemented unilaterally, mainly due to terms of trade gains, to a delayed impact on value added and export deflators, and to a low elasticity of exports to domestic price developments. Further, a higher GDP deflator helps improve public finance conditions.
2. Beyond the short term, the economic growth and employment could however be severely undermined and also positive effects on carbon dioxide global emissions could be significantly compromised. Second round effects on domestic prices, due to increases in the cost of raw materials and intermediate goods and fueled by wages indexation, can lead to a significant loss in price competitiveness. For a small economy belonging to a currency union like Italy, where price increases cannot be compensated by exchange rate movements, and in a context of globalization, with free movement of goods, services and capital, a loss in competitiveness can easily lead to an increased consumption of foreign products. In this way, production in countries with no carbon tax is enhanced, and growing flows of productive investment abroad can occur, with no gain in terms of the reduction of global emissions. On the contrary, public finance conditions are favorably affected by higher inflation that improves government accounts, as revenues

increase[9] more than expenditures, and expands the denominator of debt to GDP ratio. In the longer period, however, if economic growth is hampered, even this positive effect could vanish.

3. More favorable effects will be possible if revenues are recycled through measures enhancing competitiveness.
4. Recycling resources through income tax reduction would not prevent a significant restrictive effect on economic growth occurring in the medium term. Competitiveness loss, in fact, largely translates expansive effects on import demand and, as final effect, employment and real disposable income of households could also be reduced.

The analysis, which highlights how limiting and preventing the negative impacts of the carbon tax on economic growth is a key policy challenge, also helps to identify some policy implications.

In particular, it suggests that policy makers should aim to:

- strengthen the efforts to implement a homogenous carbon tax across countries: In this case Italy would fully benefit from terms of trade gains without significant loss of competitiveness;
- use the carbon tax revenues to reduce other production costs (i.e. to reduce labor costs, as labor is actually an overtaxed production factor);
- pay attention to effects on energy intensive trade exposed sectors;
- design a carbon tax applicable also to imported goods (border carbon adjustment etc.);
- prevent the insurgence of an inflationary spiral;
- support private and public investment in order to stimulate improvements in economic efficiency and competitiveness of domestic products in the medium term; and
- pay attention to the effects on demand of domestic versus foreign products.[10]

NOTES

1. Italian National institute of Statistics. The views expressed in this article are those of the author and do not necessarily represent those of ISTAT. I want to thank Franco Sartori, my teacher in many policy simulation analyses, and to dedicate to his memory this chapter, broadly inspired by an unpublished study we prepared together, but that was mainly the result of his great skills and professional qualities, for Legambiente in 1994.

2. For a review on the effectiveness and efficiency of different environmental policy instruments, *see* Goulder and Parry 2008; Nordhaus 2007; Metcalf 2009.
3. For the purpose of this analysis, the official version of the ISTAT macroeconometric model has been suitably modified and implemented to better take into account the fiscal measures considered and the related transmission channels.
4. For a detailed description, *see* Bacchini et al. 2013.
5. Main fiscal policy instruments are tax and social contribution rates, government consumption expenditures in nominal terms and public investment in real terms.
6. Petrol, diesel, kerosene, fuel oil, emulsified oil, LPG, lubricants, bitumen.
7. In simulation C, public subsidies increase if private investment rises, while in simulation D public investment expansion is held constant in nominal terms.
8. In the hypothesis that real gross wages are not directly affected by tax reduction.
9. Mainly indirect taxes.
10. It should be recalled, at this regard, that the government incentives for renewable sources of energy delivered in Italy in 2009–2010 led to an increase in imports of photovoltaic cells from 1 billion euros in 2008 to 9 billion euros in 2010, 2.5% of total imported goods.

REFERENCES

Bacchini, Fabio, Cristina Brandimarte, Piero Crivelli, Roberta De Santis, Marco Fioramanti, Alessandro Girardi, Roberto Golinelli, Cecilia Jona-Lasinio, Massimo Mancini, Carmine Pappalardo, Daniela Rossi, Marco Ventura, Claudio Vicarelli (2013), 'Building the Core of the ISTAT System of Models for Forecasting the Italian Economy: MeMo-It', Rivista di Statistica Ufficiale No. 1/2013.

Baumol, W.J. (1972), 'On Taxation and the Control of Externalities', *American Economic Review*, 62(3), 307–22.

Baumol, W.J, and W.E. Oates (1971), 'The Use of Standards and Prices for the Protection of the Environment', *Scandinavian Journal of Economics*, 73(1), 42–54.

Bovenberg, A.L. and R.A. de Mooij (1994), 'Environmental Levies and Distortionary Taxation', *The American Economic Review*, Vol. 84, No. 4 (September), 1085–9.

Conefrey T., J.D. Fitz Gerald, Valeri L. Malaguzzi and R.S-J. Tol (2008), 'The Impact of a Carbon Tax on Economic Growth and Carbon Dioxide Emissions in Ireland', ESRI Working Paper No. 251.

EEA (2011), 'Environmental Fiscal Reform – Illustrative Potential in Italy', EEA Staff Position Note (December 2011).

Gale W., S. Brown and F. Saltiel (2013), 'Carbon Taxes as Part of the Fiscal Solution', Urban-Brookings Tax Policy Center, March 12, 2013.

Goulder, L.H. and I.W. Parry (2008), 'Instrument Choice in Environmental Policy', *Review of Environmental Economics and Policy* Vol. 2. No. 2, 152–74.

Heine, D., J. Norregaard and I.W. Parry (2012), 'Environmental Tax Reform: Principles from Theory and Practice to Date', IMF Working Paper WP/12/180.

Metcalf, G.E. (2008), 'Designing a Carbon Tax to Reduce U.S. Greenhouse Gas Emissions', *Review of Environmental Economics and Policy*, Vol. 3, No. 1, 63–83.

Muller, N.Z. and R.O. Mendelsohn (2007), 'Measuring the Damages of Air

Pollution in the U.S.', *Journal of Environmental Economics and Management*, 54(1), 1–14.
Nordhaus, W.D. (2007), 'To Tax or Not to Tax: Alternative Approaches to Slowing Global Warming', *Review of Environmental Economics and Policy*, Vol. 1, No. 1, 26–44.
Parry, I.W. and R.C. Williams (2011), 'Moving US Climate Policy Forward: Are Carbon Taxes the Only Good Alternative?', Resources for the Future Discussion Paper 11–02.
Pearce, D.W. (1991), 'The Role of Carbon Taxes in Adjusting to Global Warming', *Economic Journal*, (407), 938–48.
Pigou, A.C. (1920), *Economics of Welfare*, London: Macmillan Publishing.
Sartori, F. and C. Brandimarte (1994), 'Una manovra fiscale per la riduzione dei consumi energetici inquinanti', ISPE.mimeo.
Sumner J., L. Bird and H. Smith (2009), 'Carbon Taxes: A Review of Experience and Policy Design Considerations', NREL Technical Report TP-6A2–47312 December.
Tol, R.S.J. (2007), 'Irish Climate Policy for 2012: An Assessment', *Quarterly Economic Commentary*, Winter 2007, 104–17.
Ulph, A., D. Ulph and J. Pezzey (1991), 'Should a Carbon Tax Rise or Fall Over Time?', University of Bristol, Department of Economics, Discussion Paper No. 91/309.

Section B

Waste management

16. Does industrial waste taxation contribute to waste reduction? Panel data analysis of the generation and final disposal of industrial waste in Japan

Toshiaki Sasao[1]

1. INTRODUCTION

Currently, more than half of Japan's prefectures enforce industrial waste taxation to promote the reduction, reuse and recycling (3Rs) principle and the proper disposal of industrial waste, even though the Japanese government is not involved in such enforcement. Industrial waste taxation is an objective tax that includes two elements: raising financial resources and promoting incentives for adhering to the 3Rs principle. The tax base refers to transporting waste into intermediate treatment facilities or landfills and includes three types of taxation at the prefecture level.

Over the past decade, the total amount of industrial waste generated in Japan has been almost constant, while the total amount of industrial waste disposed in landfills has gradually decreased. Does industrial waste taxation contribute to waste reduction? This chapter analyzes the effect of industrial waste taxation on waste generation and final disposal in Japan.

This chapter proceeds as follows. Section 2 outlines the industrial waste taxes in Japan. Section 3 provides an overview of existing relevant studies on waste taxes. Section 4 explains the estimation methods and data used in the analysis. Section 5 presents the estimation results and examines the effects of industrial waste taxes. Section 6 discusses the reasons why the industrial waste taxes have had little effect on the amount of industrial waste generated and disposed in landfills. Section 7 offers concluding remarks.

2. INDUSTRIAL WASTE TAXATION IN JAPAN

The Local Tax Law was reformed to expand the taxation autonomy of local governments following the enforcement of the Law of Decentralization in 2000. In 2002, industrial waste taxation was first introduced in the Mie Prefecture. Some of the tax revenue in most prefectures is used to subsidize research and development of the 3Rs, although the utilization of this revenue somewhat differs by prefecture. The three types of taxation at the prefecture level are described below.

Type A taxation is the declaration payment made by waste generators. Waste generators are taxed on the direct transport of waste to landfills and intermediate treatment facilities other than recycling facilities. This type of industrial waste taxation is based on the declaration of the waste generators. Two prefectures use this type of taxation by imposing a tax of 1000 yen per ton on the transport of waste to landfills.[2] This tax rate is common among the three types of industrial waste taxation in Japan. Unique to Type A, a specific coefficient is multiplied for transporting waste to intermediate treatment facilities, considering the environmental impact of final disposal. For example, a tax rate of 100 yen per ton is imposed on transporting the waste to incinerators. It is said that Type A taxation generates the strongest incentive for waste reduction among the three types of taxation because waste generators are taxed on direct waste transport to both landfills and intermediate treatment facilities other than recycling facilities.

Type B taxation is a special levy on contractors involved with the final disposal of waste. This tax is similar to the landfill tax in the United Kingdom and other countries, and it is now the most popular type of industrial waste taxation in Japan. In this type of taxation, waste generators, including the intermediate treatment facilities, are taxed on the waste transported to landfills. This type of taxation has two major characteristics. It is based on transporting waste to landfills only and final disposal contractors must levy the tax on waste generators on behalf of the prefecture government. All prefectures that have introduced this type of industrial waste taxation have applied a tax of 1000 yen per ton. The cost of Type B taxation is the least among the three types of taxation because the tax is only applied to transporting waste to landfills. On the other hand, it is said that the incentive to reduce waste is weaker than that for Types A and C, although we can still expect a reduction of waste disposal in landfills.

Type C is also a special levy on intermediate disposal contractors with incinerators and final disposal contractors. This type of industrial waste taxation has been implemented in six prefectures on Kyushu Island

and it has two major characteristics. First is that waste generators are taxed on transporting waste not only to landfills but also to incinerators. Second is that intermediate disposal contractors with incinerators are also taxed on transporting the waste (e.g., post-incineration ashes) to landfills. All prefectures that have introduced this type of taxation have placed a tax of 1000 yen per ton on transporting waste to landfills and that of 800 yen per ton on transporting waste to incinerators. Intermediate disposal contractors with incinerators and final disposal contractors must levy the tax on waste generators on behalf of their respective prefecture government. It is anticipated that the incentive to reduce the amount of waste generated is stronger than Type B, but weaker than Type A.

Table 16.1 shows that the number of prefectures enforcing industrial waste taxation increased for several years prior to 2007, but the number has held steady thereafter. Table 16.1 also shows the trend of the total amount of industrial waste generated and disposed in landfills in Japan over the past decade.

Some prefectures reduce and exempt specific types of waste or size of generators from industrial waste taxation; for example, waste transported to a generator's own landfill. Moreover, the two prefectures that have adopted Type A taxation have exempted smaller generators to reduce the cost of tax collection.

3. LITERATURE REVIEW

To assess the effectiveness of industrial waste taxes or landfill taxes on waste flow, there are two main approaches: *ex ante* and *ex post*. The former simulates the possible effectiveness of enforcing waste taxes on waste flow using an economic model, such as a computable general equilibrium (CGE) model. The latter examines actual waste management data, such as panel data, and compares data before and after taxation. This chapter uses the latter (*ex post*) approach.

Bartelings et al. (2005) exemplifies *ex ante* assessment of waste taxes and uses a CGE model of the Netherlands to show that a landfill tax could reduce the amount of waste transported to landfills by increasing incineration or recycling. Okushima and Yamashita (2005) examined the potential impact of a nationwide industrial waste tax on the Japanese economy using a CGE model.

In terms of an *ex post* assessment, Sigman (1996) used panel data for local waste taxes in the United States to examine the impact of state taxes on chlorinated solvent waste from metal cleaning. The result showed

Table 16.1 Trend of implementation of industrial waste tax, total amount of industrial waste and economic output in Japan

Fiscal year		2000	2001	2002	2003	2004	2005	2006	2007	2008	2009
Number of prefectures enforcing industrial waste taxation	Type A	0	0	1	1	2*	2	2	2	2	2
	Type B	0	0	0	3	9*	13	18	19	19	19
	Type C	0	0	0	0	0	6	6	6	6	6
Total amount of industrial waste generated (thousand tons)		406037	400243	393234	411623	417156	421677	418497	419425	403661	389746
Total amount of industrial waste disposed in landfills (thousand tons)		21547	20899	19167	17157	16659	16438	15582	13243	14077	9468
Output (million yen)	Agriculture	5274542	5157093	5384525	4839136	4829303	5079882	4861351	5102623	5471190	5047950
	Mining	855156	918670	844336	792573	694923	680039	650961	541315	478972	317714
	Ceramic and quarrying	3843833	3634604	3530834	3540048	3684216	3759533	3881526	4165327	3520320	2501832
	Pulp and paper	2716506	2557878	2490684	2409976	2490059	2529463	2513746	2457886	2223887	1984191
	Other manufacturing industries	105392456	97992132	100853963	106702843	112592038	119775029	127332754	133598780	120681216	110033357
	Construction	36531097	34512019	32685675	30595759	30629210	29342299	28792338	26095878	25796521	24604042
	Electricity, gas and water supply	20174388	20311987	20994410	20765647	21520275	22661059	22928817	21846736	22180569	22079278

Note: * Although industrial waste taxes in some prefectures were enforced in January 2004, they are counted in 2004 FY in accordance with the analysis method noted later.

that the estimated overall impact of state hazardous waste disposal taxes currently in place was small. Bartelings et al. (2005) used panel data to examine the impact of a landfill tax in the Netherlands. They showed that the landfill tax contributed to an increase in the share of recycling for the service sector, although it did not affect the generation of waste. In Japan, Sasao (2014) showed that industrial waste taxation in the neighboring prefectures was a significant factor in increasing inflows and Type B taxation could increase outflows to other prefectures for intermediate disposal.

4. ESTIMATION METHODS AND DATA

Panel data was collected at the prefecture level for all 47 prefectures from FY2000 to FY2009 to analyze the effect of local waste taxation on waste generation and the final disposal of industrial waste in Japan. This chapter examines two types of dependent variables: the amount of industrial waste generated and the disposal of waste in landfills. These data are from the Ministry of the Environment (MOE). For final disposal, the chapter considers both excluding and including waste from outside the prefecture to examine the different effects between the prefecture that implemented industrial waste taxation and the neighboring prefectures. Part of the waste, such as waste disposed by the generators themselves, is excluded due to data constraints for final disposal.

The explanatory variables are divided into two categories: industrial waste taxation and socioeconomic determinants. The analysis considers the differences in the three types of taxation (as noted in section 2) and examines two types of tax variables: the tax rate and the dummy variables that represent the time period after the introduction of taxation. For the socioeconomic variables, the chapter focuses on the output of industries that generate large amounts of waste such as agriculture; mining; ceramic and quarrying; pulp and paper; and electricity, gas and water supply.[3] Table 16.1 shows the trend of the total output of each industry in Japan. These data are from the Ministry for Internal Affairs and Communications. Table 16.2 shows the descriptive statistics of each variable. Numerical variables, except for the dummy variables, are transformed by logarithms to capture their elasticity. The models including the year dummy variables are also estimated to examine the time trend.

Following the standard procedure in panel data analysis, this chapter applies the following three models: pooled ordinary least squares (OLS); fixed effects and random effects (Hsiao 2003). In this analysis, the OLS model pools all of the data, ignoring differences between prefectures. The fixed effects model assumes that differences between prefectures are fixed

Table 16.2 Descriptive statistics of variables

Variables	Abbreviation	Mean	SD	Max	Min
Amount of waste generated (thousand tons)	gen	8 683 705	7 397 831	4.02E+07	1 395 209
Amount of waste disposed of in landfills excluding waste from outside the prefecture* (thousand tons)	fd	271.0069	318.4486	2 312	0.001
Amount of waste disposed of in landfills including waste from outside the prefecture* (thousand tons)	fd2	349.5734	391.4936	2 820	0.001
Output in agriculture (million yen)	agr	108 611.9	88 837.12	617 247	23 126
Output in mining (million yen)	min	14414.17	16 709.85	154 851	143
Output in ceramic and quarrying (million yen)	cem	76 727.81	74 697.99	479 412	2 088
Output in pulp and paper industries (million yen)	plp	51 860.16	56 986.33	291 179	1 186
Output in other manufacturing industries (million yen)	oth	2 414 797	2 508 922	1.52E+07	146 990
Output in construction (million yen)	con	637 414.5	722 002.2	4 834 920	110 873
Output in electricity gas and water supply (million yen)	ele	458 432.3	409 162.5	2 038 853	85 552
Tax rate of Industrial waste taxation type A	txra	29.78723	170.181	1 000	0
Tax rate of Industrial waste taxation type B	txrb	206.3574	401.5938	1 000	0
Tax rate of Industrial waste taxation type C	txrc	63.82979	244.7099	1 000	0

Note: *For the amount of waste disposed of in landfills 'less than 500 tonnes' and 'not applicable' in the original data are transformed to 0.25 and 0.001 thousand tons respectively.

constants over time, whereas the random effects model assumes that differences between prefectures are random variables.

Following Hsiao (2003), the optimal model is selected on the basis of three tests: F test, Hausman test and Breusch–Pagan test (BP test). The F test compares the pooled OLS and fixed effects models under the null hypothesis in that all of the prefecture constants are common. If the hypothesis is rejected, the fixed effects model is better than the pooled OLS model. The Hausman test compares the fixed versus random effect models under the null that the individual effects are uncorrelated with the other explanatory variables in the models. If the hypothesis is rejected, the fixed effects model is better than the random effects model. The BP test compares the pooled OLS versus the random effects models under the null that cross-sectional variance components are zero. If the hypothesis is rejected, the random effects model is better than the pooled OLS model.

5. ESTIMATION RESULTS

5.1 Waste Generation

Table 16.3 shows the estimation results of the amount of industrial waste generated, excluding the insignificant variables. The total number of samples is 470 (47 prefectures multiplied by 10 years) for all of the models. For industrial waste generation, the estimations of the models that include the time trend are not shown because the yearly dummy variables are not significant. The three tests mentioned above showed that the fixed effects model had the most preferred specification estimates for both the tax rate and tax dummy models. Consequently, only the results of the fixed effects model (represented by FE) are shown in the table.

Model 1–1 considers the tax rates for industrial waste taxes. Model 1–2 considers the annual effects after introducing industrial waste taxes. Because the latter model shows a higher adjusted R-squared value, we rely on Model 1–2 when interpreting the estimated results. The variables that begin with 'l' represent variables that have been transformed by logarithms.

For Type A taxation, the dummy variables are positively significant for the second–fifth, seventh and eighth years after taxation. This means that the amount of industrial waste generated has increased after taxation. This result is contrary to our prior expectation. However, because only two prefectures use Type A taxation, some special circumstances in these prefectures may affect the amount of waste generated. On the other hand,

Table 16.3 Estimation results of generation (estimated without insignificant variables)

	Model 1–1	Model 1–2
FE or RE	FE	FE
l_plp	0.0724 [3.09]***	0.0634 [2.63]**
l_txa	0.0283 [2.87]***	
tay2		0.1367 [2.34]**
tay3		0.1618 [5.11]***
tay4		0.1251 [5.70]***
tay5		0.1423 [2.44]**
tay7		0.4261 [20.04]***
tay8		0.3652 [16.98]***
tby7		−0.1337 [−2.34]**
cons	14.922 [61.84]***	15.0179 [60.31]***
Adj-R^2	0.0444	0.0715
F	F(2 46) = 8.76***	N.A.
F test	F(46 421) = 376.48	F(46 415) = 385.45
Prob > F	0	0
Hausman test	χ^2 (2) = 39.26	χ^2 (8) = 42.36
Prob > χ^2	0	0
BP test	χ^2 (1) = 1935.58	χ^2 (1) = 1934.27
Prob > χ^2	0	0

Notes: $*p < 0.1$ $**p < 0.05$ $***p < 0.01$. Values in square bracket show t-statistics by robust estimation.

a negative significant effect is only observed for the seventh year after taxation for Type B. However, a continuous reduction is not observed. For Type C, no significant effects are observed. For the socioeconomic determinants, only the output of the pulp and paper industry is positively significant.

5.2 Final Disposal

Tables 16.4 and 16.5 show the estimation results (without insignificant variables) of the amount of industrial waste disposed in landfills. The estimations of the models in these tables respectively exclude and include the waste from outside the prefecture. The total sample size is 470 for all of the models.

Models 2–1 and 2–2 consider the tax rates for industrial waste taxes, without and with the yearly dummy variables, respectively. Models 2–3 and 2–4 consider the annual effects after implementing industrial waste

Table 16.4 Estimation results of final disposal excluding waste from outside the prefecture (estimated without insignificant variables)

	Model 2–1	Model 2–2	Model 2–3	Model 2–4
FE or RE	FE	RE	RE	RE
l_agr	1.9209 [2.20]**	0.8351 [2.78]***	1.0391 [3.25]***	0.8405 [2.79]***
l_txb	−0.0654 [−4.54]***			
l_txc	−0.109 [−16.59]***			
tay2			−0.3221 [−3.49]***	
tay3			−0.7652 [−8.25]***	
tay7				0.9071 [3.60]***
tby2			−0.2046 [−2.17]**	
tby3			−0.2249 [−3.28]***	
tby7			−1.1759 [−21.71]***	
tcy1			−0.2792 [−2.00]**	
tcy2			−0.3075 [−4.16]***	
tcy3			−0.8716 [−4.33]***	
tcy4			−1.1359 [−4.38]***	
tcy5			−0.8821 [−7.50]***	
d02		−0.2856 [−2.15]**		−0.2857 [−2.15]**
d03		−0.5137 [−2.95]***		−0.5132 [−2.95]***
d04		−0.5115 [−2.86]***		−0.511 [−2.86]***
d05		−0.5482 [−3.60]***		−0.548 [−3.59]***
d06		−0.9347 [−3.02]***		−0.9342 [−3.02]***
d07		−0.9646 [−3.25]***		−0.9643 [−3.25]***
d08		−1.0833 [−3.23]***		−1.1028 [−3.24]***

Table 16.4 (continued)

	Model 2–1	Model 2–2	Model 2–3	Model 2–4
FE or RE	FE	RE	RE	RE
d09		−1.1302 [−3.71]***		−1.1299 [−3.70]***
cons	−17.0151 [−1.71]*	−4.2339 [−1.22]	−7.074 [−1.88]*	−4.2951 [−1.23]
Adj-R^2	0.0332	0.098	0.015	0.0968
F or Wald	F(3 46) = 107.21***	χ^2 (9) = 32.34***	χ^2 (11) = 190388.08***	χ^2 (10) = 1858.19***
F test	F(46 420) = 16.54	F(46 414) = 17.46	F(46 412) = 16.25	F(46 413) = 17.42
Prob > F	0	0	0	0
Hausman test	χ^2 (3) = 7.15	χ^2 (9) = 0.09	χ^2 (11) = 7.05	χ^2 (10) = 0.15
Prob > χ^2	0.0673	1	0.7954	1
BP test	χ^2 (1) = 726.81	χ^2 (1) = 818.03	χ^2 (1) = 747.65	χ^2 (1) = 818.04
Prob > χ^2	0	0	0	0

Notes: *p < 0.1 **p < 0.05 ***p < 0.01. Values in square bracket show t-statistics by robust estimation.

taxes, without and with the yearly dummy variables, respectively. Models 3–1 to 3–4 represent the same considerations as above. The three tests conducted earlier identified the fixed effects model to have the most preferred specifications when modeling the tax rate without the yearly dummy variables; namely, Models 2–1 and 3–1. However, the random effects model has the most preferred specifications for all of the models other than Models 2–1 and 3–1. On the other hand, the models with the yearly dummy variables have higher adjusted R-squares than the models without such variables. The adjusted R-squared differences between the models that consider the tax rates and the models that consider the annual effects after the implementation of the industrial waste taxes is not large. Consequently, we rely on Models 2–2, 2–4, 3–2 and 3–4 for our interpretation of the estimated results.

For Type A taxation, the tax rate is not significant for all of the models that exclude waste from outside the prefecture. Including waste from outside the prefecture, the tax rate is positively significant for Model 3–2. The dummy variable of the seventh year after taxation is positively significant in the case of excluding waste from outside the prefecture and the dummy variables from the fourth–sixth years

Table 16.5 Estimation results of final disposal including waste from outside the prefecture (estimated without insignificant variables)

	Model 3–1	Model 3–2	Model 3–3	Model 3–4
FE or RE	FE	RE	RE	RE
l_agr		0.7457 [2.66]***	0.7542 [2.59]***	0.6498 [2.14]**
l_plp			0.5092 [3.05]***	
l_ele				0.5764 [1.70]*
l_txa		0.1207 [2.71]***		
l_txb	−0.0584 [−3.82]***			
l_txc	−0.0829 [−7.58]***			
tay4			1.1005 [4.11]***	1.3269 [6.96]***
tay5			1.2058 [3.53]***	1.4648 [4.03]***
tay6			1.2594 [4.39]***	1.6299 [4.40]***
tby2			−0.1677 [−2.33]**	
tby7			−0.7515 [−15.36]***	
tcy1			−0.242 [−1.97]**	
tcy2			−0.1628 [−2.80]***	
tcy3			−0.5915 [−2.86]***	
tcy4			−0.8808 [−3.07]***	
tcy5			−0.6859 [−7.18]***	
d02		−0.1978 [−1.77]*		−0.2054 [−1.98]**
d03		−0.4284 [−2.37]**		−0.4439 [−2.46]**
d04		−0.4262 [−2.39]**		−0.4476 [−2.54]**
d05		−0.3624 [−2.74]***		−0.4377 [−3.15]***
d06		−0.6499 [−2.22]**		−0.7368 [−2.88]***
d07		−0.8117 [−2.68]***		−0.9063 [−3.21]***
d08		−0.8372 [−2.66]***		−0.8927 [−2.98]***
d09		−0.9753 [−3.11]***		−1.0417 [−3.60]***
cons	5.1191 [224.18]***	−3.0248 [−0.93]	−8.7859 [−1.97]**	−9.223 [−1.90]*

Table 16.5 (continued)

	Model 3–1	Model 3–2	Model 3–3	Model 3–4
FE or RE	FE	RE	RE	RE
Adj–R^2	0.0159	0.068	0.0266	0.0753
F or Wald	F(2 46) = 36.01***	χ^2 (10) = 24.97***	N.A.	N.A.
F test	F(46 420) = 16.54	F(46 413) = 18.42	F(46 411) = 17.23	F(46 410) = 17.55
Prob > F	0	0	0	0
Hausman test	χ^2 (3) = 7.15	χ^2 (10) = 0.08	χ^2 (12) = 5.27	χ^2 (13) = 0.64
Prob > χ^2	0.0673	1	0.9485	1
BP test	χ^2 (1) = 726.81	χ^2 (1) = 854.99	χ^2 (1) = 770.36	χ^2 (1) = 826.54
Prob > χ^2	0	0	0	0

Notes: *p < 0.1 **p < 0.05 ***p < 0.01. Values in square bracket show t-statistics by robust estimation.

after taxation are positively significant in case of including waste from outside the prefecture. These results are similar to those of waste generation. In contrast, no significant effects are observed in the four models for Types B and C. In Models 2–3 and 3–3, the adjusted R-squares are very low, although some tax dummy variables are negatively significant when excluding and including waste from outside the prefecture. These results indicate that the reduction effects have been offset by the time trend to date.

For the socioeconomic determinants, agricultural output is positively significant in all of the models. In Model 3–4, the output of electricity, gas and water supply is also positively significant, in spite of a 10 percent significance level.

6. DISCUSSION

The results of the empirical studies clearly show that industrial waste taxes in Japan have minimal significant effects on the reduction of waste generation thus far. In addition, the results show that, although there seems to be significant effects on the reduction of final disposal, whether one excludes or includes waste from outside the prefecture, the reduction effects to date have been offset by the time trend.

There seem to be at least five reasons why industrial waste taxes in Japan have little effect on the amount of industrial waste generated and disposed in landfills: (1) Due to the low tax rate, industrial waste taxes have not provided significant incentives for waste reduction by the waste generators; (2) The tax transfer from the disposal contractors to waste generators may not be sufficient; (3) Fixed contracts between the disposal contractors and waste generators may be an obstacle limiting the effectiveness of the tax; (4) The reduction of taxes and associated exemptions (as noted in section 2) may have affected such generation and disposal; and (5) an inherent factor of local area characteristics over time may have offset the effects.

For (1), it is not appropriate to consider only the tax rate because waste generators have to pay for waste disposal contracts in addition to the tax. The charges vary depending on the category and region. However, it is likely that the reduction effects tend to be weak in regions where the disposal fee including the tax is cheap. For example, most of the countries in the European Union that have implemented a landfill tax have gradually increased the tax rates. This indicates that the authorities have increased the tax rates after considering the effectiveness of the taxes on waste flow and the economy. Therefore, it is also necessary to reconsider the 1000 yen per ton tax rate in Japan. Reason (2) has been a matter of concern for Types B and C taxation. Actually, some disposal contractors may not transfer the tax to waste generators for fear that they would contract with other disposal contractors. However, the empirical results show that the reduction effect is not observed for Type A, which was expected to provide the strongest incentive for waste reduction among the three types of taxation. For (3), Bartelings et al. (2005) point out a similar issue when referring to a case in France. It is probable that final disposal contractors and generators in Japan also exchange contracts in fixed terms (e.g., years) or that disposal contractors set fixed charges (e.g., yen per truck). In such cases, disposal charges are not flexible when the disposal amount fluctuates. In terms of reason (4), some prefectures reduce or exempt taxes to lighten the burden on the generators. These measures are contrary to the original purpose of taxation; namely, waste reduction and recycling. Therefore, such measures should be minimized. In terms of reason (5), for example, the proper disposal of illegally dumped waste or waste generated by bankrupt firms temporarily increases the amount of waste. Although this result is inevitable, it indicates that the effectiveness of taxation on waste flow is insufficient.

7. CONCLUSION

The empirical results show that although such taxes seem to have a significant effect by reducing the amount of final waste disposal, the reduction effects to date have been offset by the time trend. These results indicate that the current industrial waste taxes should be reconsidered from the standpoint of reducing the waste generated or disposed in landfills. Although one solution is to increase the tax rates, it is difficult to increase such rates indiscriminately due to taxpayer opposition. Therefore, it could be argued that different tax rates are set according to waste category considering the environmental impact, even when the disposal methods are similar.

The future directions of this empirical study are as follows. Each waste category should be analyzed to provide a detailed examination of the effectiveness of taxation on waste flow. In addition, the possibility of endogeneity should be examined. If the prefectures that have introduced industrial waste taxes have common characteristics (e.g., significant waste generation before the introduction and enforcement of industrial waste taxation), the relationship between cause and effect may be misunderstood. These issues will be dealt with in future research.

NOTES

1. This study was supported by a Grant-in-Aid for Scientific Research on Priority Areas (18078005), Scientific Research (B) (21330056) and Grant-in-Aid for Young Scientists (B) (25740059) by the Ministry of Education, Culture, Sports, Science and Technology, Japan.
2. Yen is converted into US dollars assuming an exchange rate of approximately 100 yen to 1.07 dollars (the average rate in 2009).
3. These outputs are measured using a gross domestic product (GDP) deflator. I confirm that the correlations between these explanatory variables are negligible.

REFERENCES

Bartelings, H., P. van Beukering, O. Kuik, V. Linderhof and F. Oosterhuis (2005), 'Effectiveness of Landfill Taxation', *Institute for Environmental Studies*, Netherlands.

Hsiao, Cheng (2003), *Analysis of Panel Data*, 2nd edn., Cambridge, Cambridge University Press.

Okushima, S. and H. Yamashita (2005), 'A General Equilibrium Analysis of Waste Management Policy in Japan', *Hitotsubashi Journal of Economics*, 46, 111–34.

Sasao, Toshiaki (2014), 'Industrial Waste Shipments and Trade Restrictions', in T. Kinnaman and K. Takeuchi (eds), *Handbook on Waste Management*,

Cheltenham, UK and Northampton, MA, USA: Edward Elgar Publishing (in press).
Sigman, Hilary (1996), 'The Effects of Hazardous Waste Taxes on Waste Generation and Disposal', *Journal of Environmental Economics and Management*, 30, 199–217.

17. Exploring the need for direct tax incentives for plastic waste management in India

Rajiv V. Shah

1. INTRODUCTION

About 9 percent of municipal solid waste in India consists of plastic waste, which amounts to about 10,000 tons per day. This waste is landfilled, recycled or incinerated, thus creating a large amount of pollution. The few measures to handle this waste include efforts by entrepreneurs to convert the plastic waste into more usable products such as fuels and road construction material.

The policy approach to solving environmental problems has been through command-and-control measures, negotiations, economic instruments, environmental taxation and incentives. There is a fair amount of literature on the use of command-and-control measures, economic instruments and environmental taxation. While each of these has its pros and cons, there is need for a concerted policy using all or most of these measures in proportions customized to the context to achieve the environmental goal. Of these measures, there is relatively less information on the concept of direct taxes as a source of incentives to businesses engaged in cleaning up the environment or in creating positive externalities. In practice, many economies have used direct tax incentives to provide incentives for 'good' environmental behavior.

This chapter first tries to understand the importance and benefits of plastic waste management within the larger canvas of municipal waste management. It then looks at the various ways and means currently in practice to tackle environmental issues and focuses on the usage of direct tax incentives (DTI) to encourage businesses engaged in plastic waste management. Thereafter, the various provisions in the Indian Income Tax Act are studied to find out if there are adequate measures existing to encourage this activity. It then attempts to suggest provisions that could help promote these businesses and raises a set of questions to be explored in the future.

The structure of this chapter is as follows: Section 2 looks at the broad picture of waste management in India, and plastic waste management in specific. It identifies plastic waste management as the focus area of this chapter. Section 3 explores the different facets of policy instruments to help the environmental cause and makes a case for the use of DTI as one of the policy measures to help businesses engaged in plastic waste management. Section 4 reviews the existing incentives offered by the Income Tax Act, 1961 for encouraging such environment friendly activities. Section 5 consists of the concluding remarks.

2. PLASTIC WASTE MANAGEMENT

Solid waste management in India has assumed a critical status not only for environmentalists and governments but also for the common man. This is mainly due to the explosion in the amounts of waste generated each day in urban and rural centers, which is also partly due to the population growth, migration of population from rural to urban areas, income levels and changes in lifestyle. It is estimated that municipal solid waste (MSW) generated in India is about 43 million tons per annum or 120,000 tons per day (TPD). This figure is expected to reach 160.5 million tons per annum or 440,000 TPD by 2041. The growth in MSW is expected to go hand-in-hand with the increase in the gross domestic product (GDP) (Central Pollution Control Board 2008).

Almost 90 percent of the Municipal solid waste management (MSWM) budget is spent on waste collection and transport activities. Disposal of waste, a long-standing problem for municipal corporations, is mainly done by dumping the waste in low lying areas outside the cities (landfills). This waste needs to be compacted and leveled and finally the site needs to be covered with earth, which rarely happens (Sharholy et al. 2007). As a result, the waste disposal activities are quite unscientific and potentially harmful to residents around the dumping area (Gupta et al. 1998). In fact, improper handling of the gases released during the bio-degradation process in these sites can even contribute to the increase in greenhouse gases, thus hastening the global warming process. The composition of MSW in India is as shown in Table 17.1.

About 9 percent of the solid waste generated is plastic and, when seen in the context of total waste of 120,000 TPD, the quantum of plastic waste generated amounts to 10,000 TPD. If left to itself, the time taken for the waste to degrade is shown in Table 17.2.

As can be seen, plastic is among the components that need the maximum time to degrade. Plastic waste needs more scientific disposal techniques as

Table 17.1 Composition of municipal solid waste in India

Waste category	% of total municipal waste
Paper	8.13
Plastic	9.22
Metal	0.5
Glass	1.01
Rags	4.49
Inerts	25.16
Compostable material	47.43
Others	4.06

Source: Zhu et al. 2008.

Table 17.2 Time taken for waste material to degrade

Nature of waste	Time taken to degrade
Organic waste (kitchen waste)	1–2 weeks
Paper	10–30 days
Cotton cloth	2–5 months
Tin, aluminum and other such metals	100–500 years
Plastic	One million years

Source: NSWAI 2013.

it is not capable of bio-degrading naturally and hence would remain in its original form for a large number of years. Plastic waste disposal if not managed properly, can lead to the following forms of pollution, among others, as mentioned in the Central Pollution Control Board of India's website (Central Pollution Control Board 2013):

- Plastic waste, when burnt with other garbage, causes harmful and toxic gases to be released.
- It clogs up drains, landfills and interferes with other waste processing facilities.
- Recycling these plastics in a haphazard manner causes further pollution.
- It leads to spoiling the aesthetics of the area.

The problem with plastic is less of its creation and use and more of its disposal. The benefits of plastic as a consumer product are that it is strong, highly durable, economically viable and easier to process. To exemplify, a paper cup typically consumes about 12 times more steam, 36 times more electricity and twice the cooling water required for a plastic foam cup (Rebeiz and Craft 1995). Replacing plastic with paper is also fraught with danger as it would put more pressure on the existing forest wealth, which is already depleting alarmingly.

Plastic waste needs to be recycled in an environmentally sound manner, as opposed to the unscientific landfilling activities and open burning of plastic waste. Some of the environment friendly recycling measures suggested by the CPCB include:

1. *Use as road construction material.* In this method, the plastic waste is dried, cleaned and shredded and, thereafter, added to heated granite and ceramic aggregate while constructing the road. This melts the plastic waste and makes the aggregate less water friendly, leading to roads that are resistant to creation of potholes.
2. *Co-processing.* Here, the plastic waste is used as an alternative fuel due to its high calorific quality. It is mainly usable in cement and power stations and other large combustion plants. This helps the user of this waste to reduce dependence on conventional fuel.
3. *Conversion of plastic waste into fuel.* This method involves the heating of plastic waste at high temperature in absence of oxygen and in presence of additives. This depolymerizes the waste into liquid fuel, gas and sludge. Further pilot studies using this method have shown that this is considered to be a more promising way of plastic waste management due to the benefits combined with the minimal toxic output during the process.

These methods are currently in the experimentation stage and are used in pilot projects in certain places in the country (Central Pollution Control Board 2008).

Having identified plastic waste management as the problem in this chapter, we now look at the various policy measures in use to tackle such problems. The intention is to identify the best measure or combination of measures to take care of the plastic waste disposal by encouraging plastic waste management businesses.

3. TAX INCENTIVES AS POLICY INSTRUMENTS

We now see the application of various tools to the general environmental problems and try to identify the appropriate one for the selected area of plastic waste management. Traditionally, the approach to environmental protection through policy has been through market centric measures such as pollution permits or through command-and-control methods such as regulations and standards. Frequently governments also intervene by imposing green taxes on polluters and using these collections to provide a benefit to certain sections of society by reducing taxes on salaries (Kolstad 2000; Ligthart 1998). The different policy instruments that are used to protect the environment are regulations and standards, pollution permits, moral suasion, green taxes and incentives (including subsidies) (Ligthart 1998). While these instruments need to be used in tandem, this chapter looks at the role of taxation, which normally includes levying a charge on incomes and activities (green taxes), but can also be used to provide DTI to encourage certain behavior. The different policy measures include:

- *Regulations and standards.* These command-and-control measures include bans and restrictions. These could be counterproductive due to their compulsory and restrictive nature. With direct regulation, a polluting company has no incentive to pollute less than the permissible limit. Informational cost being high can make the command-and-control system more expensive and the polluter also has an incentive to misreport information. These also significantly reduce the incentive to innovate and find other ways of reducing pollution (Kolstad 2000).
- *Pollution permits.* These are part of a set of economic instruments to help control pollution and allow the polluter to buy and sell the right to pollute. However, the challenge with pollution permits is to achieve environmental transformation without being too complex and impractical. This instrument also encounters political roadblocks as the level of the fee needs to be changed over time, which is usually resisted by industry (Kolstad 2000).
- *Moral suasion and bilateral negotiations.* Moral pressure by governments or society on industry has increased of late, leading to some change in the polluting patterns. However, this method is largely voluntary and depends to a great extent on the individual polluter. The Coase theorem states that the initial distribution of polluting rights does not matter and market mechanism would ultimately lead to a Pareto optimal condition (Coase 1960). It is seen that bilateral negotiations are motivated by this principle. However, the theorem assumes that among other things, there is perfect information, the legal system for enforcing agreements is costless and there are no transaction costs (Kolstad 2000). Owing to these, the negotiations are difficult to conclude or implement.
- *Green taxes.* The primary role of any taxation system is to raise revenue to fund the general functions of government. However, an

important policy objective is also to enhance overall economic well being, while promoting fairness, and continuing to raise sufficient revenue at the same time. Taxes can be raised directly as well as indirectly. Indirect taxes are taxes such as value added tax (VAT), central excise, etc., which are levied on production or production-related activity.

Pigou (1920) stated that negative externalities caused by pollution would be internalized by the market if polluters paid a tax equal to the marginal social cost of polluting emissions. The focus was entirely on the principle 'the polluter pays'. Worldwide, 'green taxes' as they are known, are mainly taxes of the indirect kind, occurring at the production and/or sales stage. Examples would be taxes on production and sale of petroleum products and plastic products. One of the advances of the green tax theory is the 'double dividend' hypothesis, which implies that the tax policies can be revenue neutral in form by taxing polluting activities and using the increased revenues to offset a reduction in taxes on salaries. This would pay double dividends in the form of raising more revenue for the government (green dividend) and increase environmental quality (efficiency dividend) (Williams 2002; Blackman and Harrington 2000; Goulder 1995).

While governments can collect taxes from the polluting producers, these taxes still need to be ploughed back into the economy in a beneficial way. If the collected taxes are channelized back by way of reduced salary or wage taxes, there would be a compensation of sorts for the consumer for having paid a higher green tax (Schöb 1996). This move of reducing salary taxes would put more money into the hands of the consumer, thus encouraging the search for better and more environmental friendly alternatives. However, green taxes have their shortcomings.

These taxes would be ultimately borne by the consumer, irrespective of the level of income. As a result, the poor tend to pay more taxes as a percentage of their total income. If lower income groups spend a greater portion of their income on products with external social costs, such as electricity, such tax is regressive (Eskeland and Kong 1998). Further, like all indirect taxes, Pigouvian taxes, as these green taxes are also known, can also encourage smuggling and black market activities, especially if there are large differences in product prices with those in nearby areas (Okoye and Akenbor 2010). Hence, the green tax approach needs to be balanced with the positive effect of DTI.

- *Incentives and subsidies*. While the approach to green taxes has mostly been the 'stick' one, the 'carrot' part should not be ignored. Incentives such as subsidy schemes for reducing emissions, soft

> loans to buy capital equipment, etc. could prove equally effective (Ligthart 1998). These benefits could also be in the form of specific deductions, which directly relate to conservationist activities, as opposed to general deductions, which could be taken advantage of by all industries (Douglas 2002). Traditionally, tax incentives have mostly been to encourage supply, as mentioned above. They could do well to encourage demand for environmentally friendly machines, products, energy, etc. (Mann and Hymel 2006). For example, a household investing in solar water heaters could well be given rebates in their regular electricity bills, as is being done in some parts of India. A large number of government schemes in India are driven by way of incentivizing people to invest in them and get a tax benefit. For example, businesses are encouraged to buy new machinery instead of old ones and drive the machinery production industry. They are offered additional depreciation under section 32 of the Income Tax Act 1961 to compensate them for their decision to buy new machinery.

Thus, incentives in general can play an important role in reducing environmental pollution along with other measures (Ligthart 1998; Wilson 1996). We discuss the role of incentives in the form of DTI here. Combining a green tax policy with DTI would mean that the taxes collected could be used to help provide an alternative to the polluting product, or at least reduce the polluting effect of the polluting product by helping recycling it or converting it into another usable product (Gago and Labandeira 2000).

The revenues collected through green taxes on plastic products could be channelized to provide benefits to manufacturers engaged in the area of converting this plastic into reusable products. For example, there is a technology that is being worked out to convert plastic waste into fuel, gas and ash, without polluting the environment as much as regular incineration would. This action, which would help develop positive externalities, could be supported through DTI.

Next, we examine the provisions in the Indian Income Tax Act 1961 pertaining to DTI for environmental protection in general.

4. THE INDIAN INCOME TAX SCENARIO

We have discussed in the preceding sections that DTI can play a role in helping reduce pollution. The income tax provisions in India aimed at creating positive externalities are as follows:

- If specified air pollution, water pollution control equipment, solid waste control equipment or recycling and resource recovery systems are purchased, 100 percent depreciation under section 32 of the Income Tax Act 1961, is allowed to the taxpayer. This enhanced depreciation helps the entrepreneur to reduce taxable profits in the first year and if this depreciation is more than the profits, it can be carried forward to the coming years to be set off against profits till the entire depreciation is exhausted.
- Renewable energy devices including solar/wind power based equipment and other related equipment are allowed 80 percent deduction under section 32 of the Income Tax Act 1961. A similar benefit as in the above case is available to the entrepreneur in respect of the set-off against profits.
- For businesses engaged in collecting and processing or treatment of bio-degradable waste and converting into power, bio-fertilizers, bio-pesticides, etc., 100 percent of the profits from such activities are deductible from tax under section 80JJA of the Income Tax Act 1961, for a period of five years from the year in which the activity commences.

However, there are no DTI for businesses specifically engaged in plastic or non bio-degradable waste management. Nor is there any deduction for research and development in this area. Section 35 of the Income Tax Act 1961 allows for a weighted average deduction of revenue as well as capital expenses on scientific research ranging from 100 percent to 200 percent of the expenses incurred (Bakker 2009). A specific deduction for research and development in the area of plastic waste management could also help alleviate concerns regarding the reliability of the technology. Hence, there appears to be scope for introduction of such provisions.

5. CONCLUDING REMARKS

The need for plastic waste management in India is quite evident from the data available from government sites responsible for monitoring the same (Central Pollution Control Board 2013). A glance at the measures to tackle this problem shows that they are either short term and costly in nature, like dumping this waste in landfill sites, or reactionary in nature, such as banning the use of plastic itself, with less consideration to the availability of suitable material to replace it. As discussed earlier, the problem area may be the disposal and not the use of plastic. Among other measures to reach a viable solution, until such time that adequate replacement is found, DTI can play a vital role in encouraging new businesses to use this abundant plastic waste from municipal corporation dumpsites and convert it into fuel or use it as road construction material.

An advantage of DTI in this area is the reduced expenditure for municipal corporations in terms of lesser landfill sites. These savings can be used for more socially productive purposes such as the creation of amusement areas, gardens, playgrounds, etc. The municipal corporations also benefit from the reduced cost of transporting the waste from dumpsites to landfills if they allow the plastic waste manager to operate from the dumpsite and receive the waste there. From a social viewpoint, since there is a created demand for the plastic waste, households might even be tempted not to throw the waste into garbage bins but instead collect it and take it to the nearest collection center, as is the case in India with certain categories of waste such as newspapers, metal and glass. This would go a long way in creating awareness in the minds of the consumers. At a macro level, encouraging this business would go some way in reducing dependence on imported fuel. If plastic waste is converted into fuel, 10,000 tons of plastic waste per day could potentially yield about 10 million liters of fuel per day, and at a much reduced cost.

The DTI aspects suggested above need to be part of a larger policy that encompasses issues such as soft loans for this purpose, allowing businesses to set up factories on the dumping sites and encouraging research in this area. There is little literature available on the topic DTI for plastic waste management. This chapter attempts to contribute to the debate on the broader issue by bringing in the lesser discussed angle of the role of DTI to help solve the problem of plastic waste management. It aims at encouraging further studies to firm up the role of DTI as part of the broad policy package for this purpose.

REFERENCES

Bakker, A. (2009), *Tax and the Environment: A World of Possibilities*, Amsterdam, The Netherlands: IBFD.

Blackman, A. and W. Harrington (2000), 'The Use of Economic Incentives in Developing Countries: Lessons from International Experience with Industrial Air Pollution', *The Journal of Environment & Development*, 9(1), 5–44.

Central Pollution Control Board (2008), *Plastic Waste Management*, Government of India.

Central Pollution Control Board (2013), website material on plastic waste management, available at http://www.cpcb.nic.in/divisionsofheadoffice/pcp/management_plasticwaste.pdf, accessed July 17, 2013.

Coase, R.H. (1960), 'The Problem of Social Cost', *Journal of Law and Economics*, 3(October), 1–44.

Douglas, R. (2002), 'Potential Effects of Selected Taxation Provisions on the Environment', Report to the Productivity Commission, Canberra.

Eskeland, G.S. and C. Kong (1998), *Protecting the Environment and the Poor: A Public Goods Framework Applied to Indonesia, Issue 1961*, World Bank Publications.

Gago, A. and X. Labandeira, (2000), 'Towards a Green Tax Reform Model', *Journal of Environmental Policy & Planning*, 2(1), 25–37.

Goulder, L. (1995), 'Environmental Taxation and the Double Dividend: A Reader's Guide', *International Tax and Public Finance*, 2(2), 157–83.

Gupta, S., K. Mohan, R. Prasad and A. Kansal (1998), 'Solid Waste Management in India: Options and Opportunities', *Resources, Conservation and Recycling*, Vol. 24, 137–54.

Kolstad, C.D. (2000), *Environmental Economics*, Oxford: Oxford University Press.

Ligthart, J. (1998), 'The Macroeconomic Effects of Environmental Taxes – A Closer Look at the Feasibility of "Win-Win" Outcomes', WP 75, IMF–Fiscal Affairs Department, May 1998.

Mann, R. and M. Hymel (2006), 'Getting into the Act: Enticing the Consumer to Become "Green" through Tax Incentives', *Environmental Law Review*, 36(6), 10419–29.

NSWAI (National Solid Waste Association of India) (2013), Waste Portal-Municipal Solid Waste, available at http://www.nswai.com/waste-municipal-solid-waste.php, accessed May 26, 2013.

Okoye, E. and C. Akenbor (2010), 'The Pigovian Tax, Market for Pollution Rights and Environmental Pollution Control in the Niger-Delta Region of Nigeria', *Journal of Business and Financial Studies*, 2(1), 60–75.

Pigou, A.C. (1920), *The Economics of Welfare*, London: Macmillan and Co.

Rebeiz, K.S. and A.P. Craft (1995), 'Plastic Waste Management in Construction: Technological and Institutional Issues', *Resources, Conservation and Recycling*, 15, 245–57.

Schöb, R. (1996), 'Evaluating Tax Reforms in the Presence of Externalities', *Oxford Economic Papers*, 48, 537–55.

Sharholy, M., K. Ahmad, G. Mahmood and R.C. Trivedi (2008), 'Municipal Solid Waste Management in Indian Cities – A Review', *Waste Management*, 28(2), 459–67.

Williams, R.C. (2002), 'Environmental Tax Interactions when Pollution Affects Health or Productivity', *Journal of Environmental Economics and Management*, 44(2), 261–70.

Wilson, D.C. (1996), 'Stick or Carrot?: The Use of Policy Measures to Move Waste Management up the Hierarchy', *Waste Management & Research*, 14(4), 385–98.

Zhu Da, P.U. Asnani, Chris Zurbrügg, Sebastian Anapolsky and Shyamala Mani (2008), 'Improving Municipal Solid Waste Management in India – A Sourcebook for Policy Makers and Practitioners', Washington, DC: The International Bank for Reconstruction and Development/The World Bank.

Section C

Permit trading

18. Regional market-based climate policy in North America: efficient, effective, fair?

Sven Rudolph, Takeshi Kawakatsu and Achim Lerch

1. INTRODUCTION

Despite promising recent developments, after the failure of the Waxman-Markey Bill in 2010 (Pooley 2010), ambitious federal level market-based approaches in the US seems very unlikely. The same is true for Canada, which has aligned its climate policy strategy to the US (Bernstein, Brunnée and Duff 2008; GoC 2013). However, several US states and Canadian provinces have acted on their own. Besides the US Northeast, British Columbia (BC) introduced a carbon tax in 2008 and California has started its cap-and-trade program in 2013.

But can these programs be considered a sustainable alternative or at least a supplement to federal action, and which of the two programs does better under the given circumstances? In order to answer these questions, this chapter analyzes the designs and the effects of both programs in a comparative way based on modern environmental economics and climate justice arguments. By doing so, the chapter provides a comparative evaluation of two North American sub-national level market-based climate policy programs based on sustainability criteria, shows the merits and the challenges of such initiatives, identifies best-practice design elements, and provides recommendations for regional market-based climate policy design.

2. DESIGN ELEMENTS AND CRITERIA FOR SUSTAINABLE MARKET-BASED CLIMATE POLICIES

Earlier chapters have already shown how sustainability criteria and design elements can be specified and how design recommendations for a sustainable carbon market can be derived (Rudolph et al. 2012). Accordingly, coverage should be comprehensive, including all major polluters and pollutants; the cap should be scarce, adequate to the 2°C target, and set in absolute volume terms; the initial distribution of emissions rights should be done by auctioning; revenues should be used to invest in mitigation and adaptation, or as a per capita dividend; banking should be allowed, borrowing permitted, and environmentally reliable offsets limited in quantity; the market should be based on existing, well-tried infrastructure; monitoring has to be reliable using approved standards and technologies; and penalties have to be higher than the market price for allowances, while also including *ex post* compensation for excess emissions.

In the case of climate policy taxes, the task of defining criteria for sustainable policy design is still work to be done. Taxes as an instrument to internalize externalities were suggested for the first time by Pigou (1920). However, it is well known that a Pigouvian tax is, although Pareto-efficient in theory, not feasible in practice, particularly due to the problems of calculating the monetary value of externalities. Therefore, today's discussions on environmental taxes are usually based on the Standard-Price-Approach proposed by Baumol and Oates (1971): as a price for emissions to achieve a pre-set arbitrary environmental goal (instead of Pareto-efficient allocation).

The comparison of environmental taxes and emissions trading has a long history in the environmental economics literature (Tietenberg and Lewis 2010). From a theoretical perspective both instruments are equally efficient and effective if the tax and the permit price equal marginal abatement costs for achieving the given emission target. The main advantage of emissions trading certainly is the security in achieving the emission target due to the immediate amount regulation by the emission cap and thus a higher environmental effectiveness, which is achieved even without the knowledge of marginal abatement costs. A tax, on the other hand, might miss the target if the government estimates these costs incorrectly and sets the wrong price. However, it is argued, that the right tax can be found in a process of trial and error (Baumol and Oates 1971); still such a process would cause temporary efficiency losses.

One major advantage of an environmental tax is the possibility of a broader coverage by including small emitters, which in an emissions trading scheme would significantly increase transaction costs; for example, it seems easier to include the transport sector as a major emitter in a tax scheme than in emission trading. In addition, taxes grant more certainty about the marginal control costs, especially when the marginal control cost curve is rather steeply sloped while the marginal damage curve is rather flat. In this case small changes in the degree of control would have little effect on damages but a large effect on abatement costs (Tietenberg and Lewis 2010: 319). From a public choice perspective, governments might prefer taxes over emissions trading, because they are used to raising taxes but not to creating markets, because governments can have direct control over costs burdens put on emitters, and because governments are reluctant to leave allocation decisions entirely to markets. Therefore, in terms of political feasibility, taxes might be advantageous.

Still, in climate policy, as in the case of carbon cap-and-trade schemes, carbon or energy taxes' compliance with sustainability criteria largely depends on their concrete design. Major design elements of such taxes are:

- Target: Does the tax pursue a concrete absolute volume emission target, and if so which target?
- Coverage: Which emitters have to pay for which emissions?
- Tax base: Has the tax to be paid on emissions or on fuels?
- Tax rate: Fixed or dynamic; does it equal marginal abatement costs for the required target?
- Revenue spending: Are the tax revenues used for ecological purposes, for lowering distortional taxes or for social redistribution?
- Monitoring and penalties.

Applying basic arguments on sustainability criteria for climate policy instruments (Rudolph et al. 2012) to the design elements of a carbon or energy tax, the following design recommendations for climate policy taxes can be derived.

With respect to the target, as already mentioned above, it seems impossible to implement a Pareto-efficient Pigouvian tax, because damage costs cannot be exactly calculated. Applying the Standard-Price-Approach, however, economic efficiency is independent of the concrete target level, which is therefore not a question of economics, but of environmental as well as of social (particularly intergenerational) justice considerations. In order to comply with the global 2°C climate policy target with a probability of two-thirds, applying the Budget Approach (WBGU 2009) would lead to a total amount of 750 billion tons of CO_2e that can be emitted within the period of 2010 to 2050. If, additionally, aspects of social justice such as different historic responsibilities for emissions are considered, concrete emission targets for individual countries could be calculated; for example, based on the concept of Contraction and Convergence (Meyer 2000).

From an efficiency perspective, as well as in terms of ecological effectiveness, the tax should cover all polluters and pollutants. Thus, all greenhouse gases (GHG) should be taxed, whereat the tax rate could be calculated on the base of Global Warming Potentials (GWP), for example, in carbon dioxide equivalents (CO_2e). However, taxing non-CO_2 GHG can either be difficult due to measurement problems, for example, for methane from the agricultural sector, or inadequate as in the case of CFCs (where rules seems more appropriate because of their destructive effect on the ozone layer). From a social justice perspective two aspects have to be considered. In order to comply with the polluter-pays principle, all polluters as well as all pollutants should be covered. However, this could lead to a high burden for poor households, especially due to the regressive effect of energy taxes. Such problems of social justice can be dealt with in three ways: tax exemptions, the tax rate, the spending of tax revenue. While reduced tax rates or exemptions would result in significantly weakening the effectiveness, using the revenues for *ex-post* compensation would reduce the effectiveness only with respect to the income effect of the tax while the substitution effect would still remain.

In terms of the tax base, in practice environmental taxes are often paid based on pre-products containing the actual pollutant, because direct emissions are oftentimes difficult to measure. In the case of CO_2, for example, the tax base could be the carbon-containing fossil such as coal, oil, or natural gas, etc. Tax rates should then be calculated based on the different carbon contents of the fuels. In the perspective of efficiency and ecological effectiveness a strong correlation between emissions and the tax base is essential (which applies in the case of carbon content and CO_2-emissions); thus a carbon tax is preferable over a general energy tax, because the latter would also penalize renewable energies.

Ideally, the tax rate should be set at a level equal to marginal abatement costs for the emission target. In practice abatement costs are known only to individual emitters, but not to the tax-setting authority. Therefore, establishing the adequate tax rate at first try seems impossible, but a trial-and-error process may allow approximating the respective level. However, such a process would not only cause temporary efficiency losses, but also lead to less planning reliability for emitters and to inefficient investments in new technologies (Tietenberg and Lewis 2010: 313). In order to mitigate negative impacts while also considering the fact, that significant emission reduction may need time (e.g. for technological improvements), the authority should choose a dynamic tax rate starting at a low rate, which will rise over time in pre-fixed steps. This procedure would also give planning reliability to emitters due to the pre-set tax hikes, which in turn could foster the dynamic efficiency in terms of innovation incentives even better than in the case of emissions trading, where price developments are uncertain. In addition, such a procedure could also be advantageous with respect to social justice, because it leaves more time for adaptation to households.

In terms of spending the revenues, from the perspective of economic efficiency revenues should be used to reduce other distorting taxes and by that overall inefficiency of the tax system (double dividend). From the environmental perspective the revenues should be used for additional environmental measures, which could increase the ecological effect of the tax. However, from a social justice point of view, redistributing the revenues in order to mitigate adverse distributional effects seems to be preferable. In addition, due to the substitution effect, such compensations would be less harmful to the environmental effect of the tax than exemptions or low rates. However, in any case there is an obvious tradeoff. The better the tax works in reaching the environmental target of reduced emissions, the lower the tax revenues are. Therefore, using tax revenues for other than redistributional or environmental measures such as the lowering of distortional taxes or social security payments might be problematic due to uncertain revenue levels.[1]

Just as in the case of emission trading, the monitoring system has to be reliable. This includes an accurate measurement or calculation of emissions from the pre-products. Penalties have to be severe and above the tax rate, in order to prevent fines being considered as quasi prices.

3. THE CALIFORNIA CAP-AND-TRADE PROGRAM

While on the federal level a large scale cap-and-trade scheme continues to be unlikely due to the political scars of the 2010 discussion on the Waxman-Markey Bill (Pooley 2010), individual US states are more progressive in using carbon markets. Besides the Regional Greenhouse Gas Initiative (RGGI), in 2013 California, the ninth largest economy in the world and emitter of 452 Mio.t. of CO_2e in 2010, started the biggest cap-and-trade program in the US so far (CARB 2013c).

3.1 Design

In 2007, California was a co-founder of the Western Climate Initiative (WCI), a joint project of western US and Mexican states as well as Canadian provinces, with the aim of establishing a common North American carbon market to reduce GHG emissions by at least 15 percent. While most jurisdictions have lost interest, Quebec is going to link its carbon market to California's in 2014. In California, former governor Schwarzenegger issued an official order to reduce GHG emissions to the 2000 level by 2010, to the 1990 level by 2020, and 80 percent below the 1990 level by 2050. In 2006, California passed its Global Warming

Solutions Act, the Assembly Bill 32 (AB 32) (California State Assembly 2006), making the California Air Resources Board (CARB) responsible for achieving the targets and for implementing policies such as a cap-and-trade program made concrete in the 2008 Scoping Plan and the 2011 Final Order (Burtraw, McClaughlin and Szambelan 2012, CARB 2008, CARB 2011).

California's cap-and-trade program is a mixed up- and down-stream scheme, which covers all six Kyoto gases and nitrogen trifluoride, starting downstream with power generation and large industrial facilities (>25,000 t. CO_2e) and including electricity imports. From 2015 onward emissions from liquid and gaseous fossil fuel use in smaller facilities, buildings and the transport sector will also be covered upstream; compliance obligations rests with distributors. Altogether the program covers 85 percent of California's GHG emissions. Total reductions in the covered sectors will amount to 17 percent in 2020 (base 2012), achieved by gradual reductions of an annual 2 percent cap reduction between 2012 and 2013 and 3 percent thereafter.

California hands out 90 percent of its California Carbon Allowances (CCA), each worth one ton of CO_2e, for free. Two-thirds of electricity generators allowances go to investor-owned utilities (IOU), one-third goes to publicly owned utilities (POU). Basically, all electricity generating facilities receive their allowances for free on behalf of their clients. However, while publicly owned generators can directly use allowances for compliance, privately owned facilities have to auction off all their allowances and buy back the amount they need for compliance. Industrial sector allocation is calculated by using a product benchmark based on the best available technology, a cap decline factor, which aligns the cap to the reduction roadmap, and the assistance factor, taking account of carbon leakage. The initial 10 percent auctioning share is going to be increased in the future.

New entrants are provided with allowances free-of-charge from a reserve, which is filled with an increasing share of total allowances under the cap (1–7 percent). The reserve is also used for cost containment. In each case, one third of the cost containment reserve allowances can be bought quarterly at a price of US$ 40, 45 and 50; however these prices will be increased by 5 percent plus inflationary adjustment each year. Thus, California establishes a price collar ranging from the reserve price of US$ 10 to the reserve prices; but it is only binding at the upper limit as long as there are still allowances available from the reserve. Banking of unused allowances is allowed without limits, while borrowing is prohibited. Offsets are allowed up to 8 percent of an individual entity's compliance obligation. Project types are currently limited to projects within the US and to forestry, dairy digesters, and the destruction of ozone-depleting substances. Reductions will be verified by independents agents based on ambitious criteria.

Trading and compliance periods are 2013–2014, 2015–2017 and 2018–2020. The biggest secondary market is expected to be the Intercontinental Exchange. Quarterly auctions of spot and forward allowances are held by a private company, Market Northamerica, applying a reserve price of US$ 10, which increases annually by 5 percent over inflation. Unsold allowances are transferred to the reserve. Auction revenues, calculated to be at least US$ 1 billion per year, go to two different uses. At least 85 percent of the economic value of allowances handed out to utilities has to inure to the benefit of ratepayers. In the case of private utilities the Public Utility Commission (PUC) decides about the concrete spending, while in the case of public utilities the utilities decide themselves. Details of refunding are not yet decided, but there are proposals on a per capita dividend and on funding energy efficiency measures. Revenues from industry auctions are transferred to a Greenhouse Gas Reduction Account within the Air Pollution Control Fund (Burtraw, McClaughlin and Szambelan 2012). California laws demand proceeds to be spent for environmental purposes only. At least 25 percent will be allocated to energy saving projects in disadvantaged communities (CARB 2013a).

Monitoring, reporting and, verifying of emissions (MRV) is based on annual, independently verified facility reports, and trading facilities have to open accounts in CARB's Compliance Instrument Tracking System Service (CITSS). For compliance, facilities have to provide allowances for 30 percent of the previous year's emissions annually, while the remaining 70 percent have to be covered at the end of the compliance period. In the case of non-compliance, four allowances must be provided for every ton of emissions that was not covered in time. In addition, fines of up to several thousand dollars per day based on clean air regulations may apply.

3.2 Effects, Evaluation, and Recommendations

As the program has just started its operation in 2013, empirical results are limited. Still, some *ex-ante* studies have predicted the program's effects (Burtraw, McClaughlin and Szambelan 2012; CARB 2010; Next 10 2012). Depending on how the revenues are spent, the Californian gross domestic product (GDP) is calculated to change between −1.4 and +0.2 percent. Price expectations are US$ 15.90 in 2013, US$ 20.92 in 2015, and US$ 36.94 in 2020 (Synapse 2008). Household incomes might be slightly negatively influenced (<1 percent) when all sectors are covered from 2015 onwards. However, as several studies show (Burtraw, McClaughlin and

Table 18.1 Auction results 2012–2013 (US$)

	Reserve Price	Vintage 2013 Clearing Price	Vintage 2015/16 Clearing Price	Revenues
Auction 1 (Nov. 2012)	10.00	10.09	10.00	289 102 450
Auction 2 (Feb. 2013)	10.71	13.62	10.71	223 588 476
Auction 3 (May 2013)	10.71	14.00	10.71	283 794 322
Auction 4 (Aug. 2013)	10.71	12.22	11.10	275 551 457
				1 072 036 705

Source: Data from CARB 2013b.

Szambelan 2012; Dunkel and Kammen 2009), increasing energy costs for households can be compensated by purposefully recycling auction revenues. Even if allowances prices reach US$ 30, a per capita refund of the total value of allowances would lead to a net benefit for the majority of Californian households. This holds even when 50 percent of the value goes to the state; and for compensating low income households even 10–20 percent would suffice. At an allowance price of US$ 15.90, the total economic value of allowances would sum up to about US$ 3 billion in 2013, increasing to 8.7 billion in 2015 (p= US$ 20.92) and 11.7 billion in 2020 (p= US$ 34.09).

Besides *ex ante* studies, the results from the first allowance auctions (see Table 18.1) show that while prices for vintage 2013 allowances started only slightly above the reserve price, in later auctions prices increased to a level close to *ex ante* calculations. Vintage phase II allowances, however, have been sold at the reserve price level at the first three auctions and only outstripped it in August 2013. All vintage 2013 allowances on offer have been sold, while only parts of vintage phase II allowances have been sold up to the third auction; only in August 2013 were all vintage phase II allowances sold. Total revenues of the first four auctions added up to more than US$ 1 billion.

Altogether, while there is leeway for improvement, the California cap-and-trade program represents a significant step towards ambitious market-based US climate policy and it complies with major sustainability criteria. First, the program is mandatory and covers California's GHG emissions most comprehensively. Second, the 2020 reduction target of around 17 percent below 2012 emission levels achieved by a dynamic reduction path is ambitious if compared to other cap-and-trade programs. Also, most recent market developments show that there is scarcity in the market. Still, if the 25–40 percent reduction requirement (base

1990) necessary to stay within the 2°C temperature increase boundary set forth by the Intergovernmental Panel on Climate Change (IPCC) is to be taken seriously, a significant shortening of the cap might become necessary.

Third, the free-of-charge initial distribution does not comply with sustainability criteria and could be improved by a more immediate phase-in of auctioning. Although the revenue recycling may not be the most efficient, it lessens burdens for low income households and allows additional investments in climate mitigation and adaptation measures. While banking and borrowing rules are well designed, offsets rule are very generous in quantity. Thus, the integrity of these offsets has to be well guarded by government oversight.

Fourth, the program has implemented a reliable trading and monitoring infrastructure, fully in line with sustainability criteria. Still, while in cost containment the price ceiling may be acceptable from a social justice perspective and the floor price might serve mainly environmental purposes, California's price collar may hamper efficiency. However, taking into account the current price trends, this collar seems to be set at a level not to obstruct the market.

4. BRITISH COLUMBIA'S CARBON TAX

Among alternative public policies to reduce GHG emissions, a carbon tax represents a promising but often under-utilized approach, particularly in North America.[2] In Canada, however, BC, emitter of 62 Mio. t. of CO_2e in 2010, launched its 'Climate Action Plan' in 2008 with aggressive GHG targets of a 33 percent reduction from 2007 levels by 2020 and an 80 percent reduction by 2050. At the same time, the carbon tax was introduced in 2008 as a crucial component of the province's climate change strategy (GoBC 2008).

4.1 Design

Concerning the tax base, BC's carbon tax applies to GHG emissions in the province from the combustion of fossil fuels. Thus, the tax base includes all fossil fuels purchased for use in the province, or used by those importing or producing the fuel. However, it is intended that some fuels, or the use of some fuels in certain circumstances, are not to be subject to the carbon tax. Because of technical measurement problems, the tax does not apply to CO_2 emissions from industrial processes such as the production of oil, gas, and cement, as well as emissions of other GHGs from landfills and the agricultural sector. Also the tax does not apply to the combustion of biofuels. Fuels exported from BC and fuels used for inter-jurisdictional commercial marine and aviation purposes are also excluded. Competitiveness concerns of BC's industries are addressed by implementing such a border tax adjustments

Starting on July 1, 2008, the tax rates are based on C$ 10 per ton of CO_2-equivalent (CO_2e) emissions, increasing by C$ 5/t. each year for the next four years to C$ 30/t. in 2012. The specific tax rates vary for each type of fuel, depending on the amount of CO_2e released in combustion (e.g. 6.67 cents per liter for gasoline, while 7.67 cents/l for diesel).

In terms of administration, the legislation requires all businesses that make the first sale of fossil fuels in BC to have been appointed collectors like those of the existing motor fuel tax. Thus, all individuals, businesses and visitors to BC who purchase or use fossil fuel in the province are required to pay the tax at the time of retail purchase or use of fossil fuel in the province.

With respect to revenue spending, every cent generated by the carbon tax is returned to taxpayers through tax reductions and credits. According to BCMoF (2013), spending mentioned in an annual plan can be differentiated between household tax measures and business tax measures. The former includes Low Income Climate Action Tax Credit, the 5 percent reductions in the first two personal income tax rates, Northern and Rural Homeowner benefit and so forth. The latter includes the reductions in each of the general and small business corporate income tax rates, the corporate income tax small business threshold increased from C$ 400,000 to 500,000, and so forth.

4.2 Effects, Evaluation, and Recommendations

In the past four years, how have this carbon tax and revenue recycling actually impacted on the environment and economy? While there have been few studies of this kind so far, Elgie, Antakly and McClay (2012) and Elgie and McClay (2013) have presented some early *ex post* study results (see Table 18.2).

In terms of environmental effects, Table 18.2 shows both changes of fuel consumption per capita and per capita GHG emissions. BC's fuel consumption per capita has fallen every year since 2008–2009. It declined by 17.4 percent from the 2007–2008 base year to 2011–2012. Moreover, it declined 18.8 percent more than in the rest of Canada during this four year period. BC's per capita GHG emissions associated with carbon taxed fuels declined by 10.0 percent from 2008 to 2011. During this period, BC's reductions outpaced those in the rest of Canada by almost 9 percent.

Table 18.2 The environmental and economic effects of BC's carbon tax (base 2007–2008)

Per capita consumption of petroleum fuels subject to BC's carbon tax					
	2008/09	2009/10	2010/11	2011/12	2008/12 total
British Columbia	−5.4 %	−3.6 %	−2.4 %	−7.1 %	−17.4 %
Rest of Canada	−3.4 %	−0.7 %	3.9 %	1.7 %	1.5 %
Difference	−2.1 %	−3.0 %	−6.3 %	−8.8 %	−18.8 %
GHG emissions per capita from sources subject to BC's carbon tax					
	2008	2009	2010	2011	2008/11 total
British Columbia	−1.5 %	−6.7 %	−1.1 %	−2.4 %	−10.0 %
Rest of Canada	−3.6 %	−3.9 %	−0.9 %	3.9 %	−1.1 %
Difference	2.1 %	−2.8 %	−0.2 %	−6.3 %	−8.9 %
BC and Canada GDP per capita					
	2008/09	2009/10	2010/11	2011/12	2008/12 total
British Columbia	−1.16 %	−3.90 %	1.64 %	1.92 %	−0.15 %
Rest of Canada	−0.45 %	−3.38 %	1.91 %	1.38 %	−0.23 %
Difference	−0.71 %	−0.52 %	−0.27 %	0.54 %	−0.08 %

Note: While the data of per capita consumption of petroleum fuels is expressed by fiscal year (July 1–June 30), that of GHG emissions per capita is expressed by calendar year, due to data availability.

Source: Elgie and Mcclay (2013: 2, 4–5)

These GHG reductions were similar to those seen in fuel use during this same 2008–2011 time period.

Regarding economic effects, Table 18.2 shows that after four years BC's GDP has slightly outperformed the rest of the country over the period the carbon tax has been in place. The difference in GDP change is very small (0.1 percent in total from 2008–2011). BC has a carbon price that is higher than anywhere else in North America, while the data at least appears to indicate it has not had a negative effect.

However, this only means that the economy-wide impact of the tax shift seems to have been neutral or positive. It does not mean that no firms or households have experienced adverse economic impacts. Actually, it is expected in the analysis by BCMoF (2013) that the economic impact of BC's carbon tax varies by industry and that some industries with high emissions intensities, such as cement production, are more impacted than others. Unfortunately, there are yet no studies which examine the impacts of BC's carbon tax shift on outputs and jobs, differentiating by industry.

In terms of effects on households, some empirical studies exist. For example, Lee and Sanger (2008) estimated the impact of the tax on different income groups on direct and indirect consumption of fossil fuels, and also modeled the distribution of the tax cuts and credits implemented by the government. They found that BC's carbon tax is slightly progressive for 2008–2009, with credits exceeding taxes paid, although personal and corporate income tax cuts lead to net gains for the top 20 percent of households. However, as the tax increases over time, the regime will be moderately regressive from 2010–2011 with an increasing trend afterwards. Lee (2011) derives more detailed estimations for the distributional impact of BC's carbon tax and revenue recycling for households in each income decile for 2010 and 2012. The results show the income top 10 percent, on average, receive net benefits of up to 1 percent in 2012; while the bottom 10 percent face net costs of 0.5 percent. Anyway, the total effect on households is slightly positive.

Considering the above described design as well as the effects, BC's carbon tax can be evaluated as follows. First, the tax base is relatively broad. The fossil fuels included in the tax base account for 75 percent of BC's total GHG emissions. Still, if the tax would additionally cover the non-combustion industry emissions that can be accurately measured, the coverage would increase from 75 percent to 82 percent (Horne, Petropavlova and Partington 2012). This would not only enhance the environmental effectiveness of the tax but make it more social just by treating more GHG emissions sources equally. However, it is important to keep in mind that, when the carbon tax was introduced, the BC government committed to replace the tax on large industries by a cap-and-trade scheme via WCI. Part of the reason for that commitment was to address a gap in the tax's coverage in that it did not apply to non-combustion GHG emissions. BC may join in the relatively near term, but the picture is still much less clear.

Second, the tax rate starts low and increases gradually. Allowing this relatively long phase-in is intended to give people and businesses enough time to adjust their consumption patterns prior to the announcement of the tax. However, at the end, the carbon tax needs to be high enough to shift technology investments as well as behavior significantly towards cleaner and more efficient energy choices in a way that BC can meet its climate policy commitments.

Third, BC's carbon tax is revenue neutral. Therefore, if in the event of a revenue surplus, the revenue recycling plan must show how the government intends to return the surplus to taxpayers via additional tax reductions. This ensures that there is full, transparent, ongoing revenue recycling. However, BC's carbon tax regime has been 'revenue negative

(C$ −260 million)' for the years 2012 and 2013, primarily due to corporate income tax cuts. While, as a result, the general corporate income tax rate in BC is among the lowest in North America and BC's income tax rates are presently the lowest in Canada for those earning up to C$ 122,000, there is a need to find mechanisms to deal with this problem.

Fourth, low income households are protected. A refundable Climate Action Tax Credit will ensure that those households with low income are compensated for the tax, and that most will be better off than without the tax scheme. As described above, while the tax credit was large enough to more than offset any potentially negative impacts from the carbon tax on low income individuals and families in the first year, increases in the credit have not kept pace with increases in the carbon tax. To make up for this gap, the province needs to examine increases of the possible protection it provides to low income households.

Finally, the administration of the tax is simple. The carbon tax is applied and collected at the wholesale level in essentially the same way that motor fuel taxes are applied and collected. This minimizes administrative costs.

5. COMPARATIVE CONCLUSIONS

Summing up major results of this chapter, first, is has to be stated that in the present situation, British Columbia and California can be considered the North American leaders in climate policy, and even on a global scale BC's carbon tax and California's cap-and-trade program are best practice models.

Second, as national levels in North America do not seem to move, regional programs are the way to go. Not only can they, even though geographically restricted, provide significant emission reductions. They can also serve as drivers for the national level and even as best practice models for other regions.

Third, both programs are well designed, fulfilling a big share of criteria for sustainable market-based climate policy. Coverage is comprehensive and targets appear ambitious at least compared to similar programs. The long-term carbon price level of C$ 30 and above seems sufficient for generating emission reductions and innovation. In addition, both programs are fully revenue neutral, investing each and every cent either in climate protection, redistribution, or the lowering of distortional taxes.

Fourth, in comparison, California's cap-and-trade program covered 85 percent of the state's GHG emissions in 2010, while the BC carbon tax only covered 75 percent of the province's emissions in 2010. Program targets are 9 percent by 2020 (base 2007) for California's program against

6 percent for BC's tax; also, California's absolute amount emissions reductions are certain, while BC's are not. Program induced carbon price increases started in 2008 in BC and in 2013 in California, already reaching a level of around C$ 30 in BC in 2012 while being delayed until 2015 in California. However California prices may further increase to about US$ 35 by 2020, while BC's tax, at least for the time being, stays at C$ 30. Still, while price levels in BC are certain, California's allowance prices are subject to fluctuations. GDP effects in both jurisdictions are between –1.4 and +0.2 percent, but while program effects are slightly regressive, the total effect on households is positive. In terms of the apportionment of the burden, the BC carbon tax makes most polluters fully pay for their resource use, while California hands out major parts of its emission allowances for free. Hence, overall, California's program appears a little more ambitious than BC's tax in terms of environmental effects, while the latter excels in its social components.

Fifth, in terms of improvements, for sure, taking into account the IPCC's reduction requirements, both programs have to strengthen their targets by shortening the cap or increasing the tax rate. California, in addition, should accelerate the phase-in of auctioning.

Nevertheless, despite the few design flaws, both the California cap-and-trade program and BC's carbon tax might act as groundbreaking examples for sustainable sub-national climate policies. It remains to be hoped that they will also stimulate action at North America's federal level and at regional levels in other countries across the globe.

NOTES

1. In the case of inelastic demand (as for many energy sources) the trade off is minor, however. Thus e.g. the German Ecological Tax Reform has been using revenues for lowering payment to the old age pension fund with some success.
2. In Canada, the Federal Liberal Party made the introduction of a carbon tax a major issue in the federal election in 2008, but, popular support for the Liberal Party fell by 4% and the Party lost 27 seats on the House (Duff 2008).

REFERENCES

Baumol, W.J. and W.E. Oates (1971), 'The Use of Standards and Prices for Protection of the Environment', *Swedish Journal of Economics* 73(1), 42–54.

Bernstein, S., J. Brunnée and D.G. Duff (2008), *A Globally Integrated Climate Policy for Canada*, Toronto: University of Toronto Press.

British Columbia Ministry of Finance (BCMoF) (2013), Budget and Fiscal Plan 2013/14 to 2015/16.

Burtraw, D., D. McLaughlin and S.J. Szambelan (2012), California's New Gold, Resources for the Future, Discussion Paper 12–23, Washington DC.
California Air Resources Board (CARB) (2008), Climate Change Scoping Plan a Framework for Change, Sacramento, CA.
California Air Resources Board (CARB) (2010), Updated Economic Analysis of California's Climate Change Scoping Plan, Sacramento, CA.
California Air Resources Board (CARB) (2011), California Cap on Greenhouse Gas Emissions and Market-Based Compliance Mechanisms – Final Order, Sacramento, CA.
California Air Resources Board (CARB) (2013a), Cap-and-Trade Auction Proceeds Investment Plan – Fiscal Years 2013–14 through 2015–16, Sacramento, CA.
California Air Resources Board (CARB) (2013b), California Air Resources Board Quarterly Auction 1–4 – Summary Results Report, Sacramento, CA.
California Air Resources Board (CARB) (2013c), California Greenhouse Gas Emissions for 2000 to 2010 – Trends by Emissions and Other Indicators, Sacramento, CA.
California State Assembly (2006), Assembly Bill 32 – California Global Warming Solutions Act, Sacramento, CA.
Duff, D.G. (2008), 'Carbon Taxation in British Columbia', *Vermont Journal of Environmental Law* 10(1), 87–107.
Dunkel, C. and D.N. Kammen (2009), *Cap-and-Dividend*, Berkeley, CA: Energy Resources Group.
Elgie, S. and J. McClay (2013), *BC's Carbon Tax Shift after Five Years – An Environmental (and Economic) Success Story*, Ottawa: Sustainable Prosperity.
Elgie, S., D. Antakly and J. McClay (2012), *British Columbian's Carbon Tax Shift – The Four Years*, Ottawa: Sustainable Prosperity.
Government of British Columbia (GoBC) (2008), Climate Action Plan, available at http://www.livesmartbc.ca/attachments/climateaction_plan_web.pdf.
Government of Canada (GoC) (2013), Climate Change, available at http://www.ec.gc.ca/cc/Default.asp?lang=En&n=9853BFC5-1.
Horne, M., E. Petropavlova and P.J. Partington (2012), *British Columbia's Carbon Tax – Exploring perspectives and seeking common ground*, Alberta: Pembina.
Lee, M. (2011), *Fair and Effective Carbon Pricing Lessons from BC*, Vancouver, BC: Canadian Centre for Policy Alternatives.
Lee, M. and T. Sanger (2008), *Is BC's Carbon Tax Fair?: An Impact Analysis for Different Income Levels*, Vancouver, BC: Canadian Centre for Policy Alternatives.
Meyer, A. (2000), *Contraction and Convergence*, Totnes, UK: Green Books.
Next 10 (2012), *Using the Allowance Value from California's Carbon Trading System – Legal Risk Factors, Impacts to Ratepayers, and the Economy*, Washington, DC.
Pigou, A.C. (1920), *The Economics of Welfare*, London: Macmillan (4th edition 1932).
Pooley, E. (2010), *The Climate War*, New York, NY: Hyperion.
Rudolph, S., C. Lenz, A. Lerch and B. Volmert (2012), 'Towards Sustainable Carbon Markets: Requirements for Ecologically Effective, Economically Efficient, and Socially Just Emissions Trading Schemes', in Larry Kreiser, Ana Yábar Sterling, Pedro Herrera, Janet E. Milne and Hope Ashiabor (eds), *Carbon Pricing, Growth and the Environment – Critical Issues in Environmental*

Taxation, Band XI, Cheltenham, UK and Northampton. MA, USA: Edward Elgar, pp. 167–83.
Synapse (2008), *Synapse 2008 CO_2 Price Forecasts*, Cambridge, MA.
Tietenberg, T. and L. Lewis (2010), *Environmental Economics & Policy*, Boston, MA: Pearson.
WBGU (Wissenschaftlicher Beirat der Bundesregierung Globale Umweltveränderungen) (2009), Solving the Climate Dilemma, Berlin.

19. A survey analysis of company perspective to the GHG emissions trading scheme in the Republic of Korea

Sunhee Suk and Xianbing Liu

1. INTRODUCTION

The Republic of Korea (hereinafter referred as Korea) announced in November 2009 a plan to reduce its greenhouse gases (GHG) emissions by 30 percent from the business as usual (BAU) scenario by 2020. Korean industry used 61.6 percent of the country's total energy in 2011, making it a key target of climate policies (KEMCO 2013). The enactment of the 'Basic Act on Low Carbon Green Growth' in 2010 established a legal ground for the practice of market-based instruments (MBIs), i.e., a GHG emission trading scheme (GHG ETS) and carbon tax, etc. Korea adopted the mandatory 'GHG-Energy Target Management System' (TMS) in 2011 for large energy-consuming entities. The TMS paves the way for the introduction of GHG ETS in Korea. Accordingly, a bill of quasi-mandatory GHG ETS was approved in May 2012 and determined to launch the domestic GHG ETS at the beginning of 2015. More recently, a bill of carbon tax was also proposed, suggesting the introduction of this policy from 2016.

GHG ETS holds a theoretical advantage in cost efficiency and shall be effective for GHG mitigation referring to the experience of the European Union (EU) ETS as the largest example of emissions trading in operation, encompassing over 11,500 installations across 30 countries and covering approximately 40 percent of total EU emissions. This scheme has led to emissions reductions of 40–80 Mt-CO_2 per year, sharing about 2–4 percent of the total capped emissions. This amount is much bigger than the impact of most other individual policy instruments. According to the studies investigating the impact of the EU ETS based on managerial interviews at firms, EU ETS has captured the attention of decision-makers and brought some impact on the innovation and investment of low carbon technology (Laing et al. 2013). However, businesses in Korea indicate less acceptability to carbon pricing policies and show limited affordability of costs originated from the introduction of MBIs (Suk et al. 2014a; Suk et al. 2014b). Our previous survey confirmed the marginal function of the government in enhancing Korean companies' energy saving and GHG mitigation practices (Suk, Liu and Sudo 2013). The resistance from industry was identified as the largest barrier for the introduction of GHG ETS in Korea (Liu, Suk and Sudo 2012). In practice, the acceptance level of companies, as the major policy targets, is a key factor determining the actual progress and success of climate policies. It is necessary to understand viewpoints of businesses to the policies in advance. However, few studies have been conducted at the individual company level in Korea under the emerging process of carbon pricing policies.

Aiming to bridge the existing gap, a questionnaire survey to Korean companies was arranged to clarify their perspective to GHG ETS. Two topics are discussed in this chapter. One is to monitor the opinions of Korean companies to various aspects of GHG ETS. The other is to identify the difference in companies' viewpoints due to their characteristics in organizational size, sector and ownership. Three sectors, iron and steel, cement and petro-chemical industries, were targeted since they are energy-intensive and significant for realizing the country's overall goal of GHG mitigation.

The remainder of this chapter is as follows. Section 2 describes the progress of GHG ETS in Korea and the debate for the introduction of this scheme. Section 3 outlines the questionnaire survey and the samples. Section 4 discusses the survey analysis results. Lastly, section 5 concludes this survey study.

2. THE PROGRESS OF GHG ETS IN KOREA

2.1 GHG ETS Proposals and Bill of Korea

The preliminary proposal of GHG ETS was first formulated in November 2010, suggesting its introduction in 2013 with three phases. The first phase would start from 2013 and end in 2015. Two following phases would run for five years for each from 2016. In this proposal, 10 percent of the total allowances would be allocated by auction and the remaining 90 percent for free in the initial phase, with the auction proportions increased thereafter. The penalty for non-compliance emissions is less than five times the average market price of credits. This preliminary proposal received strong opposition from industry. As a result, the proposal was revised and its stringency was watered down in terms of starting time, the allocation of emissions allowances and the level of penalty, etc. The starting time was postponed to January 1, 2015 and 95 percent allowances would be allocated for free in the initial period. The penalty was decreased to less than three times the average market price and up to 100,000 KRW/t-CO_2 (about 90 US$/t-$CO_2$). The updated proposal called for an 'Allocation Committee', led by the Ministry of Strategy and Finance (MOSF), for determining the method of allowances allocation for each field and maintaining the stability of the carbon market. This proposal indicated one likely option for targeting the largest energy consumers or GHG emitters heading the list of TMS targets. Allowances transfer is allowable between different compliance periods.

This revised proposal was submitted to the parliament in April 2011. After slight revisions, the GHG ETS bill, namely the 'Act on Allocation and Trading of Greenhouse Gas Emissions Allowances', was finally approved by the parliament in May 2012. Later, the 'Presidential Decree', officially approved on November 13, 2012, clarified the commencement of GHG ETS since the beginning of 2015 and specified the management rules. Responsibility for operation lies within the Ministry of Environment, Korea (MOEK). The entities emitting over 125,000t-CO_2 and business sites emitting over 25,000t-CO_2 annually shall participate obligatorily. The legislation provides for allowances to be allocated fully for free in the first phase (2015–2017), at 95–97 percent for the second phase (2018–2020) and at 90 percent for the third phase (2021–2025). Banking within and between compliance periods, and borrowing within compliance periods, are allowed. Six years later, domestic and foreign individuals or corporations can join as parties for the transaction. The carbon leakage sectors will be given 100 percent free allocation. Early action for GHG reductions will be recognized. MOEK established the 'Emissions Trading Task Force' to prepare for the detailed allocation method for emissions allowances.

2.2 The Debate for the Introduction of GHG ETS in Korea

Cost effectiveness is viewed as the key merit for Korea to introduce GHG ETS. The evaluations of several core research institutes in Korea did indicate that GHG ETS would be more cost effective than the mandatory regulations, like TMS, and could save the cost by 44 to 68 percent for achieving the country's GHG mitigation target of 2020 (PCGG press 2011; Kim 2010; Lee 2009). On the other hand, Korea Energy Management Corporation (KEMCO) estimated that the additional production cost would be 5.6 trillion KRW (About 943 million US$) for main industries if 10 percent of the allowances were allocated by auction. Similarly, several studies revealed the additional production cost increase of overall sectors in difference allowance scenarios of the ETS introduction (Kim 2009; Lee 2010; Han, Lim and Kwak 2010, Steel & Steel 2011; Cho 2011). Referring to the estimation results above, the industry argued that GHG ETS would obviously weaken the industrial competitiveness due to the increase of production costs, and increase the burden on the Korean economy as a whole.

Korean industry also emphasized that the early action of Korea would bring significantly adverse impacts to its competitiveness in international markets, considering the laggard policy movement of major competing economies, for example, the US, China and Japan, in the pricing of carbon emissions. Korean companies pointed out that this policy effort of Korea would have virtually no contribution to the mitigation overall, given that GHG emissions in Korea only account for 1.7 percent of the global total. The other concerns of industry include the stability of carbon credit prices and the sufficient number of participants for the market to operate smoothly. Actually, the number of business sites emitting GHG emissions over 25,000t-CO_2 in 2007 was only 704 in Korea, with emissions sharing 78 percent of the total from the manufacturing sector. The top 25 business sites contributed to 40 percent of the emissions of manufacturing industry (except for the power sector). The total participants by the business sites in Korea would be no more than 600. If counted by entities, the number of GHG ETS targets would be much less. High concentration of GHG emissions emitters and small number of GHG ETS targets may cause low credit liquidity and instability of carbon prices.

Our previous study confirmed that Korean companies agree with the usefulness of governmental requirements in mandatory (Suk et al. 2014a). The companies in this survey further stated that the existing regulations of Korea are strict enough and effective considering the introduction of the GHG ETS. They strongly appeal their good performance to abide by the regulations and insist on their limited potential for energy efficiency improvement and GHG mitigation. In fact, petro-chemical, cement, and iron and steel sectors have achieved comparative levels with Japan and Germany in energy efficiency (IEA 2007). The companies thus argued that GHG ETS with high stringency would discourage their investments since they have to purchase additional credits for the increased production.

3. THE QUESTIONNAIRE SURVEY AND THE SAMPLES

Based on the understanding of the Korean situation, a questionnaire was developed with the main objectives of estimating the affordability

Table 19.1 Distribution of respondents by company characteristics

Company's characteristics		Number of samples				Number (Percentage)
		Small	Medium	Large Medium	Large	
Sector	Cement	2	6	2	1	11 (17.7)
	Steel	–	8	5	3	16 (25.8)
	Petro-chemical	–	13	13	9	35 (56.5)
Number (Percentage)		2 (3.2)	27 (43.5)	20 (32.2)	13 (21.0)	62 (100.0)
TMS target or not	TMS	2	26	17	13	58 (93.5)
	Non-TMS	–	1	3	–	4 (6.5)
Number (Percentage)		2 (3.2)	27 (43.5)	20 (32.2)	13 (21.0)	62 (100.0)

of companies on carbon prices and measuring their perspective to GHG ETS. Major components of the format include company general information; companys' energy use and management status; the acceptability level to various energy cost increases due to carbon pricing policies; and, companys' opinions of GHG ETS. This chapter summarizes the part of companies' perspective of GHG ETS.

The survey was carried out from January 25 to February 10, 2012. Questionnaires were sent via fax and email to 205 companies, including 137 TMS target companies and 68 non-TMS, intending to be filled out by environmental and energy managers. Valid answers from 62 companies were collected and used for this analysis. The distribution of the samples by company characteristics is summarized in Table 19.1.

The respondents from cement, iron and steel and petro-chemical sectors individually account for 17.7 percent, 25.8 percent and 56.5 percent respectively of the total. Twenty seven are medium-sized companies having 50–300 staff, 2 are small companies with staff numbers less than 50, and 13 are large companies with employees over 1,000. The remaining 20 companies are those with relatively larger scale than medium-sized companies but smaller than large ones, which are thus categorized as large medium-sized companies in this survey. Of the total 62 samples, 58 are TMS target companies.

Overall, the surveyed companies are large energy consumers and heavy carbon emitters. Around 95 percent of them used more than 2,000 TOE (Ton of oil equivalent) of energy in 2010. The samples consuming more than 100,000 TOE in 2010 account for 35.5 percent of the total. Most respondents (92 percent) emit over 25,000t-CO_2 annually. The companies with emissions less than 5,000t-CO_2 only share 4.8 percent. The other companies answered that their annual CO_2 emissions are between 5,000 to 15,000t-CO_2. The companies were requested to check their potential for energy saving. A majority of them evaluated that there remains limited energy saving potential. Even 40 percent of iron and steel companies selected almost no further potential. Only 3 percent of the samples in the petro-chemical sector admit that they have very high potentials.

4. RESULTS AND DISCUSSIONS

4.1 Companies' Evaluations of Merits of GHG ETS

The companies were asked to evaluate the advantages of GHG ETS to be implemented in Korea. A five-point scale was applied, with 5 = 'very appropriate', 4 = 'appropriate', 3 = 'somewhat appropriate', 2 = 'not appropriate', 1 = 'not appropriate at all'. The average scores for the six merits listed in the questionnaire are shown in Table 19.2.

The companies evaluated the advantages of GHG ETS at low degrees and almost all the merit items achieved a mean under 3.00. The samples moderately recognize GHG ETS as an effective measure for GHG mitigation, with a mean of 3.08 for MERIT01. Although the Korean government expects to make use of the advantage of GHG ETS in cost efficiency, the businesses seem not to agree with this, with the mean for MERIT02 being 2.86. The companies do not believe that GHG ETS could generate economic revenues at the current stage and present MERIT05 the lowest mean of 2.08. This result confirms the negative attitude of Korean companies to the introduction of GHG ETS in Korea.

Econometric regressions were performed for identifying the differences in companies' evaluations of GHG ETS merits due to their various characteristics. As the dependent variables, the evaluations of GHG ETS merits, MERIT01 to MERIT06, are in an ordinal measurement. An ordered logistic model is a rational choice for this analysis (Greene 1997). Company size, sector, ownership, TMS involvement and its international orientation are selected as the independent variables. The company size, SIZE, is classified into small, medium, medium-large and large, individually named as SMALL, MEDIUM, MLARGE and LARGE. Sector, SECTOR, has three categories: iron and steel, cement, and chemical, which are presented as STEEL, CEMENT and CHEMICAL. The ownership consists of two types, domestically private and foreign-funded, DOMESTIC and FOREIGN. The status of TMS involvement is indicated as TMS for the targets and non-TMS for the others. The main market

Table 19.2 Companies' evaluations of merits of GHG ETS

Item	Merits	Mean of scores			
		Overall (N=62)	Chemical (N=35)	Cement (N=11)	Steel (N=16)
MERIT01	ETS is an effective measure to mitigate GHG emissions	3.08	3.40	2.55	2.75
MERIT02	ETS is cost-effective compared with regulative policies	2.86	2.83	2.64	3.06
MERIT03	There would be an advantage to be better involved in international carbon market if introduced earlier	2.40	2.63	2.00	2.19
MERIT04	It is a global policy trend to introduce ETS	2.45	2.66	2.09	2.25
MERIT05	Compared with TMS, ETS has a possibly positive effect in generating economic revenues	2.08	2.23	1.82	1.94
MERIT06	Introducing ETS may generate the opportunities for new business and employment	2.50	2.69	2.09	2.38

of the products, EXPORT, is used as the proxy of a company's international orientation. Companies with products for the domestic market are presented a value of '0' and '1' is for the export-oriented companies. The regression coefficients are listed in Table 19.3.

The regression results of MERIT01, MERIT04 and MERIT06 are statistically significant. Compared with cement companies, the samples from the petro-chemical industry gave more positive assessment to all these three merits of GHG ETS. Company size is significantly but negatively associated with the evaluations of MERIT04. It is less likely for the companies with medium size and above to view GHG ETS as a global policy trend than the small ones. Similarly, TMS targets more negatively evaluate MERIT04

Table 19.3 Regression results of companies' evaluations of merits of GHG ETS

Independent variables		Dependent variables					
		MERIT01	MERIT02	MERIT03	MERIT04	MERIT05	MERIT06
SECTOR	STEEL	0.389	0.583	0.151	0.741	0.448	0.540
	CHEMICAL	**1.262**[a]	0.361	0.629	**1.274**[a]	0.898[c]	**0.912**[b]
SIZE	MEDIUM	−0.862	−1.291	0.577	**−1.546**[c]	−0.522	−0.812
	MLARGE	−0.407	−0.980	1.182	−1.419	−0.537	−0.594
	LARGE	−0.806	−1.325	0.918	**−1.759**[b]	−0.740	−1.305
DOMESTIC		0.301	−0.647	−0.076	0.358	0.007	0.282
TMS		−0.566	−0.217	−0.774	**−1.238**[b]	−1.426[b]	**−1.70**[a]
EXPORT		−0.178	−0.051	−0.128	−0.543	−0.126	0.208
Obs.		62	62	62	62	62	62
LR chi		**16.08**[b]	5.57	12.23	**15.42**[c]	10.16	**17.84**[b]
Pseudo R^2		0.098	0.030	0.073	0.089	0.067	0.100

Notes: a Significant at 1%; b Significant at 5%; c Significant at 10%.

and MERIT06 in comparison with the non-TMS companies. This result is consistent with intuitive perception. The companies with higher energy intensities, larger size and covered by TMS are more likely included by GHG ETS and have negative attitudes to the merits of this policy.

4.2 Companies' Evaluations of Negative Aspects of GHG ETS

In order to find out to what extent Korean businesses are concerned about the negative issues of GHG ETS, the samples were requested to evaluate 10 items of disadvantages pre-listed in the questionnaire. A five-point scale was applied, with 5 being 'highly concerned' and 1 meaning 'no concern at all'. The statistics are presented in Table 19.4.

The companies revealed high concerns about the negative aspect of GHG ETS and all the items achieved a mean of nearly 4.00 and over. Among which, NEG01 is presented the highest mean of 4.52. This implies that the companies commonly and most worry about the loss of business competitiveness due to the production cost increase if GHG ETS is phased in earlier in Korea than major competition countries. The uncleanness of the detailed operation scheme, for example, method for emissions allowance allocation (NEG02), was ranked the second, with a mean of 4.39. The surveyed companies are also concerned about other ambiguous issues of GHG ETS, including the expected contribution of this policy for GHG mitigation of the country (NEG04), the relationship between GHG ETS and the mandatory TMS (NEG03), market liquidity (NEG06), carbon price stability (NEG07) and the unclear responsibilities of related authorities for the policy implementation (NEG10). This requires the Korean government to further clear these aspects for achieving the understanding and support from the industry.

Ordered logistic analyses were carried out with companies' evaluations of disadvantages of GHG ETS, NEG01 to NEG10, as the dependent variables, and the company's characteristics as independents. The regression coefficients, as listed in Table 19.5, indicate that the results of NEG02, NEG06, NEG07 and NEG10 are statistically significant.

Company size and sector significantly determine their evaluation of negative aspects of GHG ETS. Specifically, it is less likely for chemical companies to be concerned about these three negative points of GHG ETS compared with the cement industry. Steel companies are less concerned on carbon price stability (NEG07) than their counterparts from the cement sector. In comparison with small companies, the samples of the other size categories are more likely to emphasize NEG02, NEG06 and NEG07. Additionally, foreign-funded companies tend to make clear the competent authorities and their responsibilities in implementing GHG ETS (NEG10)

Table 19.4 Companies' evaluations of negative aspects of GHG ETS

Item	Negative aspects	Mean of the scores			
		Overall (N=62)	Chemical (N=35)	Cement (N=11)	Steel (N=16)
NEG01	Premature implementation and loss of business competitiveness	4.52	4.40	4.91	4.50
NEG02	Unclearness of the detailed operation scheme including emission allowance allocation method, etc.	4.39	4.17	4.73	4.63
NEG03	Unclearness of the detailed measure to avoid the possible double burdens with TMS	4.29	4.20	4.18	4.56
NEG04	Ambiguity of the contribution of ETS to national GHG reductions	4.02	3.89	4.00	4.31
NEG05	Company's lack of capacity to cope with the implementation of ETS	4.00	3.86	4.18	4.19
NEG06	Insufficient liquidity of carbon market due to the limited credit volume in total	3.98	3.71	4.27	4.38
NEG07	Instability of carbon price and the speculative trading	4.05	3.94	4.36	4.06
NEG08	Carbon leakage problem	3.97	3.89	4.27	3.94
NEG09	Foreign companies hesitate to invest in Korea and the problem of domestic deindustrialization	4.16	4.00	4.55	4.25
NEG10	Ambiguity of the competent authorities and their responsibilities in implementing ETS	3.98	3.83	4.00	4.31

than the ones with domestic ownership. TMS targets address NEG06 more than the non-TMS ones.

4.3 Companies' Preparations for GHG ETS

The companies were asked to check the activities they have practiced or plan to do for the preparation of GHG ETS. Table 19.6 lists the percentages of samples with the answer 'YES' overall and by sector.

Table 19.5 Regression results of companies' evaluations of negative aspects of GHG ETS

Independent variables		Dependent variables									
		NEG01	NEG02	NEG03	NEG04	NEG05	NEG06	NEG07	NEG08	NEG09	NEG10
SECTOR	STEEL	−1.358	−1.076	0.440	0.423	−0.131	−0.446	**−0.937**[c]	−0.833[c]	−0.756	0.641
	CHEMICAL	−1.534	**−1.958**[a]	−0.150	−0.206	−0.676	**−1.522**[a]	**−1.209**[b]	−0.946[b]	−1.236[b]	0.002
SIZE	MEDIUM	−4.604	**2.177**[b]	0.485	1.061	0.417	**2.582**[a]	**1.716**[c]	1.434	1.110	0.823
	MLARGE	−4.852	**2.277**[b]	0.311	0.610	0.382	**2.712**[a]	**1.781**[c]	1.150	0.699	0.201
	LARGE	−4.631	**2.466**[b]	0.801	1.070	0.905	**3.217**[a]	**2.467**[b]	2.059[b]	1.059	1.078
DOMESTIC		−0.234	−0.236	−0.430	−0.556	−0.023	−0.365	−0.552	−0.343	−0.568	**−1.056**[b]
TMS		1.050	0.990	−0.122	0.182	0.810	**1.377**[b]	0.903	−0.216	−0.637	−0.976
EXPORT		0.060	−0.139	−0.392	−0.416	−0.086	−0.358	−0.089	0.078	0.445	−0.879
Obs.		62	62	62	62	62	62	62	62	62	62
LR chi		11.96	**17.37**[b]	6.55	10.73	7.59	**25.82**[a]	**14.48**[c]	10.27	11.87	**20.06**[b]
Pseudo R^2		0.110	0.146	0.052	0.079	0.057	0.175	0.106	0.077	0.087	0.138

Notes: a Significant at 1%; b Significant at 5%; c Significant at 10%.

Table 19.6 Companies' preparations for GHG ETS

No.	Preparation activities	Percentage with 'YES' (%)			
		Overall (N=62)	Cement (N=11)	Steel (N=16)	Chemical (N=35)
1	Establish a specific division for TMS and ETS	38.7	48.6	27.3	25.0
2	Sign the MOU with government for the self-implementation of ETS within the group company	4.8	8.6	0.0	0.0
3	Establish the company's inventory of GHG emissions and verify with a third party	93.5	94.3	90.9	93.8
4	Participate in the pilot project of ETS or TMS	33.9	48.6	27.3	6.3
5	Develop the offset program for achieving carbon credits	3.2	2.9	0.0	6.3
6	Plan to move the factory abroad with loose carbon regulations	4.8	5.7	0.0	6.3
7	Hire or outsource external professionals or company for necessary preparations	21.0	22.9	0.0	31.3

It is encouraging that most companies (93.5 percent) have established the internal inventory of GHG emissions, which is verified by a third party. This is because most sampled companies are targeted by the TMS launched in 2011 and TMS requires the target entities to establish their inventories of GHG emissions. Companies have made some preparations for GHG ETS by institutional arrangement. Nearly 40 percent of them established a specific division for TMS and GHG ETS. Around one-third of the samples actively participate in the pilots of TMS or GHG ETS for accumulating policy practice experience. Nevertheless, the companies have not started to act by self implementation and this activity only achieved a participation ratio of 4.8 percent. The samples did not consider achieving carbon credits by the offsetting programs, which obtained the lowest participation ratio of 3.2 percent. It is meaningful that the companies do not believe the moving of production to areas with loose regulations is an option and less than 5 percent of the samples ticked this choice.

4.4 Companies' Behavioral Changes in Response to GHG ETS

The companies' energy costs would increase while introducing GHG ETS. Aiming to understand the possible responses of companies to this policy, we requested the samples to check the possibility of taking alternative actions. A five-point scale was applied with the meanings: 5 = 'very possible'; 4 = 'relatively possible'; 3 = 'moderate possibility'; 2 = 'low possibility'; and 1 = 'completely impossible'. The statistics are listed in Table 19.7.

Table 19.7 Companies' behavioral changes in response to GHG ETS

No.	Optional actions	Mean of scores			
		Overall (N=62)	Chemical (N=35)	Cement (N=11)	Steel (N=16)
1	Strengthen internal management and save energy through management measures	3.82	3.89	3.73	3.75
2	Invest in more advanced energy-saving technologies and equipment	3.58	3.71	3.45	3.38
3	Self-investment in research and development of new energy-saving technologies and equipment	2.84	2.97	2.36	2.88
4	Try to use low carbon energies, adjust the company's energy use structure	2.90	3.09	2.09	3.06
5	Adjust product structure for reducing energy intensity per product	3.31	3.46	2.82	3.31
6	Raise the product price to transfer the increased costs	3.15	3.00	3.18	3.44
7	Increase production amount to reduce the energy cost on average	2.84	3.00	2.45	2.75
8	Reduce productions to alleviate market pressure due to cost increase	2.11	2.09	2.27	2.06
9	Relocate part or all the company to areas with relatively loose policies	2.32	2.43	2.18	2.19
10	Stop the production and business due to cost pressures	2.03	2.03	2.73	1.56
11	No specific reaction by accepting the loss due to cost increase	2.68	2.57	2.73	2.88

The companies would avoid the reactive behaviors, including to reduce production; move production to the areas with loose policy; close production facilities; and not reacting by accepting the loss. These four choices were presented average scores under 2.70. In contrast, the companies prefer to make internal efforts in energy saving to relieve the policy's negative impacts. Practicing managerial energy saving activities is the most possible choice, with the highest mean of 3.82. To invest in energy efficient technologies, self-investment in R&D and using less carbon-intensive energies are preferable options with relatively higher possibilities. Besides capping emissions, another key objective of the GHG ETS is to drive innovations in low carbon technologies, incentivize additional investments in low carbon assets and reduce investment in carbon-intensive products and processes. The companies would not like to simply transfer the policy economic burden to their clients. The option of raising product prices for cost shifting achieved a moderate mean of 2.84. De Groot, Verhoef and Nijkamp (2001) suggested that Dutch companies would more possibly charge the customers with additional costs given an energy tax increase. The different finding of this survey may be attributed to the strict competition faced by Korean companies. In this sense, our survey, to a certain degree, confirmed the effectiveness of GHG ETS in enhancing Korean companies' efforts in energy saving and GHG mitigation.

4.5 The Barriers for Companies to Implement GHG ETS

The companies were asked the difficulties they may encounter for the implementation of GHG ETS. Table 19.8 lists the percentages of samples confirming the barriers pre-listed in the survey document.

It is obvious that companies feel pressures from the introduction of GHG ETS due to the limited reduction potential, with the highest ratio of 80.6 percent. As mentioned earlier, energy intensities of the three target sectors have been improved dramatically in the past (Park and Kim 2009). The energy efficiency of the most energy-intensive petro-chemical and steel sectors in Korea has generally outpaced their counterparts in other countries (IEA 2009). The barriers with relatively high ratios of 'YES' answers are 'lack of information for the analysis of future carbon market' (64.5 percent) and 'lack of specialists on energy management and reduction potential identification' (61.3 percent). Fewer companies confirmed the 'budget shortage' (38.7 percent) and 'lack of awareness of top management' (33.9 percent) as the difficulties to implement GHG ETS.

Table 19.8 Barriers of companies for the implementation of GHG ETS

No.	Barriers	Percentage with 'YES' (%)			
		Overall (N=62)	Chemical (N=35)	Cement (N=11)	Steel (N=16)
1	Lack of information for the analysis of future carbon market	64.5	74.3	45.5	56.3
2	Lack of technology	50.0	51.4	45.5	50.0
3	Limited reduction potential	80.6	80.0	90.9	75.0
4	Lack of specialists on energy management and reduction potential identification	61.3	54.3	81.8	62.5
5	Budget shortages	38.7	48.6	45.5	12.5
6	Lack of effective incentive and support policies at national level	50.0	48.6	54.5	50.0
7	Lack of awareness at top management level	33.9	45.7	18.2	18.8

4.6 Companies' Expectations for GHG ETS

In the survey, companies were allowed to show their expectations for the implementation of GHG ETS. The results are shown in Table 19.9.

Similarly as the evaluation results of disadvantages of GHG ETS, the samples highly expect that GHG ETS could well coordinate with existing regulations, like Energy Audit and TMS (with a ticked ratio of 75.8 percent). 72.6 percent of the samples expect the government to clarify the allowance allocation method earlier for them to better understand the real policy impact. The companies are reluctant to take much economic burden from GHG ETS. Nearly three-quarters of them hope to alleviate the burdens either by reducing the penalties for the excessive emissions or by expanding the incentives in forms of tax reduction and subsidies, etc. More than half of the samples (58.1 percent) expect the government to appropriately appreciate the early actions for GHG reductions. Training programs are viewed necessary for the companies to improve their understanding of the latest policy progress and 56.5 percent of the samples expressed this expectation.

Table 19.9 Companies' expectations for GHG ETS

No.	Expectations	Percentage with 'YES' (%)			
		Overall (N=62)	Chemical (N=35)	Cement (N=11)	Steel (N=16)
1	To coordinate with existing regulations such as Energy Audit and TMS	75.8	68.6	81.8	87.5
2	To clarify the competent ministries and their specific roles	54.5	54.3	54.5	56.3
3	To provide related information	37.1	37.1	36.4	37.5
4	To conduct training programs to improve the understanding of the latest policy progress	56.5	68.6	27.3	50.0
5	To appropriately appreciate the early actions for GHG reduction such as KCER and Energy Audit	58.1	48.6	72.7	68.8
6	To diversify the offset credits	12.9	5.7	18.2	25.0
7	To clarify the allowance allocation method	72.6	80.0	63.6	62.5
8	To expand incentives policies (tax reduction, subsidies, etc.)	74.2	77.1	90.9	56.3
9	To alleviate penalties on the excessive carbon emissions	74.2	80.0	90.9	50.0

5. CONCLUSIONS

This chapter summarized the perspective of Korean companies to GHG ETS to be formally launched in 2015 in Korea. The analysis was carried out in a qualitative manner using the data collected by a questionnaire survey to energy-intensive petro-chemical, cement, and iron and steel industries. The results indicated that the companies do not appreciate the merits of GHG ETS, whereas they have strong concerns about its negative aspects. Most of the surveyed companies are still opposed to the introduction of GHG ETS although the introduction schedule has been decided by the government. Most of companies under TMS established the inventory for GHG emissions, which provides a necessary basis for the actual implementation of GHG ETS. A meaningful finding from this survey is that the companies would make internal efforts in energy saving and GHG mitigation and invest in energy efficient technologies rather than simply transfer the policy burden to their clients. This result confirms the effectiveness of GHG ETS for enhancing a company's carbon performance in Korea. Our survey also clarified the difficulties and expectations of the industry for GHG ETS. The Korean government shall make efforts to meet these expectations for the companies to overcome the barriers. Specifically, the coordination of GHG ETS with ongoing policies, declaration of the method for emissions allowance allocation, clarification of responsibilities of authorities in charge, and capacity building are the priorities. These efforts may increase the understanding and support from the industry for smooth implementation of GHG ETS in Korea.

The current bill of GHG ETS of Korea is flexible for companies in order to minimize their resistance to the adoption of this policy. On the other hand, it is essential to have an adaptation period with loose policy requirements for the arrangement of the relevant institutional infrastructure and to test the scheme's operation at the early stage of the policy introduction. As confirmed by the interview-based studies to the companies under EU ETS, the effectiveness of this scheme is dependent on its strictness. The stringency of GHG ETS of Korea should be strengthened in later phases for achieving the policy goals in carbon mitigation and low carbon technology investment as desired.

REFERENCES

Cho G.L. (2011), 'How emission trading schemes works has different economic effect' [In Korean], KERI (Korea Economic Research Institute).

De Groot, H.L.F., E.T. Verhoef and P. Nijkamp (2001), 'Energy saving by firms: decision-making barriers and policies', *Energy Economics*, 23, 717–40.

Greene, W.H. (1997), *Econometric Analysis*, 3rd edition, New York, NY: Prentice Hall.

Han K.H., D.S. Lim and D.J. Kwak (2010), 'A study on the industrial competitiveness of the GHG emission trading system in Korea' [In Korean], KIET (Korea Institute for Industrial Economics & Trade).

International Energy Agency (IEA) (2007), 'Tracking Industrial Energy Efficiency and CO_2 Emissions ENERGY', Paris: OECD/IEA.

International Energy Agency (IEA) (2009), 'Implementing energy efficiency policies: are IEA member countries on track?', Paris: OECD/IEA.

Kim, W.G. (2009), 'Development of Industry Structure and the adaptation of Emission Trading Scheme' [In Korean], KIET (Korea Institute for Industrial Economics and Trade).

Kim, Y.G. (2010), 'A study of development of effective climate change adaptation system, [2nd year anniversary symposium of Green Growth Vision]' [In Korean], MOE (Ministry of Environment), PCGG (the Presidential Committee for Green Growth).

Korea Energy Management Corporation (KEMCO) (2013), *2013 Handbook*

of Energy & Economic Statistics in Korea [in Korean], KEMCO press.
Laing, T., M. Sato, M. Grubb and C. Comberti (2013), 'Assessing the effectiveness of the EU Emissions Trading System', Centre for Climate Change Economics and Policy, Working Paper No. 126, Grantham Research Institute on Climate Change and the Environment, Working Paper No. 106, January, 2013.
Lee, J.H. (2009), 'Economic effect of the Emission Trading Scheme' [In Korean], SERI (Samsung Economics Research Institute).
Lee, S.H. (2010), 'An analysis of economic cost and institutional issues of greenhouse gas emission trading scheme' [In Korean], KERI (Korea Economic Research Institute).
Liu, X.B., S.H. Suk and K. Sudo (2012), 'GHG emissions trading schemes in Northeast Asia: an overview and analysis of current scenarios', in L. Kreiser, A.Y. Sterling, P. Herrera, J.E. Milne and H. Ashiabor (eds), *Carbon Pricing, Growth and the Environment*, Cheltenham, UK and Northampton, MA, USA: Edward Elgar, pp. 149–66.
Park, S.B. and J.Y. Kim (2009), 'An Analysis of the Energy Effective of Energy Intensive Company in Korea' [In Korean], Issue paper, SERI (Samsung Economics Research Institute).
PCGG (the Presidential Committee on Green Growth) press (2011), 'PCGG proposed the comprehensive economic impact analysis of the introduction of GHG Emission Trading Scheme' [In Korean], February 7, 2011.
Steel & Steel (2011), 'Greenhouse Gas Emissions Trading Scheme shall be discussed later 2015' [In Korean], February 28, 2011, available at http://www.steeldaily.co.kr/news/n_view.asp?NewsID=65218.
Suk, S.H., X.B. Liu and K. Sudo (2013), 'A survey study of energy saving activities of industrial companies in the Republic of Korea', *Journal of Cleaner Production* 41, 301–11.
Suk, S.H., X.B. Liu, S.Y. Lee, S.J. Ko and K. Sudo (2014a), 'Affordability of energy cost increases for Korean companies due to market-based climate policies: A survey study by sector', *Journal of Cleaner Production*, 67, 208–19.
Suk, S.H., X.B. Liu, S.Y. Lee, S.J. Ko and K. Sudo (2014b), 'Awareness and acceptability of Korean companies on market-based instruments for energy saving: A survey analysis by sectors', paper under review, *Journal of Cleaner Production*.

Index